DOSTOEVSKY AT 200

Dostoevsky at 200

The Novel in Modernity

EDITED BY KATHERINE BOWERS
AND KATE HOLLAND

UNIVERSITY OF TORONTO PRESS
Toronto Buffalo London

ISBN 978-1-4875-0863-0 (cloth)   ISBN 978-1-4875-3865-1 (EPUB)
                                   ISBN 978-1-4875-3864-4 (PDF)

Library and Archives Canada Cataloguing in Publication

Title: Dostoevsky at 200 : the novel in modernity / edited by Katherine Bowers
   and Kate Holland.
Other titles: Dostoevsky at two hundred
Names: Bowers, Katherine, editor. | Holland, Kate, editor.
Description: Includes bibliographical references and index.
Identifiers: Canadiana (print) 20210153849 | Canadiana (ebook) 2021015389X |
   ISBN 9781487508630 (cloth) | ISBN 9781487538651 (EPUB) | ISBN
   9781487538644 (PDF)
Subjects: LCSH: Dostoyevsky, Fyodor, 1821–1881 – Criticism and interpretation. |
   LCSH: Civilization, Modern, in literature.
Classification: LCC PG3328.Z6 D6285 2021 | DDC 891.73/3 – dc23

Chapter 9 includes selections from Chloë Kitzinger, "'A novel needs a hero …':
Dostoevsky's Realist Character-Systems." In *Mimetic Lives: Tolstoy, Dostoevsky, and
Character in the Novel.* Evanston: Northwestern University Press, forthcoming.
Courtesy Northwestern University Press. All rights reserved.

University of Toronto Press acknowledges the financial assistance to its
publishing program of the Canada Council for the Arts and the Ontario Arts
Council, an agency of the Government of Ontario.

Canada Council   Conseil des Arts
for the Arts   du Canada

ONTARIO ARTS COUNCIL
CONSEIL DES ARTS DE L'ONTARIO
an Ontario government agency
un organisme du gouvernement de l'Ontario

Funded by the   Financé par le
Government   gouvernement
of Canada   du Canada

To all the Dostoevsky scholars who have shaped our scholarship, especially Robert Louis Jackson, Deborah Martinsen, and Robin Feuer Miller

Contents

Acknowledgments

This volume would not have appeared without the support of a number of individuals and institutions. We are grateful to our editor, Stephen Shapiro, who helped us realize our vision and to all the authors who have written chapters for us.

The project took shape at a workshop hosted by Green College at the University of British Columbia in August 2018. There Melissa Frazier, Vadim Shneyder, and we editors discussed each chapter and helped to bring them closer in dialogue with each other. We thank Melissa and Vadim for their work in Vancouver, as well as Anna Berman and Greta Matzner-Gore for their comments on the chapters during our second, virtual workshopping phase. We are grateful to the external readers for the University of Toronto Press for the constructive comments in their reports. We also would like to thank Alison Smith for her feedback.

Chapters from the volume were presented and discussed in a variety of venues, especially at the Canadian Association of Slavists Annual Conference at UBC in June 2019, the XVII International Dostoevsky Symposium in Boston in July 2019, and in a specially organized panel at the virtual Modern Language Association Annual Convention in January 2021. We are grateful to these audiences for the discussions that followed, which helped shape our work.

The volume's creation was supported with Bridge Funding from the University of Toronto Faculty of Arts & Science and Department of Slavic Languages and Literatures as well as the UBC CENES Department's Faculty Research Fund. The publication was made possible by a grant from the UBC Scholarly Publication Fund, which provided a subvention and indexing costs. We are thankful to Oksana Vynnyk for her skilled work on our index.

We would like to acknowledge that the final revisions for the volume were completed under challenging circumstances during the COVID-19 pandemic in the spring and summer of 2020. We deeply appreciate the hard work of our authors in getting the revisions done during this time of intense stress and anxiety.

Note on Transliteration

When transliterating from Russian to English we have chosen to follow the Library of Congress system with a few exceptions. We depart from the Library of Congress system in the following cases: we use familiar English spellings of common names (such as Dostoevsky instead of Dostoevskii, Gogol instead of Gogol', Herzen instead of Gertsen, Raskolnikov instead of Raskol'nikov, and Dmitry instead of Dmitrii). We also adapt some names to aid in pronunciation (for example: Seryozha, Alyosha, Lidiya, Alyona, Grigoryevna instead of Serezha, Alesha, Lidiia, Alena, Grigor'evna). In parenthetical citations of Russian words or phrases and throughout the notes and bibliography, we have adhered strictly to the Library of Congress transliteration system.

DOSTOEVSKY AT 200

Introduction: Dostoevsky and the Novel in Modernity

KATHERINE BOWERS AND KATE HOLLAND

At the beginning of *The Idiot* [Idiot, 1869], Prince Myshkin meets Rogozhin and Lebedev in a third-class carriage on the Warsaw-Petersburg train as it approaches its destination "at full speed" [na vsekh parakh].[1] The speeding train, described in the opening sentence, seems at first just a backdrop for Myshkin and Rogozhin's introduction. Yet in fact it will be explicitly foregrounded as a symbol of catastrophic modernity. The train is a device which introduces into the novel the experience of acceleration so particular to modernity, as analyzed by Reinhart Koselleck and others.[2] As the inappropriately dressed Myshkin, coming from abroad, converses with his countrymen Rogozhin and Lebedev, the novel opens out onto time; the timeless idyll of the Switzerland Myshkin has left behind is contrasted with the chaotic Russian modernity into which he is arriving, encapsulated by the image of the impenetrable Nastasya Filippovna. This is Myshkin's first experience of historical time since his convalescence and his first experience of his home country, of which he knows nothing. As their conversation progresses in the railway carriage, time slows, and the characters become so engrossed in their discussion that the train's arrival in the station even takes them by surprise. Although Myshkin and his new acquaintances forget their train's movement, the train's presence at the beginning of the novel emphasizes that this is a novel set squarely in the present, in modern times. Later, Lebedev explicitly articulates this point when he describes the nineteenth century as "our century of vices and railways" [nash vek porokov i zheleznykh dorog] (8:315). The railway comes to represent modernity, the sense of a new temporality.

In *Measuring Time, Making History*, Lynn Hunt examines the history of the concept of modernity and how its secondary definition, that of a comprehensive departure from traditional ideas and values, has its roots in the Enlightenment and the French Revolution.[3] The experience of a radical break in temporality, expressed most explicitly in the conceptualization of the French Republican calendar, can be said to inform the nineteenth-century Russian novel from its beginnings, but it becomes much more palpable in the period following the emancipation of serfs, a moment of rupture perhaps akin to that of the French Revolution in the history of the Russian empire. Hunt emphasizes the essential core of the concept of modernity as being a new way of experiencing time, invoking Koselleck's discussion of "the peculiar form of acceleration which characterizes modernity."[4] Acceleration in Koselleck's sense, extrapolates Hunt, can be seen as "the 'constant renewal' of the difference between the 'space of experience' and the 'horizon of expectation.'"[5] In other words, there is a rupture between the experience of the past and expectations for the future. As experience and expectation grow further apart, there is an acceleration to try to rush from one to the other. This sense of acceleration can be found everywhere in Dostoevsky's novels, as it can in other nineteenth-century European texts: Baudelaire's poetry and the novels of Dickens, Balzac, and Zola, to name a few.[6] *The Idiot* is the first of Dostoevsky's novels to so explicitly contextualize this process of temporal acceleration in technological as well as social, philosophical, and economic terms. Through the device of Myshkin returning from Switzerland to St Petersburg on the train, Dostoevsky stages this moment of rupture between coherent and organized past experience and incoherent and amorphous future possibility as central to the novel that lies ahead. This volume is concerned with the ways in which the particular experience of temporality that encapsulates modernity affects the form of the novel as Dostoevsky conceives it, with the peculiar challenges the form faces as it seeks to convey the acceleration of modern life.

Dostoevsky was writing at a time of remarkable change. His return from Siberian imprisonment and exile in 1859 came on the eve of Alexander II's Great Reforms, a period of social, judicial, economic, administrative, and educational reforms that saw the emancipation of the serfs, the advent of jury trials, and the creation of a state treasury and state bank, as well as other changes. Between 1861 and 1874 the reforms led to rapid social and economic growth. At the same time, the publishing industry expanded significantly as a result of the development of a mass circulation press as well as increased literacy rates.[7] More information circulated to more people than ever before in the Russian empire. This increase in information flow gave rise to public debates about science, religion, economics, politics, philosophy, and art.[8] At the same time, new breakthroughs in the sciences, new theories in economics and politics, and new advancements in the arts engaged the growing reading public more quickly and deeply than ever before. The rapid changes in society in the 1860s and '70s were characterized by a public sense of impending crisis, of swift forward motion, but also an impetus to embrace change as a means to further reform state and society. Russia at this time was a society in transition.

The changes set into motion by the reforms helped transform literature as well. Deborah A. Martinsen has observed that, following the Reforms of the 1860s, "Russians in the 1870s felt the need to master the new facts of contemporary life and to take a personal stand. Literary genres that dealt with clarifying the relation of self to the outside world, such as confessional novels, diaries and notebooks became immensely popular."[9] Michael Holquist has demonstrated that Dostoevsky's engagement with these genres, his experimentation with form, and his fascination with subjectivity in narrative also emerges from the experience of modernity.[10] As Kate Holland has argued, this period of crisis is also linked to a crisis of form in Dostoevsky's novels of the 1860s and '70s: "[Dostoevsky] examines the tempest of modernization, which has fractured society's image into a multiplicity of fragments, so that it can no longer be imagined or visualized ... The world has taken on a new appearance that can no longer be captured by the old lenses; it requires a new way of seeing."[11] Modernity is the backdrop for all of Dostoevsky's major works, their historical context and also their engagement with the questions of form and narrative that we address in this volume. Modernity, with its crises and changes, influenced Dostoevsky's lived and intellectual experiences in innumerable ways and, in so doing, shaped not just his thinking but also his artistic practice.

Modernity was a crucial component of Dostoevsky's artistic vision. He struggled with how to convey the historical experience of modernity within the novelistic form. What does acceleration mean for the novel? In formal terms, the rupture between past experience and future possibility could be viewed as a problem of genre. Discussing *The Idiot* in his study of apocalyptic fiction, David Bethea argues that the novel's plot centres on the dissonance "between Christianity and historicism, between an atemporal ideal and the relentless march of chronos."[12] The train is a significant symbol of the novel's expression of this temporal rupture. As Bethea observes, "Dostoevsky embodies these concerns in his art not only thematically but *structurally*; he visualizes the shape of contemporary history, including what he felt to be the critical 1860s, by reincarnating the flesh-and-blood horse of biblical and folkloric tradition in the horse of modern times – the train."[13] In the beginning, the train serves to connect Myshkin's idealized Swiss idyll with the violent and artificial world of Russian urban society. As the novel progresses, Myshkin's expected assimilation into this society fails to happen. Instead, the society is drawn into the Prince's ethical frame, and collapses under its burden. As expectations are thwarted, the novel form accelerates toward an unknown end, the unknowable *obraz* [image].

In the novel, Ippolit articulates the anxiety of this apocalypticism when he crucially asks, "Can one conceive in an image [obraz], that which has no image?" Jackson's formulation of this important question is: "With what *image* – with what sense of form or perfection, inner and outer – can one look at death and disfiguration and still retain one's faith, or, more generally, maintain one's moral-psychological and spiritual integrity?"[14] At the heart of this question is the representation of this unknown and unknowable quantity in terms of its form: *obraz* [image]. Faced with the apocalypticism and speed of his present, Dostoevsky recognized his aesthetic and ethical duty to represent this moment. But to do so required new tools of representation and a transformation of the novel form.

Ever since Georg Lukács claimed, in his *Theory of the Novel* in 1916, that "Dostoevsky did not write novels,"[15] and Mikhail Bakhtin built a theory of the novel on Dostoevsky's novels,[16] there has been intense critical debate focused on the question of the relationship of Dostoevsky's novels to the traditional Western European novel. With their lack of an omniscient narrator, their careering plots, their plunging of the reader *in medias res* at the expense of extensive descriptive scene setting, their substitution of the traditional plots of marriage and inheritance with the drama of the hero's divided selfhood, Dostoevsky's novels seem rather to anticipate the fragmented experiments of the modernist novel that followed them than to adhere to realist novelistic norms. Yet at the same time, they share many of the Western European novel's preoccupations: the contested spaces of identity between self and other, the possibility of retaining one's identity in the urban jungle of the modern city, the need to compromise with social laws and conventions while at the same time never losing the ambition to transform and change them. Critics have always found rich veins to mine in the relationship of Dostoevsky's novels to the domestic literary tradition since Pushkin, finding in his works the latest iteration of the Russian novel's consistent refusal to conform to European type.[17] Dostoevsky was consciously writing in the context of the European novel, as we know from his notes to himself; for example, while working on *The Adolescent,* he wrote a note to himself to write "the anti-Copperfield" (16:22). In setting himself against the trends of the European novel, Dostoevsky deliberately set out to create new forms, to invent a new kind of literature.

Dostoevsky's representation of modernity differs from that of other writers who are concerned with its depiction like Dickens, Balzac, or Baudelaire. In Dostoevsky's works, both the temporality of modernity and a kind of attempt to recuperate the wholeness of a pre-rupture temporality coexist in the literary text. The novel itself is transformed as it becomes the repository for both these visions. The train in *The Idiot* becomes a radically ambiguous and dualistic image in its representation of both temporalities. However, the transformation of the novel occurs constantly as its form shifts to accommodate the necessary elements that are beyond it. Alyson Tapp, for example, has argued that the embarrassment of Myshkin's presence in Russian upper-class society is "incompatible with novelistic form," but demonstrates the way the social novel nonetheless accommodates this embarrassment through its own transformation.[18] In *The Idiot* the temporal rupture is never overcome, and other works that demonstrate the struggle to represent the dual temporalities of modernity – for example, *Demons* [Besy, 1872] and *The Adolescent* [Podrostok, 1875] – are similarly driven by the problem of acceleration. Of all Dostoevsky's novels, *The Idiot* is most clearly linked to modernity through its opening pages and the image of the train, but all the novels demonstrate Dostoevsky's search for new tools of representation, new forms, and new ways of approaching the problem of modernity.

Dostoevsky's final work, *Brothers Karamazov* [Brat'ia Karamazovy, 1880], is frequently seen as the culminating triumph of his novelistic art. This acknowledged masterpiece has been compared to Chartres Cathedral in that it "can never be seen or fully taken in from any single perspective ... it is manifold and changing from every point of view."[19] It is like an echo chamber in which every new sound gives rise to a multitude of echoes that give a new resonance to the original sound. If we try to isolate a theme or a plot thread, we see how it is connected to all the other themes or plot threads. Even "The Grand Inquisitor," which is frequently removed from the context of the novel and treated as a work that can stand alone, is attached to the novel by thousands of threads. This complicated and intricate work of philosophy in prose came into being through a lifetime, a career, of formal experimentation, narrative innovation, and philosophical questioning. Dostoevsky's literary career spanned around thirty-five years, an incredibly short time when we consider the number of significant works produced between 1846 and 1881: *Notes from Underground* [Zapiski iz podpol'ia, 1864], *Crime and Punishment* [Prestuplenie i nakazanie,1866], *The Idiot* (1869), *Demons* (1872), and *The Adolescent* (1875), not to mention, of course, *Brothers Karamazov* (1880). This volume is concerned less with Dostoevsky's crowning achievement, the end point of the development of his thinking about the novel, than with the complex set of aesthetic, formal, and ideological questions, problems, and issues encountered along the way. As a result, our focus is less on either the early works of the 1840s or *Brothers Karamazov*, and more on the works written in between, particularly the major novels, which have variously been praised in terms of form, but which also have been called (including by Dostoevsky), "imperfect," "failures," "messy," "confusing," and "confounding."

Just as Dostoevsky was self-consciously rethinking the boundaries of the novel as a form, so too was he engaged in an interrogation of generic concepts. For Dostoevsky, genre plays an integral role in literary creation, in creating and confounding readerly expectations. Emphasizing the link between genre and aesthetic creation, Vladimir Zakharov identifies genre as "one of the key categories of Dostoevsky's artistic thinking."[20] It ends up being far more than merely a mode of categorization; it becomes a way of looking at the world. The stakes involved in choosing a genre could not be higher. For example, we see it in the deliberate choice of subtitles that categorize works generically, from *The Double* [Dvoinik] as "A Petersburg Poem [Peterburgskaia poema]" to Ivan's *poema* in *Brothers Karamazov*, from the *zapiski* and *zametki* in *Notes from Underground* and *Winter Notes on Summer Impressions* [Zimnie zametki o letnikh vpechatleniiakh] to the "fantastic stories" in *A Writer's Diary* [Dnevnik pisatelia, 1873; 1876–77], "Bobok" [Bobok, 1873], "A Gentle Creature" [Krotkaia, 1876], and "The Dream of a Ridiculous Man" [Son smeshnogo cheloveka, 1877]. Questions of form preoccupied Dostoevsky throughout his career; he borrowed extensively from diverse generic models such as the romance, the adventure novel, the Bildungsroman, the gothic novel, hagiography, and others.[21] This borrowing goes beyond the surface level of simulation as genre becomes an essential function within the Dostoevskian novel; as Bakhtin argues, in Dostoevsky's writing, genre "is placed wholly at the service of the idea."[22] Genre becomes, for Dostoevsky, a way of shaping a particular world view. In this vein, Gary Saul Morson terms Dostoevsky's *Writer's Diary* "a threshold work," that is, "*designed* to resonate between opposing genres and interpretations."[23] Placing genres in conflict on the level of form allows Dostoevsky to explore broader ideological, social. and historical conflicts.

Plot provides the framework for the philosophical and aesthetic experiments Dostoevsky planned in his literary fiction. Through emplotment comes the structure and organizing principle of the narrative; in Robert L. Belknap's concise formulation, "plots arrange literary experience."[24] Plot is a means of structuring the episodes, speeches, and disparate narrative elements of a text that enables their meaning to take form. Peter Brooks defines it as "the design and intention of narrative, what shapes a story and gives it a certain direction or intention of meaning."[25] Dostoevsky's working notebooks reveal the central importance of plot and its construction, or emplotment, demonstrating the "intention of meaning" within his art. Within the notebooks Dostoevsky does not just set forth storyline ideas, but rigorously interrogates them.[26] In the Notebooks to *The Idiot*, for example, the character that eventually becomes Myshkin in the novel is first introduced as a rapist and arsonist who suffers from violent passions and boundless pride (9:141). Reading the Notebooks allows us to see the author's struggles to determine what shape of plot can best convey the idea that drives the novel's creation; his notes focus specifically on plot, which he mentions continuously. In one instance, after Dostoevsky decides that the Idiot character functions better as a Christ-like figure, he writes the following: "Main problem: the character of the Idiot. Develop it. That is the idea of the novel ... showing the Prince in action will be enough. But! For that the plot of the novel is needed" (9:252). Beyond this articulation of plot's central importance, the adjustments, omissions, additions, and other revisions visible in the Notebooks indelibly link Dostoevsky's emplotment with his philosophical impetus.

While plot provides the framework, characterization is the embodiment of the ideas in Dostoevsky's novelistic art. In this volume, we are interested in characterization as it relates to form. In this we move away from the strong tradition of Dostoevsky scholarship that focuses on analyzing characters from a psychological perspective. The connection between the novelistic hero and the other characters who revolve around him is particularly significant in Dostoevsky's novels, serving to dramatize the protagonist's ideological choices and their ramifications. In *Crime and Punishment*, for example, Sonya, Svidrigailov, and Porfiry Petrovich all offer opposing paths Raskolnikov might follow out of his moral and existential crisis. Similarly, in *Demons* or *Brothers Karamazov*, the protagonists create disciples who preach distorted versions of the ideas they espouse, and parallel and opposed character developments reveal the moral hierarchies of the novelistic universe. René Girard, Joseph Frank, and Robert Belknap have all examined in very different ways the significance of the structural relations between characters for larger thematic or emotional dynamics in the novels.[27] More recently, a new strain of scholarship has begun to focus on the particularities of the structural relationships among characters and between characters and narrator in Dostoevsky's novels. This has been in part a response to studies of character and the novel in English and other Western European literatures, particularly Alex Woloch's *The One versus the Many: Minor Characters and the Space of the Protagonist in the Novel* (2003), which seeks to redefine literary characterization by examining "how the discrete representation of any specific individual is intertwined with the narrative's continual apportioning of attention to different characters who jostle for limited space within the same fictive universe."[28]

The experimentalism and originality of Dostoevsky's approach to narrative perspective emerged fully with Bakhtin's claim that he created the polyphonic novel, a novelistic form that, Bakhtin argued, entailed a new relationship between author and characters, an authorial perspective on the text akin to that of a conductor leading a choir of independent voices, each autonomous in and of themselves, each insistent upon their right to have the "final word."[29] Dostoevsky experimented throughout his career with narrative form, from his first novel, *Poor Folk* [Bednye liudi, 1846], with its blending of the sentimentalist form of the epistolary novel with content more associated with Gogol or the authors of the Natural School, and his second novel, the experimental meditation on madness, *The Double*, to his penultimate novel, *The Adolescent*, with its epilogue that reflects on the novel's own form, and his experiments with journalism and fiction in *A Writer's Diary*. He was clearly attuned to the importance of narrative perspective as he debated with himself in the notebooks the question of whether to narrate *Crime and Punishment* in the first person or whether the first-person perspective would make *The Adolescent* too confused and hard to follow.[30] In the notebooks to *The Adolescent* he reminds himself that the narrator, Arkady, was not present for the events of a story he narrates: "though he didn't witness anything personally, he still tells the story *as if he had been there*, having warned the reader that it is based on hearsay and on facts gathered by him" (16:47).[31] Dostoevsky's rejection of a traditional omniscient narrator in the Tolstoian model allowed for the possibility of a variety of different kinds of narrative perspective. We have the blended omniscient/non-omniscient narrator of *Crime and Punishment* who is sometimes able to enter Raskolnikov's mind as well as the first-person narrators like the underground man and Arkady Dolgoruky whose identity crises find form in the disordered prose they narrate. Finally, the narrator-chroniclers of the late novels, whose uneasy participation in the events of the plot, conveyance of rumours, or involvement in the social circles the novels portray, raise the stakes of their narratorial contribution. They render it, on the one hand, radically unreliable, and on the other, expressive of deeper truths about the world the novel represents.

This volume, which marks the bicentenary of Dostoevsky's birth, takes the writer's art – specifically the tension between the experience of living within modernity and formal representation – as its central theme. Many critical approaches to Dostoevsky's works are concerned with spiritual and philosophical dilemmas. As Carol Apollonio observes, "Dostoevsky's writing records a struggle to express in words a truth that lies beyond the feeble powers of human reason to grasp, and of human language to convey."[32] Our focus in this volume is precisely the question of *how* this process of expression led to the creation of novels that Virginia Woolf famously described as "composed purely and wholly of the stuff of the soul."[33] To help answer this question, we turn to questions of form, design, and narrative to explore Dostoevsky and the novel from a multitude of perspectives.[34] Our title "Dostoevsky and the Novel in Modernity" underscores our approach. We are interested in situating Dostoevsky's formal choices of narrative, plot, genre, characterization, and the novel itself within modernity, that is within the particular experience of temporality of the post-emancipation moment, the sense of acceleration of the reform era. In the chapters that comprise this volume, we ask how form, narrative, and genre shape Dostoevsky's works as well as how they influence the way modernity is represented. Similarly, we consider how the experience of modernity led to Dostoevsky's particular engagement with form. Our exploration of Dostoevsky's works is not comprehensive; the early works have little coverage here, and no chapter is dedicated solely to *Brothers Karamazov.* Instead the volume focuses particularly on works that fail to conform to conventional generic categories or frames of expectation because of their hybridic, confusing, or problematic form, especially *Notes from Underground, The Idiot, Demons,* and *The Adolescent.*

Each of the chapters in the present volume deals in different ways with the experience of temporality within modernity. The volume begins with a chapter by Kate Holland, which provides an overview of one of the ways Dostoevsky conceived of emplotment through analysis of a gesture across *Notes from Underground, Demons,* and *The Adolescent.* We thus begin with a chapter that encompasses the later Dostoevsky, from his first major work after his return from Siberia to the novel that came before *Brothers Karamazov.* Holland's analysis of the slap within Dostoevsky's poetics reveals the importance of even minor narrative moments in the writer's creation of the novel. While slaps often seem like mere sensationalistic embellishment divorced from the novel's plot, Holland demonstrates that they have, at their core, a connection to the Romantic duel plot and its attendant honour code. Dostoevsky's slaps are intentional. The slap, in Holland's reading, becomes a manifestation of semiotic and social breakdown, a symptom of the crisis and uncertainty present in the historical systems at work in late imperial Russia.

Anna A. Berman's chapter examines another aspect of Dostoevsky's engagement with plot: his complex treatment of the marriage plot. Focusing particularly on *Brothers Karamazov,* Berman suggests that Dostoevsky's marriage plots resist the "genealogical imperative," rejecting the idea of the formation of new family and focusing instead on its retention, on the re-establishment of old relations along new lines. Berman's exploration of Dostoevsky's novels' refusal to engage in reproductive futurity finds conceptual support from an unexpected quarter: queer theory, specifically queer temporality, which here serves to cast new light on Dostoevsky's resistance to the traditional family plot. While Berman rejects many of the conceptual implications that a queer theory approach to Dostoevsky's novels might bring, she nonetheless finds the idea of a queer futurity useful as a lens through which to examine Dostoevsky's resistance to the narrative closure imposed by the traditional marriage plot.

Vadim Shneyder also draws on the context of social history in his examination of an aspect of the economic imaginary at work in Dostoevsky's fiction. Shneyder juxtaposes two characters who are also businesswomen – Alyona Ivanovna from *Crime and Punishment* and Grushenka from *Brothers Karamazov* – and contextualizes them not just in their roles in the novel, but also in their historical moment. In studying the small descriptive details used to represent the two women, Shneyder uses the characters as case studies to illustrate facets of the broader representation of women and monetary systems in Dostoevsky's novels, the way the businesswomen become both economic subjects and objects of forces beyond their control. Shneyder's analysis ultimately reveals the way Dostoevsky's economic imaginary is gendered; metaphorically, the businesswomen may resemble their money, as do the businessmen, but the women are unable to hold their shapes and shift into new forms by the end of their narratives.

Shneyder's discussion of metaphor's function in Dostoevsky's poetics complements Melissa Frazier's chapter, which examines the role of allegory in Dostoevsky's critique of positivist science and contextualizes it within a more general late nineteenth-century European movement to do away with the opposition of mind and matter. This movement is encapsulated in George Henry Lewes's understanding of dual-aspect monism, the idea that the mental and the physical are two perspectives on the same substance and exist in a non-hierarchical relationship. Frazier argues that this dual-aspect monism finds expression in *Crime and Punishment* and *Demons*, specifically in Dostoevsky's multifaceted response to Chernyshevsky's vulgar materialism. Dostoevsky breaks down the opposition between materialism and utopia, rejecting the primacy of matter over mind or vice versa and, in the process, remakes allegory in a way that reflects his own more complex understanding of the world.

Examining Dostoevsky's relationship with another of his contemporaries, Alexey Vdovin reads *Notes from Underground* alongside I.M. Sechenov's influential scientific work *Reflexes of the Brain* [Refleksy golovnogo mozga, 1863]. While *Notes from Underground* is often read as a psychological novel, Vdovin's investigation demonstrates not only that Dostoevsky wrote psychological prose, but also that he drew on contemporary empirical scientific research in creating his narratives. *Notes from Underground* is commonly read as a text that demarcates the early, more Romantic Dostoevsky from the later, more psychological Dostoevsky. Vdovin's chapter demonstrates that this shift is not just perceived, but rather predicated on Dostoevsky's engagement with the natural sciences and investment in the polemics surrounding empiricism and evolutionism.

Complementing these more scientific approaches to Dostoevsky, Sarah J. Young maps the narrative mechanics of senses and embodiment in *Crime and Punishment* and *The Adolescent*, particularly hearing and seeing. In this, she presents a new approach to the question of how Dostoevsky's characters experience their world. Young argues that, through patterns of indirect presentation, these ways of understanding the external world – sensory experience and embodiment – are relegated to the margins of consciousness, displaced spatially and temporally. The subjective self (or the relationship between self and other) forms a large subset of Dostoevsky scholarship, but Young's approach closely connects the representation of self and spatiality within narrative. Ultimately Young's chapter argues that Dostoevsky's novelistic approach requires the self to be uncovered only indirectly, from the outside, demarcating the limits of the material world and realist potential.

In a different approach to sensory experience and spatiality, Katherine Bowers's chapter takes as its focus the duality of the image in *The Idiot*. The chapter considers the well-trod topic of the meaning of Holbein's painting *Body of the Dead Christ in the Tomb* (1521–22) in comparison with the symbolism of the Mazurin murder case that informs several corpses depicted in the text. Reading the painting and these murder victims as gothic bodies, she breaks the novel down into three significant episodes, which rely on gothic narrative force generated by the abject effect of the corpses. As a gothic body, *Dead Christ*, she argues, creates a meaning-laden space in the novel, which enables Dostoevsky to move beyond the depiction of images to prose that, through its very structure and employment of genre, goes beyond the image, engaging the reader on an affective level. In this way, Bowers's reading of Dostoevsky's novel demonstrates the utility of genre as a tool that connects emotional response with realist representation, but also serves to facilitate the duality central to the novel's plot.

Where Bowers uses genre to decode Dostoevsky's mode of emplotment, Greta Matzner-Gore's study takes a more contemporaneously informed approach to the topic; Matzner-Gore examines Dostoevsky's interest in nineteenth-century statistics and probability in *Crime and Punishment* and the ways this engagement shapes the novel's narrative. As

Matzner-Gore argues, in *Crime and Punishment* Dostoevsky rejects "statistical fatalism," which concludes, through statistics, that free will is illusory and, instead, valorizes statistical outliers, odd people, and unusual events. Matzner-Gore identifies a "poetics of probability," predicated in the social statistics work being published in Dostoevsky's time, which she demonstrates informs the novel's methods of characterization, the structure of its individual scenes, and even the improbable ending of the novel, which sees Raskolnikov's moral resurrection. In this poetics of (im)probability, Matzner-Gore finds narrative openness and temporal potential.

Matzner-Gore examines narrative through the prism of improbability, while Chloë Kitzinger focuses on illegitimacy in her examination of Dostoevsky's approach to the problem of novelistic realism. In her analysis of *The Adolescent*, Kitzinger engages with the idea, developed by Lukács, Bakhtin, and Ivanov, among others, that Dostoevsky's characters lack the mimetic qualities of such protagonists of novelistic realism as Tolstoy's heroes, that they are less fully fledged embodied characters, and more theoretical entities, idea-principles. She argues that this longing for embodiment finds expression through the voice of Arkady Dolgoruky, the narrator-protagonist of *The Adolescent*. Kitzinger demonstrates that Arkady's illegitimacy becomes a model through which Dostoevsky explores new aesthetic and narrative possibilities for the novel within the context of the new pressures of modernity.

Finally, rounding out the volume, Ilya Kliger's chapter examines two of Dostoevsky's novels, *Crime and Punishment* and *Demons*, as responses to autocratic power and sovereignty. As Kliger points out, Dostoevsky had his own experience with autocratic power in his staged execution. Setting his argument against the long tradition of theory that sees the novel as a social art form, Kliger is interested instead in the novel as a political art form. Beginning his analysis with Dostoevsky's Siberian odes (1854–56), very rarely examined by critics, he contends that the novels explore how the symbolic apparatus of sovereignty and power affect questions of identity and the possibility of action. This allows him to read Raskolnikov's and Stavrogin's crimes in a new way, as sites contested by the symbolic regimes of sovereignty and socialization. This interpretation allows Kliger to analyze the differences between the Russian novel, the product of an autocratic society, and the Western European novel, the product of liberalizing and democratizing societies. In the larger debates about the history of the European novel as a form and theorizing of the realist tradition, there has been much discussion of how to account for both the Russian novel's similarities with the broader tradition and its differences. We end with Kliger's chapter

because it provides one possible way of accounting for those common-
alities and differences, pointing towards the ways in which Russia's
particular historical and political trajectory might have helped shape
a different version of the realist novel's general concerns and preoccupations. Future accounts of Dostoevsky's novels and the Russian novel
more generally might opt to follow Kliger's lead or else find other explanations for the particularities of the Dostoevskian novel's complex
account of Russian modernity.

The chapters presented here are not organized in terms of their
chronological or thematic coverage, but, rather, so that they logically
flow from one to the next in terms of their approach to Dostoevsky's
poetics. They focus on formal elements like emplotment, narrative, characterization, and genre, but also analyze Dostoevsky's engagement with
form within the specific experience of temporality in the broader context of modernity from different perspectives. As a result, the chapters
also read Dostoevsky in the context of nineteenth-century social change,
scientific and economic theories, and the socio-historical development
of the literary text.

We have deliberately placed the chapters in this order, but each chapter opens up a myriad of connections with the other chapters, not just
those that bookend it. For instance, Holland and Berman's opening
chapters take a broad view on how Dostoevsky's approach to emplotment reflects the transitional historical moment within which his novels were written. Holland provides a perspective on emplotment that
encompasses Dostoevsky's works of the 1860s as well as his late novels
and deals with a kind of crisis of emplotment. Berman shows how this
crisis creates new possibilities for old plots, while Shneyder shows how
the transformative historical moment and the new economic relations
it engenders create new possibilities in the area of narrative, categorization, and description. Metaphor becomes a crucial category for Shneyder, while Frazier finds allegory more useful in demonstrating the
difference between Dostoevsky's understanding of the relations between
language and the world and that of his vulgar materialist opponents.
Vdovin's chapter also deals with scientific and literary discourse, showing
how their intermingling forges new developments in narrative. Young's
chapter is also concerned with narrative, and both she and Bowers focus
on spatial and temporal categories and their significance for Dostoevsky
as a novelist. Where Bowers returns us to the realm of generic systems
and their shaping of readers' expectations, Matzner-Gore shows how
Dostoevsky was working with, and against, different kinds of predictive
systems, namely nineteenth-century developments in statistics and mathematical probability and their implications for narrative.

While all the chapters consider aspects of characters in some way, from Holland's study of gesture to Shneyder's examination of metaphor, from Young's emphasis on sensory experience to Matzner-Gore's consideration of predictable action, Kitzinger's chapter is the only one to focus on characterization. Kitzinger's argument that Dostoevsky's characters are idea-principles yearning for embodiment leads in to the question of Dostoevsky's contribution to the novel as a genre, which forms the focus of Kliger's contribution. The questions each chapter asks connect with those posed in other chapters, yet each offers a unique perspective in its consideration of Dostoevsky's poetics of the novel and, specifically, his narrative exploration of the experience of modernity.

As a cohesive volume, *Dostoevsky at 200: The Novel in Modernity* demonstrates the importance of form for Dostoevsky's novelistic art, and, more importantly, it provides a framework for reading each of Dostoevsky's novels as a significant development in the praxis of the novel. Completed during a global pandemic marked by a palpable sense of accelerating modernity, the sudden transfer of almost all communications to a virtual mode, and the repeating patterns that prompt the uncovering of the memory of past pandemics, *Dostoevsky at 200*, and the novelist whose bicentenary it is marking, remind us of the difficulty and yet the necessity of finding an image in that which, as yet, has no image.

NOTES

1 F.M. Dostoevskii, *Polnoe sobranie sochinenii v tridtsati tomakh*, ed. G.M. Fridlender et al. (Leningrad: "Nauka," 1972–90), vol. 8, 5. Subsequent volume and page number references to this edition will be indicated in the text in parentheses: (vol.:page). All translations in the introduction are our own, unless specified otherwise.

2 Reinhart Koselleck, *Futures Past: On the Semantics of Historical Time*, trans. Keith Tribe (Cambridge, MA: MIT Press, 1985). For more discussion of this, see Lynn Hunt, *Measuring Time, Making History* (Budapest: Central European University Press, 2008), 47–91.

3 Hunt, *Measuring Time, Making History*, 47–48, 65–72.

4 Ibid., 75.

5 Ibid., 76.

6 See Marshall Berman, *All That Is Solid Melts into Air* (New York: Verso, 1983).

7 On the rise of the newspaper, see Louise McReynolds, *The News under Russia's Old Regime: The Development of a Mass Circulation Press* (Princeton: Princeton University Press, 1991). On literacy and the social and cultural developments it engendered, see Jeffrey Brooks, *When Russia Learned to Read: Literacy and Popular Literature, 1861–1917* (Princeton: Princeton

University Press, 1985) and Damiano Rebecchini and Raffaella Vassena, eds., *Reading Russia: A History of Reading in Modern Russia*, vol. 2 (Milan: Ledizioni, 2020).

8 On the influence of new scientific discoveries on Dostoevsky's novels, see Liza Knapp, *The Annihilation of Inertia: Dostoevsky and Metaphysics* (Evanston: Northwestern University Press, 1996). On the influence of the changing status of religion, see Harriet Murav, *Holy Foolishness: Dostoevsky's Novels and the Poetics of Cultural Critique* (Stanford: Stanford University Press, 1992), and Linda Ivanits, *Dostoevsky and the Russian People* (Cambridge: Cambridge University Press, 2008). On the changing relationship of literature and economics and their significance for Dostoevsky's novels, see Jonathan Paine, *Selling the Story: Transaction and Narrative Value in Balzac, Dostoevsky and Zola* (Cambridge, MA: Harvard University Press, 2019), and William Mills Todd III, "Dostoevsky as a Professional Writer," in *The Cambridge Companion to Dostoevsky*, ed. W.G. Leatherbarrow (Cambridge: Cambridge University Press, 2002) 66–92; "The Brothers Karamazov and the Poetics of Serial Publication," *Dostoevsky Studies* Old Series, no. 7 (1986): 87–93. On developments in philosophy and their significance for Dostoevsky's novels, see James P. Scanlan, *Dostoevsky the Thinker* (Ithaca: Cornell University Press, 2002), and Svetlana Evdokimova and Vladimir Golstein, eds., *Dostoevsky beyond Dostoevsky: Science, Religion, Philosophy* (Boston: Academic Studies Press, 2019). On the relationship between Dostoevsky's novels and parallel developments in the fine arts, see Molly Brunson, *Russian Realisms: Literature and Painting, 1840–1890* (DeKalb: Northern Illinois University Press, 2016).

9 Deborah A. Martinsen, "Dostoevsky's 'Diary of a Writer': Journal of the 1870s," in Deborah A. Martinsen, ed., *Literary Journals in Imperial Russia*, (Cambridge: Cambridge University Press, 1998), 152.

10 See Michael Holquist, *Dostoevsky and the Novel* (Princeton: Princeton University Press, 1977).

11 Kate Holland, *The Novel in the Age of Disintegration: Dostoevsky and the Problem of Genre in the 1870s* (Evanston: Northwestern University Press, 2013), 4.

12 David M. Bethea, *The Shape of Apocalypse in Modern Russian Fiction* (Princeton: Princeton University Press, 1989), 67.

13 Bethea, *The Shape of Apocalypse*, 71.

14 Robert Louis Jackson, *Dialogues with Dostoevsky: The Overwhelming Questions* (Stanford: Stanford University Press, 1993), 52–3. Italics in original.

15 Georg Lukács, *The Theory of the Novel*, trans. Anna Bostock (Cambridge, MA: MIT Press, 1971), 152.

16 Mikhail Bakhtin, *Problems of Dostoevsky's Poetics*, trans. Caryl Emerson (Minneapolis: University of Minnesota Press, 1984).

17 See, for example, William Mills Todd III, "The Ruse of the Russian Novel" in *The Novel*, vol. 1: *History, Geography and Culture*, ed. Franco Moretti, (Princeton: Princeton University Press, 2006), 401–13; Gary Rosenshield,

Challenging the Bard: Dostoevsky and Pushkin, a Study of Literary Relationship (Madison: Wisconsin University Press, 2013).

18 Alyson Tapp, "Embarrassment in *The Idiot*," *Slavic and East European Journal* 60, no. 3 (2016): 422–46.

19 Robert Louis Jackson, "Preface," in *A New Word on* The Brothers Karamazov, edited by Robert Louis Jackson, ix (Evanston: Northwestern University Press, 2002).

20 V.N. Zakharov, *Sistema zhanrov Dostoevskogo: tipologiia i poetika* (Leningrad: Izdatel'stvo Leningradskogo universiteta, 1985), 5.

21 Leonid Grossman identifies a number of genres to which Dostoevsky is indebted, which are then explored in great detail by later critics. See Leonid Grossman, *Poetika Dostoevskogo* (Moscow: 39-aia tip. Internatsional'naia "Mospoligraf," 1925); on the adventure plot and genre more broadly, see Bakhtin, *Problems*, 101–80; on Dostoevsky's engagement with Romanticism, see Donald Fanger, *Dostoevsky and Romantic Realism: A Study of Dostoevsky in Relation to Balzac, Dickens, and Gogol* (Cambridge, MA: Harvard University Press, 1967); on the gothic novel in Dostoevsky's works, see especially Robin Feuer Miller, *Dostoevsky and* The Idiot*: Author, Narrator, and Reader* (Cambridge, MA: Harvard University Press, 1981), 108–25; Katherine Bowers, *Writing Fear: Russian Realism and the Gothic* (Toronto: University of Toronto Press, forthcoming, 2021), and Bowers's chapter in the present volume; on the *Bildungsroman*, see Lina Steiner, *For Humanity's Sake: The Bildungsroman in Russian Culture* (Toronto: University of Toronto Press, 2011), 134–73; on hagiography, see Valentina A. Vetlovskaya, "Alyosha Karamazov and the Hagiographic Hero," trans. Nancy Pollak and Suzanne Fusso, in *Dostoevsky: New Perspectives*, ed. Robert Louis Jackson (New York: Prentice Hall, 1984), 206–26; and Harriet Murav, *Holy Foolishness*, 17–31 and ff. These examples constitute only a handful of a multitude of rich studies of Dostoevsky and genre.

22 Bakhtin, *Problems*, 105. The quote specifically addresses the utility of the adventure plot in Dostoevsky's works, but the example of the adventure plot is representative of the writer's engagement with genre more broadly in Bakhtin's study.

23 Gary Saul Morson, *The Boundaries of Genre: Dostoevsky's* Diary of a Writer *and the Traditions of Literary Utopia* (Austin: University of Texas Press, 1981), 182. Italics in original.

24 Robert L. Belknap, *Plots* (New York: Columbia University Press, 2016), 3.

25 Peter Brooks, *Reading for the Plot: Design and Intention in Narrative* (Cambridge, MA: Harvard University Press, 1984), xi.

26 Robin Feuer Miller's reading of Dostoevsky's Notebooks for *The Idiot* is a good example of the way they can be analyzed to determine the writer's design choices; see Robin Feuer Miller, *Dostoevsky and* The Idiot, 46–89.

27 René Girard, *Mensonge romantique et vérité Romanesque* (Paris: Grasset, 1961), English translation: *Deceit, Desire and the Novel: Self and Other in Literary*

Structure (Baltimore: Johns Hopkins University Press, 1966); Joseph Frank, "The Masks of Stavrogin," *The Sewanee Review* 77, no. 4 (Autumn, 1969): 660–91; Robert Belknap, *The Structure of* The Brothers Karamazov (The Hague: Mouton, 1967).

28 Alex Woloch, *The One vs. The Many: Minor Characters and the Space of the Protagonist in the Novel* (Princeton: Princeton University Press, 2003), 13. See, for instance, Greta Matzner-Gore, *Dostoevsky and the Ethics of Narrative Form: Suspense, Closure, Minor Characters* (Evanston: Northwestern University Press, 2020), 71–102. See also the 2014 mini-forum in *Slavic and East European Journal* with articles by Jillian Porter, Eric Naiman, and Greta Matzner-Gore: "Mini-Forum: Money and Minor Characters in Dostoevsky's *The Double* and *The Brothers Karamazov*," *Slavic and East European Journal* 58, no. 3 (Fall 2014): 376–436: Jillian Porter, "The Double, The Ruble, The Real: Counterfeit Money in Dostoevsky's "Dvoinik"; Eric Naiman, "Kalganov"; Greta Matzner-Gore, "Kicking Maksimov out of the Carriage."

29 Bakhtin, *Problems*, 48–56.

30 In the notebooks to *The Adolescent*, Dostoevsky writes, "Give it a good deal of thought. Color. Will I succeed in giving life to this character? If I write the novel in the first person, this will undoubtedly give it more unity, and less of that what Strakhov has been criticizing me for, i.e., too many different characters and subjects. But what about the style and the tone of the Youth's narrative? This style and tone may help the reader in anticipating the denouement" (16:87).

31 The English translation of the notebooks is taken from Fyodor Dostoevsky, *The Notebooks to* A Raw Youth, trans. and ed. Edward Wasiolek (Chicago: University of Chicago Press, 1969). Italics are Dostoevsky's, reproduced in the translation.

32 Carol Apollonio, *Dostoevsky's Secrets: Reading against the Grain* (Evanston: Northwestern University Press, 2009), 3.

33 Virginia Woolf, "The Russian Point of View," in *The Essays of Virginia Woolf*, vol. 4: *1925–1928*, ed. Andrew McNeillie (Orlando: Harcourt Books, 2008), 186.

34 This focus also informs our individual critical work on Dostoevsky to date. See, for example, our monographs: Sarah J. Young, *Dostoevsky's* The Idiot *and the Ethical Foundations of Narrative: Reading, Narrating, Scripting* (London: Anthem Press, 2004); Ilya Kliger, *The Narrative Shape of Truth: Veridiction in Modern European Literature* (University Park: Pennsylvania State University Press, 2011); Kate Holland, *The Novel in the Age of Disintegration: Dostoevsky and the Problem of Genre in the 1870s*; Anna A. Berman, *Siblings in Tolstoy and Dostoevsky: The Path to Universal Brotherhood* (Evanston: Northwestern University Press, 2015); Greta Matzner-Gore, *Dostoevsky and the Ethics of Narrative Form: Suspense, Closure, Minor Characters*; Vadim Shneyder, *Russia's Capitalist Realism: Dostoevsky, Tolstoy, and Chekhov* (Evanston: Northwestern University

Press, 2020); Chloë Kitzinger, *Mimetic Lives: Tolstoy, Dostoevsky, and Character in the Novel* (Evanston: Northwestern University Press, forthcoming, 2021); Katherine Bowers, *Writing Fear: Russian Realism and the Gothic.* Additionally, the following articles and chapters by volume authors take this approach: Sarah J. Young, "Holbein's *Christ in the Tomb* in the Structure of *The Idiot,*" *Russian Studies in Literature* 44, no. 1 (2007): 90–102; Ilya Kliger, "Shapes of History and the Enigmatic Hero in Dostoevsky: The Case of *Crime and Punishment,*" *Comparative Literature* 62, no. 3 (2010): 228–45; Ilya Kliger, "Dostoevsky and the Novel-Tragedy: Genre and Modernity in Ivanov, Pumpiansky and Bakhtin," *PMLA* 126, no. 1 (January 2011): 73–87; Katherine Bowers, "The City through a Glass, Darkly: Use of the Gothic in Early Russian Realism," *Modern Language Review* 108, no. 4 (2013): 1237–53; Greta Matzner-Gore, "Kicking Maksimov out of the Carriage: Minor Characters, Exclusion, and *The Brothers Karamazov,*" *Slavic and East European Journal* 58, no. 3 (Fall 2014): 419–436; Kate Holland, "From the Pre-History of Russian Novel Theory: Alexander Veselovsky and Fyodor Dostoevsky on the Modern Novel's Roots in Folklore and Legend," in *Persistent Forms: Explorations in Historical Poetics,* ed. Ilya Kliger and Boris Maslov (New York: Fordham University Press, 2015), 340–68; Melissa Frazier, "The Science of Sensation: Dostoevsky, Wilkie Collins, and the Detective Novel," *Dostoevsky Studies* New Series, no. 19 (2015): 7–28; Sarah J. Young, "Hesitation, Projection and Desire: The Fictionalizing 'As If' in Dostoevskii's Early Works," *Modern Languages Open* 1 (2018), http://doi.org/10.3828/mlo.v0i0.183; Vadim Shneyder, "Myshkin's Millions: Merchants, Capitalists, and the Economic Imaginary in *The Idiot,*" *Russian Review* 77, no. 2 (2018): 241–58; Anna A. Berman, "Incest and the Limits of Family in the Nineteenth-Century Novel," *Russian Review* 78, no. 1 (2019): 82–102; Melissa Frazier, "Minds and Bodies in the World: Dostoevskii, George Eliot, and George Henry Lewes," *Forum for Modern Language Studies* 55, no. 2 (2019): 152–70; the cluster of articles by Katherine Bowers, Kate Holland, and Eric Naiman, with Afterword by Robin Feuer Miller, on the Epilogue to *Crime and Punishment* in *Canadian Slavonic Papers* 62, no. 2 (2020): 95–153: Katherine Bowers, "Plotting the Ending: Generic Expectation and the Uncanny Epilogue of *Crime and Punishment,*" Kate Holland, "The Clash of Deferral and Anticipation: *Crime and Punishment*'s Epilogue and the Difficulties of Narrative Closure," Eric Naiman, "'There Was Something Almost Cruel about It All …' – reading *Crime and Punishment*'s Epilogue Hard against the Grain," Robin Feuer Miller, "Afterword. In the end is the beginning"; and M. Vaisman, A. Vdovin, I. Kliger, and K. Ospovat, eds., *Russkii realizm XIX veka: Mimesis, politika, ekonomika* (Moscow: Novoe literaturnoe obozrenie, 2020).

1 The Poetics of the Slap: Dostoevsky's Disintegrating Duel Plot

KATE HOLLAND

In the world of Dostoevskian gesture, public slaps and the challenges they may or may not engender are the last remaining currency of a value system that no longer exists in the world of the late nineteenth century: the honour code.[1] Transposed into Dostoevsky's novels, gestures and acts that once carried symbolic value become decontextualized, transformed into the absurdities of the Underground Man's bumping duel or Stavrogin biting the governor's ear.[2] Such gestures frequently recur in the notebooks to the novels; they clearly play an important role in Dostoevsky's aesthetic conceptualizations of his novels, but they often seem to make little sense on the level of plot or characterization, eliding conventional causality, and often migrating from character to character. In what follows, I argue that the slap motif and the duel plot play a crucial role in Dostoevsky's late novels in revealing the state of semiotic crisis within which his heroes function.[3] While slaps and duels seem to evoke the fixed values and symbolic meaning-making system of the honour code, in fact they uncover the semiotic and social ruptures of the post-reform era, revealing the breakdown of the honour code and the lack of any other mutually agreed-upon semiotic system. The physical violence of Dostoevsky's late novels lies on the boundary between ritual and chaos, revealing the social flux of the new historical moment inhabited by his heroes.

According to the rules of the honour code, a slap functions as an insult which should draw a challenge. In *Notes from Underground* [Zapiski iz podpol'ia, 1864], the Underground Man explains the semiotic significance of the slap as an act of branding as he fantasizes about slapping Zverkov, the friend who has humiliated him:

> Still, I'll slap him first: it'll be my initiative; and according to the code of honor, that's everything; he's branded now, and no beating can wash away that slap, only a duel. He's going to have to fight.[4]

The slap publicly shames the slapped person, and according to the honour code, that shame can be effaced only by the ritualized violence of a duel. The duel creates a structure by which the insult can be translated into a contest of social equals where violence is tamed, ordered, and transformed into an easily readable sign. Traditionally a slap escalates but ultimately resolves a conflict over an individual's wounded honour. Intended to provoke a challenge to a duel, it allows the insulted party to translate his own wounded pride into a physical demonstration of superiority, to impinge on another's physical inviolability, but also to transfer the insult to the symbolic plane, allowing the violence to be ritualized and thus translated into a rule-bound system mutually intelligible to slap perpetrator and victim.[5] In Dostoevsky's works the mutually agreed upon conventions of the honour code frequently break down, and the slap and the duel lose their symbolic power.

In her extensive study on Russian duelling in the nineteenth century, Irina Reyfman has shown how Dostoevsky's use of the slap marks a new stage in the duel plot in nineteenth-century Russian literature. For Reyfman, the significance of the slap in Dostoevsky lies in its position at the intersection of two ethical-semiotic systems, the Christian non-resistance of the Sermon on the Mount on the one hand, and the honour code of the duel plot on the other.[6] The slap, she argues, threatens the victim's physical inviolability; it must result either in shame that can be effaced only by means of a duel, or by a radical Christian rejection of the honour code, a symbolic proffering of the other cheek for a slap. The latter scenario, suggests Reyfman, shows the slap victim's refusal to recognize his own bodily autonomy and his appeal to a larger ethical whole; we see this in the examples of Prince Myshkin and Father Zosima, both of whom are able to extricate themselves from duel plots without shame.[7] These Christian renunciation plots notwithstanding, the duel plots of Dostoevsky's late novels mostly end in scandal, in the subversion of expectation, the failure to shoot, and in the exacerbation of shame rather than its exorcism. I argue here that the unanswered slaps and failed duel plots of *Demons* [Besy, 1872] and *The Adolescent* [Podrostok, 1875] reveal more than just the collision of the honour code and Christian teachings; they reveal a world in a state of semiotic crisis, where the honour code has broken down but there is nothing to replace it. Where Reyfman's analysis of the duel in Dostoevsky underlines the writer's conservatism, asserting that he never condemned the honour code or duelling culture outright, mine emphasizes his radicalism, his persistent investigation of a new historical moment rather than a nostalgia for the old and his rejection of the honour code.[8] Rather than resolving ethical and semiotic conflicts and plots or allowing resolution on the symbolic plane, I suggest, Dostoevskian slaps open up new semiotic quandaries. Instead of appealing to the fixed semiotic values of the honour code, they draw attention to coexisting and contradictory semiotic systems and open up contradictions between them.

I argue here that the collapse of the honour code leads to a crisis of emplotment in Dostoevsky's late novels. Theoretically, when the honour code is followed, the duel simplifies both the complexity of human relations and the multiple emplotment possibilities that such complexities entail. A duel has a fixed and finite set of outcomes. Yet in Dostoevsky's novels the duel complicates emplotment rather than simplifying it, diffuses the shame instead of containing it. Already in *Notes from Underground*, as the Underground Man fantasizes about challenging the friends who have humiliated him to a duel, we see the difference between the clarity the duel fantasy is supposed to provide, and the shame that it engenders as the Underground Man realizes that he lacks the resources (imaginative as well as social) to issue a challenge to Zverkov or his companions. Continuing to anticipate impediments in his mind, he envisages the difficulties he will have finding seconds, and the multiple obstacles that stand in the way of the duel ever taking place. The Underground Man still maintains the boundary between ritualized violence, with its attendant and readable codes, and random violence, being beaten by his opponents without warning. This boundary becomes increasingly porous in Dostoevsky's later novels, where violence threatens to lose the ordered semiotic and clarifying power invested in it by the honour code.

In what follows, I first examine the foundations of the slap motif and duel plot in *Notes from Underground* and the mobilization and rejection of Romantic models, then trace two different slap motifs through the notebooks and the finished versions of *Demons* and *The Adolescent*, examining the vestigial plots each brings into play, as well as the quintessentially Dostoevskian approach to emplotment that each reveals. In both novels, I suggest, the clear and acknowledged link to concrete Romantic texts that we find in *Notes from Underground* and *The Idiot* [Idiot, 1869] have been effaced. The slap motif, I contend, serves to evoke a plot that is never borne out in reality, that remains vestigial, and that invokes the genre memory of a Romantic plot while insisting on the incomplete nature of that plot. Slaps and failed duel plots serve as crucial elements in the staging of the dramas of Dostoevsky's two great aristocratic anti-heroes, Nikolai Stavrogin and Andrei Versilov, and in the two late novels that struggle most explicitly with the problem of changing social and semiotic codes in the age of modernity, *Demons* and *The Adolescent*.

Notes from Underground: Rewriting the Romantic Duel Plot

The slap emerges as a potent symbol of the Underground Man's shame in the first part of *Notes from Underground*.[9] He introduces the contradictions of his underground consciousness, revealing that, despite his self-love, he might nonetheless derive pleasure from being slapped (5:103). Here the slap is introduced as an isolated motif, unconnected to a duel plot, yet it carries unmistakable semiotic echoes of the honour code. The duality it projects immobilizes the Underground Man, rendering him unable to return the insult and symbolizing his incapacity to act. It emerges again following the analogy of the insulted mouse, the ultimate sign of hyperconsciousness, as the Underground Man imagines his reader-interlocutor implying that he himself must have received a slap and makes the claim that he has never been slapped (5:105). This claim, motivated solely by spite, undermines both the structure of his own argument and the reliability of his own claims about himself. The slap functions here both as the decisive proof of the palpability of the Underground Man's shame, and as something elusive, ontologically unstable yet semiotically stable. A slap is the ultimate sign of disgrace, and the Underground Man is defined by this disgrace, yet the shameful certainty of an actual slap eludes him; it remains within the realm of the theoretical, the impersonal. He is defined not by *having been* slapped, but by the *desire to be* slapped; therein lies his hope and his despair. The problem of clarifying the status, meaning, and significance of the slap as sign and its connection to larger social and historical systems becomes a central aspect of its use in Dostoevsky's later novels.

The slap fantasy recurs in the second part of *Notes from Underground* as the Underground Man, smarting from the disaster of Zverkov's birthday dinner at the Hôtel de Paris, dreams of revenging himself on the friends who have abandoned him for the brothel. His duel fantasies are inseparable from the dreams of humiliation that begin with his envy of the man he sees being thrown out of a tavern window one evening. That envy inspires him to seek out a fight, and when he is pushed aside by an officer at a billiard table, he experiences his desired shame and proceeds to plan his revenge. He imagines challenging his opponent to a duel, but becomes unmoored by the complexities of the honour code and by the gulf between theory and practice.[10] While that fantasy leads first to the "bumping duel," a motif that semiotically cross-fertilizes the rational egoism of the Chernyshevskian new man with the rule-bound practices of the honour code, rendering both equally absurd, it emerges once more following the dinner with his schoolfriends and his shame-filled apology for his actions, when Ferfichkin casts aspersions on his fitness as a duellist and his self-loathing leads him to beg Simonov for money.[11]

After he is abandoned by his friends, the Underground Man insists, "So this is it at last: a collision with reality" (5:148; 81). Yet far from grounding himself in this supposed reality, he retreats into a duel fantasy which even he recognizes as inspired by Romantic literary models, most notably Pushkin's "The Shot" [Vystrel, 1831] from *Belkin Tales* and Lermontov's *Masquerade* [Maskerad, 1835]. The slap the Underground Man imagines is located at the intersection between the reality he seeks and the fantasy he cannot abandon: it offers a physical embodiment and palpable proof of his presence – which his friends repeatedly seemed to deny throughout the dinner – also promising a readable honour plot scenario that will allow resolution for the Underground Man. At the same time, it remains within the realm of his imagination, leading only to a vestigial, fantasy duel plot which is never realized within the story, as well as precipitating the reader's questioning of the Romantic models he references. As Reyfman points out, ultimately the Underground Man fails to slap Zverkov or challenge him to a duel because of his hyperconsciousness, the constant need to reflect, which renders him incapable of the kind of decisive action the honour code requires.[12]

The Underground Man imagines his duel scenario playing out in the following way: he will be arrested, exiled to Siberia, and then return fifteen years later to demand his revenge before offering forgiveness. Here the fantasy flounders on the Underground Man's failures of imagination. He admits that the plot of the deferred revenge is taken from another source, Pushkin's "The Shot":

> I was on the point of tears, although I knew perfectly well at that instant that all of this was out of Silvio and Lermontov's *Masquerade*. And all at once I became terribly ashamed, so ashamed that I stopped the horse, climbed out of the sledge, and stood there in the snow in the middle of the street. (5:150; 84)

Pushkin's "The Shot" and Lermontov's *Masquerade* serve as the two main examples of the honour code not just for the Underground Man, but for many of Dostoevsky's characters.[13] Given the overall theme of Part Two of *Notes from Underground*, the intellectual origins of the Underground Man's hyperconsciousness in Romanticism, the invocation of two of Russian Romanticism's most canonical anti-heroes, Silvio and Arbenin, is not surprising.[14] However, these two texts provide highly ambiguous and non-standard examples of the duel plot, and their centrality to the system of representation of the duel plot raises more questions than it answers.

"The Shot" tells the story of a duel plot deferred, in which Silvio, the protagonist, cuts short the duel he has provoked against his enemy, the Count (whose slap serves as the pretext for the challenge), and waits several years to enact his revenge at an unexpected future moment. The honour code is at first egregiously flouted, then awkwardly recuperated by the end of the story as Silvio saves the Count's life again but also redeems his honour. Pushkin's story ultimately reveals a gulf between human relations as organized through the honour code and the messiness of those relations outside of the code, and serves as a usable model for registering historical change.[15] In *Notes from Underground* and later in *Demons* and *The Adolescent*, the motif of deferral of the duel gets repurposed by Dostoevsky for a new historical moment that yearns for the order of the honour code, but in which multiple new codes of behaviour have begun to operate simultaneously and messily. The deferral motif offers both the genre memory of Pushkin's story, with its suggestions of narrative order and control, and a sense of anticipation of the porous boundary between the duel plot and random violence, which is hinted at in "The Shot," but which becomes explicitly thematized in Dostoevsky's late novels.

If "The Shot" offers a discordant and ambiguous model of the duel plot and the honour code, Lermontov's *Masquerade*, with its Russian rewriting of the *Othello* plot, provides an even less clear-cut model of the honour code. When Arbenin, the play's protagonist (and former gambler), discovers that his wife Nina's bracelet is missing and in the possession of Prince Zvezdich, he suspects his wife of infidelity and his first instinct is to challenge the Prince to a duel. However, he decides instead to invite him to a gambling den, where he cheats and humiliates him at cards, refuses to fight a duel with him and forces him to live with his shame.[16] As Ian Helfant observes, while the Prince behaves in accordance with a strict adherence to the honour code, and Arbenin's fellow gambler, Kazarin, is guided only by extreme cynicism, Arbenin is an ambiguous figure who doesn't subscribe to a particular code of behaviour, whose actions reflect a continually shifting set of social codes.[17] During the rigged card game that results in the injury to the Prince's honour, Arbenin tells him the story of a husband who takes revenge on his wife's lover by slapping him in the face:

ARBENIN: So are you curious to know
  What her husband did? He chose some minor pretext
  And slapped his foe in the face ...

And you, my Prince? If you were in his place,
What would you do?
PRINCE: I would do the same. And later?
Did they square off with pistols?
ARBENIN: No
PRINCE: Did they fight with swords?
ARBENIN: (*smiling bitterly*) No, no
KAZARIN: Did they make up then?
ARBENIN: Oh, no.
PRINCE: And so, what did he do?
ARBENIN: The husband was avenged,
And closed the case.
And left his foe.
With that slap in the face.
PRINCE: (*laughing*) But that is against all the rules.
ARBENIN: What code contains the law or prescription for hatred and
vengeance?[18]

Here the slap serves as an ambiguous sign that is read at cross purposes by the Prince and by Arbenin and the husband. According to the honour code it should be the immediate grounds for the challenge, forcing the lover's hand and allowing the husband to fight his rival and avenge the insult to his honour, and this is what the Prince anticipates. In fact, the slap becomes the sole form of vengeance; the duel plot is aborted, and the situation remains unresolved. According to the honour code, the shame is never truly effaced. Arbenin, like the husband, rejects the honour code, leaving his opponent's and his own honour stained. This foreshadows the card sharping that will allow Arbenin to refuse to fight the Prince, another serious violation of the honour code. As Helfant explains, "Arbenin forestalls each attempt by Zvedich to gain any authority over the narrative they are now performing"; he names Zvedich "a scoundrel who has forfeited his right to participate in social discourse with honorable men."[19] In fact, Arbenin's insistence on the Prince's dishonour masks his awareness of his own shame, which, together with his guilt at the murder of his wife, eventually drives him to madness.

Arbenin's final question in the passage quoted above reveals the gulf between his own self-aggrandizing Romantic ideology that rejects all fixed systems, and the honour code.[20] His manipulation and repurposing of particular elements of the honour code in order to disguise his own cowardice and weakness is a central element of his Romantic personality. In his simultaneous mastery of and rejection of social codes as well as in his shame masked by pride, Lermontov's card sharp has much in common with Dostoevsky's Underground Man; the invocation of *Masquerade* reveals Arbenin as one of the Underground Man's literary progenitors. However, where Arbenin's manipulation of the honour code makes him unique within Lermontov's play, a character ahead of his time and at odds with his world, the Underground Man's retreat into the honour code and simultaneous recognition of its disintegration harmonizes with and reflects the new post-Emancipation world to which he belongs.

It is clear that Dostoevsky's Romantic models undermine the honour code and the duel plot more than they exemplify them. The deferred duel plot of "The Shot" and the polysemic slap and aborted duel of *Masquerade* inform the half-baked fantasies of the Underground Man, undergirding the instabilities of the slap and the fragmented duel plot in *Notes from Underground*. At first sight the references to "The Shot" and *Masquerade* seem to suggest nostalgia for a functional honour code, a retreat into a world of readable signs and legible codes where the Underground Man can symbolically re-establish his injured selfhood. On closer examination, these textual examples offer no semiotically stable ground, no lost unity, seeming rather to bolster the idea that shame cannot be effaced. Furthermore, they are invoked at moments in the text that threaten to undermine the possibility of semiotic stability. In Dostoevsky, Romantic models offer no defence of the honour code, but they do offer possible models of emplotment that can be repurposed and filled with new content reflective of a moment of new semiotic challenges and conflicts.[21] If even in the duel's heyday, it apparently offered little hope for the re-establishment of fractured selfhood, Pushkin's and Lermontov's ambiguous slaps and deferred shots herald a sense of semiotic uncertainty that by the time of *Notes from Underground* has become era-defining, and that helps to explain how the Romantic fantasist of Part II became the hyperconscious protagonist of Part I.

Where *Notes from Underground* openly acknowledges its models and thematizes the breakdown of the Romantic duel plot as part of the ideological and narratological journey of the Underground Man from disillusioned Romantic to divided and impassioned poet of the dependence of the self on the other, Dostoevsky's later novels go further in their representation of the dissolution of the honour code and the semiotic instability of the slap motif and the duel plot, resisting the immediate acknowledgment of Romantic models and the direct mobilization of the duel plot. In these works, the slap becomes dislodged from its place within the duel plot and takes on a life of its own. It becomes a motif that evokes the duel plot, but which resists mobilizing it fully.

Demons: Deformation of the Duel Plot

A slap, the ensuing mark of shame, and a deferred duel plot, which violates the honour code, play a crucial role in *Demons* in revealing both the moral and psychological fractures at the heart of the novel's elusive protagonist, Stavrogin, and the contradictory set of semiotic codes according to which the novelistic action unfolds. Shatov slaps Stavrogin soon after his return from abroad and Stavrogin fails to respond. Characterized as a coward by the son of a man he had previously insulted, Gaganov, he then issues a challenge to the latter, thus substituting the original slap for the later insult. He refuses to follow the rules of the duel and shoots into the air, enraging his opponent and leaving the conflict unresolved. The slap motif is central to Dostoevsky's plans for the novel, first appearing in the early plans for *Demons* but recurring throughout (11:32, 34, 51, 54). As is the case with Myshkin in *The Idiot*, the slap is a test of the protagonist's moral qualities, yet from the earliest notebooks for *Demons,* the social shame it generates is emphasized. In a story begun in 1868, a slap brings shame to the titular Kartuzov, a character who shares many traits with the future Captain Lebyadkin. Altogether, in the notebooks, variants of the word "slap" [poshchechina] appear fifty-six times. Although initially the Prince is the one slapping the teacher, later Shatov (11:68, 81, 82, 83, 84, 89, 96, 117, 118, 123, 126, 127), he soon becomes the one on the receiving end of Shatov's slap (11:131, 133, 134). The gesture becomes part of a putative duel plot in March 1870, when we find the formulation, "slap and duel without a shot," [poshchechina i duel'bez vystrela] (135). Though in "Kartuzov," the slap is invariably coupled with the duel that must inevitably result from it, which must efface the shame it evokes, it soon begins to appear in and of its own right, functioning as a motif severed from its broader plot, yet carrying with it suggestions of the duel plot (11:136, 137, 140, 142, 145, 154, 176). This action becomes one of the central motifs of the notebooks, together with the hero's action of hanging himself and his rape of the girl, later Matryosha, a defining characteristic of the Prince, later Stavrogin, as he develops over time. (12:163)

In the finished version Shatov administers his slap to Stavrogin in front of a large audience at the end of the scandal scene that concludes Part I of the novel. The blow and its aftermath, including Lizaveta's faint, serve as cliffhangers at the end of the section, creating suspense for characters and readers alike. By bringing shame and conflict out into the open with a violent incursion into another's space, it promises a resolution of that shame and conflict and a clear plot progression. Though the blow generates a host of questions about motive and plot, it also creates the expectation that those questions will soon be answered. It cuts through the hermeneutic tension which the narrator has been building throughout his confused and confusing account of the prehistory of the main plot in Part I of the novel and promises clarification, a clearing away of the obstacles to interpretation that have been accumulating throughout Part I.[22] However, instead of dissipating emotional and hermeneutic tensions, the slap aggravates them.

The blow itself is half-slap, half-punch, lending it an ambiguous status on the boundary between the ritualized violence of the first element and the base violence of the second:

> Shatov had a particular way of delivering the blow, not at all the way a slap on the cheek is usually delivered (if one may put it that way); not with the palm of the hand, but with the whole fist. (10:164)[23]

Stavrogin's failure to respond to the blow reveals a rupture between the social reputation he has gained over time and the inexplicable image he currently projects within the town, between past and present Stavrogin.[24] When he eventually responds to an insulting letter sent by the son of the man whose nose he had pulled, but then flouts the duelling code by firing off to the side, the whole duel plot is revealed as just one more of the destabilizing plot developments that threaten to undermine the novel's very structure. Stavrogin's gradual disintegration in the prehistory of the novel's main plot, from follower of the honour code to instigator of inexplicable violent outbursts, prepares the ground for the aborted duel. Early on the narrator reveals Stavrogin's history with excessive duelling during his time in Petersburg, when he simultaneously upheld the honour code and transgressed it, fought two duels, killed one opponent and crippled another, and was reduced in the ranks (10:36). His excessive penchant for duelling is abruptly transformed into chaotic violence that seems to completely transgress all the rules of physical inviolability:

> Suddenly our prince, for no apparent reason, carried out two or three impermissible outrages against various people, – the important thing being, in other words, that these outrages were completely without precedent, completely unimaginable, completely unlike anything usually done, completely rotten and childish, and the Devil knows why, completely without provocation. (10:38; 49)

Stavrogin's two strange and violent gestures – his act of pulling Gaganov round by the nose and his act of biting the Governor's ear – resist being read according to the legible script of the honour code. Both acts deform and reframe the face, marking it as no longer sacrosanct, and thus create a more lasting shame than the simple incursion of the slap. They set the stage not only for Stavrogin's complete rejection of the plots of the honour code but also for the ambiguity of Shatov's blow. Stavrogin's and Shatov's gestures belong to a moment of semiotic transition and cause confusion in those who receive and witness them.[25]

The culminating scene of the shame plot in *Demons* is when Shatov delivers his blow to Stavrogin at his mother's house in front of Lizaveta Nikolaevna and her entourage as well as his mother. The scene unfolds in slow motion, the narration saturated with temporal expressions, and is partially focalized through the perspective of Lizaveta Nikolaevna, who "is dominated by some kind of new impulse" [ovladelo kakoe-to novoe dvizhenie], whose face is the first marker of emotion and who serves to register the shame that accrues. Shatov's half-slap, half-punch carries with it the suggestion of uncontrolled violence, rather than functioning as a readable stage in an unfolding orderly duel plot. As Reyfman points out, the emphasis is on Stavrogin's face, which first seems to disintegrate into its constituent parts following impact with Shatov's fist and then comes together again in a mask-like covering.[26] The long and strange scene, in which the passing of time is repeatedly mentioned, ends in a staring contest between Shatov and Stavrogin and then Liza's faint. The narrator's focalization of the scene through Lizaveta Nikolaevna's perspective, combined with the description of Shatov's unorthodox move, creates a moment of true potentiality. While Lizaveta's response points towards the expected sense of shame, Shatov's fist and Stavrogin's failure to respond either by returning it or challenging Shatov to a duel lead out of the world of the honour code and into semiotically uncharted waters.

The opening chapter of Part II reveals a shift in the narrator's focus as the slap becomes the pretext for an examination of the progression of rumours and gossip rather than an attempt to get to the truth behind the blow itself (10:231). The question of why Stavrogin was slapped is subordinated to the problem of how the story of the slap is being told. This has the effect of undermining causal mechanisms within the novel and reorienting its focus from narrating the plot to reflecting on the possibilities of such narration. As Anne Lounsbery has observed, a central dynamic of *Demons* is the illusion of a vast and nebulous network of vague connections between people and events, which models the revolutionaries' "belief in a vast web of conspiracy, linking and controlling everything and everyone."[27] The slap as response to some chain of events is swept aside in favour of the slap as narrated event, the beginning of a new story, rather than the playing out of an old one. The motive for the slap falls out of the narrator's zone of inquiry, as does its ability to provide insight into Stavrogin's character and motivations.

The origin of the rumours is revealed as Gaganov, who is desperate to avenge the insult to his father five years before, sends a letter that refers to Stavrogin's "slapped mug" [bitaia rozha]. Using Shatov's slap as a pretext, Gaganov attempts to insert himself into Stavrogin's shame plot and re-establish the honour code. By invoking the plot of the deferred duel, *Demons* evokes the memory of "The Shot," and Silvio's delayed revenge, but the duel plot that plays out looks quite different. Gaganov has left the army, partly as a result of the stain on his family's reputation after the incident with Stavrogin. He has just spent a month insulting Stavrogin in an attempt to provoke a duel. As a prelude to the narration of the duel, the narrator-chronicler provides a predictably colourful account of the background to Gaganov's conflict with Stavrogin in which he traces Gaganov's sense of shame to the Emancipation of the serfs:

> Strange though it is to write it, this initial intention, or rather, impulse, to retire came from the manifesto of February nineteenth on the emancipation of the peasants. Artemii Pavlovich, the wealthiest landowner of our province, was himself capable of being convinced of the humaneness of the measure and almost of understanding the economic advantages of the reform, suddenly, after the appearance of the manifesto, felt himself personally offended, as it were. This was something unconscious, like a sort of feeling, but all the stronger the more unaccountable it was. (10:224; 316)

The fact that the narrator tells us that Gaganov has not lost much revenue as a result of the Emancipation is significant; the "manifesto of February nineteenth" functions here not as a real historical event but as a sign of a historical event.[28] Gaganov is shaken not by a loss of income but by the Emancipation's semiotic reverberations, by the suggestion of the transformation of the meaning of himself and of his social estate. He thus falls back on semiotic certainty – provoking a duel that will serve as a grand substitution and allowing him to erase not only the shame inflicted on his father by Stavrogin, but also the shame inflicted on himself and his estate by the Emancipation and its changes. The slap and the duel here do not function as motifs within a coherent honour code plot; instead they serve as vessels of potential new plot generation, or vestigial Romantic plot fragments that are repurposed to deal with a new historical moment and a new crisis of semiosis.

The duel plot here is a red herring that generates false expectations about Gaganov's motives and the possibilities of effacing the shame of his social position. Gaganov, as a post-reform aristocrat, seeks the meaning and certainty in the honour code that he fails to find in service following the Emancipation. The duel offers him the possibility of effacing the concrete shame of his father's past humiliation instead of the shapeless shame of his own present socio-historical humiliation. He fears that the duel will not take place and demands absolute fidelity to the duelling code, rebuffing Kirillov's attempts to effect a reconciliation. Uncertainty and lack of definition are his greatest fear, and when Stavrogin insists on firing into the air, even after Gaganov has grazed his finger with his first shot, Gaganov is overcome with a new kind of shame that can no longer be effaced. A post-Emancipation Russian aristocrat with a penchant for medieval pageantry, Gaganov is himself a historical anachronism, and his shame is formless and indefinable, suffused throughout the novel's fluctuating networks, rather than easily definable and effaceable. This is the duel as farce, but also as a plot adrift, only nebulously connected to the slap motif, conducted in order to reverse the imminent historical extinction of his social estate and its modes of behaviour.

The slap and the "duel without a shot" in *Demons* continue the process of the disintegration of the honour code begun in *Notes from Underground*. In *Notes* Dostoevsky depicts a world with a tangible memory of the honour code, where Romantic models still theoretically offer the Underground Man the promise of rehabilitating his honour (though this promise is occluded by a closer examination of those models). *Demons* depicts a world where such a memory no longer exists other than as empty comfort for those such as Gaganov, who declare vengeance on historical progress itself. The slap becomes distorted, its symbolic meaning attenuated by ambiguity and the suggestion of raw violence with no possibility of resolution. The slap motif and the aborted duel plot symbolize the semiotic confusion that characterizes the broader atmosphere of a world adrift, unmoored by moral or philosophical values.

The Adolescent: Decoding the "Slap at Ems"

The story of the slap sustained by Versilov in *The Adolescent* and the duel plot it engenders also reveals the semiotic confusion of a world on the brink of modernity. Here too the slap is also present from the very earliest period of work on the novel and occurs twenty-nine times in the notebooks. Unlike in *Demons*, it is not always associated with the same protagonists; rather, various characters perform the slap: the young prince, later Arkady, a little boy who later commits suicide, the princess who is involved with him (16:7, 10, 12, 17, 18, 21, 23, 27, 35). However, it is always performed on the predatory type, the future Versilov. As Jacques Catteau observes, "Dostoyevsky is not so much interested in the person who performs the action as in the one who suffers it."²⁹ Like Myshkin and Stavrogin before him, Versilov absorbs the slap and then fails to respond, leading to social shame, his estrangement from society, and an aborted duel plot in which his son involves himself. Short-hand, in the notebooks it becomes the "the story of the slap. The bearing of the slap," [istoriia poshchechiny. Perenesenie poshchechiny] marked by the potentiality of emplotment that it offers (16:17). Though the notes seem to prefigure the slap as Versilov's burden, connecting him with the ideological and spiritual legacy of Stavrogin, in the novel itself it functions differently, becoming a marker of plot potentiality, the node of two different historically determined and mutually anachronistic scenarios. As with Shatov's slap and Gaganov's duel, an old honour plot is reworked here to respond to new historical and social needs.

The slap appears first as part of a story Arkady has heard through rumour in his first month in Petersburg. Versilov is supposed to have committed some kind of scandalous act the previous year in Germany, and to have received a slap from one of the Princes Sokolsky (soon revealed as Prince Seryozha, who is defined as "the man who gave him a slap"), to which Versilov never responded with a challenge and for which he is punished by social ostracism:

> Everybody turned away from him, including, by the way, all the influential nobility … owing to rumors of a certain low and – what's worst of all in the eyes of the "world" – scandalous act he was supposed to have committed over a year before in Germany, and even of a slap in the face he had received then, much too publicly, from one of the Sokolskii princes, and to which he had not responded with a challenge. (13:18)³⁰

"The slap at Ems" as it becomes known, exists at the intersection of two different codes of behaviour and interpretation within the novel (13:88; 105). On the one hand, Arkady reads Versilov's failure to issue a challenge within the terms of the old honour code as a mark of shame on Versilov, a proof of his lack of honour. On the other, he is aware that Versilov is engaged in a court case over an inheritance against the very same Prince Seryozha. The litigation is the marker of a rule-bound society where the honour code has become superfluous, even meaningless, so Versilov's refusal to issue the challenge reveals him as a man of the modern age. The slap and its possible outcomes become a staging ground for Arkady's understanding of his own position in the world. Versilov's response to the slap becomes a test into which is inscribed Arkady's desire to see his father enact his aristocratic destiny and his own filial responsibility to make up for his father's failures but also his awareness of the semiotic absurdity of such a response in the new world to which Arkady belongs. Arkady is no Gaganov, longing for a pre-Emancipation world, yet he longs for the narrative certainties he sees as his father's legacy, a contrast from the story of his own life as product of an accidental family.[31] The slap becomes a moment of pregnant possibility on the level of both *siuzhet* and *fabula*, on the level of both Arkady's autobiographical notes and Dostoevsky's novel; it reveals the breach between the world Arkady yearns for, in which he can overcome his illegitimacy and inherit his father's semiotic certainties, and the one he inhabits, in which semiotic values are in flux.

Versilov's failure to extract vengeance on the Prince becomes a twofold possibility for Arkady's own plotting. His planned challenge becomes the opportunity to claim Versilov as his father by defending his honour and also to efface the ambiguities of his social identity as Versilov's illegitimate son. As he tells Zveryev when he asks him to be his second:

> I knew the objections and at once explained to him that it was not at all as stupid as he supposed. First, it would be proved to the insolent prince that there were still people of our estate who understood honor, and second, Versilov would be shamed and learn a lesson. And third, and most important, even if Versilov, owing to certain convictions of his own, was right not to have challenged the prince and to have decided to bear with the slap, he would at least see that there was a being who was able to feel his offense so strongly that he took it as his own, and was ready even to lay down his life for his interests ... in spite of the fact that he had parted from him forever. (13:116; 136)

The anticipated duel carries the traditional semiotically restorative function, the "wiping away of shame" that we saw in the Underground Man's fantasy, but is meant to restore not Versilov's honour, but rather Arkady's legitimate social status. Fighting a duel in Versilov's stead would imply his right to be considered a social equal of both Versilov and Prince Seryozha. To move to the level of emplotment, Dostoevsky again borrows the motif of the deferred duel from "The Shot" but substitutes one of the duellists, thus deconstructing the Romantic plot once again. The duel never comes to pass, since Zveryev refuses to be Arkady's second, objecting to the fact that Versilov is involved in a court case against the Prince. Instead of providing semiotic clarity, here the duel brings only semiotic confusion, the fragments of another zombie plot that will be filled with new content and adapted to fit the new historical and semiotic conditions of Russia in the mid-1870s, in all its post-reform semiotic confusion.

As the duel plot develops, it becomes increasingly distanced from the original slap at Ems and takes on a life of its own. Arkady's desire to fight the duel soon becomes emblematic of his naivety and his ignorance of the true relations between his father, the Prince, and the many other participants in the drama at Ems. He is unaware of the circumstances of Seryozha's insult to Versilov, rendering his perspective increasingly unreliable as the stakes of Versilov's involvement in the plot gradually rise. The rumoured slap opens and closes emplotment possibilities, revealing the extent of Arkady's ignorance. The villain Stebelkov tells him about the "nursing baby" of Lidiya Akhmakov and claims Versilov fathered it, and so Arkady assumes that the slap was a punishment for this impregnation. His sister Liza then points out that it was not Versilov's baby before Vasin tells him that the baby was Prince Seryozha's, thus reopening the question of motive for the slap. Arkady also wonders about his own mother's involvement in the plot. Lidiya's baby's uncertain paternity becomes an extension of Arkady's own illegitimacy and the duel seems to mark the only possibility of effacing that shame. The shame of Arkady's birth comes to substitute for the shame of the slap at Ems.

When Arkady speaks to the Prince about his intention to challenge him, he reveals that the court case has been resolved, and that Versilov has now decided to challenge Prince Seryozha. The deferred duel plot from "The Shot" emerges once more, removing the need for Arkady to fight, and hence denying him the certainty and clarity he so desires. An hour later, though, Versilov rescinds his offer. If the duel plot traditionally simplifies and narrows down emplotment possibilities within a text, here it creates new plots and new outcomes, complicating, rather than simplifying emplotment possibilities. *The Adolescent* is the messiest of Dostoevsky's novels, and like the rest of its plots, such as the document and the blackmail plots, the duel plot careens out of control. Disappearing for a while, it emerges once again later in the novel when Versilov writes a letter to Katerina accusing her of sexually corrupting Arkady, provoking her fiancé to challenge him to a duel before ultimately deciding that he is insane and should be sent to a hospital ward to recover. The slap motif ultimately serves as the source of a vast proliferation of plots and subplots, all of which serve to confuse rather than clarify, and which reveal a world that exists according to multiple contradictory codes and systems.

In conclusion, while slaps and the duel plots they engender seem at first to suggest semiotic and narrative stability in Dostoevsky's novels, a nod to the mutually comprehensible rules of the honour code, in fact they serve as markers of semiotic confusion, of the coexistence of the multiple codes and slippages between them. In *Notes from Underground* Dostoevsky reveals the Romantic models that underlie the honour code plot, but those models themselves are shown to be unstable, signifying narrative uncertainties and shifting semiotic values. The Underground Man's duel fantasies and desire to be slapped mark his attempt to look for familiar landmarks in a semiotic territory that is changing beyond recognition. *Demons* shows a world where Romantic models are unrecognizable and emptied of content. The slap Shatov gives Stavrogin in *Demons* is emblematic of the gestural poetics of Dostoevsky's late novels. It generates the expectation of narrative and semiotic clarity while in fact complicating emplotment and distancing the reader from any understanding of Shatov or Stavrogin and their motivations. As the story of the slap takes over from the slap itself and the duel plot disintegrates as a result of the substitutions of participants and motives, it becomes a marker not of clarity but of obscurity. The aborted duel becomes nothing more than the refuge of an aristocrat who has lost social identity and meaning in a post-Emancipation age. *The Adolescent* takes this peculiar mode of gestural poetics even further: while the story of a slap serves as the source of rumours, the apparent key to the mystery of Arkady's father, Versilov, and to Arkady's own identity, it turns out to be an empty plot, a narrative dead end. The slap and the duel fantasy it engenders serve as the last chain of identity connecting Arkady to Versilov. Moving beyond the slap and the semiotic limitations of the outdated honour code allows Arkady the freedom to operate within the multiple codes of the changing world he inhabits and grants him the possibility of emancipation from the physical and psychological limits of the honour code and its legacy. Ultimately the shifting meanings and poetics of the slap in Dostoevsky's post-Siberian works work to highlight a broader crisis in semiosis in the post-Emancipation era.

NOTES

I would like to express particular thanks to my co-editor Katherine Bowers for her careful reading of this chapter in its various forms, and my gratitude to colleagues in the Historical Poetics Working Group, to whom I presented the first version of this chapter at a conference at Columbia University in December 2018, as well as to colleagues at the Department of Slavic Languages and Literatures at Yale University, to whom I presented another in the same month. I presented a subsequent version of the talk at the Canadian Association of Slavists Annual Conference at UBC in June 2019, and at the the XVII International Dostoevsky Symposium in Boston in July 2019.

1   The most comprehensive analysis of Dostoevsky's representation of duels and the honour code, including the role of the slap, can be found in Irina Reyfman, *Ritualized Violence, Russian Style: The Duel in Russian Culture and*

Literature. (Stanford: Stanford University Press, 1999), 192–261. On the cultural history of Russian duelling more generally, see Iurii M. Lotman, "Duel'," in *Besedy o russkoi kul'ture: Byt i traditsii russkogo dvorianstva* (XVIII–nachalo XIX veka (St Petersburg, 1994), 164–79. On the duel in Russian literature, see Christina Scholle, *Das Duell in den russischen Literatur: Wandlungen und Verfall eines Ritus* (Munich: Peter Lang, 1977).

2 Notable slaps in Dostoevsky's oeuvre include Vanya's slap of Valkovsky in *The Insulted and the Injured,* the Underground Man's fantasies of slapping Zverkov in the second part of *Notes from Underground,* Ganya's slap of Prince Myshkin in *The Idiot,* Shatov's slap of Stavrogin in the face in *Demons,* the unavenged slap Versilov receives in a German spa town in *The Adolescent,* and finally, in *Brothers Karamazov,* Father Zosima's slap of his servant right before his conversion moment and his pulling out of the duel he was supposed to fight the next day, and Fyodor Karamazov's failure to respond to a slap from an opponent, which horrifies his second wife.

3 By this I mean that Dostoevsky's heroes inhabit a world where sign systems are in flux and are continually being interrogated. A rich strain of recent scholarship has begun to deal with how Dostoevsky's realism responds to the transformation of monetary signs and economic values in mid-nineteenth century Russia: see Jillian Porter, "The Double, The Rouble, The Real: Counterfeit Money in Dostoevskii's *Dvoinik,*" *Slavic and East European Journal* 58, no. 3 (2014): 378–93; Vadim Shneyder, "Myshkin's Millions: Merchants, Capitalists, and the Economic Imaginary in *The Idiot,*" *Russian Review* 77, no. 2 (2018): 241–58.

4 F.M. Dostoevskii, *Polnoe sobranie sochienii v tridtsati tomakh,* ed. G.M. Fridlender et al. (Leningrad: "Nauka," 1972–90), vol. 5, 149. Subsequent volume and page number references to this edition will be indicated in the text in parentheses: (vol.:page). Fyodor Dostoevsky, *Notes from Underground,* trans. Boris Jakim (Grand Rapids, MI, and Cambridge, UK: William B. Eerdmans Publishing, 2009), 81–2. Translation adapted. From here on I will indicate the translation parenthetically in the body of the text, following the volume and page number for the *PSS* and set off by a semicolon.

5 As Reyfman points out, "the honour code presumes that one is concentrating on the act's symbolic meaning and thus discourages the aggressor from focusing on the face he is about to slap," *Ritualized Violence,* 230.

6 Ibid., 228–61, especially 228–31.

7 Ibid., 232–9, 253–5.

8 Ibid., 260–1.

9 This is not the first slap in Dostoevsky's works (there is one in *The Village of Stepanichikovo* and another in *The Insulted and the Injured*) but this is the first instance of the slap as an *idée fixe* that dominates a character's thoughts or a subplot.

10 See Reyfman on the Underground Man's contradictory and self-serving excuses for why he cannot challenge the officer, *Ritualized Violence*, 216–21.

11 Tzvetan Todorov makes the argument that Romantic models are parodied and reframed within situations taken from the literature of the 1860s. This dissonance of form and content can also be seen in the playing out of the duel fantasies within the context of the Underground Man's pecuniary difficulties and the arrival at the brothel. Tzvetan Todorov, *Genres in Discourse* (Cambridge: Cambridge University Press, 1990), 81–2.

12 Reyfman, *Ritualized Violence*, 225–7.

13 In *The Idiot*, Kolya makes the following comment about Ganya's attempt to slap Varya, "Some madman, or fool, or villain in a state of madness, gives a slap in the face, and the man is dishonored for the rest of his life and can only wash it off with blood, or if the other one begs forgiveness on his knees. I think it's absurd and despotism. Lermontov's play *The Masquerade* is based on it and – stupidly so, in my view" (8:100–1). English translation mine. Wacław Lednicki enumerates a number of other Romantic and post-Romantic texts with which the Underground Man engages in Part II of *Notes*: Gogol's *Notes of a Madman*, Turgenev's *Diary of a Superfluous Man* (1850), and "The Bully." To these, Reyfman adds Lermontov's *Princess Ligovskaia* and Tolstoy's "A Billiard-Marker's Notes" (1855). Waclaw Lednicki, *Russia, Poland and the West: Essays in Literary and Cultural History* (Port Washington, NY: Kennicat Press, 1966), 180–248; Reyfman, *Ritualized Violence*, 215–16.

14 Joseph Frank argues that *Notes from Underground* "is a diptych depicting two episodes of a symbolic history of the Russian intelligentsia." See Joseph Frank, *The Stir of Liberation, 1860–1865* (Princeton: Princeton University Press, 1986), 316.

15 On the structure of "The Shot" and its place within *The Tales of Belkin*, see Paul Debreczeny, *The Other Pushkin: A Study of Alexander Pushkin's Prose Fiction* (Stanford: Stanford University Press, 1983), 103.

16 M.Iu. Lermontov, *Sobranie sochinenii v chetyrekh tomakh*, 2nd ed., 4 vols, ed. V.A. Manuilov et al. (Leningrad: Nauka, 1980), vol. 3, 76–84.

17 Ian Helfant, *The High Stakes of Identity: Gambling in the Life and Literature of Nineteenth Century Russia* (Evanston: Northwestern University Press, 2002), 73.

18 Lermontov, vol. 3, 80–1. English translation mine.

19 Helfant, *High Stakes*, 79.

20 Elizabeth Cheresh Allen argues that Arbenin is not a Romantic hero, but is rather a Romantic ideologue, a character whose self-image is Romanticized. Her analysis of the way in which Arbenin incorporates Romantic ideals and attributes invites parallels with the Underground Man. Elizabeth Cheresh Allen, "Unmasking Lermontov's *Masquerade*: Romanticism as Ideology," *Slavic and East European Journal* 46, no. 1 (Spring 2002): 75–97.

21 In his chapter in the present volume, Alexey Vdovin shows how Dostoevsky uses Sechenov's mode of argumentation and thought experiments in similar ways, as forms to be parodied and filled with new content.

22 There is a huge bibliography on the role of the narrator-chronicler in creating the narrative instabilities of *Demons*. See, for instance, Slobodanka B. Vladiv, *Narrative Principles in Dostoevskij's Besy: A Structural Analysis* (Bern: Peter Lang, 1979), and Adam Weiner, *By Authors Possessed: The Demonic Novel in Russia* (Evanston: Northwestern University Press, 1998). For a recent account that provides a rehabilitation of a sort for a narrator frequently seen merely as a victim of the novel's deeper account of possession, see David Stromberg, "The Enigmatic G-v: A Defense of the Narrator-Chronicler in Dostoevsky's *Demons*," *Russian Review* 71, no. 3 (July 2012): 460–81.

23 Fyodor Dostoevsky, *Demons*, translated by Robert Maguire (London and New York: Penguin Classics, new edition, 2008), 225. From now on, page numbers from this translation will be placed in parentheses following the *PSS* page numbers.

24 As Ilya Kliger points out in his chapter in the present volume, Stavrogin's choice not to respond also underlines the extent of his power.

25 The community at first attempts to decode these gestures by medicalizing and pathologizing them. When Stavrogin is diagnosed with brain fever, his previously inexplicable acts are then fitted into a madness plot that normalizes them and exculpates Stavrogin, but also serves to destabilize and redefine semiotic values within the novel.

26 Reyfman, *Ritualized Violence*, 240.

27 Anne Lounsbery, "Dostoevskii's Geography: Centers, Peripheries and Networks in *Demons*," *Slavic Review* 66, no. 2 (Summer 2007): 211–29.

28 On the symbolic and cultural reverberations of the Emancipation, see Irina Paperno, "The Liberation of the Serfs as a Cultural Symbol," *Russian Review* 50, no. 4 (October 1991): 417–36.

29 Jacques Catteau, *Dostoyevsky and the Process of Literary Creation*, trans. Audrey Littlewood (Cambridge: Cambridge University Press, 2005), 292.

30 *The Adolescent*, trans. Richard Pevear and Larissa Volokhonsky (New York: Knopf, 2003), 20. All quoted material from *The Adolescent* in the chapter is from this translation and, from now on, pages from it will be included following a semicolon in the parenthetical citations.

31 For a fuller examination of Arkady's relation to his father's narrative legacy, see Kate Holland, *The Novel in the Age of Disintegration: Dostoevsky and the Problem of Genre in the 1870s* (Evanston: Northwestern University Press, 2013), 101–30, as well as Chloë Kitzinger's chapter in the present volume.

2 Dostoevsky and the (Missing) Marriage Plot

ANNA A. BERMAN

From the tense relations between Raskolnikov and his mother and sister to the parricidal desires of the Karamazov brothers, Dostoevsky's novels explore kinship relations at their most raw and revealing. While the novels present a wide array of family constructions, spanning from the warm intimacy of the Yepanchins and Snegiryovs, to the neglect, absence, and illegitimacy of the Karamazovs, Versilovs, and Verkhovenskys, Dostoevsky's focus stays primarily on consanguineal kin: parents and children or siblings. Yet in the history of the novel, conjugal relations have arguably been a far greater generator of plots. Getting heroes and heroines to the altar, following adulteresses away from the family hearth, or watching the virtuous wife at risk of straying: these are among the central concerns of the nineteenth-century novel.[1] The Russian tradition, while offering its own twists, shared these concerns.

Critics have generally approached the novelistic family through highlighting one of two generic plots: generational or marriage, with Dostoevsky's critics falling firmly in the first camp.[2] This chapter will take the opposite approach, looking at the first crucial step in the formation of family: the coupling of male and female – traditionally in marriage – that serves as the kernel of each new nuclear unit. The Russian tradition is exceptional in its rate of failures: while courtship is at the heart of many novels, most plots about a prospective romantic couple do not lead to union.[3] Chernyshevsky famously blamed this on Russian men's weakness and indecision, lamenting that: "the hero is very daring so long as there is no question of action and one need merely occupy spare time, fill an empty head or empty heart with conversation and dreams; but when the time comes to express one's feelings and desires directly and precisely, the majority of heroes begin to waver, and are stricken dumb."[4] While his argument applies to many novels by Turgenev (Chernyshevsky was writing specifically about *Asya* [Asia, 1858]), Herzen, Goncharov, Krestovsky (pseud.), Pomialovsky, Pushkin, Lermontov, etc., it does not explain Dostoevsky's heroes, who *are* capable of acting on their ideas. Nor do Dostoevsky's novels follow the model of authors like Tur, Druzhinin, Smirnova, and Pavlova, who placed greater emphasis on societal pressures and failures in women's education and life experience to explain the unhappy outcomes of their marriage plots.

Dostoevsky's novels are different at a structural level as well as an ideological one. He decentralizes his potential marriage plots in a way that subverts nineteenth-century genre expectations.[5] While many of his characters are involved in prospective courtships, these are rarely their primary concern.[6] His heroes' failure to marry and produce heirs stems not from the inability to act, overly romantic mentality, failure to appreciate the elevated soul of the heroine, or her naivety about her potential suitors (as we find in other Russian novels). Instead, I believe this failure is related to Dostoevsky's distinctive conception of the family and the new relationship he forged between familial and novelistic form. True to the Russian tradition, Dostoevsky emphasized affective ties, rather than blood or legal bonds. But unlike the families of Tolstoy and others, in Dostoevsky's novelized families those ties came not through shared experience and familiarity, but through active love. His novels emphasize kinship ties in the present, not as a means towards a (reproductive) end, restricting the significance of courtship as a narrative propulsion.

How one depicts the family is inseparable from how one constructs a novel. In the words of literary scholar Barry McCrea: "The ideas of narrative and family are so closely interwoven that it is hard to separate them. Narrative and family both attempt to plot a relationship between what came before and what comes after; both organize the unknowable jumble of events and people who preceded us into a coherent array of precedence, sequence, and cause."[7] The family's natural narrative or plotline is that of its own continuity, parents begetting children who will, in turn go on to beget still more, a process Edward Said calls "filiation."[8] Tolstoy draws attention to this in *Anna Karenina* (1878) when describing Levin and Kitty's newborn son: "like a small flame over a lamp, wavered the life of a human being who had never existed before and who, with the same right, with the same importance for itself, would live and produce its own kind."[9] In writing of this process of filiation, Said claims: "This line and this sense of heritage [...] stands at the absolute center of the classical novel."[10]

A characteristic explication of this theme appears in Thackeray's *Vanity Fair* (1847) when George Osborne's father anticipates his son marrying a rich girl: "His blood boiled with honest British exultation, as he saw the name of Osborne ennobled in the person of his son, and thought that he might be the progenitor of a glorious line of baronets."[11] As we find in Osborne's reflections, the traditional path that leads us to these glorious lines of progeny is the marriage plot.[12] While the marriage plot may seem synchronic in focus (both actors are of the same generation), explicitly or implicitly, the nineteenth-century marriage union was also designed to produce the much sought-after heir, implicating marriage in the process of family continuity. In McCrea's words: "With its implicit promise of biological reproduction, marriage is the embodiment of the happy end, i.e., an end that is also a beginning."[13]

Neither marriage nor reproduction seems to be of great concern to Dostoevsky's heroes (though their mothers may care). They never fret about having progeny or about the legacy they will pass on to their heirs, aside from intangible family pride or honour.[14] Snegiryov cares about his son's respect *in the present* just as Versilov suddenly seeks intimacy with Arkady "now" after having ignored him for his whole upbringing.[15] Many are poor, but even the wealthy Fyodor Pavlovich concerns himself with money to seduce a concubine, not with the inheritance for his sons. Similarly, young Dostoevskian heroes may obsess about love and passion, but not about matrimony, which carries with it the promise of future obligation. Perhaps following their lead, as noted above, Dostoevsky scholars have focused little on marriage and procreation. To note one illustrative example, Susanne Fusso's brilliant chapter on "Dostoevskii and the Family" in *The Cambridge Companion to Dostoevskii* (2002) does not mention the marriage plot even a single time. Staying true to Dostoevsky's primary concerns, the essay explores Dostoevsky's vision of the breakdown of the Russian family, centring on the failures of the father–son relationship. Fusso contextualizes Dostoevsky's novelistic depictions of family with his non-fiction pronouncements in his *Writer's Diary* [Dnevnik pisatelia, 1876–7, 1880–1] and notebooks, where statements about "the family" are primarily directed at parents and children, not spouses.

The marriage plot in Dostoevsky's novels seems to (almost) disappear. *Brothers Karamazov* [Brat'ia Karamazovy, 1880] offers an illustrative example. The generational plot has received by far the most attention as its dominant family plot, and certainly one of Dostoevsky's central concerns was to depict the breakdown of the patriarchal order and the failure of the father, a theme he wrote about frequently in his *Writer's Diary*.[16] But as Carol Apollonio reminds us, *Brothers Karamazov* "is so obviously an exploration of the question of fatherhood that the reader may be excused for forgetting that the Karamazov brothers had mothers – two, and possibly even three, of them."[17] A consanguineal family cannot be created without procreation. And for the children to be legitimate, this requires the conjugal knot, a fact that plagues Smerdyakov throughout the novel. These earlier marriages – or their lack – catalyze the novel's plot.

Just as we forget the mothers who brought the Karamazov family into being, we also tend to overlook the different versions of the marriage plot for the sons that are central to the text and yet have for the most part evaded rigorous scrutiny. There are women in love with each of the Karamazov brothers, each of whom is living out her own courtship drama.[18] Katerina Ivanovna begins in a failed marriage plot, abandoned by her fiancé, Dmitry, yet also entangled in a mutual attraction with Ivan.[19] Lise Khokhlakova, writing her innocent love letter to Alyosha, is living the plotline of an ingénue like Pushkin's Tatyana Larina. Grushenka is in a classic "fallen woman" plot: betrayed by her Polish officer and forced to become a kept woman, while still virtuous and pure at heart.

However, Dostoevsky's psychological focus on pride and suffering creates female characters who invert these standard plotlines, responding to their situations in ways quite unlike a classic family novel heroine would. Katerina Ivanovna's engagement to Dmitry comes after he wins a battle of pride and will, choosing to be magnanimous at the moment he could have taken advantage of her. Her proposal to him – in a letter following this event – is a submission of will: "I love you madly, [...] even if you do not love me – no matter, only be my husband. Don't be afraid, I shan't hinder you in any way, I'll be your furniture, the rug you walk on ... I want to love you eternally, I want to save you from yourself" (14:107; 116). Despite her reference to household decor, Katerina Ivanovna has no pretensions to setting up house or creating a family with Dmitry. Her proposal of marriage is not about intimacy, affection, or even truly about love (as both later realize), but about an abnegation of will and a wish for suffering.[20] Neither is seeking domestic life and progeny in their potential union; indeed, they have no thought of a concrete future together.

Each of the young women in the novel creates – or contributes to – her own torment. Katerina Ivanovna refuses to accept that her affections truly lie with Ivan; determined to sacrifice herself for Dmitry, she struggles with her (untranslatable) *nadryv*. As Alyosha senses, she and Ivan seem to derive some kind of pleasure from the psychological games they are playing. Katerina uses the informal *ty* in speaking to Ivan in a moment of heightened emotion (15:37) and he acknowledges the truth of Alyosha's assertion that she is in love with him, yet claims: "I don't care for her" [ia do nee ne okhotnik] (15:39; 600). However, readers have every reason to doubt the coolness of his feelings. Meanwhile, after (almost) engaging herself to Alyosha, Lise writes letters offering herself to Ivan, and tells Alyosha, "I want someone to torment me, to marry me and then torment me, deceive me, leave me and go away. I want to be unhappy" (15:21; 581). This desire for abandonment and suffering goes directly against the reproductive drive of the classic novel. Lise appears to wish she were in a Russian novel with its tradition of failures, or to want to rewrite Pushkin and be Tatyana married to Onegin. And finally, Grushenka torments Fyodor Pavlovich and Mitya as she waits for her "former one" [prezhnii], unlike a traditional meek heroine. Yet even when he returns, one could never imagine her settling down with him into married life and motherhood, and she is only too happy to escape back to Mitya at the first chance.

One unique feature of Dostoevsky's treatment of these marriage plots – which I believe allows them to disappear – is the narrative perspective. Dostoevsky tell them from the point of view of the men. In Tur's *A Mistake* [Oshibka, 1849], we watch the breakdown of Olga's engagement through her perspective, just as in V. Krestovsky (pseud.)'s *Anna Mikhailovna* (1849) we share Anna's understanding of the catastrophe unfolding.[21] The reader's view is aligned with the narratives these women believe they are living. Even in novels with a male hero – like Turgenev's *Rudin* (1857) and *Noble Nest* [Dvorianskoe gnezdo, 1859], or Goncharov's *Oblomov* (1859) – the author still leaves us sympathetic to the woman's perspective. However, in *Brothers Karamazov* we learn the stories of the women through men's views of them. Katerina Ivanovna's story is literally narrated to us by her betrayer (Dmitry), not the proud woman herself. We see Lise through Alyosha's eyes and the disparaging comments of Ivan. Dostoevsky even uses the marginalization of these women's plotlines to comic effect at times. Dmitry is so caught up in his generational-rivalry plotline with his father, that he is completely oblivious to the fact that Grushenka is living out a "fallen woman" plot and waiting for her former one, even though she has explicitly told him this!

Another way Dostoevsky can hide these marriage plots in plain view is that they are essentially "plot-less," by which I mean that they do not advance. Ivan and Katerina Ivanovna can play mind games and keep each other both near and at bay, but their "courtship" – if it could even be called that – does not progress. Smerdyakov woos Mariya Kondratyevna with a serenade in the garden, but Michael Katz calls this "a broad parody of a heterosexual courtship," and suggests that Smerdyakov "represents the final and fullest exploration of the male homosexual stereotype in Dostoevsky's fiction."[22] Even if Smerdyakov did prefer the fairer sex, he ends his serenade with the verse: "I don't care what you say / For I'm going away, / I'll be happy and free / In the big cite! / And I won't grieve, / No, I'll never grieve, / I don't plan ever to grieve" (14:206; 226). This is hardly the path to a romantic union. Grushenka has devoted herself to Dmitry by the end of the novel, but there is too much uncertainty for them to plan a concrete future; he vaguely imagines tilling the soil with her in America, not raising a family.

Alyosha and Lise actually share a chapter titled "Betrothal" [Sgovor], yet everything about their interaction seems out of kilter with such an event. First Lise claims her love letter was a joke, then that it was serious. After Alyosha surprises Lise with an attempted kiss, he admits that "I see it came out silly" and she laughs at him doing it "in that dress!" (14:198; 218). Before five minutes have passed, Alyosha is confessing that he may not believe in God, and the conversation has returned to its usual Dostoevskian (unromantic) themes. Did an engagement actually take place? As Alyosha leaves, he agrees with Lise's eavesdropping mother that her words were "foolishness, foolishness, and more foolishness!" yet he still seems serious that he will someday marry her (14:201; 221). It is hard to tell whether the pair actually became betrothed or not, and their relations never progress beyond this ambiguity, with Lise soon offering herself to Alyosha's brother.

While for many authors marriage and procreation were indelibly intertwined, almost all the babies born in Dostoevsky's novels are illegitimate, breaking this connection.[23] In *Demons* [Besy, 1872], Stavrogin weds an invalid in a marriage that remains unconsummated, while he spreads his seed outside of wedlock.[24] Among his conquests is Shatov's wife, who returns to her husband on the night she gives birth to Stavrogin's illegitimate child. When Shatov announces the baby will not be sent to an orphanage as the midwife had assumed, she asks if Shatov is adopting him, forgetting the child is legally – though not biologically – a Shatov (10:452). In *The Adolescent* [Podrostok, 1875], Arkady's unwed sister Liza is carrying Prince Sokolsky's child, and the reader learns of a whole convoluted back story involving Versilov caring for an infant that turns out not to be his own illegitimate baby but another of Prince Sokolsky's. Dostoevsky's families also include many illegitimate older children or young adults, like Nelli (*The Insulted and Injured* [Unizhennye i oskorblennye, 1861]), Arkady and Liza (*The Adolescent*), and Smerdyakov (*Brothers Karamazov*), who are mature enough to wrestle with the shame of their birth and rejection – or ultimate acceptance – by their biological fathers. These children of accidental families must each determine for themselves what defines a family relationship: is bloodline enough if there has been no contact or acknowledgment?

The link between procreation and family is actively challenged in *Brothers Karamazov* during Dmitry's trial. The defence attorney offers up the pro-forma answer a typical youth is given as to why he should love his father:

"He begot you, you are of his blood, that is why you must love him." The young man involuntarily begins to think: "But did he love me when he was begetting me?" he asks, wondering more and more. "Did he beget me for my sake? He did not know me, nor even my sex at that moment, the moment of passion, probably heated up with wine, and probably all he did for me was pass on to me an inclination to drink – so much for his good deeds ... Why should I love him just because he begot me and then never loved me all my life?" (15:171; 745)[25]

The act of begetting a child is here separated from the creation of a family.[26] Sex is not the originary act. Instead, as Dostoevsky claimed in his *Writer's Diary*: "The family is created by the untiring labor of love" (22:70).[27] In other words, its creation is a continuous process, but not one with a beginning or any kind of progressive movement. It also cannot be completed, keeping the emphasis on the present.

When we consider Dostoevsky's families in the context I have been outlining – that of the standard family plot of matrimony and reproduction – a strange truth emerges: the Dostoevskian family resists the "genealogical imperative." They exist outside of what Bakhtin calls "biographical time" and the spaces of traditional family life: "Dostoevsky was least of all an estate-domestic-room-apartment-family writer. In comfortably habitable interior spaces, far from the threshold, people live a biographical life in biographical time: they are born, they pass through childhood and youth, they marry, give birth to children, die. This biographical time Dostoevsky also 'leaps over.'"[28] Protagonists tend to appear already as young adults whose childhoods we see only in brief snatches. What do we know of the "family life" of Raskolnikov before he came to St Petersburg? In *Demons*, *The Adolescent*, and *Brothers Karamazov* such family life never existed, as the characters spent years apart and only come together when the "children" are already young adults.[29] *Crime and Punishment* [Prestuplenie i nakazanie, 1866], *Demons*, *The Adolescent*, and *Brothers Karamazov* all begin with a family "reuniting" after years apart.[30] And even their family life in the present tends to lack roots, as many families in Dostoevsky's novels are living in rented rooms rather than an ancestral home (*Poor Folk* [Bednye liudi, 1846], *The Insulted and Injured*, *Crime and Punishment*, *The Gambler* [Igrok, 1866], *The Adolescent*).

Just as Dostoevsky's families have "leapt over" biographical time, they also resist the narrative propulsion towards a future.[31] None of them produce an heir. The death of Shatov's wife and illegitimate child right after they have been reunited is emblematic of this absolute negation of family continuity. In *The Adolescent*, Liza miscarries the illegitimate child she is carrying. Prince Sokolsky's other illegitimate child survives, but is orphaned and being raised by Versilov, who is neither legally nor biologically his kin. So this hardly qualifies as family continuity.[32] Jennifer Wilson's study of the *skoptsy* in Dostoevsky's novels reveals a counterintuitive truth: while *skoptsy* might be thought to be resisting futurity through castration, Dostoevsky "often connected [them] to ideas of prophecy, premature aging, accumulation of wealth (all ways of engaging the future), whereas Dostoevsky elsewhere depicts characters focused on questions of family as preoccupied with the present moment."[33] Dostoevsky contrasted the non-reproducing *skoptsy*'s future-oriented greed and hoarding "with the [present-oriented] generosity of those fully enmeshed in family affairs."[34]

Thus, the family drama for Dostoevsky is not the *formation* of new family, but the *re*formation or retention of family, "the untiring labor of love" family requires, to again use Dostoevsky's words. This shifts the emphasis to relations in the present, with no recourse to the future as a point of narrative or moral resolution. Family love can have no aim or goal beyond itself; it is not productive, just as it is not reproductive.[35] What matters in the Dostoevskian family is not the future child who would symbolize the continuity of the family line, but being thy brother's keeper in the here and now. And one cannot love this brother because of a shared past and warm childhood memories – the Tolstoy model – because that past does not exist. The "conflict of generations" plot – so central to Dostoevsky's final three novels – is only about two generations. There is no possibility of a third and no recourse to the ones that preceded the generation of the "fathers."

This does not mean that the family remains static, but growth happens laterally – adding members in the present – rather than extending across time. The Ichmenevs take in first Vanya then Nelli; Pulkheria Alexandrovna announces that Razumikhin is kin; Lizaveta Prokofyevna calls Myshkin her brother; General Ivolgin decides he is a relation of Lebedev; Rogozhin and Myshkin exchange crosses as a sign of their brotherhood; Versilov and his family raise Prince Sokolsky's illegitimate child; Grushenka makes Alyosha her brother ... These examples expand the family circle in the present, but do not extend the genealogical line.[36] I do not mean to suggest that Dostoevsky did not care about the future. He was deeply concerned about it, but this future was not about individual families, but about a broader form of unity, the universal brotherhood he ecstatically preached in his Pushkin speech. It is the children who will bring about this dreamed-of brotherhood, but it does not matter specifically whose children. Dostoevsky envisioned a communal future, where family unity would spread to the whole of Russia, and then the Russians could in turn bring brotherhood to Europe. In this vision, there is no significance for the future of an individual family line.

What does it mean to write of the family without reproductive futurity? Dostoevsky's reframing of standard family plots has vast implications for narrative form as well as for the ethics of time in the novel. Bakhtin popularized a view of Dostoevsky's novels as defined by "fundamental open-endedness" and a principled resistance of narrative closure for characters and dialogue, though he acknowledged "a *conventionally literary, conventionally monologic* ending" for most of the novels.[37] Yet Dostoevsky avoided the "conventionally literary" ending of marriage and childbirth. In light of Bakhtin's reading, one might ask: would the birth of a child have provided too much narrative closure for Dostoevsky, or in reverse, would it have added to the "open-endedness" by leaving a future to unfold beyond the novel's pages?

Greta Matzner-Gore explores the tension Bakhtin raises between dialogic openness and monologic endings, revealing the links between Dostoevsky's formal and ethical concerns. Taking *The Adolescent* as her case study, she explains:

> In *The Adolescent* [Dostoevsky] shows that highly open-ended stories leave their audience without ethical or intellectual guidance, uncertain of how to interpret them or what to do next. By contrast, narratives about contemporary life that resolve their tensions too quickly and easily are both unrealistic and potentially dangerous, because they imply that harmony can be achieved without suffering or sacrifice.[38]

A balance must be struck. Matzner-Gore observes that Dostoevsky "wavers from hope to doubt, referring to the possibility of future closure on the one hand and of continued uncertainty on the other."[39] One could say almost the same thing of the complicated families in these novels. Each is still struggling to form itself in the present, and none has an heir to carry it forward into the next generation. In this sense, the future is less than open; we do not know if these families will have a future at all – although the possibility has not been totally foreclosed.

Such a narrative structure that resists futurity has been theorized in a context far removed from the nineteenth-century Russian novel. Recently in literary studies, when faced with family models that do not match the standard of married parents with biological offspring, the theoretical model most often invoked is queer theory.[40] Early pioneers like Jack Halberstam and Lee Edelman – writing from the American context in the wake of the AIDS crisis – defined "queer" in opposition to the family, focusing on its lack of heterosexual reproduction.[41] Halberstam explains that queer time is "about the potentiality of a life unscripted by the conventions of family, inheritance, and child rearing."[42] In other

words, such time resists the temporal framework of the traditional nineteenth-century novel, which many scholars have called heteronormative,
organized around the rituals of marriage and reproduction (the point
with which this essay began).[43]

Clearly, Dostoevsky has resisted this kind of genealogically oriented
time in his novels and is exploring life outside "the conventions of family, inheritance, and child rearing," focusing on relations in the present.
Family in his novels is not constructed through heterosexual reproduction, but through active love. Many of the most stable and enduring
kinship bonds are "intentional": instances when characters choose to
make others kin without blood or legal bonds (as discussed above).[44]
This possibility of creating intentional kin is actually facilitated by the
"accidental" nature of the Dostoevskian family; without a shared family
past, one has little more in common with a biological sibling than with
a chosen one. This type of alternative family construction aligns with
Holly Furneaux's writings about *Queer Dickens*. Arguing against earlier
scholars, who saw queerness as a rejection of the family, Furneaux sees
it as an alternative way of constructing kinship: "I define queer as that
which demonstrates that marriage and reproduction are not the only, or
indeed the dominant or preferred, modes of being, and, in doing so, un-
does an unhelpfully narrow model of identity as determined by a fixed
point of sexual orientation."[45]

Like the English novels in Furneaux's study, Dostoevsky's similarly explore "other forms of intimacy, affinity, and family formation" than the
biological family.[46] So can her conception of queer help us make sense of
Dostoevsky's present-oriented family constructions that resist providing
narrative closure through marriage and reproduction? There are rea-
sons to be hopeful that it might. Just as Furneaux grounds her study in a
re-evaluation of the Victorian family and the Victorian novel that points
to "the abundance of non-heterosexual and non-reproductive families in
Victorian fiction based around the figure of a single male" or the scarcity
of households consisting of married parents, children, and no other rel-
atives, we could look to the way Russians at mid-century were challenging
ideas about the traditional, patriarchal structure of the family.[47]

Dostoevsky was deeply concerned about the historical state of the family in the reform decades when he was writing, and sex and gender roles
certainly played a role in his engagement with these issues. He critiqued
"today's fathers" again and again, yet his fiction failed to offer up a positive model of what the modern Russian father should look like.[48] In both
his fiction and non-fiction, Dostoevsky returned time and again to scenes
of women and children being abused, and he attacked Russian law and
the new courts, which provided so little protection. Barbara Alpern

Engel notes: "As did proponents of the 'woman question,' Dostoevsky highlights the link between women's economic need and their sexual vulnerability."[49] Yet, as she also reminds us: "the term 'woman question' figures ambiguously, at best, in Dostoevsky's work."[50]

Just as Dostoevsky was not blind to issues of sex or gender, nor did he ignore alternative sexual orientations (to the hetero-norm). As many scholars have noted, Dostoevsky explores the issue of same-sex desire in a number of his fictional works, from female love in *Netochka Nezvanova* (1849), to male desire in *Notes from the House of the Dead* [Zapiski iz mertvogo doma,1862] through *Brothers Karamazov*.[51] There are homosexual minor characters in many of the novels, and in *The Adolescent*, even the title character explores feelings of desire for other young men. Fusso has convincingly argued that while "Arkady's experiments with nonstandard sexuality might seem at first to be yet another example of the novel's obsession with the disorder that threatens the Russian family and social structure," ultimately Dostoevsky does not "prosecute" homosexuality "with the same fury as adultery, capitalism, and child abandonment."[52] Fusso even suggests that: "Homosexuality can lead to the creation of 'accidental families' in the best sense, families based on elective affinities, not on blood."[53] I would challenge this because in my reading of Dostoevsky's fiction, his homosexual unions are more fleeting and less stable than the types of bonds he believes the family should embody. The strongest "intentional kinship" bonds in Dostoevsky's novels are non-sexual. But even if they are not based on homosexuality, following Furneaux's definition, families based on elective kinship, rather than biological reproduction, could still be considered "queer."

Yet if the shoe fits, that does not always mean one should wear it. Although this congruence between queer theory and Dostoevsky's praxis exists, I find it potentially problematic to label Dostoevsky's novels "queer." Halberstam calls queer time and space "useful frameworks for assessing political and cultural change in the late twentieth and early twenty-first centuries."[54] One could add that they were designed to assess specifically the American context. So what does it mean to bring them back in time and into a radically different culture? I believe that Furneaux does it successfully in Victorian England, where Dickens's fictional families truly did challenge Victorian ideas about gender roles and sexuality. But "queerness" is always defined in opposition to a norm, and Russian norms were not the same as those in Britain.[55] As noted at the start of this essay, Russian marriage plots tend to fail. Rather than ending with a wedding and baby, most heroines end up single, dead, almost immediately widowed, or unhappily married without children. If Dostoevsky belongs to this broader Russian pattern, is he part of "the norm," or is the whole Russian tradition "queer" because it does not follow the Anglo/American reproductive model?

There are additional sticking points. Some scholars now claim "queer temporality" is anything that offers an alternative to "progressive, and thus future oriented, teleologies as aligned with heteronormative reproduction," but most queer theorists believe the term should in some way relate to the realm of sex/sexuality/gender.[56] I do not see gender or sexuality as the burning issue in Dostoevsky's novels that serves as the obstacle to reproductive futurity.[57] As noted above, Dostoevsky may have been concerned about women's limited economic options, but he was not a radical and he was not trying to overthrow patriarchal norms. He attacked Chernyshevsky for his ideas about replacing the conjugal couple with the ménage à trois and for his ideas about emancipated women (see Lebezyatnikov's speeches in *Crime and Punishment* for a scathing parody). Radical socialist rejections of the family in *Demons* are parroted by a female student who makes a mockery of them (10:307). Dostoevsky believed in the family, and he believed in men and women fulfilling different roles within it. I see nothing queer in his calls for increased legal rights and protections for women or his desire to end patriarchal tyranny.[58] His concern was child abuse and the suffering of innocents.

Furthermore, in most of the novels, the presence of non-heterosexual forms of desire seems unrelated to Dostoevsky's resistance to hetero-normative reproductive time. Prince Myshkin, whose doctors have confirmed his unweddable status, is a clear outlier. Dostoevsky draws explicit attention to his sexuality when Myshkin tells Rogozhin "because of my congenital illness I don't have any experience of women at all" (8:14).[59] But for other heroes, this link is absent. If Ivan Karamazov never confesses his love for Katerina Ivanovna and their potential courtship plot does not progress, it is not because Ivan is sexually repressed or challenging gender norms. He has other – arguably weightier – things on his mind. Raskolnikov and Sonya are far from thinking about domestic life and reproductive futurity not as a negation of this kind of time but because of the presence of something else. That *else* is what makes a Dostoevsky novel a Dostoevsky novel ... and potentially a Russian novel.

But here again, the issue becomes more complicated, as different conceptions of "queerness" encompass broader conceptions of futurity. An alternative strand of queer theory argues that: "Queerness is a longing that propels us onward, beyond romances of the negative and toiling in the present. Queerness is that thing that lets us feel that this world is not enough, that indeed something is missing."[60] Scholars like José Muñoz, just quoted, argue for a queer futurity that exists always on the horizon, much like Dostoevsky's Ridiculous Man's vision of a utopia that could come in a moment through faith and love, yet we know will never be attained. The "prop[ulsion] onward, beyond the romances of the negative and toiling in the present" could describe just about every one of Dostoevsky's heroes: Ivan "turning back the ticket" to God's world because he cannot accept the suffering of innocents, Mitya dreaming of the "wee one" crying in the burnt-out village and of being reborn through suffering, Raskolnikov looking to the future with hope after his spiritual revelation by the river with Sonya, Prince Myshkin trying to share his ecstatic vision before his epileptic fit at the soirée ...

Dostoevsky's novels offer a challenge to "the classical frameworks of narrative" that McCrea defines as "the rites and rituals of genealogy – marriage and paternity."[61] He narrativizes family without the "love, marriage, childbearing, a peaceful old age for the in-laws, [and] shared meals around the family table" that Bakhtin deems central to the family novel.[62] But whether this is a queer challenge is – to my mind – still an open question. And the first step in answering it is to give greater credence to the way Dostoevsky subverts our expectations for the marriage plot and to give it its due place alongside the drama of fathers and children in our understanding of the Dostoevskian family drama.

NOTES

1 As E.M. Forster claimed in a 1927 lecture: "If you think of a novel in the vague you think of a love interest – of a man and woman who want to be united and perhaps succeed." See Forster, *Aspects of the Novel* (London: Penguin, 1963), 61. Among the most famous studies that claim the centrality of marriage in the novel tradition, see: Ian P. Watt. *The Rise of the Novel: Studies in Defoe, Richardson, and Fielding* (Berkeley and Los Angeles: University of California Press, 1957); Tony Tanner, *Adultery in the Novel: Contract and Transgression* (Baltimore: Johns Hopkins University Press, 1979); and Joseph Allen Boone, *Tradition Counter Tradition: Love and the Form of Fiction* (Chicago: University of Chicago Press, 1987).

2 The two approaches are discussed by Sharon Marcus, *Between Women: Friendship, Desire, and Marriage in Victorian England* (Princeton: Princeton University Press, 2007), 73. Classic studies that focus on the generational plot include: Janet L. Beizer, *Family Plots: Balzac's Narrative Generations* (New Haven: Yale University Press, 1986); Michael Ragussis, *Acts of Naming: The Family Plot in Fiction* (New York: Oxford University Press, 1986); Edward W. Said, *Beginnings: Intention and Method* (New York: Basic Books, 1975); Ross Shideler, *Questioning the Father: From Darwin to Zola, Ibsen, Strindberg, and Hardy* (Stanford: Stanford University Press, 1999). Studies that focus on

the marriage plot include: Joseph Allen Boone, *Tradition Counter Tradition*; Jenni Calder, *Women and Marriage in Victorian Fiction* (New York: Oxford University Press, 1976); Evelyn J. Hinz, "Hierogamy Versus Wedlock: Types of Marriage Plots and Their Relationship to Genres of Prose Fiction," *PMLA* 91, no. 5 (1976): 900–13; and Tony Tanner. *Adultery in the Novel*. A notable exception in Dostoevsky scholarship is Liza Knapp's analysis of *The Adolescent* as a novel of adultery; see Liza Knapp, "Dostoevsky and the Novel of Adultery: *The Adolescent*," *Dostoevsky Studies* New Series, no. 17 (2013): 37–71.

3 Barbara Heldt observes that "Gogol', Turgenev, Goncharov, Tolstoy, Dostoevsky, and Chekhov all describe marriages that don't happen, often against the background of bad or ordinary ones that do." See Heldt, *Terrible Perfection: Women and Russian Literature* (Bloomington and Indianapolis: Indiana University Press, 1987), 21.

4 N.G. Chernyshevsky, "The Russian at the *Rendez-vous*," in *Belinsky, Chernyshevsky, and Dobrolyubov: Selected Criticism*, ed. Ralph E. Matlaw (New York: E.P. Dutton, 1962), 112.

5 Kate Holland has astutely explored Dostoevsky's challenge to the "'noble family novel,' which he saw encapsulated in the works of Tolstoy, Turgenev, and to a lesser extent Goncharov," through looking at the formal issue of fragmentation, tracing parallels between the breakdown of the family and the disintegration of narrative form. See Kate Holland, *The Novel in the Age of Disintegration: Dostoevsky and the Problem of Genre in the 1870s* (Evanston: Northwestern University Press, 2013), 103.

6 As Ilya Kliger notes in chapter 10 of this volume, in *Demons*, the wishes of Stavrogin's mother and former tutor that he "come to his senses, marry a beautiful heiress, and become a brilliant member of society" are completely out of touch with "the novel's more authentic preoccupations" (211).

7 Barry McCrea, *In the Company of Strangers: Family and Narrative in Dickens, Conan Doyle, Joyce, and Proust* (New York: Columbia University Press, 2011), 8.

8 Said, *Beginnings*, xiii. For Bakhtin, time in the family novel is defined by "family-as-genealogy." See "Forms of Time and of the Chronotope in the Novel," in *The Dialogic Imagination*, trans. Caryl Emerson and Michael Holquist, ed. Michael Holquist (Austin: University of Texas Press, 1981), 231.

9 Lev Tolstoi, *Polnoe sobranie sochinenii (Iubileinoe izdanie)*, 90 Vols. (Moscow: Gosudarstvennoe izdatel'stvo "Khudozhestvennaia literatura," 1928–59), 19:294. English translation: Leo Tolstoy, *Anna Karenina*, trans. Richard Pevear and Larissa Volokhonsky (New York: Penguin Books, 2000), 716.

10 Said, *Beginnings*, 93.

11 William Makepeace Thackeray, *Vanity Fair* (London: Penguin, 2012), 250.

12 In Barry McCrea's words: "The English nineteenth-century novel from Austen on seems, structurally at least, to be in the thrall of a sort of fertility cult,

where all sense of beginnings and endings are predicated upon marriage and procreation," *In the Company of Strangers*, 7.

13 McCrea, *In the Company of Strangers*, 8. Many English novels end with a marriage and the birth of a child in the final pages, epitomizing this ending cum beginning. On the Russian side, the arrival of an heir is not always at the very conclusion of the novel, but Aksakov's *Family Chronicle* [Semeinaia khronika, 1856], Turgenev's *Rudin* (1857), Goncharov's *Oblomov* (1859), Tolstoy's *Family Happiness* [Semeinaia schast'ia, 1859], *War and Peace* [Voina i mir, 1869], and *Anna Karenina* (1877), and Stulli's *Twice Married* [Dva raza zamuzhem, 1875] all feature the arrival of children in their later pages. Aksakov's *Family Chronicle* closes with the long-desired heir's name being penned into the family's genealogical tree – bringing the narrative full circle, as this infant would grow up to become the author of the chronicle.

14 This does not mean that Dostoevsky ignored genetic inheritance. The Karamazov brothers, for example, make repeated references to their shared blood, what Ivan calls "the Karamazov force" [karamazovskaia sila] (14:240; 263). All references to Dostoevsky are to F.M. Dostoevskii, *Polnoe sobranie sochinenii v tridtsati tomakh*, ed. G.M. Fridlender et al. (Leningrad: "Nauka," 1972–90). Subsequent volume and page number references to this edition will be indicated in the text in parentheses: (vol.:page). Where an English translation is used, the page number is provided following the *PSS* and set off by a semicolon. Translations from *Brothers Karamazov* are from Richard Pevear and Larissa Volokhonsky, trans., *The Brothers Karamazov* (London: Vintage Books, 2004).

15 In the scene of their coming together, the word *teper'* appears thirty-four times (and *segodnia/shnee* seven times). Yet at the same time, Arkady asks to hear his origin story – how his father and mother first became a couple. He wishes to understand the family past he never had.

16 Dostoevsky's critique responded to the lives and ideas of Herzen and Chernyshevsky, who challenged the traditional, patriarchal family structure, as well as to Turgenev's landmark *Fathers and Children* [Ottsy i deti, 1862]. In his *Writer's Diary*, Dostoevsky explained that *The Adolescent* was his first attempt at writing his own *Fathers and Children* (22:7). See also Susanne Fusso, "Dostoevskii and the Family," in *The Cambridge Companion to Dostoevskii*, ed. William J. Leatherbarrow (Cambridge: Cambridge University Press, 2002), 175, 177.

17 Carol Apollonio, *Dostoevsky's Secrets: Reading against the Grain* (Evanston: Northwestern University Press, 2009), 144.

18 I discuss this in "Lateral Plots: Brothers and the Nineteenth-Century Russian Novel," *Slavic and East European Journal* 16, no.1 (2017): 21.

19 Dostoevsky refers to Ivan's passion for her after his return from Moscow, and notes: "it could all serve as the plot for another story, for a different

novel, which I do not even know that I shall ever undertake" (15:48, 610–11).

20 The dynamics of their relationship receive a brilliant treatment by Yuri Corrigan, who points out that "Dmitry's fear of his unexplored interior darkness and his incapacity for self-direction thus make him ideally suited to fall under Katerina Ivanovna's administrative guidance." See Yuri Corrigan, *Dostoevsky and the Riddle of the Self* (Evanston: Northwestern University Press, 2017), 127. Yet at the same time as Katerina plans to "be his god, to whom he will pray," Corrigan notes that "part of her bizarre intention [is] to dissolve herself into Dmitry as a mere extension of his personality: 'I will turn myself simply into a means for his salvation… into an instrument, into a machine for his happiness, and that for my whole life' (14:172)." See Corrigan, *Riddle of the Self*, 127–8.

21 Similarly, in English literature we see the seduction of Gaskell's *Ruth* (1853) – the classic English fallen woman – through *her* eyes, just as in Austen we learn that Wickham and Willoughby have no honest matrimonial intentions only when Elizabeth and Marianne themselves discover the truth: *Pride and Prejudice* (1813); *Sense and Sensibility* (1811).

22 Michael Katz, "Dostoevskii's Homophilia/Homophobia," in *Gender and Sexuality in Russian Civilization*, ed. Peter I. Barta (London: Routledge, 2001), 249, 247–8.

23 Illegitimacy was a much greater concern in the eighteenth-century English novel than in the nineteenth, and the extramarital affairs could be treated with humour, as in Fielding's *Tom Jones* (1749).

24 Vyacheslav Ivanov provides a symbolic reading of Stavrogin's marriage to Mariya Shatova, seeing her as the embodiment of Russia and Stavrogin as Russia's betrayer. See V.I. Ivanov, "Ekskurs osnovnoi mif v romane 'Besy,'" in Ivanov, *Sobranie sochinenii* (Brussels, 1987), vol. 4, 442–3.

25 While in *Brothers Karamazov*, this idea that love must be earned is actively challenged (the chapter containing the defence attorney's speech is titled "An Adulterer of Thought"), Fusso notes in her discussion of the Kroneberg trial, Dostoevsky "refuses to admit an *a priori* sacredness for the family": see "Dostoevskii and the Family," 185. The difference, she argues, is that Dmitry's lawyer was trying to help him evade responsibility, whereas in the Kroneberg case, Dostoevsky wanted to *make* the father responsible for torturing his daughter.

26 In *Demons*, Stepan Trofimovich similarly claims: "I find I have so little right to be called a father," after noting how long it has been since he's seen "Petrusha" (10:75; 92). English translation from Richard Pevear and Larissa Volokhonsky, trans., *Demons* (London: Vintage, 2006).

27 In her study of memory, Diane Oenning Thompson arrives at this point through its inverse: forgetting one's children as a form of neglect and "a

critical index of morality." See Diane Oenning Thompson, The Brothers Karamazov *and the Poetics of Memory* (Cambridge: Cambridge University Press, 1991), 165.

28 Bakhtin, *Problems of Dostoevsky's Poetics*, trans. Caryl Emerson (Minneapolis: University of Minnesota Press, 1984), 169. Robin Feuer Miller notes that *The Idiot* provides an exception to this general rule in *Dostoevsky and "The Idiot": Author, Narrator, and Reader* (Cambridge, MA: Harvard University Press, 1981), 97.

29 See Fusso, "Dostoevskii and the Family," 179. Holland writes that *The Adolescent* "presents an all-pervasive present" and "takes as its starting point a blank slate, the denial of memory, but gradually acknowledges that without memory form is not possible." See *Novel in the Age of Disintegration*, 122. I am grateful to Greta Matzner-Gore for pointing out Arkady's confusion with genealogical time when he refers to Versilov as his "future father" (13:17).

30 As Corrigan has noted: "the dramatic crises of Dostoevskii's major novels […] are all, without exception, catalyzed by his characters' sudden confrontation with the distant past: Raskolnikov's discovery that his mother and sister are coming to Petersburg in *Crime and Punishment*; Myshkin's return to Russia in *The Idiot*; Stavrogin's arrival in his hometown in *Demons*; Arkady's reunion with his family in *The Adolescent*; and the brothers' homecoming in *The Brothers Karamazov*." See Yuri Corrigan, "Dostoevskii on Evil as Safe Haven and Anesthetic," *Slavic and East European Journal* 63, no. 2 (2019): 229. While Corrigan is interested in the characters' "reckoning with the past," these are also important moments of family reunion.

31 Here I am disagreeing with Semenov, who argues that the conflict of fathers and children is a conflict of the present and future. E.I. Semenov, *Roman Dostoevskogo 'Podrostok': problematika i zhanr* (Leningrad: Nauka, 1979), 138.

32 The one seeming exception is in Dostoevsky's very first novel, *Poor Folk* [Bednye liudi, 1846], where Bykov's express purpose in marrying Varenka is to produce an heir. But as Varenka reports, his true motivation – that he openly explains to her – is that "he had, as he put it, a 'no-good nephew' whom he had sworn to deprive of his inheritance, and that it was for this very reason – that of acquiring some lawful inheritors – that he sought my hand" (1:100; 118). English translation by David McDuff, *Poor Folk and Other Stories* (London: Penguin Books, 1988). He is not actually concerned with creating his own line. Varenka, in turn, departs the novel as if going to her death, her final words to Devushkin being: "My tears are choking me, breaking me. Farewell. God, how sad! Remember, remember your poor Varenka!" (1:106, 127). We have no indication of whether the sought-after heir ever materializes.

33 Jennifer Wilson, "Dostoevsky's Timely Castration," *Transgender Studies Quarterly* 4, no. 5 (2018): 567.

34 According to Wilson, the *skoptsy* "provide an example of queer time that is not belated, delayed, or without a future but one that rushes to the future, unencumbered by the quotidian demands of the present. It is precisely this overwhelming futurity that makes them antisocial to Dostoevsky." Wilson, "Dostoevsky's Timely Castration," 570.

35 There are also no family businesses to carry on as, for example, in Dickens's *Dombey and Son* (1848), Charlotte Brontë's *Shirley* (1849), or Gaskell's *North and South* (1855). There are, however, family estates that the men must steward for the good of their children. Tolstoy emphasizes this in *Anna Karenina*, contrasting Oblonsky's failures with Levin's successes.

36 This lateral expansion provided Dostoevsky's path towards the universal unity for which he strived. As I have argued elsewhere, for Dostoevsky: "Family can expand when the ties that bind it are active love, which can be bestowed on all, not something shared – childhood memories, clan, race, nationality – which will ultimately prove to be a restricting and dividing force." See Anna A. Berman, *Siblings in Tolstoy and Dostoevsky: The Path to Universal Brotherhood* (Evanston: Northwestern University Press, 2015), 130.

37 Bakhtin, *Problems of Dostoevsky's Poetics*, 39. Italics in original.

38 Matzner-Gore, *Dostoevsky and the Ethics of Narrative Form*, 44.

39 Ibid., 62.

40 Duc Dau and Shale Preston discuss the implications of applying a queer theory lens to Victorian depictions of the family in their "Introduction" to *Queer Victorian Families: Curious Relations in Literature* (New York: Routledge, 2015).

41 Edelman, for example, specifically objects to "the trope of the child as figure for the universal value attributed to political futurity," and the "absolute privilege of heteronormativity" that accompanies it. See: "The Future is Kid Stuff: Queer Theory, Disidentification, and the Death Drive" *NARRATIVE* 6, no. 1 (1998): 18–30 (here 19); *No Future: Queer Theory and the Death Drive* (Durham: Duke University Press, 2004), 2.

42 Judith Halberstam, *In a Queer Time and Place: Transgender Bodies, Subcultural Lives* (New York: New York University Press, 2005), 2.

43 Halberstam defines "the time of inheritance" as an "overview of generational time within which values, wealth, goods, and morals are passed through family ties from one generation to the next. It also connects the family to the historical past of the nation, and glances ahead to connect the family to the future of both familial and national stability." See *In a Queer Time and Place*, 5.

44 'Intentional kin" is explained by the sociologist Margaret K. Nelson in her "Fictive Kin, Families We Choose, and Voluntary Kin: What Does the Discourse Tell Us?" *Journal of Family Theory & Review* 5 (2013): 269. In relying on a conception of family that is not based on biology or legal state

sanction, Dostoevsky is closer to twenty-first-century sociologists' social constructionist definitions of the family. These definitions approach family as a social construct and set of behaviours, shifting the emphasis to the affective bonds, actions, and activities that *create* familial relationships rather than bloodline or legal unions (e.g., Dostoevsky's claim that "family is created by the untiring labor of love."). See Braithwaite et al., "Constructing family: a Typology of Voluntary Kin," *Journal of Social and Personal Relationships* 27, no. 3 (2010): 388–407.

45 Holly Furneaux, *Queer Dickens: Erotics, Families, Masculinities* (Oxford: Oxford University Press, 2009), 9.

46 Ibid., 10. According to Barry McCrea "the rites and rituals of genealogy – marriage and paternity – are the basis for the classical frameworks of narrative." See *In the Company of Strangers*, 8.

47 Furneaux, *Queer Dickens*, 26.

48 While not specifically concerned with family roles, Connor Doak sees masculinity as a central issue in Dostoevsky's novels. His study of Prince Myshkin offers an early attempt to use queer theory to make sense of some of the ambiguities in Dostoevsky's treatment of gender in *The Idiot*. See Connor Doak, "Myshkin's Queer Failure: (Mis)reading Masculinity in Dostoevskii's *The Idiot*." *Slavic and East European Journal* 63, no. 1 (2019): 1–27.

49 Barbara Alpern Engel, "The 'Woman Question,' Women's Work, Women's Options," in *Dostoevsky in Context*, ed. Deborah A. Martinsen and O.E. Maiorova (Cambridge: Cambridge University Press, 2015), 59.

50 Ibid., 61.

51 For a thoughtful, meticulously researched and historically grounded treatment of the subject, see Suzanne Fusso, *Discovering Sexuality in Dostoevsky* (Evanston: Northwestern University Press, 2006), 42–54. Her footnote 7 on p. 45 includes a list of relevant scholarship on homosexuality in Dostoevsky's novels.

52 Indeed, Fusso goes further in suggesting a positive place for homosexuality, noting that the moments of "tender friendship" between (homosexual) Trishatov and other men "stand out from the generally bleak landscape of human relationships in [*The Adolescent*]." See *Discovering Sexuality*, 54.

53 Ibid.

54 Halberstam, *In a Queer Time and Place*, 4.

55 In support of this, David M. Halperin argues explicitly that "queer" "acquires its meaning from its oppositional relation to the norm," and must be thought of as "a positionality vis-à-vis the normative." See Halperin, *Saint Foucault: Towards a Gay Hagiography* (New York: Oxford University Press, 1995), 62.

56 The issue is summarized in Carla Freccero, "Queer Times," *South Atlantic Quarterly* 106, no. 3 (2007): 489.

57 Connor Doak does see Dostoevsky as critiquing masculinity, arguing that (in *Demons*) "Dostoevsky found it impossible to imagine a masculinity that could unite an active sexuality with moral goodness in his fictional world." See Connor Doak, "Masculine Degeneration in Dostoevsky's *Demons*" in *Russian Writers and the Fin de Siècle: The Twilight of Realism*, ed. Katherine Bowers and Ani Kokobobo (Cambridge: Cambridge University Press, 2015), 116. Although moral exemplars like Father Zosima and Prince Myshkin are celibate, I would question whether the issue is combining sexuality with moral goodness, or just conceiving of a true moral model who is also active in the world. Razumikhin is one of Dostoevsky's most positive and active figures and he clearly has no lack of sexual passion for Dunya.

58 For a feminist reading of Dostoevsky's views on women that treats the question of women's rights, see Nina Pelikan Straus, *Dostoevsky and the Woman Question* (New York: St Martin's Press, 1994).

59 See Doak's discussion of Myshkin's queer challenge to norms of masculinity ("Myshkin's Queer Failure," 1–27).

60 José Esteban Muñoz, *Cruising Utopia: The Then and There of Queer Futurity* (New York: New York University Press, 2009), 1.

61 McCrea, *In the Company of Strangers*, 8.

62 Bakhtin, "Forms of Time and of the Chronotope in the Novel," 232.

3 The Greasy-Haired Pawnbroker and the Capitalist *Raskrasavitsa*: Dostoevsky's Businesswomen

VADIM SHNEYDER

Dostoevsky's Businesswomen

Women's unusually strong property rights in Imperial Russia had important consequences both for Russian society and for Russian literature. Russian women retained the right to own and acquire separate property in marriage.[1] As the nineteenth-century feminist writer and critic Mariya Tsebrikova explained, "The pecuniary independence of the Russian woman – for she is mistress of her own fortune, as I have already stated – has led to her obtaining the few other privileges which she enjoys. As she owns property, she pays taxes, and therefore participates in the choice of the members of the municipal council (*gorodskaia ouprava*) [*sic*] which expends her money."[2] Nineteenth-century Russian literature offers numerous examples of economically independent women, from the landowners Korobochka in Nikolai Gogol's *Dead Souls* [Mertvye dushi, 1842] and Arina Petrovna Golovlyova in Mikhail Saltykov-Shchedrin's *The Golovlyovs* [Gospoda golovlevy, 1880] to owners of enterprises like Vera Pavlovna in Nikolai Chernyshevsky's *What Is to Be Done?* [Chto delat'?, 1863] and a number of characters in stories by Anton Chekhov. In this respect, Dostoevsky may be unusual only in terms of the relative frequency with which wealthy women appear in his works.

Scholars examining Dostoevsky's representation of women have come to different conclusions regarding his treatment of women's property. Sally Livingston argues that nineteenth-century Russian women writers could posit alternatives to the marriage plot for their female protagonists, while Dostoevsky and other male writers responded by portraying "propertied heroines as dangerous and controlling."[3] Ultimately, argues Livingston, Dostoevsky "neutralizes the women of property, subjugating their wealth to spiritual redemption," so that they come to function as "vehicles through which Dostoevsky conveys his larger message about the evils of money."[4] On the other hand, Nina Pelikan Straus emphasizes the ways that money allows some of Dostoevsky's female characters to resist their own commodification. Writing about *Brothers Karamazov* [Brat'ia Karamazovy, 1880], Straus argues that "Katerina and Grushenka differ from these women [i.e., women who are forced by poverty to acquiesce to purchase by men] in a major respect [...] Each has money and therefore more choice; neither Grushenka nor Katerina can be 'bought' like Nastasya Filippovna or the poverty-stricken gentle creature."[5] Furthermore, "each woman actively participates in culturally symbolic transactions involving money that allow her to remain independent of men's evaluations of her to some extent."[6]

Perhaps Livingston and Straus are both right: women of property in Dostoevsky often lose their property in order to embark upon their own redemption or to become vehicles for the redemption of others. At the same time, women who control property exert power over men. Indeed, propertied women in Dostoevsky's fictions are frequently both economically active subjects and objects of desire, coercion, and violence. The aim of the following pages is to examine this subject/object duality in the broader context of Dostoevsky's economic plots and to deepen our understanding of the ways that money, gender, and power interact in Dostoevsky's fictions. In the process, this chapter focuses, to a large extent, on apparent *melochi* – insignificant details. Two case studies – one drawn from *Crime and Punishment* [Prestuplenie i nakazanie], the other from *Brothers Karamazov* – will aim to show how details pertaining to the description of two exemplary businesswomen link them to their characteristic forms of money. At the same time, these details – the greasy hair of the pawnbroker Alyona Ivanovna and the curiously abstract "curve" expressed in the body of the (part-time) moneylender Grushenka – also illustrate the other crucial dimension of each Dostoevskian businesswoman: her status as an object of male observation and violence. Each of these telling details is isomorphic with a type of money and, more broadly, a character type within Dostoevsky's taxonomy of economic elites.

In Dostoevsky's fictions, most rich characters resemble their money.[7] This applies to the two major categories of these characters, who can be distinguished as merchants and capitalists (a distinction that does not necessarily hold in the works of other nineteenth-century Russian writers or in Russian history). Alyona Ivanovna and Grushenka generally correspond to merchants and capitalists, and their characteristic details point to their function within two quite different novelistic economies. Whereas Alyona Ivanovna is linked, like Dostoevsky's merchant characters, to immobile, unexchangeable money, Grushenka is connected to the model of Dostoevsky's capitalists, who are linked to abstract, fungible capital. At the same time, in their imperfect correspondence to these models of economic activity, with their related narrative forms, the cases of Alyona Ivanovna and Grushenka also reveal how Dostoevsky's economic imaginary is gendered.

Capitalists and Merchants in Dostoevsky's Economic Imaginary

Dostoevsky's character system accommodates a considerable number of pawnbrokers, landlords, lawyers, merchants, and businesspeople loosely labelled "*delovye liudi.*" Within this range of characters largely defined by their relationship to money, there are, broadly, two types, whom I have categorized elsewhere as capitalists and merchants.[8] It is in *The Idiot* [Idiot, 1869] that Dostoevsky offers the clearest differentiation of these types. Among the St Petersburg super-rich in that novel there is a somewhat indistinct man named Afanasy Ivanovich Totsky, known for being "a landowner and arch-capitalist [raskapitalistom], a member of companies and societies."[9] What is an arch-capitalist? This distinctive locution enters the novel through the speech of the verbally excessive civil servant Lebedev. It appears to be Dostoevsky's neologism, alongside other nouns augmented with the intensifying prefix *-raz: razarestant* (arch-prisoner), *razgenii* (arch-genius), *razmillioner* (arch-millionaire).[10] It is, moreover, one that appears only once in all of Dostoevsky's oeuvre.[11] Despite its unique application to him, this word tells us rather little about Totsky. We learn almost nothing about his biography, except that, many years earlier, he became the guardian of the adolescent Nastasya Filippovna and used his position to rape her. He fears exposure of this single biographical fact and tries to bribe an ambitious and acquisitive young suitor, Gavrila Ardalionovich, into marrying Nastasya Filippovna with a dowry of 75,000 rubles. When a scandal ensues at her name-day party, he makes a quiet exit from the novel, but reappears in the narrator's recollections at the very end, at which point we learn that he, unlike the novel's protagonists – Myshkin, Rogozhin, and Nastasya Filippovna – is, by all indications, doing fine at the novel's conclusion. When his money is no longer significant to the plot, Totsky vanishes, but unlike the characters in this novel who make their exits by dying, going mad, or being sentenced to hard labour, Totsky leaves the novel unharmed. This ability to slip away is a telling feature of Dostoevsky's capitalists.

The very lack of description that makes Totsky so illegible within the novel and so easily dismissed form its plot associates him with the endlessly mobile, amorphous wealth that he derives from his activities as an arch-capitalist. This money is generated somewhere on the fringes of the novel's diegesis and flows from these undescribed "companies and societies" into unspecified repositories where it remains available, if Totsky needed to deploy it at a narratively pivotal moment. He does not need to bring his 75,000 rubles to Nastasya Filippovna's apartment; everyone believes that he has the money, and that is enough. Diametrically opposed to capitalists like Totsky are the Dostoevskian merchants, of whom Rogozhin is the most fully elaborated example. In general, the merchants tend to be suspicious and conservative. They build their insular lives around their wealth, which has a tendency to assume the form of cash, and they hoard this cash in their massive, solid houses. The merchants are merchants somehow ontologically – immobile, isolated, and, at extreme points, tending to fuse with their possessions, like Kuzma Kuzmich Samsonov in *Brothers Karamazov*, who has become immobile and sits permanently inside his house. These merchants owe much to traditional miser types in European literature, although Dostoevsky imbues his most prominent merchants, like Rogozhin, with tempestuous interior depths: he is a "usurer ... with poetry," as a draft to *The Idiot* puts it (9:142).[12]

Dostoevskian capitalists are less like the traditional misers of European literature. They are always busy, constantly accumulating new capital through ceaseless activity that usually involves manipulating the institutions of modern society. General Yepanchin, another prominent capitalist in *The Idiot*, is a self-made man, a soldier's son who rose from such disreputable activities as tax farming to owning expensive rental properties in St Petersburg and a factory on its outskirts, as well as participating in a joint-stock company. His wealth is abstract like Totsky's, consisting of assets that stretch across the novel's imaginary topography. Likewise, Luzhin in *Crime and Punishment* is a modern type of capitalist. He is a lawyer, benefiting from the newfound relevance of his profession in the wake of the 1864 legal reform. Like his counterparts in other works of Russian fiction of the time, Luzhin seeks to turn his legal expertise into a remunerative business.[13] While the merchants hoard, the capitalists invest. The economic immobility of Dostoevskian merchants tends to fix them narratively as well. The capitalists, on the other hand, range far and wide in their novels, and their narrative future tends to remain open at the end.

Dostoevsky's businesswomen broadly fit into these two categories of economic elites. Although Alyona Ivanovna does not belong to the merchant estate, she shares their key features, such as the physicality of their wealth and their harmony with their interior spaces. Grushenka, on the other hand, shares important traits of the capitalists.[14] Although her description by the narrator of *Brothers Karamazov* is considerably more detailed than that of most of the capitalists who inhabit Dostoevsky's novels, her physicality bears traces of the capitalists' distinctive abstractness. These similarities notwithstanding, Dostoevskian businesswomen differ from their male counterparts in several significant ways. They tend to have a narrower range of occupations. Both Alyona Ivanovna and Grushenka collect debts (although Grushenka does not loan money).[15] Other, more marginal, characters, like Zarnitsyna, Raskolnikov's landlady, own real estate. More significantly, unlike businessmen in Dostoevsky's novels, the businesswomen are never just businesswomen. Whereas wealthy men are largely defined by and congruent with their wealth, there seems always to be a descriptive excess associated with the businesswoman. In each case examined here, in the course of introducing the character, the narrator will come to a telling detail, which will complicate the connection between the woman and her moneymaking by defining her in part as an object of a (male) character's actions or desires. In their constantly oscillating status as, alternately, agents and objects of economic transactions, Dostoevskian businesswomen do not fit their milieus quite as snugly as do their male counterparts.

Interior Description and Essence

We can see a clear example of the differing degrees of correspondence between character and milieu by comparing the relationship of two characters and their homes. Once again, *The Idiot* furnishes the best material for comparison. In Part 2 of that novel, Prince Myshkin pays a visit to the house where Rogozhin lives with his elderly mother. Myshkin explains to Rogozhin that he was able to identify the building from the street on account of a mysterious similitude between its appearance and the essence of its owners:

> Your house has the physiognomy of your whole family and your whole Rogozhin life. But ask me why I came to this conclusion, and I won't be able to explain it at all. It's nonsense, of course. It even frightens me that this concerns me so much. Before, I would not have even thought that you live in such a house, but once I saw it, it immediately occurred to me: "Yes, why he has to have a house exactly like this!" (8:172)

Myshkin finds that the house's details are legible, and what he reads in them is the nature of the Rogozhin family: the dark recesses, the thick, almost windowless walls, and the money-changing booths run by *skoptsy* on the lower floors all say something about the Rogozhins and about Parfyon Semyonovich in particular.[16] William Comer summarizes the metonymic links joining the house and its occupants as follows: "secretive gloom – the house – the 'Castrates' – Rogozhin."[17] The Rogozhin family essence, objectified in the house, also suggests Rogozhin's destiny. The encounter with Nastasya Filippovna sets Rogozhin on a path of public confrontation and wanton expenditure, but even his passionate desire for her ultimately assumes the form of greed. As Michael Holquist puts it, "he is a miser who takes very seriously the grim joke of Nastasya Filippovna's sale of herself to the highest bidder in the auction that concludes the first book of the novel. Having bought her, he seeks to hoard her – because she possesses him."[18] In the end, Rogozhin's essence reasserts itself and pulls him back into the world of his family home – which is where his story ends in a deranged embrace with Myshkin beside Nastasya Filippovna's body.

At first glance, every detail of Alyona Ivanovna's appearance seems to indicate that she fits her apartment just as well as Rogozhin corresponded to his house. Although she is a minor character, we learn a gread deal about her details. Near the beginning of *Crime and Punishment*, Raskolnikov pays a visit to the apartment from which Alyona Ivanovna conducts her business. He has prepared for this meeting – this trial run for the murder – by deliberately dwelling on the danger posed by insignificant details (*melochi*) to his carefully reasoned plan. Walking through Haymarket Square, he is singled out by some passerby on account of his grotesque hat. "Some stupid little thing, some banal little detail could ruin the whole idea!" Raskolnikov reflects (6:9). The word *meloch'* occurs four times on this page as Raskolnikov reflects: "It's precisely these little details that always bring ruin to everything." This is, in a certain sense, precisely what will happen later. Raskolnikov forgets to close the door after he kills Alyona Ivanovna, and this *meloch'* means that Lizaveta enters silently when he is in the other room. As far as he is concerned, she – and, possibly, her unborn child as well, since Raskolnikov overhears that Lizaveta is "constantly pregnant" (6:54) – are likewise *melochi* – and to such an extent that he famously forgets about them.[19] But for now, he meticulously registers every detail of the building in which the pawnbroker lives.

When Alyona Ivanovna responds to his knock by opening the door to her apartment, he looks inside, and this motivates the first of the novel's interior descriptions.[20] The pawnbroker's apartment, filled with suffocating air and furnishings all tinged with yellow, is itself a metonym of the febrile city suffering under a July heatwave. In addition to the intensification of the urban atmosphere, as focalized through Raskolnikov's tormented subjectivity, this glimpse of the apartment also incorporates Alyona Ivanovna into the novel's system of social classification.[21] Like Rogozhin's house, this apartment gives material expression to a particular social category: in this case, the apartments of "cruel and old widows" (6:9). Observing the old and oddly shaped objects in the apartment (including a "round table of an oval shape"), Raskolnikov notices that, despite the obvious age of the furnishings and the signs of poverty and decay, "everything was very clean: both the furniture and the floors were polished to a shine; everything gleamed" (6:9). The pawnbroker's tyrannical will has evidently imposed itself upon all the objects in this apartment (and upon Alyona Ivanovna's half-sister Lizaveta, who tends to them and keeps everything shiny and free of dust). Later, after the murder, when Raskolnikov rummages through the pledges in the pawnbroker's lockbox, he will find that the apparent disorder in which they are scattered among items of clothing in fact gives way to a systematic organization of carefully wrapped and hidden objects. It turns out that everything in this small and poor interior has its place. Even a cracked saucer has found purpose as a soap holder, which Raskolnikov finds while he is trying to scrub the blood from the handle of his ax. Everything in this space is rigorously controlled, and the space itself is totally sequestered from the outside by numerous locks and bolts.

In most respects, Alyona Ivanovna is like the space she inhabits. Her clothing, faded and yellowed, seems in harmony with the apartment's yellow wallpaper. The flannel and fur that she wears intensifies the sensation of heat that pervades these rooms. The adjectives that the narrator attaches to Alyona Ivanovna's physical description likewise suggest that she belongs in this hot and desiccated environment: she is "a dry little old lady, about sixty, with sharp and cruel eyes and a sharp little nose" (6:8). A dried-up, suspicious old woman, living out her life inside a tiny, hermetically sealed apartment with her accumulated wealth: Alyona Ivanova is a familiar type. She clearly descends from the misers of European literary tradition, which, as Jillian Porter has shown, adapted to the formal and thematic demands of Russian realism even as other traditional types tended to obsolesce.[22] Like Rogozhin, she dwells and hoards in secret.

The particular similitude that obtains between Alyona Ivanovna and her interior stems from several sources. One of these is likely Balzac. In his novel *Eugénie Grandet* (1834), whose Russian translation was Dostoevsky's first published work, the protagonist, a miser's daughter, ends up succumbing to the rigorous discipline of monetary accumulation: "money was destined to impart its cold glitter to her angelic life and to inspire a mistrust of feeling in a woman who was all feeling."[23] At the end of the novel, the narrator informs us that Eugénie, now the widowed Madame de Bonfons, lives in solitude in the house where she grew up. "The house at Saumur, sunless, devoid of warmth, gloomy, and always in the shade, reflects her life."[24] Notably, both the passages about the cold glitter of money and the description of the gloomy house in Saumur were absent from the published text of Dostoevsky's translation as it appeared in the journal *Repertoire and Pantheon*, although it is unclear if this absence reflects Dostoevsky's choice or the editor's.[25] Regardless, Dostoevsky undoubtedly read these descriptions as he carefully worked his way through Balzac's text. While he opted to emphasize Eugénie's "suffering self-denial" and her sentimental relationship with her servant Nanon, rather than her relationship to money, the image of a woman shaped and transformed by money comes back forcefully twenty years later in the figure of Alyona Ivanovna.[26] In his translation, Dostoevsky does make one suggestive lexical change: whereas Balzac attributes to the aging Eugénie "the rigidity [raideur] of the old maid," Dostoevsky translates *raideur* as *sukhost'* (dryness), which anticipates the miserly dryness of the pawnbroker in *Crime and Punishment*.[27]

Furthermore, certain textual details suggest that Alyona Ivanovna is related to another character type intimately linked to interior spaces in realist novels: the landlady. Elisa Frost has observed that within the intricate system of doubles in *Crime and Punishment*, several plot details – stairs, debts, apartments, the alternation of Raskolnikov's thoughts – link Alyona Ivanovna to his landlady Zarnitsyna, and, by extension, to what Frost calls the "landlady topos" in Russian fiction.[28] Insofar as Alyona Ivanovna functions as a quasi-landlady in the character system of *Crime and Punishment*, she brings to mind another character from Balzac: Madame Vauquer, the quintessential landlady from *Father Goriot* [Le Père Goriot, 1835]. The deep connections between this novel and *Crime and Punishment* have been examined extensively.[29] As for Madame Vauquer, Erich Auerbach provided the classic analysis of the essential connection, the "harmony," that obtained between the landlady and her boarding house.[30] What asserts the connection between the landlady and her property is, as Hayden White suggests, the perspective of the implied author, with his interest in social taxonomy.[31] An observer's consciousness establishes the link between the woman and the interior space she inhabits, identifying her as a type linked to a particular environment. In the case of *Crime and Punishment*, Raskolnikov, who seeks both to scrutinize and to kill, focalizes the narrative perspective that establishes a similar kind of harmony between Alyona Ivanovna and her interior. It is also because of the prominent place of Raskolnikov's subjectivity in this scene that the accummulated details of Alyona Ivanovna's description will eventually disrupt the Balzacian harmony between her and her environment.

Alyona Ivanovna's Hair

Among the things that Raskolnikov notices as he glances over the apartment is Alyona Ivanovna's hair: "Her blond hair, with just a bit of gray, was thickly covered in grease" (6:8). The greasiness of her hair is sufficiently noteworthy to merit a second mention when Raskolnikov returns to the apartment to murder her (6:63). This time, nothing else about Alyona Ivanovna or her home attracts the narrator's attention, here again focalized through Raskolnikov's subjectivity: only her hair, which Raskolnikov presumably notices moments before striking her head with the ax. This little bit of obdurate detail drives a tiny wedge between Alyona Ivanovna and her apartment. While all the objects are spotlessly clean, her hair is greasy. In this novel, and in particular in these scenes where Raskolnikov's preoccupation with *melochi* causes everything to overflow in semiotic excess, the pawnbroker's greasy hair is unlikely to be merely an inert bit of nineteenth-century realia.

I think that we can gain insight into the meaning of this greasy hair by way of a distant source: twentieth-century existential phenomenology. Near the end of *Being and Nothingness*, Jean-Paul Sartre examines the tactile quality of *viscosité*, which can be translated as sliminess or stickiness.[32] What makes this material property so notable for Sartre is its capacity to simultaneously define and threaten the boundaries of the embodied self and the world it inhabits:

> There is something like a tactile fascination in the slimy. I am no longer the master in *arresting* the process of appropriation. It continues. In one sense it is like the supreme docility of the possessed, the fidelity of a dog who *gives himself* even when one does not want him any longer, and in another sense there is underneath this docility a surreptitious appropriation of the possessor by the possessed.[33]

Although one may choose the moment when one touches a slimy or sticky substance, one does not have the same degree of choice in disengaging from it. Its traces remain on one's fingers for a long time, a reminder that one has been changed by this contact, which cannot be undone. The same property of lingering contact, which resists the body's attempts to extricate itself, also obtains in the case of the greasy, and this, I think, is where the deeper significance of Alyona Ivanovna's hair becomes apparent. Grease spreads to surfaces it contacts, and it is not soluble in water, a substance with no shortage of symbolic resonances in *Crime and Punishment*.[34] Once Raskolnikov commits murder, traces of this act, and of his victim, will cling to him like the blood that contaminates the fringes of his clothing. But this persistence of Alyona Ivanovna has meaning only for Raskolnikov: she continues to exist, in a sense, but only as his nightmares and torments. In other words, Alyona Ivanovna's greasy hair, which severs the link between her and her milieu, simultaneously makes her an object for Raskolnikov to observe, to murder, and to think about later as he takes his slow path from error to redemption.

Sticky and greasy substances will continue to adhere to Raskolnikov throughout the novel.[35] The one other appearance of a person explicitly described as greasy takes place between Raskolnikov's two visits to Alyona Ivanovna's, when he steps into the bar where he meets Marmeladov. In that case, the bar's proprietor has a face "as if smeared in grease, just like an iron lock" (6:10). This greasy proprietor is congruent with his bar, where the tables are sticky and the food smells rotten. Moments later, in this environment where everything sticks and becomes contaminated, Raskolnikov will encounter Marmeladov, the ex–civil servant whose sugary name is also redolent of stickiness, and the two men will become morally and narratively entangled. The sticky, beer-encrusted table on which Raskolnikov rests his sleeves just before his conversation with Marmeladov seems likewise to contain the implication that Raskolnikov has not fully removed himself from the intersubjective density of his social surroundings. Later, Raskolnikov will help carry the dying Marmeladov to his family's apartment. Afterward, Nikodim Fomich, the police officer, notes that Raskolnikov is covered in blood:

> "You are all soaked in blood," noted Nikodim Fomich, observing several fresh stains on Raskolnikov's vest in the light of a street lamp. "Yes, I got soaked ... I am all covered in blood!," said Raskolnikov with some special look, then he smiled, nodded his head, and went down the stairs. (6:145)

This "special look" refers, of course, to Raskolnikov's awareness that he has been covered in blood before. But this sticky blood also reifies the persistent stickiness of social connections in this novel.

Like the sticky tabletop in the bar, which itself adumbrates Marmeladov's sticky blood, Alyona Ivanovna's greasy hair turns out to be more than a mere *meloch'*. It is what Naomi Schor has called a "diegetic detail," that is, one belonging to "that class of details which is situated on the evenmential[36] plane of the text, and which involves those prosaic objects whose exchange and communication constitute the classical realist narrative."[37] Unlike those apparently non-signifying details exposed by Roland Barthes that duly proclaim "we are the real,"[38] the diegetic detail establishes a link between background and foreground, object and subject. This particular detail, the greasy hair, pulls Alyona Ivanovna out of the "semantic matrix" of her room and into the accreted associations in Raskolnikov's mind.[39] That grease becomes one of the many substances in this novel that leave traces on Raskolnikov, whether materially or mentally. That is to say, the notable greasiness of Alyona Ivanovna's hair becomes a sign of her own transformation into an object for Raskolnikov's hypertrophied consciousness.

This is the kind of objectification that Dostoevsky's characters often seek to avoid by means of accumulating money. In an 1880 note, Dostoevsky wrote: "Wealth (Hard to save oneself [or to be saved – spastis']). Wealth is the augmentation of the individual [or subjectivity – lichnosti], a mechanical and spiritual satisfaction, thus, separation of the individual from the whole" (27:49). In the novels, Dostoevsky's money-loving characters often desire money because of the hypertrophied individual power that it can grant them. This is, for example, the dream of Arkady Dolgoruky in *The Adolescent* [Podrostok, 1875].[40] But if Alyona Ivanovna, as a Dostoevskian miser, had sought isolation in her rigorously separated and compartmentalized apartment, that ceased to be a possibility when she became the object of Raskolnikov's contemplation and, eventually, his murder victim. Her money could not shield her from this process, a sort of dissolution, whereby she became the vehicle for Raskolnikov's redemption.[41] This transformation of her into an object of another's will makes it impossible for her to remain solely a miser in harmony with her hoard. This does not happen to Dostoevsky's businessmen.

From *Raskapitalist* to *Raskrasavitsa*

Alyona Ivanovna broadly corresponds to Dostoevsky's secretive, avaricious merchants. While she is evidently not of merchant origin, she shares a common literary ancestor with characters like Rogozhin in the traditional misers of European literature. There is also at least one Dostoevskian businesswoman who similarly corresponds to the capitalists. This is not the woman actually called a capitalist by other characters: in *Demons* [Besy, 1872], the estate-owning Varvara Petrovna earns this unflattering label for attempting to found a literary journal and allegedly "exploiting" workers' labour in the process (10:22).[42] Likewise, it is not the woman who has the most to say about capitalism: the landowner Madame Khokhlakova, who discourses about the problems besetting the Russian financial system while Mitya desperately seeks three thousand rubles. Both of these wealthy landowners reside in the old world of Russia's pre-capitalist economy, which survives in the provinces even as Dostoevsky's Petersburg hurtles into a future ruled by non-noble wealth. Their association with capitalism is faintly ridiculous. It is Grushenka, an impoverished young woman who grew up under the tutelage of a merchant, who most clearly exhibits the the abstraction characteristic of a Dostoevskian capitalist. In the chapter titled "The Little Onion," in Book Seven of *Brothers Karamazov*, we learn about Grushenka's current living arrangements and business activities in the provincial town of Skotoprigonevsk. After she was abandoned by her fiancé, the seventeen-year-old Grushenka found a patron in the local merchant Samsonov. She now rents a room belonging to a relative of his, an old spinster. Grushenka lives under the watchful eye of this woman, but it turns out that the surveillance is unnecessary because she exhibits some of Samsonov's own habits. She is shrewd, calculating, minimizes contact with other people, and devotes herself to making money. The narrator informs us that, in the course of four years, Grushenka has grown quite wealthy through her business. We learn that she grew up into a woman "having good sense in money, acquisitive, miserly, and cautious, who had already managed, by fair or unfair means, as people said about her, to knock together a little fortune of her own" (14:311). Her financial skill has earned her a reputation as a "Jewess" [zhidovka], and she has teamed up with Fyodor Pavlovich Karamazov to buy up discounted promissory notes and collect the debts at a considerable profit.

"Acquisitive" Grushenka is thus a successful businesswoman who has proven herself capable of accumulating a considerable capital by earning large profits. Although the narrator does not call her a capitalist, she belongs to the capitalist type within Dostoevsky's taxonomy of rich people, even if she does not rise to the heights of a millionaire like Totsky. In mid-nineteenth-century Russian usage, a capitalist was someone who was, in Vladimir Dal's definition, "a rich person, one who has a great deal of money, a large amount of capital [velik istinnik]."[43] In Dostoevsky's works, this word refers either to markedly modern entrepreneurs, or, with discernible irony, to those who obviously are not, such as Varvara Petrovna in *Demons* or Samsonov himself, whom Mitya tries to flatter in hopes of borrowing three thousand rubles: "If only you would lend me these three thousand ... since who is a capitalist [kapitalist] compared to you in this little town?" (14:335). Samsonov is shrewd and calculating, but he exhibits the characteristic ponderousness of Dostoevsky's merchants – in his case, this is manifested physically in his inability to walk. Grushenka, on the other hand, is dynamic and adaptable and has grown rich with minimal financial support from Samsonov. She has evidently even managed to outwit the old merchant by making herself indispensable to him ("Grushenka stunned him, so that he could not live without her") (14:311). It is this ability of Grushenka to profit from her own status as a desired commodity that distinguishes her from the male capitalists.

Although Grushenka belongs to a lower rank of capitalists than the *raskapitalist* Totsky, the narrator assigns her comparable status in an altogether different category. A few lines before we read the details of her financial activities, the narrator makes use of the same prefix, favoured by Dostoevsky, to relate that Grushenka has grown into a "*raskrasavitsa*," a superlative beauty.[44] In the difference between a *raskapitalist* and a *raskrasavitsa*, the shifting meaning of the businesswoman in Dostoevsky's fiction emerges. In the course of describing Grushenka's business activities, the narrator notes how unusual it is for her to reward any man with positive attention. The narrator observes that there are many in the town who sought the "acquisition" [priobretenie] of this acquisitive woman's good graces (14:311). This repetition carries the strong suggestion that Grushenka is both the subject and object of the same transactional logic. While she exercises considerable economic power, she also belongs to the category of "beautiful female commodities whom men attempt to buy as though they were prostitutes."[45]

Grushenka's status as both a businesswoman and a commodity becomes apparent in her interactions with Mitya. In the story of their meeting, she emerges as the unlikely successor to Alyona Ivanovna. When Mitya first tells Alyosha about her, he relates how she "she likes to earn money, earns it by lending at evil rates, she is a swindler, a rouge, merciless [den'gu nazhit' liubit, nazhivaet, na zlye protsenty daet, proidokha, shel'ma, bez zhalosti]" (14:109). Mitya's first meaningful encounter with Grushenka takes places when he goes to her house with the intention of beating her, because his father had transferred to her a promissory note in Mitya's name. Mitya intends to harm Grushenka out of anger that she now possesses his debt, not for some thought experiment like Raskolnikov. Nevertheless, the parallels between these two plot situations are considerable. The crucial difference is what happens occurs when Mitya arrives at Grushenka's house. As we learn from Mitya's account to Alyosha, Grushenka, like Alyona Ivanovna, has a distinctive physical attribute: a certain curve [izgib] of her body. Once he sees this curve, Mitya falls in love with Grushenka. Instead of beating her in accordance with his plan, he goes carousing with her and spends three thousand rubles entrusted to him by Katerina Ivanovna. We hear no more of the promissory note, and the financial relationship, in which Mitya had become Grushenka's debtor, has given way to a relationship of desire, so Mitya will now go to extreme lengths to acquire three thousand rubles not to pay his debt to Grushenka, but to acquire her. Since Fyodor Pavlovich has already fallen in love with Grushenka in the course of their joint enterprise, the debt collector becomes the object of competition between father and son, and each seeks to entice her with the promise of money, even though, as a contemporary reviewer complained, three thousand rubles would not have meant much to the rich businesswoman.[46]

In the course of this competition, Grushenka takes her place among the diverse objects in the novel – including a lawyer's fees and a café-restaurant in Moscow – whose postulated price happens to be three thousand rubles.[47] This price, in turn, takes its place in a register of commodified women in Dostoevsky's fiction, including Nastasya Filippovna in *The Idiot*, as well as both Sonya Marmeladova and Avdotia Raskolnikova in *Crime and Punishment*, Varenka in *Poor Folk* [Bednye liudi, 1846], and many others. Grushenka's designation as a *raskrasavitsa* posits her as a supremely desirable object, but her apparent price is the same as several utterly disparate objects. The extraordinary fungibility of the three thousand rubles in *Brothers Karamazov* merits more detailed examination than is possible here.[48] What matters for the present argument is Grushenka's connection to this kind of amorphous, endlessly motile money. Much of the drama in the trial scene at the end of the novel rests on Mitya's inability to prove that the money he had been carrying around his neck did not come from the bundle of money stolen from Fyodor Pavlovich's room. Money from any source could have served as the projected payment for Grushenka according to the economic logic that predominates in this novel.

Grushenka's resemblance to this untraceable money is apparent in the distinctive nature of her physical form. Despite Mitya's quite concrete attraction to her, the particular object of his obsession is curiously abstract – a curve that is reproduced fractally on every level of her body: "I'm telling you: a curve. Grushenka, that rogue, has this curve in her body, it's reflected on her foot and even in her left pinky toe" (14:109). This structure, endlessly reduplicating itself, and, furthermore, somehow linked to her penchant for trickery, seems to describe Grushenka's essence as much as her body. Indeed, she will prove, in the course of the novel, to be an elusive, amorphous person. By the end, she apparently gives up her business, but what remains is the resemblance between her form – each curve like every other – and the flow of endlessly self-similar money that at times falls under her control and at other times absorbs her.

Whereas the money in *Brothers Karamazov* is difficult to authenticate, its origins disappearing in the course of its circulation, the money that initiates the causal chain of events in *Crime and Punishment* remains inextricable from its physical context. Like the blood that contaminates all of Raskolnikov's rags, the money and valuables that he takes from the dead pawnbroker's apartment prove to be tainted by their origin and incapable of being spent or exchanged. Having justified his crime as a means to acquire start-up capital, Raskolnikov ends up being unable to do anything with the money he has stolen except to hide it: the rationalized robbery becomes, in desperation, a burial. Separated from her money, Alyona Ivanovna lingers on as the ineradicable trace of crime. She meets a bad end like the Dostoevskian merchants generally do, but her fate is not to die on her moneybags. It is, rather, to become pure object, a faint trace of greasiness. Grushenka's fate, like that of the capitalists, remains open at the end of her novel. In her commitment to follow Mitya into Siberian exile, she appears to shake off all traces of her capitalist activity.[49] In this respect, Grushenka, as a female character, appears to be less locked in to the circulation of capital than are her male counterparts.

Although having money means that Alyona Ivanovna and Grushenka exercise considerably more power than the numerous poor women in Dostoevsky's novels, neither of them remains sequestered from the relentless expansion of commodification, which spreads though the language of Dostoevsky's works, even capturing the most seemingly unpecuniary concepts in its orbit.[50] Whereas the male capitalists, like Totsky and Yepanchin, pass through the plot of *The Idiot* ultimately unaffected by what has taken place around them, both of the businesswomen examined here remain, despite their money, linked to a world of people and objects. In the case of the (male) merchants and capitalists, money functions as an extension of the man and resembles him accordingly. On the other hand, Alyona Ivanovna and Grushenka both lose contact with their money by the end of their respective stories. In the process, however, they come to resemble money in another of its Dostoevskian guises: a kind of substantivized metaphor, capable of taking on the resemblance of seemingly disparate things. The desiccated pawnbroker metamorphoses into an unremovable stickiness. The *raskrasavitsa* becomes a *raskapitalistka*, and vice versa.

NOTES

1   For an overview of the situation of Russian noblewomen, see Michelle Lamarche Marrese, *A Woman's Kingdom: Noblewomen and the Control of Property in Russia, 1700–1861* (Ithaca: Cornell University Press, 2002), 1–9. Marrese focuses on the period before 1861. For an examination of women's economic activity over the course of the whole nineteenth century, see Galina Ulianova, *Female Entrepreneurs in Nineteenth-Century Russia* (London: Routledge, 2009).

2   Marie Zebrikoff, "Chapter XIV: Russia," in *The Woman Question in Europe: A Series of Original Essays*, ed. Theodore Stanton (London: Sampson Low, Marston, Searle, and Rivington, 1884), 400. This essay is also cited in Sally

A. Livingston, *Marriage, Property, and Women's Narratives* (New York: Palgrave Macmillan, 2012), 121.

3 Livingston, *Marriage, Property, and Women's Narratives*, 133.

4 Ibid., 136.

5 Nina Pelikan Straus, *Dostoevsky and the Woman Question: Rereadings at the End of a Century* (New York: St Martin's Press, 1994), 124–5.

6 Ibid., 124–5.

7 It is notable, but beyond the scope of this chapter, that so much wealth in Dostoevsky's fictions is contained in money rather than landed property. Much of that money also belongs to characters who are not nobles. For more on this issue, see Vadim Shneyder, *Russia's Capitalist Realism: Tolstoy, Dostoevsky, and Chekhov* (Evanston: Northwestern University Press, 2020), chapters 3 and 4.

8 For a detailed examination of capitalists and merchants in *The Idiot*, and the relationship between their distinctive forms of money and the development of the novel's narrative form, see Vadim Shneyder, "Myshkin's Million: Merchants, Capitalists, and the Economic Imaginary in *The Idiot*," *The Russian Review* 77, no. 2 (March 2018): 241–58.

9 F.M. Dostoevskii, *Polnoe sobranie sochinenii v tridtsati tomakh*, ed. G.M. Fridlender et al. (Leningrad: "Nauka," 1972–90), vol. 8, 11. Subsequent volume and page number references to this edition will be indicated in the text in parentheses: (vol.:page). All translations in this chapter are mine unless specified otherwise.

10 I.V. Ruzhitskii, "Atopony Dostoevskogo: K proektu slovaria," *Voprosy leksikografii* 1, no. 5 (2014): 64.

11 According to the *Statisticheskii slovar' iazyka Dostoevskogo*, ed. A.Ia. Shaikevich et al. (Moscow: Iazyki slovianskoi kul'tury, 2003), 342, *raskapitalist* appears only once in his entire oeuvre. See also the article on *kapital* in Dostoevsky's writings: *Slovar' iazyka Dostoevskogo: Leksicheskii stroi idiolekta*, issue 1, ed. Iu.N. Karaulov et al. (Moscow: "Azbukovnik," 2001), 186–9. On the productivity of the prefix *-raz* in the Russian literary language of the 1830s and '40s, including in Dostoevsky's early works, see L.I. Shotskaia, "Leksiko-semanticheskie gruppy s narodno-razgovornymi slvoobrazovatel'nymi priznakami v proze 30–40-kh godov XIX veka," in *Voprosy stilistiki russkogo iazyka*, ed. L.I. Shotskaia et al. (Irkutsk: Irkutskii Gosudarstvennyi Pedagogicheskii Institut, 1973), 10–17. Shotaskaia notes that nouns of this type tend to be "situational, stylistically motivated" and "unreproducible in literary language" (16).

12 Of course, Rogozhin is more than a miser. His willingness to spend extravagantly in order to impress Nastasya Filippovna leads to conflict with his father. It also makes his money, as a tactile object, central to the plot of *The Idiot*.

13 A particularly striking, albeit neglected, example is P.D. Boborykin's *Del' tsy* (1870–1), which features a larger-than-life lawyer-capitalist named Salamatov, who makes tens of thousands of rubles a day writing up commercial documents that exploit various loopholes in the law.

14 To be clear, "merchants" and "capitalists" are convenient names for two literary types, rather than sociological categories. That Alyona Ivanovna does not come from a merchant family is arguably less important than her typological similarity (although, as we will see, not perfect identity) with merchant characters from other novels by Dostoevsky.

15 Nathan Rosen has catalogued the major moneylenders and usurers in Dostoevsky's novels; aside from the two women, these include Ptitsyn in *The Idiot*, Liamshyn in *Demons*, and Perkhotin and Fyodor Pavlovich Karamazov in *Brothers Karamazov*. See Nathan Rosen, review of *Dostoevsky and the Jews*, by David I. Goldstein, *Dostoevsky Studies* Old Series, no. 3 (1982): 200–2.

16 For an analysis of the ways in which Dostoevsky foregrounds the gothic in his discussion of the Rogozhin house and how this spatial description informs the novel's narrative structure, see Katherine Bowers's chapter in this volume.

17 William J. Comer, "Rogozhin and the 'Castrates': Russian Religious Traditions in Dostoevsky's *The Idiot*," *Slavic and East European Journal* 40, no. 1 (Spring 1996): 90.

18 Michael Holquist, "Gaps in Christology: *The Idiot*," in *Dostoevsky: New Perspectives*, ed. Robert Louis Jackson (Englewood Cliffs, NJ: Prentice-Hall, 1984), 142. For a different reading of Rogozhin, one according to which he departs from the trajectory of the miser, see Gary Rosenshield, *Challenging the Bard: Dostoevsky and Pushkin, a Study of Literary Relationship* (Madison: University of Wisconsin Press, 2013), 221–2.

19 Several scholars have examined Raskolnikov's telling forgetfulness. See Richard Peace, *Dostoyevsky: An Examination of the Major Novels* (Cambridge: Cambridge University Press, 1971), 39–40; Deborah A. Martinsen, "Shame and Punishment," *Dostoevsky Studies* New Series, no. 5 (2001): 60; and Olga Meerson, *Dostoevsky's Taboos* (Dresden: Dresden University Press, 1998), 56–7. On the significance of *melochi* – including Lizaveta, see Robin Feuer Miller, *Dostoevsky's Unfinished Journey* (New Haven: Yale University Press, 2007), 64–7.

20 Sarah J. Young examines the importance of interior spaces in *Crime and Punishment* as locations where characters become embodied – often through the mediating effect of a concealed eavesdropper. See her chapter in this volume.

21 Donald Fanger, *Dostoevsky and Romantic Realism: A Study of Dostoevsky in Relation to Balzac, Dickens, and Gogol* (Evanston: Northwestern University Press, 1998), 197.

22 Jillian Porter, *Economies of Feeling: Russian Literature under Nicholas I* (Evanston: Northwestern University Press, 2017), 113–14.

23 Comparisons of Dostoevsky's translation to Balzac's original were long marred by inattention to the edition that Dostoevsky used – the 1834 edition, which differs in significant ways from the edition of 1843, which has become canonical. See Vera Nechaeva's discussion of the various editions of *Eugénie Grandet* and her convincing conclusion that Dostoevsky used the edition of 1834 in V.S. Nechaeva, *Rannii Dostoevskii 1821–1849* (Moscow: Nauka, 1979), 106–7. When quoting from Balzac, I have checked the modern English translation against this edition: M. de Balzac, *Eugénie Grandet*, in *Études de mœurs au XIXe siècle. Scènes de la vie de province*, tome 5, vol. 1 (Madame Charles-Béchet, 1834), 381. English translation from Honoré de Balzac, *Eugénie Grandet*, trans. Sylvia Raphael (Oxford: Oxford University Press, 1990), 192.

24 Balzac, *Eugénie Grandet*, 380; *Eugénie Grandet*, trans. Raphael, 191–2.

25 By Nechaeva's count, the cuts imposed by the editors amounted to 10–15 pages out of 150 pages of text. The final pages of the novel contain some of the most significant paraphrases and omissions, some evidently made out of consideration of the censor. See Nechaeva, *Rannii Dostoevskii*, 110–12.

26 The quotation comes from Dostoevsky's translation of *Eugénie Grandet* in the new edition of the *Complete Collected Works*: F.M. Dostoevskii, *Polnoe sobranie sochinenii i pisem v tridtsati piati tomakh*, 2-e izdanie, ispravlennoe i dopolnennoe, ed. V.E. Bagno et al. (St Petersburg: Nauka, 2013) vol. 1, 466. While taking issue with claims that Dostoevsky's translation was loose and unfaithful to the original, Nechaeva notes that he emphasizes Eugénie's moral elevation above her social surroundings and reduces her complexity somewhat. The overall result, Nechaeva concludes, is that Dostoevsky "departed from Balzac's naturalistic depictions of the everyday and went in the direction of deepening the characters psychologically, while giving sentimentalism its due with a heightened emotional, occasionally melodramatic tone in the representation of his heroes' experiences" (*Rannii Dostoevskii*, 126).

27 Balzac, *Eugénie Grandet*, 380. Dostoevskii, *PSS* 2nd ed., vol. 1, 465.

28 Elisa S. Frost, "The Hut on Chicken Legs: Encounters with Landladies in Russian Literature" (PhD diss., University of Wisconsin Madison, 2002), 239–43.

29 See Priscilla Meyer, *How the Russians Read the French: Lermontov, Dostoevsky, Tolstoy* (Madison: Wisconsin University Press, 2008), 119–23, and Leonid Grossman, *Bal'zak i Dostoevskii*, in *Poetika Dostoevskogo* (Moscow: 39-aia tip. Internatsional'naia "Mospoligraf," 1925), 92–107.

30 Erich Auerbach, *Mimesis: The Representation of Reality in Western Literature*, trans. Willard R. Trask (Princeton: Princeton University Press, 2003), 470–3.

31 Hayden White, "Auerbach's Literary History," in *Figural Realism: Studies in the Mimesis Effect* (Baltimore: Johns Hopkins University Press, 1999), 92–3.

32 Jean-Paul Sartre, *Being and Nothingness: An Essay on Phenomenological Ontology*, trans. Hazel E. Barnes (New York: Washington Square Press, 1966), 765–80. I have chosen to follow Barnes in rendering *visqueux* as "slimy."

33 Ibid., 776. Italics in original. Sartre's discussion of sliminess is accompanied by explicit associations of the slimy with the feminine – associations that have been examined in detail by feminist critics. See Margery L. Collins and Christine Pierce, "Holes and Slime: Sexism in Sartre's Psychoanalysis," *Philosophical Forum* 5, nos. 1–2 (Fall–Winter 1973–4): 112–27.

34 See, for instance, George Gibian, "Traditional Symbolism in *Crime and Punishment*" *PMLA* 70, no. 5 (December 1955): 982–5.

35 The meaning and function of sticky and greasy substances in the symbolic matrix of Dostoevsky's works deserve more detailed examination. Particularly notable among the multifarious meanings of stickiness is the image of the "sticky little leaves," which, as Robin Feuer Miller has pointed out, can serve as a "tag phrase identifying Ivan Karamazov," which indicates that he, too, is still sticky – still "susceptible to experience." Miller, *Dostoevsky's Unfinished Journey*, 179, 182.

36 That is, the plane of events.

37 Naomi Schor, *Reading in Detail: Aesthetics and the Feminine* (New York: Methuen, 1987), 142.

38 Roland Barthes, "The Reality Effect," in *The Rustle of Language*, trans. Richard Howard (Berkeley: University of California Press, 1989), 141–8. This is the sort of realist detail from which Schor distinguishes the diegetic detail.

39 I borrow this term from Faith Wilson Stein, "Wallpapering the Novel: Economics, Aesthetics, and the Realist Home" (PhD diss., University of Illinois at Urbana-Champaign, 2013), 150.

40 See Yuri Corrigan, *Dostoevsky and the Riddle of the Self* (Evanston: Northwestern University Press, 2017), 108.

41 Straus reads Raskolnikov's relationship to women in *Crime and Punishment* with a different emphasis. "Bakhtinian feminism re-engages the question of Raskolnikov's motives by suggesting that his 'self' is not a self-sufficient entity, but is constituted by the variously assimilated voices of others: his mother's and Dunia's voice, the intellectual's voice associated with 'Napoleon,' and Sonya's voice, to name just a few." Nina Pelikan Strauss, "'Why Did I Say 'Women'?' Raskolnikov Reimagined," *Diacritics* 23, no. 1 (1993): 55.

42 Another time, Pyotr Stepanovich Verkhovensky explains the transactional nature of the relationship between Varvara Petrovna and his father, Stepan Trofimovich: "I proved to her, like two times two, that you lived to mutual advantage [na vzaimnykh vygodakh]: she as a capitalist and you as her sentimental fool" (10:239).

43 V.I. Dal', *Tolkovyi slovar' zhivogo velikorusskogo iazyka* (Moscow: Tipografiia lazaretskogo instituta vostochnykh iazykov, 1865), vol. 2, 704.

44   In all its forms, *raskrasavitsa* appears eleven times in Dostoevsky's fictional works. See *Slovar' iazyka Dostoevskogo*, ed. Iu.N. Karaulov (Moscow: "Azbukovnik," 2012), 294. The word is applied by various speakers to Katerina Ivanovna and Grushenka in *Brothers Karamazov*, Avdotia Romanovna in *Crime and Punishment*, and Nastasya Filippovna and an undetermined beauty whom Totsky would like to marry in *The Idiot*. Outside of Dostoevsky's works, *raskrasavitsa* was a relatively common word in nineteenth-century Russian literature. It occurs, for example, in Nikolai Leskov's *The Enchanted Wanderer* [Ocharovannyi strannik, 1873], which features another *raskrasavitsa* named Grushenka, and in Andrei Melnikov-Pechersky's *On the Hills* [Na gorakh, 1875–81], as a component of folksy, colloquial formulas: "Well, he is a nice young fellow, and you are a maidenly beauty [raskrasavitsa-devitsa]," said Patap Maksimych. "Now, by the testament of your grandfathers and great-grandfathers, we ought to kiss for love, counsel, and a long and happy life. Be so kind as to conclude the Lord's blessing by your kiss." P.I. Mel'nikov-Pecherskii, *Na gorakh*, Part 4, in *Sobranie sochinenii v vos'mi tomakh* (Moscow: Izdatel'stvo "Pravda," 1976), vol. 7, 96–7.

45   Straus, *Dostoevsky and the Woman Question*, 127.

46   Oniks [V. Petersen], "Vstuplenie k romanu angela," *Literaturnaia gazeta* 6 (1881), quoted in V. Zelinskii, *Kriticheskii komentarii k sochineniiam F.M. Dostoevskogo. Sbornik kriticheskikh statei. Chast' chetvertaia: "Brat'ia Karamazovy,"* 3rd ed. (Moscow: Tipo-lit V. Rikhter, 1906), 504.

47   See Jacques Catteau, *Dostoyevsky and the Process of Literary Creation*, trans. Audrey Littlewood (Cambridge: Cambridge University Press, 1989), 164–5.

48   For more on the adventures of the three thousand and their broader meaning for *Brothers Karamazov*, see Jonathan Paine, *Selling the Story: Transaction and Narrative Value in Balzac, Dostoevsky, and Zola* (Cambridge, MA: Harvard University Press, 2019), 156–82, and Shneyder, *Russia's Capitalist Realism*, chapter 4.

49   In following Mitya into Siberian exile, Grushenka enters into a different kind of Dostoevskian narrative paradigm: the open-ended and ambiguous romantic relationships that Anna Berman examines in chapter 2 of the present volume. There is nothing that precludes capitalists from having families in Dostoevsky's novels: General Yepanchin in *The Idiot* has a happy family life with a wife and three daughters. But the danger and uncertainty of life with Mitya – possibly in America – distinguishes her future path from that of the male capitalists, who carry on their steady accumulation.

50   See Susan McReynolds, "'You Can Buy the Whole World': The Problem of Redemption in *The Brothers Karamazov*," *Slavic and East European Journal* 52, no. 1 (Spring 2008): 87–111.

4 Allegories of the Material World: Dostoevsky and Nineteenth-Century Science

MELISSA FRAZIER

In *Demons* [*Besy*, 1872] Shatov rails against what he calls "half-science." "Half-science is a despot such as has never been seen before," he tells Stavrogin: "A despot with its own priests and slaves, a despot before whom everything has bowed down with a love and superstition unthinkable till now, before whom even science itself trembles and whom it shamefully caters to."[1] What Shatov disparages as "half-science" is better known as Nihilism, a combination of Comte and the "vulgar" materialists together with a dash of Claude Bernard that lays claim to both an abstract mathematical rationality and a strict empiricism. Dostoevsky's antipathy to this highly popular but entirely contradictory approach to the material world is often so extreme in its expression that readers have only recently begun to discern the richer and more complete science that his realism advocates.[2] In *Demons* this more capacious nineteenth-century science reveals itself most importantly in a complicated symbolic practice.

As Nikolai Chernyshevsky demonstrates in his compendium of Nihilist thought, *What Is to Be Done?* [Chto delat'?, 1863], "half-science" entails its own constellation of literary devices, including most notably a plot driven by the ideas and actions of a set of scientist-heroes who purport to explain and also manifest the "laws" of nature. As his enlightened heroes work to refashion their world along properly socialist lines, Chernyshevsky undermines his own claims to a world of matter alone, a paradoxical stance that finds its most striking literary realization in his frequent and invariably heavy-handed allegories: the allegory of the bride, the allegory of the cellar or underground, the allegorical function of the four dreams. If any figure of speech implies two levels of meaning, Chernyshevsky's allegories are remarkable for their attempt to collapse the two into one, as Chernyshevsky tries and fails to reconcile his commitment to material monism with a utopian insistence that the ideal be made real. In *Demons* the characters' often absurd allegorical assertion of matter as the only measure of reality serves as a direct mockery of the Chernyshevskian world view, not that Dostoevsky rejects either materialism or allegory altogether. Dostoevsky instead reconfigures allegory to better accommodate a material world that his Underground Man calls "living life" [zhivaia zhizn'] (5:178).[3]

As Dostoevsky with his undergraduate training and life-long reading in the sciences was well aware, the most significant of nineteenth-century scientists from Charles Darwin (1809–82) through Hermann von Helmholtz (1821–94) and James Clerk Maxwell (1831–79) tempered their scientific desire for natural "law" with an equally scientific recognition of the fundamental multiplicity and even indeterminacy of a material world that includes the material underpinnings and implications of our own minds. This commitment to relativity also marks the work of pioneering physiological psychologist George Henry Lewes (1817–78). While Lewes is most often remembered as George Eliot's common-law husband, during his lifetime he was famous in his own right as the author of scientific works read across Europe, from *The Physiology of Common Life* (1859) to the partly posthumously published *Problems of Life and Mind* (1875–79). In the early twenty-first century, his star is also once more on the rise. Although Lewes as a practising scientist was necessarily committed to the premise of a real and really knowable material world, he was also clear in his still cutting-edge belief that scientific knowledge is not the reproduction of an already-existing and "objective" reality, but a link to what Bruno Latour in *Pandora's Hope* (1999) calls an "aligned, transformed, constructed world."[4] Lewes's great contribution to a newly emerging science of physiological psychology was the "dual-aspect monism" that claimed, in Richard Menke's words, that "physiology and psychology, nerves and neuroses, are best understood as, respectively, the objective and subjective presentations of what are in fact the same phenomena."[5] For Lewes the dual workings of mind and matter both complicate our understanding of cause and effect and also guarantee the impossibility of a single objective reality "out there." As Lewes firmly explained in *Problems of Life and Mind*: "objective existence *is* to each what it is felt to be."[6]

Dostoevsky's realism incorporates the insights of Lewesian physiological psychology in its own attentiveness to the interactions of minds and bodies, including the reader's own as we thrill to the twists and turns of his suspenseful and often crime-ridden plots. The scientific instability of "dual-aspect monism" also finds reflection in a different kind of allegory. Certainly Dostoevsky derides the Nihilist urge to conflate reality as it is with reality as it might be, above all in *Demons*, where his mockery culminates in the "pathetic, trite, giftless, and insipid allegory" that is the quadrille of literature at the ball that is itself an allegory and that precipitates the series of calamities that conclude the novel: as the fête descends into chaos, the town goes up in flames, Shatov is killed and Stavrogin commits suicide, Dostoevsky reveals the Nihilist insistence on a single and yet ideologically correct reality as not just ridiculous, but an actual dead end (10:389; 508).[7] At the same time and in direct contrast to the would-be flatness of this failed allegory, Dostoevsky's own symbolic practice claims clearly defined yet multiple meanings in a duality that doesn't depart from material reality, but more fully expresses it.

Allegory in a Fallen World

While, in its simplest terms, as Angus Fletcher writes, allegory "says one thing and means another," as opposed to other forms of figurative language, allegory is usually also defined in terms of a certain lack of flexibility; as J. Hillis Miller argues, the "true" meaning of allegory is one, and it most often lies outside the text.[8] With significant exceptions – C.S. Lewis's *The Chronicles of Narnia* (1950–56) come to mind – the device also largely went out of fashion with the advent of Romanticism. It was first Goethe who famously distinguished allegory, "where the particular serves only as an example of the general," from the truly poetic device of symbol, "where the particular represents the more general, not as a dream or a shadow, but as a living momentary revelation of the Inscrutable."[9] Coleridge then made Goethe's claim into a distinction between what he termed "mechanic" and "organic" form. Allegory for Coleridge "is but a translation of abstract notions into a picture-language, which is itself nothing but an abstraction from objects of the senses"; symbol, on the other hand, "always partakes of the reality which it renders intelligible; and while it enunciates the whole, abides itself as a living part in that Unity of which it is the representative."[10] It is against this background that Chernyshevsky's reliance on allegory is all the more striking. It is also Chernyshevsky himself who draws attention to his use of the device.

When Mariya Alexeyevna drops hints about his supposed fiancée, Lopukhov asks himself, "Why did I devise such an allegory – it wasn't needed at all!"[11] If it wasn't needed, however, the allegory continues, first as Vera Pavlovna enters into a fictional marriage with Lopukhov and then as the "Bride of Her Bridegrooms" in Vera Pavlovna's fourth dream again represents the future of Vera Pavlovna herself. The didacticism that marks allegory as opposed to other, more open forms of figuration, already insists on a singular meaning; as Fletcher explains, since allegory "implies a dominance of theme over action and image ... the mode necessarily exerts a high degree of control over the way any reader must approach any given work."[12] Chernyshevsky makes very sure of that control, however, most often through the simple device of repetition.

In her first dream, for example, Vera Pavlovna sees herself "locked up in a damp, dark cellar [podval]" when the door "suddenly" flies open and "she finds herself in a field, running about and skipping."[13] After she recounts her dream to Lopukhov, it promptly comes true, as she says, "So, my dear, you are liberating me from this cellar," and she then makes the same allegorical reference again and again: "I now know that I'm leaving this cellar"; "I shall escape from this cellar!"; How did I manage to breathe in that cellar?" until the allegory migrates to the narrator who addresses us, his readers: "Come up out of your godforsaken underworld [iz vashei trushchoby], my friends."[14] As Chernyshevsky forcefully urges his readers to flatten the two halves of his allegory into one reality, the connection with his social-utopian aspirations is clear: allegory in Chernyshevsky allegorizes what the novel presents as the function of art more generally, which is to make real its own fictions. Chernyshevsky's own claims to the contrary, the reification of "abstract notions" that his allegory attempts is then also the guiding principle of his science.

What Is to Be Done? is very obviously a story of science, not just because the heroes all practise science, but because their conversations are littered with physiological jargon. Lopukhov and Kirsanov discuss their work on the "optical nerve" and the production of "artificial albumin," while Kirsanov in particular offers long, apparently scientific disquisitions on the workings of sensation and the relationship of mind to body. "The intensity of sensation is in proportion to the level of feeling from which it evolves in the organism," he tells Vera Pavlovna, or: "Statistics have already demonstrated that the female organism is more resilient. You've read these conclusions only in life-expectancy tables. If you add physiological evidence to the statistical data, then the difference emerges as much greater."[15] Our narrator also emphasizes the material dimensions of his heroes – Lopukhov's broad frame, Vera Pavlovna's well-developed bust – as well as the actual functioning of their bodies, for example when a troubled Lopukhov takes two morphine pills to help him sleep and finds that "the spiritual travail was roughly equivalent in strength (according to Lopukhov's materialist viewpoint) to four cups of strong coffee."[16] This story of science is also one that derives from a few well-known sources.

By the 1860s Auguste Comte (1798–1857) was no longer quite as celebrated in progressive circles as he once was, so much so that Chernyshevsky's merry picnic-goers adopt "Auguste Comtean" as an expression of apparently mild disparagement.[17] As even this usage suggests, however, it was Comte's Positivism that lay behind the Nihilist commitment to both mathematical quantification and a strict if proximate cause and effect. Chernyshevsky's narrator also vouches for Kirsanov's fictional credentials with reference to both the real German cell biologist Rudolf Virchow (1821–1902) and the real French physiologist Claude Bernard (1813–78), the latter especially well known for his codification in his *Introduction to the Study of Experimental Medicine* [Introduction à l'étude de la médecine expérimentale, 1865] of what we would now call the scientific method. When it comes to a "materialist viewpoint" that would equate a certain amount of "spiritual travail" with "four cups of strong coffee," however, the Western European science that mattered most for Chernyshevsky was the material monism that we know as "scientific" or, in Friedrich Engels's wonderful phrase, "vulgar itinerant preacher materialism."[18]

The "vulgar" materialists were a trio of once-famous scientists and science writers, Ludwig Büchner (1824–99), Jakob Moleschott (1822–93), and Karl Vogt (1817–95). For Engels, the three were "vulgar" above all in that they failed to anticipate the fundamentally dualistic Marxist view that the material world is only a symbol of the "real" reality of economic relationships. They were also "vulgar" in that they were extremely popular. By Frederick Gregory's count, Büchner's 1853 *Matter and Force* [Kraft und Stoff], for example, went through twelve editions in seventeen years and was translated into seventeen foreign languages, including Russian; as readers of Russian literature may recall, the book even makes a brief appearance in Ivan Turgenev's *Fathers and Children* [Ottsy i deti, 1862] when Kirsanov senior spends too much time reading Pushkin, and Bazarov suggests that Arkady give him Büchner instead. Despite their materialist claims, the three were finally "vulgar" in that their work was so ideologically driven as to hardly qualify as "scientific."

Like Büchner, Vogt was known for an engagement in radical politics that came at the expense of his career as an actual practising scientist. Despite his own inclination towards mind over matter, Vogt is best remembered for a single line from 1846, his inflammatory and highly reductive claim that "those capacities that we understand by the phrase psychic activities (Seelenthätigkeiten) are but functions of the brain substance; or, to express myself a bit crudely here, that thoughts stand in the same relation to the brain as gall does to the liver or urine to the kidneys."[19] Of the three, it is Moleschott who achieved the most in the way of actual institutional credentials, including a prestigious position as professor of anatomy and physiology at the University of Zurich. Even so, as Dmitry Pisarev's popular review of what was already a work of popular science, Moleschott's relatively late *Physiological Sketchbook* [Physiologisches Skizzenbuch, 1861], would suggest, Moleschott's reputation again rested on the largely unsubstantiated assertion of a radically simple form of material monism.

In his review of the *Sketchbook* Pisarev makes a point of offering his readers an array of facts gleaned from his reading: "blood is made up of a combination of nitrogen, carbon, hydrogen, oxygen, potassium, sodium, calcium, magnesium, iron, sulfur, phosphorus, chlorine and fluorine," he explains; or: "In raw meat the meat fibers are surrounded by a sort of juice consisting of a solution of protein, various salts and nitrogeneous creatine [Fleischstoff]."[20] For all the complicated pseudo-scientific jargon that Pisarev, like Chernyshevsky, a graduate in philology, clearly enjoys, the thrust of Moleschott's argument in the *Sketchbook* as elsewhere is extremely simple. As Ludwig Feuerbach wrote in his review of Moleschott's earlier *Die Lehre der Nahrungsmittel: Für das Volk* (1850; translated into English in 1856 as *The Chemistry of Food and Diet, with a Chapter on Food Adulterations*): "Man is what he eats," and in his review of the *Sketchbook* Pisarev quotes from *Die Lehre* to hammer this point home: "Can lazy potato blood possibly lend muscles the strength for work and impart to the brain the life-creating impulse of hope?" his Moleschott cries, "Poor Ireland! Your poverty gives birth to poverty! You cannot remain unconquered in the struggle with a proud neighbor to whom plentiful herds impart power and boldness!"[21]

As this quote makes clear, the "vulgar" drive to equate living organisms with the inanimate matter that they ingest and excrete offers remarkably easy answers to what might seem complicated questions, from the apparently inevitable outcomes of British imperialism to the workings of plot and characterization in *What Is to Be Done?*. These answers also tend to suit the unfailingly left-wing politics of the so-called "scientists," so much so, in fact, that it would seem obvious that the theoretical conclusions of "vulgar" materialism precede or even act entirely in the absence of any empirical evidence. As their would-be material monism reverts always to a set of theoretical assumptions, a now quasi-scientific over-determination has the curious effect of emptying "vulgar" materialism of any real matter at all; as Coleridge warns, it also tends to empty living organisms of any actual life. Like "life-expectancy tables" and "statistical data," references to "nitrogeneous creatine" and even "potato blood" only pretend to engage with actual living matter while really offering pseudo-scientific abstraction, a retreat from the very life that their science purports to explain. This reversal is still more striking in Bernard's *Introduction*.

While Claude Bernard was a far more serious and scientifically grounded advocate of material determinism, still his attempt to reduce all of life to the law-like effects of quantifiable material conditions produces a similarly "vulgar" result. Although physiology, as Bernard explains, is "the science whose object is to study the phenomena of living beings and to *determine* the material conditions in which they appear," Bernard was controversial in his own day for the practice that he delicately termed "dissociation," and in the *Introduction* he tackles the issue head-on.[22] "If a comparison were required to express my idea of the science of life," he writes, "I should say that it is a superb and dazzlingly lighted hall which may be reached only by passing through a long and ghastly kitchen."[23] As he explains, over the course of his work the physiologist might "detach living tissues, and ... place them in conditions where we can better study their characteristics." "We occasionally isolate an organ by using anesthetics to destroy the reactions of its general group," he adds, or "reach the same result by cutting the nerves leading to a part, but preserving the blood vessels"; as he notes in another section, "This is what we observe when we place a small animal under an air pump; its lungs are obstructed by the gases liberated in the blood."[24] Unfortunately for the small animals under the physiologist's care, "[t]o extend his knowledge," Bernard writes, "he has had to increase the power of his organs by means of special appliances; at the same time he has equipped himself with various instruments enabling him to penetrate inside of bodies, to dissociate them and to study their hidden parts."[25] In *What Is to Be Done?* bodies en route to the Crystal Palace most often need to be disciplined by the rigours of theory, especially in the case of female bodies with their often unruly emotions, or Rakhmetov with his bed of nails. In the *Introduction*, those same bodies appear actually cut up into parts, as Bernard's science of life, like Coleridge's allegory, entirely fails to "partake[] of the reality which it renders intelligible."[26]

The Romantic response to the Enlightenment as an earlier iteration of Chernyshevsky's combined rationalist and empiricist project was to reject allegory altogether in favour of what Murray Krieger calls "a form-making power that could break through the temporal separateness among entities, concepts, and words to convert the parade of absences into miracles of co-presence."[27] To quote Goethe again, it is only symbol "where the particular represents the more general, not as a dream or a shadow, but as a living momentary revelation of the Inscrutable."[28] More recently, Paul de Man simply accepts the belatedness of language. As Krieger argues, the postmodern attempt to recuperate allegory returns us to the same "vulgar" belief in a "bedrock existential reality," only now combined with an embrace of the inevitable non-coincidence of sign and signified that a "bedrock" reality makes necessary; for de Man, the great virtue of allegory is not its drive to make dreams real, but its open acknowledgment of "the fallen world of our facticity."[29] If we cast mind as part of a material world that is itself multiple and even shifting, however, allegory can serve other ends, including Dostoevsky's project of a more complicated kind of realism. It is exactly this possibility that Lewesian science offers.

The Nineteenth-Century Science of Mind and Body

Although Bernard et al. were and remain highly popular, even by the mid-nineteenth century material monism was far from the only game in town. Just as physicist James Clerk Maxwell wrote that "the only laws of matter are those which our minds must fabricate, and the only laws of mind are fabricated for it by matter," so physicist and physiologist Hermann von Helmholtz's work on sound emphasized not just the source from which the sound emanates, but also the receiving capacity of the human ear; the same refusal to set the human mind apart from the natural world that it would consider is also reflected in Helmholtz's (qualified) dissemination of a non-Euclidean geometry that cuts off from the world as we know it to imagine other possible spaces.[30] What Aileen Kelly has recently described as Darwin's "theme of contingency" also undermines any strict notion of natural "law."[31] As Gillian Beer writes, "Darwin was much wounded by Herschel's description of his theory as 'the law of higgledy-piggledy,' but the phrase exactly expresses the dismay many Victorians felt at the apparently random – and so, according to their lights, trivialized – energy that Darwin perceived in the natural world."[32] Lewes offers a particularly striking example of this other strain of nineteenth-century thought, not least in the wide range of his intellectual activity. That activity is also not easy to characterize.

In an age when science was just beginning to become a professional pursuit, Lewes was self-taught and unaffiliated with any institution. He also refused to specialize, as Lewes not only actively fostered the career of his novelist-wife George Eliot, but was himself the author of a much-noted biography of Goethe, histories of philosophy and of theatre, a great deal of literary criticism, and even a few early novels. At the same time, in his experimental work Lewes, like Bernard, was an active and vocal vivisectionist; as a one-time advocate of Comte and like the "vulgar" materialists, Lewes was also often associated with left-wing politics, especially in Russia, indeed, so much so that he even makes a brief appearance in *Crime and Punishment* [Prestuplenie i nakazanie, 1866] when Lebezyatnikov recommends that Sonya read his *Physiology of Common Life*. While Dostoevsky was evidently well aware of Lewes's reputation in Nihilist circles, still a highly positive if unsigned review of *The Physiology of Common Life* that appeared in Dostoevsky's own journal *Time* [Vremia] in 1861 rightly argues that the real complexity of Lewes's thought often eluded his Russian readers. That complexity is already on view in Lewes's early novel *Ranthorpe* (1847), published in Russia in 1859 as *Zhizn' poeta* [A Poet's Life].

In its broadest terms Lewes's novel offers a retelling of Honoré de Balzac's *Lost Illusions* [Illusions perdues, 1837–43] with Percy Ranthorpe a Lucien de Rubempré who ends on a happier note. *Ranthorpe* also includes a proto-Chernyshevskian medical student, a "mixture of the gentleman and the Mohock" whose "dark eye was full of fire and intelligence; his open laughing face was indicative of malicious mirth and frankness; and the resolution about his brow, and sensibility about his mouth, redeemed his slang appearance, and showed the superior being, beneath the unprepossessing exterior."[33] Harry Cavendish's first act in the novel is to knock to the ground a peddler who "was beating his donkey in so brutal a manner that several people were crying 'Shame! shame!'"; in a chapter prefaced by an epigraph from Georges Sand's *Jacques*, Harry ends by breaking his engagement with Isola when he realizes that she loves Percy instead.[34] In between, Harry solves a violent murder wrongly attributed to Percy, and it is in this "sensational" subplot that Lewes's pioneering science of mind and body comes into play.

Like Raskolnikov in *Crime and Punishment*, Oliver Thornton apparently commits the perfect murder only to find himself overwhelmed with guilt: "He had thought of flying to America, but was afraid, lest it should look suspicious ... Such was his suffering, that he was often on the point of blowing his brains out, and so ending his misery"; "Every knock at the door went to his heart, as if it announced his arrest. Every noise in the street sounded like the mob coming to seize him. He read the morning and evening paper with horrible eagerness. Every line respecting the murder made him thrill."[35] This "thrill" is equally a matter of body and of mind, as is his initial motivation for the crime. As Lewes's narrator explains:

> His uncle's death soon became a fixed idea with him ... He must either become a murderer or a monomaniac! The tyrannous influence of fixed ideas – of thoughts which haunt the soul, and goad the unhappy wretch to his perdition – is capable, I think, of a physiological no less than of a psychological explanation ... In proportion to the horror or interest inspired by that thought, will be the strength of the tendency to recurrence. The brain may be then said to be in a state of partial inflammation, owing to the great affluence of blood in one direction. And precisely as the abnormal affluence of blood towards any part of the body will produce chronic inflammation, if it be not diverted, so will the current of thought in excess in any one direction produce monomania. Fixed ideas may thus be physiologically regarded as chronic inflammations of the brain.[36]

The "tyrannous influence of fixed ideas" is exactly balanced by the "affluence of blood" and "chronic inflammations of the brain," as Oliver's murderous "monomania" is neither a product of thought alone nor a purely physical effect. The psychological and the physiological instead operate together and at the same time: as Lewes put it in his much later *Problems of Life and Mind,* "every mental phenomenon has its corresponding neural phenomenon (the two being as the convex and concave surfaces of the same sphere, distinguishable yet identical)."[37] "Dual-aspect monism" shows mind and body to work in tandem, as simultaneously both cause and effect. It also implicates both mind and body in a material world that comes into being only through the medium of our own perceptions.

What Lewes calls his "Reasoned Realism" in fact collapses any distinction between objects as they are and objects as they seem to be. As Lewes writes, "the external world exists, and *among* the modes of its existence is the one we perceive"; for what he calls "other forms of Sentience (if there are such) than our own," reality takes on a very different shape that is no less real. [38] In Lewes's argument, the "senses don't directly apprehend – or *mirror* external things." Instead, "[e]ach excitation has to be *assimilated,*" first in terms of the material reality of our particular perceptual apparatus, and then as a reflection of the subject's own evolving history.[39] "What the Senses inscribe on [the mind]," Lewes writes, "are not merely the changes of the external world; but these characters are commingled with the characters of preceding inscriptions. The sensitive subject is no *tabula rasa;* it is not a blank sheet of paper, but a palimpsest."[40] Either way and as Latour claims in *Pandora's Hope,* phenomena "are not found at the *meeting point* between things and the forms of the human mind." They are instead "what *circulates* all along the reversible chain of transformations" that makes us one with the material world.[41]

Lewesian physiological psychology finds literary expression most obviously in Dostoevsky's own representation of bodies and minds, above all in *Crime and Punishment.* Like so many of Dostoevsky's young heroes, Raskolnikov makes the Nihilist mistake of attempting to separate his mind from a material world that includes his own body. Despite his often "greedy" consumption of soup, bread, tea, and beer, despite even his fainting fits, his fever, and what we know to be his "disturbed and already excited organism," Raskolnikov remains committed to an abstract theory; as Porfiry Petrovich explains, "There are bookish dreams here, sir, there is a heart chafed by theories" (6:46, 54). [42] Where his friend Razumikhin, like the Underground Man, seeks "the *living* process of life," Raskolnikov accordingly finds only death, not just the death of the old pawnbroker and her sister, but also his own. As he tells Sonya, "I killed

myself, not the old crone!" (6:197, 322; 256, 420). Long before Raskolnikov comes to that intellectual conclusion, however, his body rejects the
deed that his rational mind has led him to perform. In his meetings with
Porfiry Petrovich, Raskolnikov's nerves "hum" and his knees "tremble";
Raskolnikov is also driven to return to the scene of the crime by a desire
to experience again "that spinal chill [kholod-to etot v spinnom mozgu]"
(6:343; 449), and overwhelmed by a series of bodily "sensations" that he
fully acknowledges only at the very end of the novel when a new "sensation" "seized him all at once, took hold of him entirely – body and mind"
(6:347; 456) and he bows down at the crossroads to kiss the earth (6:405;
525). While words like "spinal cord" [spinnoi mozg] and "sensation"
[oshchushchenie] deliberately invoke the central nervous system and
bodily responses that bypass cognition, Dostoevsky like Lewes offers not
bodies without minds, but minds and bodies functioning together in the
world as two aspects of a single whole. Dostoevsky also doesn't just tell a
story of "dual-aspect monism," but enacts one.

This enactment is most immediately a matter of the marked attention
that his "psychological" novels give to his readers' own bodies. For all
his materialist claims, when Chernyshevsky wants to gain our attention,
he employs the highly rational expedient of simply and repeatedly addressing his "perspicacious" [pronitsatel'nyi] reader. To the dismay of
his Nihilist critics with their theoretical bottom line, however, Dostoevsky instead draws on an emerging and partly Lewesian-inspired novel of
sensation to provoke a visceral reaction. As a scandalized Pyotr Tkachev
described what he saw as Dostoevsky's approach in his 1873 review of
Demons, "Give us more and more gossip, scandal, irritate all the more
strongly the reader's spinal cord make his hair stand on end, entertain
him, amuse or frighten him, but just don't make him think or look up
from the page."[43] According to a 2001 survey in Chelyabinsk, readers
to this day associate Dostoevsky not just with physical items (axes) and
topoi (St Petersburg), but also with a range of "sensations" [oshchush-
cheniia] and "states" [sostoianiia], including "pain," "sickness," "nerves,"
and "hysteria," as well as a generalized feeling of "discomfort" [diskom-
fort].[44] If the force of that physical reaction is evidently still felt, Dostoevskian "dual-aspect monism" is equally importantly at work in an allegory
that serves not to conflate real and ideal, but to hold two different and
equally valid realities in place at the same time.

Dostoevskian Realism

Although their intent is not always the same, Dostoevsky's variously
left-leaning characters recur to the very terms "allegory" and "allegorical"

with truly remarkable frequency.[45] This tendency reaches an extreme in *Demons*, where the characters as a whole, both fathers and sons, suffer from a recognizably social-utopian conflation of present words with much-desired future realities. When our chatty narrator insists that his friend Stepan Trofimovich really did pound the walls in frustration, he explains, "This occurred without a trace of allegory, so that once he even broke some plaster from the wall" (10:12; 14), while one of the guests at the ill-fated fête takes a little too much care to explain what would seem a very ordinary figure of speech: "I am speaking al-le-gor-i-cally," he clarifies, "but I went to the buffet and am glad to have come back in one piece," (10:388; 506); "These are all nonsensical allegories," an angry Varvara Petrovna tells Lebyadkin, "These are allegories, and, besides, you choose to speak too floridly" (10:140; 176). Along with an insistence on a particularly flat kind of matter as the only measure of reality, their usage reflects a gnawing concern that the "real" significance of words might lie elsewhere, an anxiety entirely appropriate to a novel where double meanings run rampant. The characters' often absurd recourse to "allegory," however, only serves to make a bad situation worse.

While Shatov as a recovering revolutionary is largely innocent of allegorical intentions, he is nonetheless not entirely immune to the practice of figuration, for example when he refers to his serfdom both literal and metaphorical. "Once I was simply born of a lackey, but now I've become a lackey myself, just like you," Shatov says. "Our Russian liberal is first of all a lackey and is only looking for someone's boots to polish." The narrator's immediate turn to "allegory," however, doesn't clarify Shatov's meaning, but only indicates his own or perhaps also our inability to see where that figure might lie: "What boots?," Anton Lavrentievich asks, "What kind of allegory is that?" (10:111; 138). Fortunately, even as the heroes of *Demons* repeatedly generate not just more confusion, but finally even death in their attempt to reduce the multiplicity of "living life" to a single level of reality, another option remains available to the novel's readers. Rather than remain mired in the non-coincidence of sign and signified that so afflicts his characters, we can accept scientific instability instead.

Russell Valentino notes what he calls the novel's "ambivalent orientation towards its own allegorical status," an ambivalence apparent even at the fête, where words, as it turns out, do have tangible effects; as the now truly mad von Lembke rightly says, "Governesses have been used to set houses on fire ... The fire is in people's minds, not on the rooftops" (10:538; 516).[46] With Lewes in mind, however, it is not so much ambivalence, as it is two different kinds of allegories in operation at once. Where his characters repeatedly attempt an allegory of the familiar, "vulgar" sort, Dostoevsky himself uses allegory to point to multiple "real" realities that are simultaneously also symbolic. This multivalence is most immediately evident in the novels as a whole in the different meanings that Dostoevsky himself attaches to space.

In a perfect illustration of "dual-aspect monism," the "underground" [podpol'e] that Dostoevsky erects in direct response to Chernyshevsky's "cellar" [podval] renders a philosophical stance in material terms, just as the narrow confines of Raskolnikov's room function both as the material environment that determines his actions and as a representation of the cramped spaces of his own mind. What Raskolnikov needs, as Porfiry Petrovich tells him, is "air, air!," both the fresh air that the city of St Petersburg lacks in real as in metaphorical terms, and the spiritual way out that is materialized in a choice between two geographical locations, America and Siberia, that again enjoy a symbolic dimension: Siberia is life and America an allegorical image of death made real, as where Chernyshevsky's Lopukhov only pretends to kill himself and emigrates to America, Dostoevsky's Svidrigailov announces his departure for America only to commit suicide (6:351; 460). Lest we think that we know the one way to interpret these already complicated images, the same contrast abruptly softens in *Brothers Karamazov* [Brat'ia Karamazovy, 1881] when Dmitry in his final scene proposes that he escape to America only to return once he's mastered English "as well as any downright Englishman"; in Dostoevsky's last and longest novel, it is Lopukhov again, but America is no longer an image of death alone (15:186).[47] In *Demons* this same play of clearly defined and yet multiple and even contradictory meanings operates most aggressively at the novel's very end when Stepan Trofimovich attempts to apply the parable of the Gadarene swine to his own Russian reality.

As his Bible-selling companion at his request reads from the Gospel according to Luke, Stepan Trofimovich is struck by what he calls "*une comparaison*" [a comparison]: "It is us, us and them, and Petrusha ... *et les autres avec lui* [and the others with him], and I, perhaps, first, at the head, and we will rush, insane and raging, from the cliff down into the sea, and all be drowned," he says, "But the sick man will be healed and 'sit at the feet of Jesus'" (10:499; 655). The "*comparaison*" proves a happy one, not least because it turns out to have shaped our reading all along; as the narrator now takes a moment to remind us, the passage from Luke that Stepan Trofimovich finds so meaningful is the very one that the narrator himself placed at the beginning of the novel. While Stepan Trofimovich and the narrator together seem to have unlocked the allegory that is the novel as a whole, the very circularity of our own evidently over-determined reading renders that meaning a little suspect; up to the very end with his Gallicisms and his inveterate "quotation," Stepan Trofimovich also remains the deeply untrustworthy wielder of words that he has been all along. To the dismay of the "perspicacious" reader of the Chernyshevskian type, as the allegorical interpretation of *Demons* as those demons, the ones from Luke, is both offered and withheld, our way forward is neither easy nor open to debate. As the equally unreliable "Petrusha" says twice, "*Avis au lecteur* [Reader take notice]": our only choice is to read the novel both ways at once (10:279; 359).

The mistake of "vulgar" materialism is the reification of what, on closer look, reveals itself to be a largely ideological "abstraction from objects of the senses"; as Chernyshevsky's allegory exactly reflects, while the material monists lay claim to a single objective reality, their very refusal to acknowledge the mutual implication of mind and matter makes duality inevitable. Allegory in Dostoevsky, on the other hand, posits multiple meanings in operation at the same time and with the same degree of "objective" reality: exactly like Lewes's nerves and neuroses and as challenging as it may be for Dostoevsky's readers, even two diametrically opposed readings serve "as the convex and concave surfaces of the same sphere, distinguishable yet identical." The oscillation between different expressions of what is nonetheless the same reality that in Dostoevsky and especially in *Demons* approaches a kind of whiplash suggests a particularly demanding form of Romantic irony, which is to say, Dostoevsky's project shares a great deal with Goethe's and Coleridge's. His recourse to the more rigorous form of allegory, however, also makes the case for a particular kind of realism.

Scholars often struggle to fit Dostoevsky into a realism that we define in scientific terms a little narrowly. Mimesis in the nineteenth century always implies a scientific world view, even when that science takes the form of Comte's "social physics"; as René Wellek explains, what he calls "the objective representation of contemporary social reality" relies on "the orderly world of nineteenth-century science, a world of cause and effect, a world without miracle, without transcendence even if the individual may have preserved a personal religious faith."[48] Nineteenth-century realists often make these scientific underpinnings clear, when Balzac frames *The Human Comedy* [La Comédie humaine, 1842] with reference to zoology, for example, or when Émile Zola claims the mantle of Bernard in his "experimental" novel. In its Russian version, realism is explicit in its scientific ambitions not just when Chernyshevsky writes of "artificial albumin" and four cups of coffee, but also in the claims of the so-called Natural School and the equally aptly named genre of the "physiology"; this is a realism defined by its apparent lack of literary artifice in an imitation of a science that is supposedly one with what it describes. Allegory in what Goethe, Coleridge, and even de Man have taught us to see as its open artificiality would seem an artifact of another way of writing, one that emphasizes "theory" over "fact," sign over signified, and often it is, even in Chernyshevsky. Lewesian science would argue, however, that a different sort of allegory serves not as an anti-realist device, but as an expression of what Latour calls "a more 'realistic realism.'"[49]

In an 1868 letter to his friend Apollon Maikov, Dostoevsky himself acknowledged that he held "[c]ompletely different ... notions ... of reality and realism than our realists and critics" (28.2:239; my translation). As Liza Knapp argues, Dostoevsky claimed more than once that the distinctive feature of his realism was his commitment to presenting reality "as *he* experienced it";[50] for Molly Brunson, Dostoevsky's "realism in a higher sense" offers a "transcendent alternative to a more grounded, objective recording of phenomenal reality, one capable of accessing truths far higher, or deeper, than those of the material world."[51] We don't need to cut off from the material world, however, to find truths "far higher, or deeper" than Wellek's "orderly world of nineteenth-century science" would allow. From Lewes's entirely scientific point of view, after all, the material world manifests itself in multiple ways, including in "fantastic" perceptions and in ways altogether beyond the reach of our particular perceptual apparatus. Even in the twenty-first century, the lessons of this other sort of science don't come easily, but they restore the figurative possibilities of language as they open us to a "living life" that always operates on multiple levels at once: to follow Dostoevsky's lead is to embrace allegory not because the material world is impoverished, but because minds and bodies in the world really work that way.

NOTES

1 F.M. Dostoevskii, *Polnoe sobranie sochinenii v tridtsati tomakh*, ed. G.M. Fridlender et al. (Leningrad: "Nauka," 1972–90), vol. 10, 199. All subsequent references to this edition will appear in parentheses in the text with first the volume, then the page number. This translation is from Fyodor Dostoevsky, *Demons*, trans. Richard Pevear and Larissa Volokhonsky (New York, Vintage, 1994), 251. All subsequent references to this translation will appear in the text set off by a semicolon following the *PSS* reference.

2 Anna Kaladiouk (Schur) offers a shining example of the work, in her words, to "restore to the science of Dostoevsky's times some of its intellectual range and complexity," see A.S. Kaladiouk, "On 'Sticking to the Fact' and 'Understanding Nothing': Dostoevskii and the Scientific Method," *The*

Russian Review 65, no. 3 (July 2006): 420; see also Alexey Vdovin's and Greta Matzner-Gore's contributions to this volume.

3 *Notes from Underground,* trans. Boris Jakim (Grand Rapids, MI, and Cambridge, UK: William B. Eerdmans, 2009), 124.

4 Bruno Latour, *Pandora's Hope* (Cambridge, MA: Harvard University Press, 1999), 71, 79.

5 Richard Menke, "Fiction as Vivisection: G.H. Lewes and George Eliot," *ELH* 67, no. 2 (Summer 2000): 623.

6 George Henry Lewes, *Problems of Life and Mind: First Series, the Foundations of a Creed,* vol. 1 (Boston: Houghton, Osgood, 1875–1880), 175–6. Italics in original.

7 In the original Russian: "Trudno bylo by predstavit' bolee zhaluyu, bolee poshluiu, bolee bezdranuiu i presnuiu allegoriiu." Note that Yuliya Mikhailovna herself describes her "economical little German ball" as "solely an allegory" [samym ekonomicheskim, nemetskim balkom … edinstvenno dlia allegorii] (10:356; 465).

8 Angus Fletcher, *Allegory: Theory of a Symbolic Mode* (Ithaca, NY: Cornell University Press, 1962), 2; see J. Hillis Miller, "The Two Allegories" in *Allegory, Myth, and Symbol,* ed. Morton W. Bloomfield (Cambridge, MA: Harvard University Press, 1981), 355–70.

9 René Wellek, *A History of Modern Criticism,* vol. 1 (Cambridge: Cambridge University Press, 1955), 325nn54, 55; Fletcher, *Allegory,* 13n24.

10 Fletcher, *Allegory,* 16n29.

11 N.G. Chernyshevskii, *Chto delat'?* (Leningrad: Nauka, 1975), 62; Nikolai Chernyshevsky, *What Is to Be Done?,* trans. Michael Katz (Ithaca, NY: Cornell University Press, 1989), 106.

12 Fletcher, *Allegory,* 304.

13 Chernyshevskii, *Chto delat'?,* 81; Katz, trans., 129–130.

14 Chernyshevskii, *Chto delat'?,* 92, 97, 100, 122, 233; Katz, trans., 143, 149, 151, 179, 313.

15 Chernyshevskii, *Chto delat'?,* 274, 258–9; trans. Katz, 358, 340.

16 Chernyshevskii, *Chto delat'?,* 183; trans. Katz, 252.

17 Chernyshevskii, *Chto delat'?,* 143; trans. Katz, 204.

18 Friedrich Engels, "Old Preface to Dühring. On Dialectics" in Karl Marx and Friedrich Engels, *Collected Works,* vol. 25 (New York: International Publishers, 1975), 340.

19 Carl Vogt, *Physiologische Briefe für Gebildete aller Stände* (Stuttgart, 1846), 206, http://www.mdz-nbn-resolving.de/urn/resolver.pl?urn=urn:nbn:de:b-vb:12-bsb10477770-0; Frederick Gregory, *Scientific Materialism in Nineteenth Century Germany* (Boston: D. Reidel, 1977), 64.

20 D.I. Pisarev, *Polnoe sobranie sochinenii i pisem v 12-i tomakh,* vol. 3 (Moscow: Nauka, 2001), 155, 162; translations mine.

21 Gregory, *Scientific Materialism*, 92; Pisarev, vol. 3, 158.

22 Claude Bernard, *Introduction à l'étude de la médecine expérimentale* (Paris: Garnier-Flammarion, 1966), 107; Claude Bernard, *An Introduction to the Study of Experimental Medicine*, trans. Henry Copley Greene (New York: Dover, 1957), 66. Italics in original.

23 Bernard, *Introduction*, 44; trans. Greene, 15.

24 Bernard, *Introduction*, 138, 174; trans. Greene, 88–9, 120.

25 Bernard, *Introduction*, 2; trans. Greene, 5.

26 I remain grateful to the students in my Fall 2013 seminar "Dostoevsky and the Age of Positivism," and especially Matthew Gonzales, for their sharp response to Bernard's "ghastly kitchen."

27 Murray Krieger, "'A Waking Dream': The Symbolic Alternative to Allegory" in *Allegory, Myth, and Symbol*, ed. Morton W. Bloomfield (Cambridge, MA: Harvard University Press, 1981), 4.

28 Wellek, *A History of Modern Criticism*, 325n55; Fletcher, *Allegory*, 13n24.

29 Krieger, "A Waking Dream," 16.

30 Ivan Tolstoy, *James Clerk Maxwell: A Biography* (Chicago: University of Chicago Press, 1981), 77.

31 Aileen Kelly, *The Discovery of Chance: The Life and Thought of Alexander Herzen* (Cambridge, MA: Harvard University Press, 2016), 6.

32 Gillian Beer, *Darwin's Plots: Evolutionary Narrative in Darwin, George Eliot and Nineteenth-Century Fiction* (New York: Cambridge University Press, 2009), 6–7.

33 George Henry Lewes, *Ranthorpe* (Athens: Ohio University Press, 1974), 6.

34 Ibid., 7.

35 Ibid., 208, 222, 221.

36 Ibid., 202–3.

37 Ibid., *Problems*, 103–4.

38 Ibid., 168. Italics in original.

39 Ibid., 113. Italics in original.

40 Ibid., 149.

41 Latour, *Pandora's Hope*, 71. Italics in original.

42 These translations are from Fyodor Dostoevsky, *Crime and Punishment*, trans. Richard Pevear and Larissa Volokhonsky (New York: Vintage, 1993), 348, 456. All subsequent references to this translation will appear in the text set off by a semicolon following the *PSS* reference.

43 P.N. Tkachev, 'Bol'nye liudi: 'Besy,' roman Fedora Dostoevskogo, v trekh chastiakh,' in *Kritika 70-kh godov XIX veka*, ed. S.F. Dmitrenko (Moscow: Olimp, 2002), 74. Translation mine.

44 M.V. Zagidullina, "Dostoevskii glazami sootechestvennikov," in *Roman F.M. Dostoevskogo 'Idiot': Sovremennoe sostoianie izucheniia*, ed. T.A. Kasatkina (Moscow: Nasledia, 2001), 527. Translations mine.

45 See, for example, Lebedev's "allegoricheskii svitok" ["allegorical scroll"] in *The Idiot* (8:168). Translation mine. See also when Versilov in *The Adolescent* [Podrostok, 1875] smashes an icon and shouts, "Ne primi za allegoriiu," only to add, "A vprochem, primi xot' i za allegoriiu; ved' eto nepremenno bylo tak!..." ["Don't take it as an allegory! ... But, anyhow, why not take it as an allegory; it certainly must have been"] (13:409). This translation can be found in Fyodor Dostoevsky, *The Adolescent*, trans. Richard Pevear and Larissa Volokhonsky (New York: Knopf, 2003), 508. All subsequent references to this translation will appear in the text set off by a semicolon following the *PSS* reference.

46 Russell Valentino, *Vicissitudes of Genre in the Russian Novel* (New York: Peter Lang, 2001), 117. Kate Holland has similarly argued that Lebedev's laughable claims in *The Idiot* in no way undermine the significance of his apocalyptic vision, and I am still responding to her "Hurrying, Clanging, Banging and Speeding for the Happiness of Mankind: Railways, Metaphor and Modernity in *The Idiot*" (presentation, Annual Convention of the American Association for Slavic, East European and Eurasian Studies, Chicago, IL, 9–12 November 2017).

47 Fyodor Dostoevsky, *The Brothers Karamazov*, trans. Richard Pevear and Larissa Volokhonsky (New York: Farrar, Straus and Giroux, 1990), 765.

48 René Wellek, *Concepts of Criticism* (New Haven: Yale University Press, 1963), 241. For further reconsideration of Dostoevsky's contributions to the mimetic project, see Sarah J. Young's and Chloë Kitzinger's chapters in this volume.

49 Latour, *Pandora's Hope*, 15.

50 Liza Knapp, "Realism," in *Dostoevsky in Context*, ed. Deborah A. Martinsen and O.E. Maiorova (Cambridge: Cambridge University Press, 2016), 235. Italics in original.

51 Molly Brunson, *Russian Realisms* (DeKalb: Northern Illinois University Press, 2016), 163.

5 Dostoevsky, Sechenov, and the Reflexes of the Brain: Towards a Stylistic Genealogy of *Notes from Underground*

ALEXEY VDOVIN

TRANSLATED BY ANDRIY BILENKYY

It is customary to consider *Notes from Underground* [Zapiski iz podpol'ia, 1864] as the first text that anticipates Dostoevsky's subsequent great novels in combining psychological, ideological, and philosophical features with narrative experimentation. While the genesis and content of the philosophical ideas espoused by the Underground Man have been studied extensively,[1] almost no research has been done on the connection of the novella with contemporaneous psychology and physiology. One may wonder whether there is a good reason to study these matters. What could this approach tell us about the poetics of Dostoevsky and the evolution of the novelistic form in nineteenth-century Russia? In this chapter I will juxtapose *Notes from Underground* with the most prominent Russian text on physiology produced at the beginning of the 1860s, Ivan Sechenov's *Reflexes of the Brain* [Refleksy golovnogo mozga, 1863], to explain how Dostoevsky succeeded in creating not only an influential philosophical text, but also an experimental narrative that expands the capacities of psychological prose.

In short, the answer lies in Dostoevsky's understanding of Sechenov's article as an intellectual challenge, and, at the same time, as a *discursive model* for a literary response, namely, *Notes from Underground*, a novella written in January–May of 1864. It is peculiar insofar as Dostoevsky both polemicizes with Sechenov's theory, which postulates that free will and voluntary human action are entirely predetermined, and uses Sechenov's rhetorical and narrative models in his fiction to demonstrate why this theory is false and how it can be improved.

In implanting physiological discourse into his fictional world, Dostoevsky might have been motivated by polemical considerations; and yet, in doing so, he expanded the capacity of prose narratives for depicting long chains of psychological reactions structured in a way akin to the reflex arc. Juxtaposing Sechenov's scientific narrative and Dostoevsky's prose reveals the genesis and specific features of the narrative techniques used by the novelist to depict the mental and psychical lives of his characters.[2] On the one hand, Dostoevsky inherits the techniques characteristic of the psychological confessional prose of the 1850s such as Ivan Turgenev's "The Diary of the Superfluous Man" [Dnevnik lishnego cheloveka, 1850],[3] and absorbs the method, familiar to the writers of that generation, whereby the character's subjectivity is conveyed through the social and psychological determination of the character's acts. On the other hand, scholars are justified not only in positing a gap between Dostoevsky's psychological prose style of the 1860s and that of the psychological prose of the 1850s, but also in proposing a qualitative difference between the two periods of Dostoevsky's writing career. The present chapter argues that this difference can be described as a transition in respect to the representation of physical processes, from what can be branded as the "Romantic" type of representation to the rationalized and positivist one, the latter guided by the discourse, metaphors, and cognitive frameworks offered by mid-nineteenth-century physiological and biological sciences.

Such an approach to the study of the interaction between scientific and artistic discourse during the age of positivism, natural sciences, and realism has long been practised by English literature scholars. Gillian Beer's classic study *Darwin's Plots* (1983) explained that the language, metaphors, and evolutionary thinking peculiar to the author of *On the Origin of Species* (1859) changed not only the way people conceived the world around them, but also the manner of plot construction in Victorian novels. For example, in a chapter on *Middlemarch* (1872), Beer demonstrates how Darwin's evolutionary concept of an "inextricable web of affinity" influenced George Eliot's plot, which depicts the dwellers of a small town with closely interconnected lives. Characters are related to each other not only generically, economically, and socially, but also by virtue of a remarkably complex system of psychological correspondences, attributes, and repetitions of identical situations with ubiquitous variability.[4]

Among recent studies I must also mention the scholarship of Nicholas Dames. Of particular importance for my discussion of Sechenov and Dostoevsky is his article "The Network of Nerves" (2011). Here Dames demonstrates that the physiological psychology (Lewes, Dallas, Bain) that dominated British science in the middle of the nineteenth century developed its own physiological theory of the psychological self that prioritized non-conscious and involuntary bodily impulses rather than the subconscious, as in the works of Sigmund Freud. Dames claims that "much of the tone and leisurely length of Victorian narrative is owed to this new epistemological split between a knowing narrator and characters who are constitutively, perhaps even ontologically, unaware of the basis of their motives. Free indirect style, which had been such a valuable tool for Austen and which would flourish in writers like Flaubert and Joyce, and as a result became foregrounded in theories of the novel influenced by modernist practice, is a much less marked presence within mid-Victorian fiction."[5]

Dames's discovery, which sheds new light on the history of the Victorian novel and the reading practices it engendered in the nineteenth century, opens new possibilities for the study of the Russian novel as well. So far, little has been done in this area, even though the importance of nineteenth-century scientific physiological theories for literary genres and discourses has been acknowledged by scholars, in some cases, extensively. One may consider, for example, Michael Holquist's remarkable description of the influence exerted by Sechenov's book upon the discursive space of the 1860s. Analyzing *Fathers and Children* [Ottsy i deti, 1862], Holquist argued that Turgenev tested a new type of discourse, scientism, "the language of facts," which Sechenov had championed since 1860 in his lectures at the Medical and Surgical Academy. Turgenev's novel, however, anticipated the arrival of Sechenov's book, and gave life to an influential discourse that shaped the reception of *Reflexes of the Brain* in the 1860s as a Nihilist book and precipitated a ban on it.[6] Yet, since Holquist's groundbreaking study, there has been little progress in the research on the mutual influence of scientific discourse, narration, and the plot structure of the Russian novel. The sole exception is Valeria Sobol's *Febris Erotica* (2011), which analyzes *Reflexes of the Brain*, but only as part of the public polemics of the 1860s that updated the language used to articulate conceptions of human nature.[7] The present chapter probes the major connections of this system, its basal ganglia, so to speak, by using *Notes from Underground* as a case study. It also sets priorities for future studies of the emergence of Dostoevsky's signature style.

Dostoevsky and Sechenov

In 1966, in his doctoral thesis, R.G. Nazirov observed that Dostoevsky was familiar with Sechenov's article and responded to it polemically in the first chapter of *Notes from Underground*. Nazirov argues that the Russian writer used the expression "dispassionate wish" [besstrastnoe khotenie], which he borrowed from the physiologist.[8] However, Nazirov offered no further development of his insight, nor was it discussed by any other Dostoevsky scholars, despite the fact that the 1990s and 2000s were marked by the publication of the noted monographs by Harriet Murav (1992) and James Scanlan (2002) that explored the way Dostoevsky reacted to the scientific discourses and theories of his time.[9] Murav does mention Sechenov's book, a special 1866 edition of which was present in Dostoevsky's personal library, but only in the context of a general overview of "rational egoism" and the positivist theories of the 1860s.[10] Only G. Kichigina, in her recent book (2009) on the history of experimental physiology in the Russian empire, mentions briefly that Dostoevsky's *Notes from Underground* challenges the physiological discoveries that reject the freedom of the human will.[11]

The history of Dostoevsky's reception of Sechenov's study is an example of a situation where the answer to the question "did the author read the text by another author" serves merely as a starting point for further inquiry, helping one focus on the problems of poetics and the narrative structure of the text. Thanks to the note in Dostoevsky's notebook, which reads "Memory of feeling (Sechenov's article)" [Pamiat' chuvstva (stat'ia Sechenova)] (20:170), we know that he read the article, published in the October 1863 issue of the *Medical Bulletin*, in November–December of that year, roughly a month before writing the first chapter of *Notes from Underground* in January–February of 1864 (5:375).[12] Dostoevsky's notebooks of the early 1860s did not preserve his views on Sechenov's personality or research. Only later, in 1877, in a letter to A.F. Gerasimova, did Dostoevsky provide his assessment of this famous scientist:

> It is not the same in Europe; there you can meet Humboldt and Bernard and other such people with universal ideas, with tremendous education and knowledge not only in their own specialty. In our country, however, even very gifted people, for instance, Sechenov, are basically ignorant and uneducated outside of their own subject. Sechenov knows nothing about his opponents (the philosophers), and thus he does more harm than good with his scientific conclusions. As for the majority of students, whether male or female, they are an ignorant lot. What is the benefit in this for mankind?[13]

Dostoevsky's reproach of Sechenov and his colleagues for their lack of erudition is overgeneralized and prejudiced. Sechenov's intellectual biography, reconstructed in the twentieth century, demonstrates that, in addition to conducting research in the laboratories of Paris, Vienna, and Berlin, in collaboration with Claude Bernard, Carl Ludwig, and other luminaries of nineteenth-century European physiology, he also read extensively in the literature of philosophy, psychology, and the natural sciences. For example, in letters to his future wife M. Bokova, sent from Europe in 1867–68, Sechenov mentions reading works by Fichte, Kant, Schelling, Hegel, Herbart, and Helmholtz.[14]

Nevertheless, as early as 1863, Dostoevsky perceived Sechenov and his article as an ideological adversary whose theory he could not endorse. Throughout his entire subsequent writing career, Dostoevsky used Sechenov's name and the expression "reflexes of the brain" as a symbol of a false world view and *Notes from Underground* became the first text to reflect this attitude. By juxtaposing the novella with Sechenov's article, we arrive at several conclusions. First of all, one can't help but notice that Dostoevsky evidently polemicized with the famous physiologist on an ideological and discursive level, engaging in a debate regarding free will. This polemic presupposes that the text of *Notes* is saturated with marked words and expressions that allude to the physiological discourse generally associated with the works of Sechenov and other positivists. Second, as I intend to show here, the complex reflex arc discovered by the physiologist, the model of mental processes built on the basis of this physiological phenomenon, and, finally, their description in *Reflexes of the Brain* influenced the narrative technique of *Notes from Underground* and shaped the methods which Dostoevsky used to depict the character's mental life.

The Underground Man's Theory as a Polemic with Sechenov

The Underground Man's ideology and his attack on the theories of rational egoism have been covered exhaustively in Scanlan's monograph, which demonstrates convincingly that the character challenges both variations of rational egoism: psychological and normative.[15] Arguing against hypothetical ideological opponents – positivists, evolutionists, socialists – the Underground Man plays his trump card by positing the person's "free wish" [svobodnoe khotenie] as that which makes them a free individual. Nazirov accurately noted that "the confession of the Underground Man, offered in the novella's first chapter, is a paradox of free will and determination."[16] Following Nazirov, I will argue here that the word "wish" [khotenie] itself, aside from its obvious connection to the well-known Russian proverb "na khotenie est' terpenie," [there is patience in wishes, or "all good things come to those who wait"] could be borrowed by Dostoevsky from the final section of Sechenov's article, where it is abstracted into a concept and presented as a token of self-deception, a characteristic of modern individuals who view themselves as bearers of free will and masters of their own "wishes" [khoteniia] and "desires" [zhelaniia].[17]

As demonstrated by historians of physiology, in *Reflexes of the Brain* Sechenov sought to discredit the philosophical foundation of the concept of free will, offering to replace it with a purely scientific, physiological foundation derived from empirical experiments.[18] At the same time, the famous scientist not only eliminated thought and consciousness from the process of sensation-formation (excitation and inhibition), but also built them into a complex chain of reflexes.[19]

Unlike desire, which is often seen as capricious, wishing, in Sechenov's interpretation, "is often regarded as an act of will," "Being tired, I am sitting; I should like to lie down, but I remain seated."[20] Sechenov analyses cases where a person, when wishing dispassionately, can even act "against his desire," for example: "I am tired and am sitting, I should like to stretch out, but I get up and begin to work." According to Sechenov, wishing is a brain reflex that is nearly devoid of passion. Desire, also a reflex, is, by contrast, accompanied by a clear manifestation of passion. Sechenov concludes that the concepts that exist in ordinary language fail to precisely characterize a more complex phenomenon and develops a new descriptive language: "The reader will see therefore that there is a certain confusion either in the usage of words which express sensations or in the sensations themselves and in the concepts and words associated with them."[21] Enthusiastic about popularizing his ideas, and, at the same time, keen on developing new terminology, Sechenov often operated with concepts borrowed from everyday life, such as "wish" [khotenie], "passion" [strastnost'], and "love" [liubov']. As Sechenov's famous student, Ivan Pavlov, noted perceptively, Sechenov used everyday language when he wrote *Reflexes of the Brain* for *The Contemporary* [Sovremennik] because he was passionately in love with his future wife, Mariya Bokova.[22] Following Pavlov's line of thought, one could add that *Reflexes* speaks so much about human life and passion precisely for that reason, as Sechenov, while writing the article, was not only pondering reflexes, but also reflecting on his feelings towards Bokova.

Sechenov's article reaches its high point in a thought experiment centred on the most routine situation of everyday life, in which the author's hypothetical interlocutor voluntarily bends his finger. This procedure, Sechenov continues wryly, is considered to be an apotheosis of free will, the triumph of the personal wish, which is supposedly independent of external circumstances. Sechenov, however, rejects this conception. First, the interlocutor bends his finger in a machine-like fashion; second, their exchange takes place not in an abstract space, but under the circumstance where the interlocutor has already bent his finger involuntarily a thousand times before, albeit without noticing. Finally, the finger is a human "organ" that is often bent involuntarily. Thus, as Sechenov's thought experiment is meant to demonstrate, even such vivid manifestations of "wishing" as bending one's finger are determined by long chains of involuntary reflexes.

Famously, the first chapter of Dostoevsky's novella offers the Underground Man's step-by-step refutation of the thesis that one's psychical life is totally predetermined by one's physiology. There is no doubt that the Underground Man aims some of his pronouncements directly and personally at Sechenov and his theory.[23] Below is the first passage where the protagonist alludes to a position that rejects free will and offers the laws of nature as an alternative explanation:

> That's not all: then you say, science itself will teach man ... that in fact he doesn't have – and never has had – *any will or caprice of his own*, and that he himself is nothing more than something *like a piano key* or an organ stop; and that, above that, the world also includes the laws of nature, so that everything he does is done *not because he desires it* [vovse ne po ego khoten'iu], *but of itself, according to the laws of nature.* (5:112)[24]

Then, as the exchange between the Underground Man and his hypothetical opponent becomes even more heated, the conversation hints directly at the theory of reflexes:

> "Ha, ha, ha! But desire, in essence, if you will, doesn't even exist!" you interrupt me, laughing loudly. "Science has succeeded in anatomizing man to such an extent that we now know that desire and so-called free will are nothing more than ..."
> "Wait, gentlemen, that's exactly how I wanted to begin. I admit, I was even frightened. I was just about to shout who in hell knows what desire depends on, and that maybe thank God for that, but then I remembered science and ... stopped dead in my tracks. And then you started talking. Well, actually, if some day they do in fact find *some formula for all our desires and caprices – that is, a formula describing what they depend on, the precise laws that determine how they arise, how they multiply, what they're directed at in such and such a case, etc., etc. – that is to say, a real mathematical formula* – then maybe man will immediately stop desiring; what's more, maybe he'll definitely stop. Really, who would want to desire with reference to a mathematical table? As if that's not enough, he'll immediately be transformed from a man into an organ stop or something of the sort, because what is man without desires and without will if not an organ stop? (5:106; 31; italics mine.)

It seems to me that the first remark was to culminate in the scandalous word "reflexes," meant to appear after the ellipsis, but, since the Underground Man was interrupted by his "inner" interlocutor, it was left to the reader to decipher the hint. The clue that points to our interpretation comes from the verb *razanatomirovat'*. In Russian the verb's prefix and root render it something like "to anatomize," which alludes to physiology and the dissection of frogs, i.e., to images that, in the mid-1860s, were associated inextricably with Sechenov and his activities.[25]

These passages exemplify the way Dostoevsky thematizes the concept of "desiring," along with adjacent terms such as "caprice" [kapriz], as a parody of Sechenov's scientific language. Wishing becomes a leitmotif of the Underground Man's behaviour, and, in the second chapter of *Notes*, the main character and his adversaries often manifest their will through the verbs "to wish" [khotet'] and "to be able to" [moch'], and the concepts of "power" [vlast'], tyranny, dominance, slavery, and submission. This lexicon simply offers a discursive embodiment of the problem of free will, as this problem is realized through situational plot elements based, as shown by Tsvetan Todorov, on the Hegelian master–slave dialectic.[26]

Contemporary scholars of Dostoevsky have expanded the philosophical context of the problem of free will in *Notes from Underground* beyond Hegel, incorporating Fichte, Kierkegaard, Schopenhauer, and Henry Thomas Buckle into it as well.[27] While it is quite likely that the novelist read the former two before 1864, his familiarity with Schopenhauer's philosophy was evidently general at best, as he drew upon synopses provided in articles by Dmitry Pisarev, Nikolai Strakhov, and Varfolomei Zaitsev.[28] From this point of view it becomes clear that Sechenov's pointed discreditation of the very notion of free will had exhausted Dostoevsky's patience, triggering a response based on the body of reflection that formed over the years of Dostoevsky's intensive journalistic work at *Vremia*, when he immersed himself enthusiastically in the world of "thick" journals, reading and reviewing them.

Accepting Sechenov's provocative challenge, Dostoevsky "teaches" his character Sechenovian language and confers on him a remarkable talent for reaching into the depths of his sensations and feelings, dissecting them into the most minuscule components, and documenting them in writing. The Underground Man famously explains his inability to end the train of self-analysis by claiming that he fails to find the first cause, and, in this, recalls the logic and rhetoric of Sechenov's scientific reflections in *Reflexes of the Brain*, which proceed from the superficial and visible causes of human behaviour to "the first causes of any behaviour." The backbone of Sechenov's investigation is the scientific epistemology of discovering things buried deeply beneath the surface and establishing their true causal connections, so, unsurprisingly, the word "cause" [prichina] occurs there 165 times.[29]

Thus, Dostoevsky expands the Underground Man's discursive vocabulary by borrowing from the stock of terms and concepts Sechenov uses to record deep psychological processes. Among these terms are the "first cause" [pervaia prichina] and "hyperreflexia" [usilennyi refleks], the latter possibly converted by Dostoevsky into the concept of hyperconsciousness [usilennoe soznanie].[30] Of great interest is the expression "the memory of feeling," noted by Dostoevsky in his notebook, which refers to the model of human memory and its activity developed by Sechenov. According to the latter, human beings possess four types of memory: visual and tactile (spatial) and aural and muscular (temporal).[31] Sechenov explains that mental reproduction of sensations through memory can occur when the subject is influenced by objects or images positioned before their eyes.[32] The article proceeds by providing vivid examples meant to demonstrate the reflex nature of some of the associations that occur to people. For example, thoughts about the emperor of China, which Sechenov entertained consciously at night, occur to him again when he stretches out on his bed during the day.[33] It seems possible that Dostoevsky was impressed by these explanations, and, for that reason, wrote them down in his notebook.

One may think that the importance of these and other occurrences of scientific terms in *Notes from Underground*, a work of fiction, lies only in the way they shed light on the character's ideologically motivated attacks on much-despised positivist theories. Yet, similarly to the reflexes of Darwin's style of thinking in the British novel, *Notes from Underground* offers us a phenomenon of significantly greater complexity.

In dissecting sensations down to their most minuscule aspects, just as a physiologist dissects a frog, in differentiating between "wish," "caprice," and "desire," in modelling situations of ordinary life, Sechenov invented and publicized a sophisticated Russian anatomical language that did not exist before. Like the language of any groundbreaking scientific theory, it had great potential, since it could describe new phenomena of physical reality, not only those previously hidden under the cover of human flesh, but also those inaccessible to human consciousness and cognition. As I will demonstrate below, Dostoevsky accepted Sechenov's challenge and put his invention to good use.

New Style Emerging

Sechenov's possible influence on Dostoevsky is manifested most intriguingly at the narrative level that represents the emotions, motives, and affect of the Underground Man. When it comes to genre and speech, Dostoevsky follows Sechenov in constructing the character's confession as a dialogue with imaginary opponents that always doubt the truthfulness of his claims. Since *Reflexes of the Brain* was addressed to a wide audience,

Sechenov had to mould his scholarly article into a lively dialogue with readers, set, as it were, in an anatomical theatre or at a public lecture, such as those delivered by this famous scientist at St Petersburg's Medical and Surgical Academy. This observation allows us to supplement Mikhail Bakhtin's conception of the dialogical nature of form in Dostoevsky's works, in general and, particularly, in *Notes from Underground.* It must be acknowledged that in adopting this form Dostoevsky's influence was not works of philosophy such as those by Diderot.[34] Instead he drew upon works of popular science written by contemporaneous authors, as they frequently constructed their narratives as dialogues between a pontiff of science and his incredulous listeners.

Aside from this fairly superficial resemblance, it is possible that Dostoevsky, in structuring his character's self-description, employed the tripartite scheme used in Sechenov's description of a voluntary reflex:

1 emotional excitation
2 particular psychical act
3 muscular movement[35]

Careful analysis of the second part of the novella, in which its protagonist describes his reactions to events in his internal and external life, reveals a remarkable regularity. It turns out that some of these fragments are arrayed according to a single narrative template that resembles Sechenov's tripartite schema. Thus, the character begins by narrating how an external impulse is delivered into his consciousness; then, he describes how his consciousness analyses it laboriously; after that, the character usually presents himself as committing an act ("muscular motion"), but, most importantly, this act oftentimes does not happen in accordance with the initial impulse. Here is the way such narrative segments are structured. Let us consider a scene from the second part of the novella, Zverkov's dinner party.

> (**I**) *(1)* "Now's the time to throw a bottle at their heads," *(2)* I thought to myself as I picked up the bottle … *(3)* and filled my glass.
> "… No, I'd better sit it out to the very end!" I kept thinking. "You'd be delighted, gentlemen, if I left. But nothing doing! I'll purposely go on sitting here and drinking to the very end, as a sign that I don't think you of the slightest consequence. I'll go on sitting and drinking, because this is a tavern and I paid good money to get in. (**II**) *(1)* I'll go on sitting and drinking, because I consider you to be so many pawns, so many non-existent pawns. I'll go on sitting and drinking …*(2)* and singing if I want to, yes, sir, singing, because I have the right … to … to sing … hmm!"

(3) But I didn't sing. I just tried not to look at any of them: I assumed the most carefree poses and waited impatiently for them to speak to me *first*. But alas, they didn't speak to me! (5:146; 77–8).

Roman numerals I and II are used here to mark the two segments of the narrative that convey the train of thoughts and impulses flashing through the character's mind, and the physical act or its absence that follows them. Within each segment, Arabic numerals between 1 and 3 are used to mark the three stages of the character's actions, (1) his emotional excitation (usually an occurrent thought or an external impulse); (2) a secondary thought or motion that adjusts the initial impulse; and (3) the final muscular motion or its absence that manifests itself as a complete opposite of the initial impulse.

This passage demonstrates that the character always lives in a state of extreme excitation, which propels his thought to operate with increased intensity, and that, in turn, stimulates his imagination. But none of the character's initial desires (to throw a bottle at the detested companions or to sing) is realized, because something, which is not verbalized in the text of the novella, is always blocking the character's impulses, forcing him to act contrary to his initial motives.

Let us consider another scene from the second part of the novella.

No one paid any attention to me, and *(1)* I sat crushed and humiliated.

"Lord in heaven, why am I associating with these people?" I thought. "And what a fool I've made of myself in front of them! I let Ferfichkin go too far, though. The numbskulls think they're doing me an honor by letting me sit down at their table; they don't understand that it's just the opposite: I'm doing them an honor! 'I've grown thinner! My clothes!' My damn trousers! Zverkov immediately noticed the yellow stain on my knee ... But what's the use! *(2)* I should get up right away, this very minute, take my hat, and just leave, without saying a word ... Out of contempt! And tomorrow, a duel. The scoundrels! As though I cared about the seven roubles. They may think ... To hell with it! I don't care about the seven roubles. I'm leaving this very minute!

(3) It goes without saying that I stayed.

In my misery I drank Lafite and sherry by the glassful. (5:144–5; 75)

This example presents a similar sequence of the character's emotions and affective motions, where the state of suppression and humiliation triggers a strong reflection that results in a passionate desire to leave the restaurant abruptly. Nevertheless, the character ends up doing quite the opposite; not only does he remain at the table, but, moreover, he begins drinking more.

It is easy to notice that the three stages in Dostoevsky's novella are not entirely consistent with Sechenov's model. The moment that marks the transition from the second to the third stage is the point of contention in Dostoevsky's polemic with Sechenov, as the Underground Man constantly acts against self-interest, against the familiar norms of rationality, and against his initial desires and even physiological reflexes. As the quotes demonstrate, the third, muscular, phase is usually set apart from the other two graphically, by an ellipsis, which symbolizes the discrepancy between Sechenov's theory, which rejects the freedom of the will, and the Underground Man's real behaviour, which, as one may think, manifests his own will and "desire." From this point of view, the entire second part of "Apropos of the Wet Snow" can be read as a literary refutation of Sechenov's theory, since each subsequent act, committed by the Underground Man, must be demonstrably illogical, absurd, and harmful, and must express the triumph of the character's "desiring" and his subconscious over the impulses of his reflexes.

Such an interpretation of Dostoevsky's polemic with Sechenov would seem to go against Robert Louis Jackson's well-known and convincing interpretation of the novel. Jackson argues that the will of the Underground Man manifests only in words, whereas in his actions and in communication with other people the hero becomes a victim of his own complexes and phantasms: "The irony of the bumping duel episode (like the irony of Raskolnikov's experiment) is clear: there are no manifestations of freedom of will here. Far from being a master of his fate, the Underground Man in his very efforts to declare his independence from the laws of nature demonstrates his enslavement to them."[36] And, elsewhere, "As we see him in part two in his own representation of his life – a drama he understands very well – nothing remains episodic. Every attempt to introduce the irrational into his life and to bring an illusion of authentic freedom, choice, self-determination, every attempt to play with the plot of his life only further underscores his subjection to the power of blind destiny."[37] As I noted earlier while commenting on the passages, it seems that an unknown force blocks the character's impulses and forces him to commit acts that contradict his advantage and, at the same time, undermine his own theory of free wishing as the chief criterion of his humanity and individuality, or, in other words, of his own self.

In fact, there is no contradiction between Dostoevsky's polemic with Sechenov and Jackson's assertion. The paradoxical situation, when the hero constantly manifests his wishes and at the same time slavishly depends on his whims and complexes, can be explained by the combination of two perspectives, the complex dialectic of domination and slavery. On one hand, at the discursive level the Underground Man demonstrates the triumph of free desire, because, thanks to his eloquence and reflexivity, he exercises rhetorical power on those around him (Apollon, Liza, his former friends). On the other hand, at the level of the plot (siuzhet), its context, and its author's position, the hero is perceived by the other characters and readers as a slave of his caprices and inordinate pride, that is, his own *self.* It is his self, ultimately, that both appears as the force that blocks the hero's natural, reflexive impulses and forces him to perform actions which go against his own interests.

The position of Dostoevsky the thinker, as is well known, does not correspond to the ideology put forward by the Underground Man. It also differs from Sechenov's scientific doctrine. True freedom of will and control over reflexes, according to Dostoevsky, are only possible within the framework of Christian self-abnegation and love. Wishing can, and, indeed, must be governed not by reflexes, but by the Christian faith and its compassion and humility. Hence, unsurprisingly, the scene of Liza's final visit, her embrace, and the character's weeping offer is the only part of the story marked by the collapse of the usual model of his unpredictable and unreasonable reactions, as, for the first time in the course of his confession, he meets another person's natural, Christian act with a reaction that is logical and natural.[38] The narrator, as if echoing Sechenov's rhetorics, concludes the second part of the novella by addressing those readers who would say that "all this is inconceivable."

Paradoxically, and in a twist of historical irony that coloured Dostoevsky's polemic with Sechenov, just as the apologia for faith in Christ from *Notes from Underground* suffered on account of censorship, so did the apologia for love in *Reflexes of the Brain.* The article's last paragraph, which described the love of one's neighbour as a necessary attitude that must underlie the foundations of morality, had to be removed in compliance with the censor's demands:

> The teaching which I have expounded does not destroy the value of human virtue and morals: the foundations of our love for one another are eternal; in the same way, man will always value a good machine better and will prefer it to a bad one when he has the choice. But in addition to this negative merit of my teaching let me point to a positive one: only my point of view explains how man can acquire the greatest of all human virtues – all-forgiving love, that is, complete indulgence toward one's neighbor.[39]

Although Dostoevsky could not know about this hymn to love and empathy, it is characteristic that, although overall he disagrees with the revolutionary discoveries Sechenov makes in reflexology, he plays with the same scientific argument in the fictional world of *Notes from Underground* in order to prove the same idea: all-forgiving love.

One may object, perhaps justifiably, to my model of the development of Dostoevsky's new method of representing affect by hypothesizing that the writer had already tested a narrative technique of this sort in his early psychological novellas. This hypothesis, however, is not fully substantiated. Indeed, *The Double* [Dvoinik, 1846], Dostoevsky's early psychological masterpiece, occasionally features passages that, describing Golyadkin Senior, accentuate rapid changes in his intentions and behaviour. All of these (numbering four or five in total) are found in chapters 1 to 4 of both the 1846 and the 1866 editions. Thus, for example, the first chapter narrates how Golyadkin, while standing in front of Dr Rutenshpitz's door, reached out for the doorbell and, suddenly,

> reasoned that tomorrow would be better, and that now, for the time being, there was no great need. But, suddenly hearing someone's footsteps on the stairs, Mr. Goliadkin immediately changed his new resolve and, just by the way, though maintaining a most resolute air, rang at Krestyan Ivanovich's door. (1:114)[40]

While in this case the character's abrupt change of motivation could be attributed to his indecisive and suspicious nature, the following two passages reveal a discrepancy between what the character says and what his body does,

> "... Why don't I go home? Devil take it all! I'm going, and that's that!" Having thus resolved his situation, Mr. Goliadkin quickly moved forward, as if someone had touched a spring inside him; in two steps he was in the pantry, he threw off his overcoat, removed his hat, hastily shoved it all into a corner, straightened and smoothed himself out; then ... then he moved to the morning room, from there he flitted to yet another room, slipping almost unnoticed among the passionately engrossed gamblers; then ... then ... here Mr. Goliadkin forgot everything that was going on around him and directly, like a bolt from the blue, appeared in the ballroom. (1:132; 36)
>
> Mr. Goliadkin, however, seemed to hear nothing, to see nothing, he could not look ... not for anything would he look; he lowered his eyes to the ground and just stood like that, having given himself in passing, however, his word of honor to shoot himself somehow that same night. Having given himself this word of honor, Mr. Goliadkin said to himself mentally: *"Here goes!" and, to his own greatest amazement, quite unexpectedly began suddenly to speak.* (1:133; 37)

It is notable that the second and the third passage emphasize the somatic affects that the characters cannot control; the second, by a mechanistic comparison with a spring, and the third, by an expression that stresses the character's astonishment at the fact that an utterance came out of his own mouth. While describing the gap and discrepancy between Golyadkin's cognitive and affective spheres, Dostoevsky is keen on presenting his mind and personality as bifurcated, creating an effect that, at first glance, may appear identical to the phenomenon of underground consciousness in *Notes from Underground*.[41] Yet, the stylistic and narrative embodiment of bifurcation in *The Double* differs qualitatively from that of the 1864 novella. In *The Double*, aside from the four or five cases described above, it is represented through the fantastical redoubling of the protagonist, namely, through the emergence of his alter ego, which embodies his ambitions.[42] In *Notes from Underground*, Dostoevsky, by rejecting the fantastical and turning towards a new approach to narrative construction, is prompted to develop a type of psychological representation that is best described as *zooming in*, where psychological reactions are split into several phases, each of them depicted in detail, to be followed by the character's multi-stage reflection, with the number of stages much greater than that in *The Double*.

Keeping in mind the way Sechenov's scientific discourse had possibly affected Dostoevsky's imagination, we can reconsider the traditional view of the genealogy of his "fantastical realism" in respect to its stylistic aspect. A keen follower of the latest developments in the natural sciences throughout his life, Dostoevsky not only polemicized with empiricism and evolutionism,[43] but also deployed some scientific metaphors, concepts, and narrative models to represent the mental and cognitive life of his characters with greater sophistication.

NOTES

The chapter is a revised and extended version of my Russian text: A. Vdovin, "Dostoevskii i refleksy golovnogo mozga: "Zapiski iz podpol'ia" v svete otkrytii I. M. Sechenova," in *Russkii realizm XIX veka: obschestvo, znanie, povestvovanie*, edited by M. Vaisman, A. Vdovin, I. Kliger, and K. Ospovat (Moscow: Novoe Literaturnoe Obozrenie, 2020), 431–51. This research is an output of a research project implemented as part of the Basic Research Program at the National Research University Higher School of Economics in 2021 (HSE). The translation of this chapter was supported by a Bridge Grant from the University of Toronto Faculty of Arts and Science and the Department of Slavic Languages and Literatures. The author and volume editors are grateful to Andriy Bilenkyy.

114   Alexey Vdovin

1 See comments in F.M. Dostoevskii, *Polnoe sobranie sochinenii v 30 tomakh*, ed. G.M. Fridlender et al. (Leningrad: "Nauka," 1972–90), vol. 5, 374–86. Subsequent references to this edition will be indicated in the text with volume and page numbers. In the newest *Polnoe sobranie sochinenii i pisem v 35 tomakh*, the commentary section is updated substantially on account of studies conducted between the 1980s and the 2010s. See F.M. Dostoevskii, *Polnoe sobranie sochinenii i pisem v 35 tomakh*, ed. V.E. Bagno et al. (St Petersburg: "Nauka," 2013), vol. 5, 479–532. The best study covering the philosophy and ideology of *Notes from the Underground* is still James Scanlan, *Dostoevsky the Thinker* (Ithaca, NY: Cornell University Press, 2002), 59–80.

2 The representation of consciousness is a key technique for realism and modernism. See Dorrit Cohn, *Transparent Minds: Narrative Modes for Presenting Consciousness in Fiction* (Princeton, NJ: Princeton University Press, 1978); Monika Fludernik, *The Fictions of Language and the Languages of Fiction. The Linguistic Representation of Speech and Consciousness* (London; New York: Routledge, 1993); *Towards a "Natural" Narratology* (London; New York: Routledge, 1996), 19–22.

3 G.A. Bialyi, "O psikhologicheskoi manere Turgeneva (Turgenev i Dostoevskii)," *Russkaia Literatura* 4 (1968): 34–50.

4 Gillian Beer, *Darwin's Plots: Evolutionary Narrative in Darwin, George Eliot and Nineteenth-Century Fiction*, 2nd ed. (Cambridge: Cambridge University Press, 2000), 156, 164.

5 Nicholas Dames, "1825–1880. The Network of Nerves," in *The Emergences of Mind: Representation of Consciousness in Narrative Discourse in English*, ed. David Herman (Lincoln: University of Nebraska Press, 2011), 227. For the intersection of physiology and fiction see also his book: Nicholas Dames, *The Physiology of the Novel: Reading, Neural Science and the Form of Victorian Fiction* (Oxford: Oxford University Press, 2007).

6 M. Holquist, "Bazarov and Secenov: The Role of Scientific Metaphor in Fathers and Sons," *Russian Literature* 6, no. 4 (1984): 359–74, 362, 367, 373. On the censorship office's meddling in the printed edition of *Reflexes of the Brain*, see the newest study of Sechenov's scholarly biography: G. Kichigina, *The Imperial Laboratory: Experimental Physiology and Clinical Medicine in Post-Crimean Russia* (New York: Rodopi, 2009), 240–1.

7 Valeria Sobol, *Febris Erotica: Lovesickness in the Russian Literary Imagination* (Seattle: University of Washington Press, 2011), 123–33.

8 R.G. Nazirov, "Sotsial'naia i eticheskaia problematika proizvedenii F. M. Dostoevskogo 1859–1866 godov" (Kand. diss., Moscow, 1966), 397. The same thesis is repeated, albeit with some abbreviations, in his later monograph: R.G. Nazirov, *Tvorcheskie printsipy F.M. Dostoevskogo* (Saratov, 1982), 54.

9 See Harriet Murav, *Holy Foolishness: Dostoevsky's Novels and the Poetics of Cultural Critique* (Stanford, CA: Stanford University Press, 1992) and Scanlan, *Dostoevsky the Thinker*.

10 Murav, *Holy Foolishness*, 35–9. A very general description of Dostoevsky's attitude towards the science of his time is given in Diane Oenning Thompson, "Dostoevskii and Science," in *The Cambridge Companion to Dostoevskii*, ed. William J. Leatherbarrow (Cambridge: Cambridge University Press, 2002), 193–202. On Dostoevsky's notion of science, see also Melissa Frazier's chapter in this volume.

11 G. Kichigina, *The Imperial Laboratory*, 302.

12 I.M. Sechenov, "Refleksy golovnogo mozga," *Meditsinskii vestnik* 47 (1863): 461–84; 48, 493–512. English translation: I.M. Sechenov, *Reflexes of the Brain*, trans. S. Belskii (Cambridge, MA: MIT Press, 1965).

13 The English translation is cited in K.S. Koshtoyants, *Essays on the History of Physiology in Russia*, trans. D.P. Boder et al. (Washington, DC: American Institute of Biological Sciences, 1964), 170.

14 Kh.S. Koshtoyants, *Ocherki po istorii fiziologii v Rossii* (Moscow, 1946), 246–50.

15 Scanlan, *Dostoevsky the Thinker*, 68–73.

16 R.G. Nazirov, "Ob eticheskoi problematike povesti "Zapiski iz podpol'ia," in *Dostoevskii i ego vremia* (Leningrad, 1971), 145–6.

17 Sechenov, "Refleksy golovnogo mozga," *Meditsinskii vestnik* 48 (1863): 509–10; Translation: Sechenov, *Reflexes of the Brain*, 100–1.

18 Daniel Philip Todes, "From Radicalism to Scientific Convention. Biological Psychology from Sechenov to Pavlov" (PhD diss., University of Pennsylvania, 1981), 240–1.

19 Ibid., 259–61.

20 Sechenov, "Refleksy golovnogo mozga," 48 (1863): 509; Sechenov, *Reflexes of the Brain*, 100–1.

21 Ibid.

22 On this topic, see G. Kichigina, *The Imperial Laboratory*, 232–4.

23 This remark, and others like it, particularly those where the protagonist mentions mathematics, the unified calendar, logarithms, and science, were used by V.N. Belopol'skii to support a persuasive hypothesis, according to which Dostoevsky also engaged in a polemic against *The Course in Positive Philosophy* by Auguste Comte. See V.N. Belopol'skii, "S kem polemiziroval Dostoevskii v povesti 'Zapiski iz podpol'ia'?" in *Dostoevskii i filosofiia. Sviazi i paralleli* (Rostov on Don, 1998), 20–30. This is not inconsistent with my thesis, since the Underground Man refers both to mathematics and to anatomy and physiology

24 Fyodor Dostoevsky, *Notes from Underground*, trans. Boris Jakim (Grand Rapids, MI and Cambridge, UK: William B. Eerdmans Publishing, 2009), 29 (my italics). From here on, all citations will give the *Polnoe sobranie sochinenii v 30 tomakh* reference first, followed by the page numbers for this translation.

25 By 1863, Dostoevsky's interest in the problem of the free will was already sparked by digests and reviews published by N.N. Strakhov in the *Svetoch*

journal. A.S. Dolinin has discovered that "free wishing" is close to some ideas expressed in Strakhov's review on the *Sketches of the Questions of Practical Philosophy* by P.L. Lavrov (*Svetoch* 7 [1860]: 1–13). Strakhov claims that "the true engine driving truly human activities always was and always will be ideas," that human behaviour neither ought to be influenced by the environment nor is, in fact, influenced by it. "Substantively and necessarily, the will is subordinated only to one thing: the very idea of its freedom, and the idea of insubordination, autonomous and conscious self-determination." Dostoevsky's *Notes from Underground* would soon be constructed around this thought or idea of "insubordination" and "autonomous self-determination." See A.S. Dolinin, "F. M. Dostoevskii i N. N. Strakhov," in *Shestidesiatye gody* (Moscow: Izdatel'stvo Akademii nauk SSSR, 1940), 240.

26 Tsvetan Todorov, *Genres in Discourse* (Cambridge: Cambridge University Press, 1990), 82–6.

27 M.S. Gus, *Idei i obrazy Dostoevskogo* (Moscow: Gosudarstvennoe izdatel'stvo khudozhestvennoi literatury,1971), 265–9; O.G. Dilaktorskaia, *Peterburgskaia povest' Dostoevskogo* (St Petersburg: Dmitrii Bulanin, 1999), 280–1. In the preface to his *History of Civilization in England* Buckle refuted Kant's metaphysical concept of "free will" and postulated that it was the special internal social laws that determine people's actions. These laws were discovered by Adolphe Quetelet. On Dostoevsky's polemics with Quetelet and Buckle see Greta Matzner-Gore's contribution to this volume.

28 V.N. Belopol'skii, *Dostoevskii i drugie: Stat'i o russkoi literature* (Rostov on Don: Foundation, 2011), 80.

29 The count is based on the book edition of 1866. I suspect that it occurs with less frequency in the newspaper edition of 1863.

30 Sechenov, "Refleksy golovnogo mozga," 47 (1863): 483; Sechenov. *Reflexes of the Brain*, 58.

31 Sechenov, "Refleksy golovnogo mozga," 48 (1863): 498; Sechenov, *Reflexes of the Brain*, 74.

32 Sechenov, "Refleksy golovnogo mozga," 48 (1863): 499; Sechenov, *Reflexes of the Brain*, 76.

33 Sechenov, "Refleksy golovnogo mozga," 48 (1863): 500; passage absent from Sechenov, *Reflexes of the Brain*.

34 Dostoevskii, *Polnoe sobranie sochinenii i pisem*, vol. 5, 522.

35 Sechenov, "Refleksy golovnogo mozga," 47 (1863): 477; Sechenov, *Reflexes of the Brain*, 41.

36 Robert Louis Jackson, *The Art of Dostoevsky: Deliriums and Nocturnes* (Princeton, NJ: Princeton University Press, 1981), 175.

37 Jackson, *The Art of Dostoevsky*, 187.

38 On the idea of Christian self-abnegation, meant to appear explicitly in the character's confession, but deleted by the censorship office, see

N.F. Budanova, "Zapiski iz podpol'ia: zagadki tsenzurnoi istorii povesti," *Dostoevskii: Materialy i issledovaniia* 21 (2016), 236–45; Dostoevskii, *PSS*, vol. 5, 497–8.

39 Translated in: M.N. Shaternikov, "The Life of I. M. Sechenov," in *I.M. Sechenov. Biographical Sketch and Essays*, ed. Howard Gardner and Judith Kreiger Gardner (New York: Arno Press, 1973), xxii. Quoted in: Todes, *From Radicalism to Scientific Convention*, 264. Based on this deleted passage, Todes concludes that Sechenov, in his political views, was not a radical.

40 Fyodor Dostoyevsky, *The Double; The Gambler*, trans. Richard Pevear and Larissa Volokhonsky (London: Everyman's Library, 2005), 9. All translations of *The Double* are from this source, with occasional modifications by the translator of the present chapter.

41 It is no accident that in the 1870s Dostoevsky said that "Goliadkin is my chief underground type" (1:488). On the connection between *The Double* and *Notes from the Underground* also see the comments section in the newest full collection of works: Dostoevskii, *Polnoe sobranie sochinenii i pisem*, vol. 5, 484–5.

42 Jillian Porter, *Economies of Feeling: Russian Literature under Nicolas I* (Evanston, IL: Northwestern University Press, 2017), 50.

43 Lidiya Ginzburg, in analyzing ways of representing human psychology through biological determinism, found in the Russian novel, noted that "Dostoevsky's position stands out among his contemporaries in that he turned a metaphysical understanding of the freedom of the will into the constructive principle of his novels, the engine that drove his character's behaviour." See Lidiya Ginzburg, *O literaturnom geroe* (Leningrad: Sovetskii pisatel', 1979)), 83. The newest studies, however, demonstrate that Dostoevsky had, in fact, absorbed quite a few positivist ideas, and used them while defending the necessity of faith in Christ. On this topic, see the remarkable article by Anna (Schur) Kaladiouk, "On 'Sticking to the Fact' and 'Understanding Nothing': Dostoevsky and the Scientific Method," *The Russian Review* 65, no. 3 (2006): 417–38.

6 Deferred Senses and Distanced Spaces: Embodying the Boundaries of Dostoevsky's Realism

SARAH J. YOUNG

In critical considerations of Dostoevsky's model of selfhood, examination of the psychic tensions within – and between – the characters has tended to dominate. Similarly, investigation into the effect of the characters' surroundings has largely focused on the symbolic significance of space, and its impact on the inner lives of Dostoevsky's heroes.[1] By comparison, the question of *how* his characters experience the world, and each other, has received little attention.[2] Yet the mechanisms of that experience are significant on various levels. The framework of Dostoevskian self-consciousness frequently implicates the visual sphere, as in *Poor Folk* [Bednye liudi, 1846], when Makar Devushkin catches sight of himself in a mirror. Bakhtin's identification of "how agonizingly the Underground Man eavesdrops on all actual and potential words others say of him," and of Stavrogin's dislike of being "spied upon," indicates the extent to which sense perception underlies both self-consciousness and dialogic interaction.[3] Relations between Dostoevsky's characters are often established through visual perception, as in *The Idiot* [Idiot, 1869], when Prince Myshkin becomes fascinated with Nastasya Filippovna through looking at her photograph. She equally emphasizes the role of vision in reciprocating that interest: "for the first time I've seen a human being!"[4] In the wider context of characters' experience of, and response to, their surroundings, the effect of St Petersburg on Raskolnikov owes as much to the sounds and smells that assault him as it does to the oppressive influence of the myth of the city's foundation. These visceral elements play a major role in bringing the spaces of the Imperial capital – both exterior and interior – to life for the reader.

References to sense perception not only locate characters in the outside world, but also allude to the "relation of inner essence to outer substance," due to the role of the sense organs as the "primary routes of ingress" into the body.[5] Dostoevsky firmly rejected the view of human beings as physiological machines espoused by Nikolai Chernyshevsky.[6] Yet the interiority for which he is so famous does not deny physical being, but to the contrary implies the existence of an exterior. The poor reception of his early experiments at anchoring his protagonists primarily in the psychic realm, in *The Double* [Dvoinik, 1846] and *The Landlady* [Khoziaika, 1847], proved the necessity of addressing the material aspects of existence, if such characters were not simply to resemble phantoms. In the aftermath of the publication of *The Double*, and while working on *The Landlady*, Dostoevsky acknowledged the importance of both dimensions in his own life: "The *external* must be balanced by the *internal*. Otherwise, in the absence of external phenomena, the internal will come to a dangerous crescendo. Nerves and fantasy will take up too much space" (28.1:138).[7] Undoubtedly, his art favours the internal, and insistently probes the consequences of losing that balance. Yet Dostoevsky never returned to the outright phantasmagorias of his early period. The healthy physicality of Alyosha Karamazov – in contrast to the sickness and ethereal nature of Prince Myshkin – suggests that ultimately he saw a spiritual existence grounded in the real world, rather than divorced from it, as the solution to the crisis of faith he associated with the age and depicted in his works.

In this chapter, I explore how the relations of self, other, and space are constructed through sense perception. I will show that references to the senses in Dostoevsky's fiction – in particular to hearing and vision – serve to embody not only the perceiving consciousness, but also the object(s) of their perception, whether those be other characters, or the spatial arrangements in which they are placed. Indeed, it is very frequently the way that characters are positioned relative to space that creates the impression of them as embodied beings. In order to elucidate Dostoevsky's approach to embodiment, and his protagonists' perceptions of the outside world and its actors, the analysis will focus on *Crime and Punishment* [Prestuplenie i nakazanie, 1866], with reference also to *The Adolescent* [Podrostok, 1875]. The latter represents Dostoevsky's longest true first-person narrative, with the narrator at the centre of the action (by contrast, the narrator-chroniclers of *Demons* [Besy, 1872] and *Brothers Karamazov* [Brat'ia Karamazovy, 1880] remain peripheral figures). Dostoevsky also originally planned to write *Crime and Punishment* in the first person. Although he ultimately reworked his material as a third-person omniscient narration in order to overcome some of the limitations of that form, the final version nevertheless retains traces of its earlier conception. The narrator's closeness to Raskolnikov's psyche means that for much of the novel, the hero is more than just the focalizer; in terms of point of view, narrator and protagonist are frequently almost indistinguishable.

By assessing the role of sense perception in accessing the other and constructing the spaces in which they operate in these texts, I aim to show how the author uses embodied characters to make the fantastic and imaginary more real, and to de-realize the everyday dimension. I will argue that embodiment and sense experience in Dostoevsky's fiction are relocated to the edges of consciousness. They are displaced temporally and spatially through patterns of indirect presentation, and deflected through the appearance of a "third person" within the text. This results in the removal of the notion of realism from the everyday realm, making the distanced, and dislocated, more real than the surrounding representation of the "normal" world. Never simply a stylistic choice, this shift to the boundaries makes experience (and therefore the self) only indirectly accessible to both consciousness and the narrator. This, in turn, impacts significantly on our understanding of the characters and their motivation, as well as on the narrative form. The absence of direct embodiment, or access to the senses, becomes a primary problem for Dostoevsky's characters. It creates obstacles to Arkady's writing in *The Adolescent*, and to Raskolnikov's confession, as well as underlying the murder itself in *Crime and Punishment*. I will show that this type of separation from the self, and of the self from the other, is the source of the "not I" that pervades Dostoevsky's oeuvre, from Mr Golyadkin's "it's not me at all, not me, and that's that" (1:113),[8] to the "[t]hat person is not I, but someone else entirely" with which the author distances himself from the narrator of "Bobok" (21:41).[9] Dostoevsky conceived of his novelistic approach as one "of [find]ing the person in the person with complete realism" (27:65). But in his framing of embodied space, and relations to self and others, through sense perception, neither that source of the person, nor their experience of the world, is available directly. Both must be found without, rather than within.

Mentally Sensing the Self

Many of Dostoevsky's characters are endowed with a bodily presence through detailed physical descriptions, but the degree to which their perception of their environment and other characters is recorded varies considerably.[10] In *Crime and Punishment*, Raskolnikov is highly susceptible to his surroundings.[11] However, it quickly becomes apparent that his sense perception and experience of both his own body and environment, although acute, are subject to significant distortion. The murder scene, the violence of which one might expect to generate the greatest sense of the characters' corporeal existence, is instead largely marked by a feeling of unreality, references to blood notwithstanding. Outside the moneylender's door, Raskolnikov feels his heart beating, but otherwise, "he was almost completely unaware of his body" (6:61).[12] He wields the axe "scarcely feeling a thing," and Alyona Ivanovna's blood pours out in notably abstract fashion, "as if from an overturned glass" (6:63; 70). Far from appearing in the episodes we would most readily associate with the physical dimension, sensual experience at such moments is minimized, distancing the characters from the embodied realm.

Nevertheless, from the start of *Crime and Punishment*, the distortion of Raskolnikov's acutely physical experience is apparent, for example after his "rehearsal" of the murder:

> He walked along the pavement like a drunken man, not seeing the passers-by, bumping into them […] Looking around him, he found that he was close to a drinking den, with steps leading down from the street to the basement […] his head was spinning and he was tormented by a burning thirst […] he ascribed his sudden weakness to hunger. (6:10; 9)

The bodily dimension is immediately associated with the abnormal states of drunkenness and weakness, which themselves cause physical contact with others. These states are further concretized by Raskolnikov's eventual awareness of his environment, as he stumbles upon a drinking establishment "like a drunken man." The reversal of causality, through which Raskolnikov is drunk *before* he enters the tavern, disrupts standard conceptions of bodily functions, further associating the working of the senses with abnormality. The affiliation of emphasis on the physical senses, material surroundings, and distorted bodily states continues in the next chapter, as vodka fumes and the stench of the food on the bar create an atmosphere sufficient to render anyone drunk (6:12).

The concomitance of unhealthy sense perception and awareness of the noxious environment's spatial dimensions is also foregrounded the morning after the murder, with reference to stuffy rooms and staircases, and the overwhelming smell of oil from the fresh paint. The allusion to Raskolnikov's sickness – "the usual sensations of someone with a fever who suddenly emerges out of doors on a bright sunny day" (6:74; 85) – establishes delirium as the source of his strong sense of both his own body and the physical world. This supports Raskolnikov's notion (6:60; 67) of the heightened consciousness of the man awaiting execution (later developed in *The Idiot*), but challenges Svidrigailov's idea that "A healthy person is the most earth-bound kind of person, and […] is obliged to live a purely earth-bound life" (6:221; 255). Raskolnikov's close attention to his surroundings is associated precisely with the acute phase of his illness. The restoration of his health – even if only partial – is linked with a *loss* of sense perception and observation of the outside world. From part 3 of the novel onwards, references to both the topography of the city and its street life, particularly the sounds of the itinerate musicians he periodically encounters, disappear.[13] At least in the abnormal atmosphere of St Petersburg, healthier bodily states paradoxically appear to preclude direct access to corporeal experience, or a sense of embodiment within the city's spaces.

In line with the heightened senses associated with delirium, dreams present a concentration of sensual perception. Before the first of Raskolnikov's dreams, the narrator opines on the "unusually real and vivid, and extraordinarily lifelike nature" of dream states associated with delirium (6:45; 49). The violence of Raskolnikov's dreams in itself implies a strong degree of embodiment, but its representation takes an indirect form. The dream of his landlady being beaten by Ilya Petrovich is overloaded with references to sounds and hearing:

> Never in his life had he heard such an unearthly noise, such a howling, wailing, grinding, weeping, such blows and curses. [Takikh neestvennykh zvukov, takogo voia, voplia, skrezheta, slez, poboi i rugatel'stv on nikogda eshche ne slykhival in ne vidyval.] [...] The fighting, bellowing, and swearing only got louder and louder [...] He was kicking her, banging her head against the stairs, you could hear that quite clearly from the sounds, from her screams, from the blows! [On b'et ee nogami, kolotit ee golovoiu o stupeni, – eto iasno, eto slyshno po zvukam, po vopliam, po udaram!]. (6:90–91; 104)

The dream then expands to introduce other listeners: "You could hear [Slyshno bylo] all the people on all the floors, up and down the staircase [kak vo vsekh etazhakh, po vsei lestnitse], crowding together, you could hear [slyshalis'] their voices, their exclamations, hear them running upstairs, knocking on doors, slamming doors, running hither and thither in a body [...] he could hear it only too clearly! [on slishkom iasno slyshit!] (6:91; 104). As hearing is repeatedly emphasized, climaxing with the homophonous *slishkom iasno slyshit*, the actions associated with the sounds embody first the protagonists of his dream, and then the building itself, as the other inhabitants' movements bring its threshold spaces into focus. His later dream in which he repeatedly tries to kill Alyona Ivanovna similarly focuses on sounds (the footsteps on the stairs above him), and on the spatial arrangement of her apartment: "Everything was as it had been – the chairs, the mirror, the yellow divan, the little pictures in their frames" (6:213; 245). This dream too widens out to reveal other people beyond the door, in the hallway and stairs, their laughter giving shape to the space.

While the dreams themselves access an intensity of sense-experience seldom attained in the waking life of the characters, the embodiment of the dream state spills over into the real world. Following Raskolnikov's dream of the horse being beaten, "He awoke covered in sweat; his hair was damp. He got up, panting with horror [...] His body ached all over [...] Leaning his elbows on his knees, he rested his head in both hands" (6:49; 54). At such points the boundaries between fantasy and reality are not so much blurred as reversed. Through the vivid evocation of sense perception in dreams and states of illness in *Crime and Punishment*, Dostoevsky associates the embodiment of characters and space with the abnormal and the unconscious. In this way, his depiction of the material world reaches beneath the surface of reality that realism usually occupies.

In the narration of *The Adolescent*, direct references to senses or the spaces they define are relatively infrequent. The only exception involves the chapters before Arkady's illness, after he receives the news of his sister Liza's pregnancy by Prince Seryozha. In this section of the novel a much stronger sense of his embodiment is apparent, notably in the descriptions of Arkady's fisticuffs with Baron Byoring (13:257–8), and his attempt to climb over a fence to set fire to a woodpile (13:268–70). This conforms largely to the type of delirious heightened sense experience we see in *Crime and Punishment*; Arkady notes that "delirium had undoubtedly begun to take hold" (13:268).[14] However, elsewhere in *The Adolescent* a different type of mental embodiment dominates. In large part due to its form as a first-person text recording events in the narrator's past, embodiment here is associated foremost with memory. Arkady conjoins bodily sensations with reference to memory on numerous occasions. His own physical responses are framed in this way, as when he learns of Kraft's suicide: "I remember being gradually overcome by quite a perceptible nervous tremor" (13:130; 171). The scenes with Baron Byoring and Arkady's accident while climbing cited above, are also framed with reference to memory. This suggests a distancing from Arkady's own sense of self, an idea that is emphasized as he deflects his own bodily sensations onto others, as in his rendezvous with Katerina Nikolaevna: "She listened to this whole wild tirade with big, wide open eyes; she saw that I was trembling" (13:203; 271). Memory for Arkady is even more strongly linked with the touch of others, in particular Versilov: "I remember him squeezing my hand" (13:171; 228). Such formulations indicate a desire to fix the moments when the relationship between the father and his illegitimate son appears solidified. Yet they also imply that Arkady does not quite trust the reality of the relationship.

Similar associations of memory and the senses also occur in *Crime and Punishment*, notably with hearing, the sense that becomes most significant for Raskolnikov,[15] as suggested by the dream discussed above of his land-lady being beaten. When he arrives at Alyona Ivanovna's apartment to rehearse the murder, and rings the doorbell: "He had forgotten the sound of this bell, and now its particular clink suddenly reminded him very vividly of something" (6:8; 6). A further reference to remembering the sound of the doorbell when he returns to the scene of the crime is more explicable (6:134). However, this first mention, already framed as a memory, implies that Raskolnikov has a recollection of the murder he has not yet committed. As with his drunkenness before the fact, this reversal distances Raskolnikov's sense perception from the concrete reality he occupies. In both novels, memory of the senses reifies experience in a way that everyday contact with the external world does not.[16]

Embodying the Other in Space

If dreamed and delirious embodiment makes these states more real than "normal" existence, they at the same time represent a distancing of the senses that cannot be accessed from everyday, healthy states of mind. Memory of sense experiences introduces temporal distancing as well. Both forms of distancing throw doubt upon the possibility of direct experience of the senses, and with them of the self. The feeling of detachment that this engenders is extended to the second form of deferred embodiment, which is framed primarily by the spatial dimension.

The idea of distancing senses from the self by projecting them onto the other is already apparent in Arkady's comment cited above, "she saw that I was trembling." As with many of the narrator's references to his own bodily sensations, invocations of the other provide a reality to his self that otherwise appears absent; in this instance, Katerina Nikolaevna's role as a witness matters as much, if not more, than his own physical response. In *The Adolescent*, that conception of witnessing takes on a greater significance through the aural dimension, as eavesdropping becomes a central device in the novel's revelation of its convoluted plot.[17] The first such scene, as Arkady waits at Vasin's apartment, relates to matters peripheral to the main storyline. It is therefore significant not so much in terms of the conversations overheard (concerning Versilov's contact with Olya) but rather for the dynamic it establishes on the boundaries of the private and the public.[18] Beginning with a detailed description of the apartment, including Arkady's position on a chair by the window (13:117), the episode consistently emphasizes the spatial arrangements and the movement of characters: doors open and close, heads poke out into the corridor in response to screams (indicating the presence of other listeners), and unknown figures are glimpsed.[19] When Vasin's stepfather Stebelkov, who "has been listening with relish" (13:122; 160), joins the women – moving position from overhearer to overheard – the visual aspect of the scene disappears. The focus shifts to Arkady's aural perception of movement and space: "all of a sudden, in the middle of a loud peal of laughter, someone, exactly as before, jumped up from a chair; this was followed by both women shouting; you could hear [slyshno bylo] Stebelkov leap up to, and hear him say something in a different voice" (13:123; 161). The substantive content of the conversation is evidently less significant here than either Arkady's act of overhearing, or the movement of the speakers that gives the scene a strong spatial dimension.

In subsequent scenes a similar dynamic continues, emphasizing interior space and movement of the characters as much as, and at times more than, the information revealed. In the very next subchapter following the extended eavesdropping incident at Vasin's, Arkady provides a detailed description of the spatial arrangement of Tatyana Pavlovna's apartment. This alerts the reader to what is about to happen, because he admits that, "All these details are necessary to understand the stupid thing I did." (13:126; 165).[20] The ensuing conversation between Tatyana Pavlovna and Katerina Nikolaevna is, this time, more relevant to the development of the plot.[21] But the overt doubling of the eavesdropping dynamic in consecutive scenes also highlights the importance of the spatial dimension, which frames an indirect mode of representation of the other. Rather than being embodied in a direct form, characters in these scenes gain embodiment relative to the construction of the spaces in which they are moving and interacting. They are accessible to the narrator only at a distance: in another room, physically separated by walls and doors, and via the auditory medium.

In *Crime and Punishment*, eavesdropping is similarly associated with the representation of interior space.[22] Unlike *The Adolescent*, in which the concealed listener – as narrator – presents his own point of view, here the third-person narration focuses on the unaware, overheard parties. (Raskolnikov's visits to the pawnbroker are an exception as, for example, he listens carefully to the sounds she makes in the bedroom in order to visualize the furniture and its distribution in the room (6:9).) Notably, at the end of the scene in Sonya's room where she reads the Raising of Lazarus to Raskolnikov, the revelation that Svidrigailov has been listening from the adjacent apartment is first made with reference to the spatial arrangement of the rooms: "Behind the door on the right, the one that separated Sonya's lodging from Gertruda Karlovna Resslich's flat, there was another room, which had long stood empty" (6:253; 292–3). Svidrigailov's presence, and in particular his decision to bring a chair up to the door to listen in more comfort on the next occasion, parallels the dynamics of the eavesdropping scenes in *The Adolescent*. Moreover, long before we are aware that Raskolnikov's conversation with Sonya has been overheard, the meticulous evocation of the interior space with which the chapter begins, and the consistent references to the movement and position of the two characters vis-à-vis each other and the furniture in the room, signal, as in *The Adolescent*, that the scene has been set up precisely in order to be overheard.[23] Naiman interprets the revelation concerning Svidrigailov's eavesdropping in terms of voyeurism, related to his conception of this and the subsequent confession scene as developing a physical as well as emotional intimacy between Raskolnikov and Sonya.[24] Yet these voyeuristic connotations are not dependent on the late disclosure of eavesdropping. Indeed, they would arguably be greater, if we knew the scene were being overheard from the start. Rather, precisely because of the revelation of Svidrigailov's concealed presence at the end of the episode, the significance of the eavesdropper is related to the form of the narrative and position of the narrator. We initially read the Raising of Lazarus scene as being channelled – like much of the rest of the text – through the omniscient third-person narrator, with Raskolnikov as the focalizer. The opening description of the layout of Sonya's room, beginning, "He cast a rapid glance over the room" (6:241; 279), indicates that it is framed from Raskolnikov's point of view. But the culminating announcement of the eavesdropper's presence reformulates the entire scene as being from Svidrigailov's point of view. From the convention of the narrator as hidden eavesdropper, revealing the characters' secrets to drive forward the plot, Svidrigailov takes the narrator's place to become the third person within the text.[25] As I will show, the question of the third person becomes significant in relation not only to the characters' embodiment within interior spaces, but also to wider issues relating to both novels' narrative form and ethics.

The following chapter of *Crime and Punishment* repeats the motif of the concealed listener, on this occasion the artisan who has accused Raskolnikov of murder. The space of Porfiry Petrovich's office is demarcated, and the character himself embodied, by the examining magistrate's bizarre movement around it: "By now he was almost running around the room, his podgy little legs going faster and faster, his eyes fixed on the ground, his right hand shoved behind his back while his left waved this way and that" (6:260; 299).[26] As in *The Adolescent*, the repetition of eavesdropping scenes that focus so strongly on the depiction of interior space – and the movement of characters within it – begs attention. Overt implications regarding the position of the narrator are absent in this second iteration. However, the common feature of the two consecutive scenes, foregrounding references to space and movement, suggests the necessity of a concealed third person to actualize those features. Both scenes function as if the additional presence of a third character in itself creates an extra dimension that turns paper persons into embodied characters. The implications of this differ in the two novels. In *The Adolescent*, Arkady is the first-person narrator, but only by turning himself into the third person in eavesdropping scenes can he have a story to tell, and make it real – the problem with which he begins the novel and addresses repeatedly throughout the text. Tellingly, he perceives eavesdropping as the primary route to knowledge of the other. In his first real conversation with Versilov, he notes, "There were moments when it seemed to me [...] that he'd been sitting somewhere or standing behind the door each time during the last two months: he knew every gesture, every feeling beforehand" (13:223; 295). As with his representation of his own self through contact with the other, he introduces the eavesdropping dynamic to reflect back on himself here. This indicates its importance to his own understanding not only of the plots around him, but also of how others view, and know, him.

In *Crime and Punishment*, the sense of embodiment in the two overheard scenes in Sonya's room, actualized through repeated reference to the characters' physical interaction and movement around the space, and reinforced by the presence of a third person as (aural) witness, has a transformative effect on Raskolnikov. Previously, as we have seen, the distortion of his sense experience renders the hero's concrete reality unreal, including endowing the murder scene itself with a strong sense of abstraction. Raskolnikov's continued perception of the murder in the same abstract terms enables him to deny the humanity of the victim:[27] "it's not about her! [...] it wasn't a person that I killed, but a principle!" (6:211; 243). In the scenes with Sonya, her verbal emphasis on the concrete person challenges Raskolnikov's reduction of others to abstractions: "That louse was a human being!" (6:320; 368). But Sonya's embodied presence and physical proximity to Raskolnikov also confront him with the reality of other human beings, including – perhaps especially – those, like herself, whom society considers of little or no account.

The connection between Sonya and Lizaveta has already forced Raskolnikov to acknowledge the murder that cannot be theorized away. At the end of the Raising of Lazarus scene, read from Lizaveta's New Testament, this is already apparent, as he pointedly preludes his confession with, "I'll tell you who killed Lizaveta" (6:253; 292). At their subsequent meeting, Raskolnikov's first recollection of killing Lizaveta – rather than Alyona – emphasizes her physical reaction. This reiterates the role of memory in embodying the senses discussed above: "He had a vivid memory of Lizaveta's expression on that day, as he advanced towards her with the axe in his hand, and she backed away from him towards the wall, stretching out her arm in front of her [vystaviv vpered ruku]" (6:315; 363). Sonya immediately replicates Lizaveta's fearful movements, as she "suddenly stretched out her left arm [vystaviv vpered levuiu ruku], pressing her fingers ever so lightly against his chest, and slowly began to get up from the bed, edging further and further away from him" (6:315; 363). In doing so, she further concretizes the idea of the victims – now plural – as embodied beings like herself.

Raskolnikov's crime may be a product of his rejection of the other's humanity. But beyond the conscious roles of Sonya and Porfiry in moving him towards confession, the presence of a hidden third person in these scenes suggests that this triangular dynamic overturns the unreality of the murders to contribute to Raskolnikov's restoration by indirectly creating embodied space and giving physical form to the characters. Bakhtin suggests that "The semantic point of view of a 'third person,' on whose territory a stable image of the hero is constructed, would destroy this atmosphere, and therefore such a point of view does not enter into Dostoevsky's creative world."[28] However, the role of the hidden witness in creating a sense of embodiment in the scenes with Sonya suggests that, to the contrary, Raskolnikov *needs* the stability of the third person in order to restore him from his orientation towards the self and denial of reality outside him. The hero at such moments is no longer able to treat others as abstract entities to be disposed of at will.

Indirect Witnessing

Eavesdropping thus impacts significantly on the representation of the hero, but it remains an ambivalent device in both *Crime and Punishment* and *The Adolescent*. The dubious motivation of Svidrigailov renders the truth vulnerable to his manipulation. Porfiry's ultimate aim may be the truth, but his opaque method appears to undermine his efforts, as his careful set-up backfires. The ignorance of Arkady,[29] which leaves him at risk of being set up (as does indeed happen), potentially subverts the truth value of supposedly revelatory scenes, exacerbating the plot confusion. Nevertheless, the embodied dimension associated with eavesdropping, and related types of indirect witnessing, leads to other kinds of truth.

The connection of embodiment to witnessing is revisited shortly after Porfiry's thwarted revelation, when Dunya's jilted fiancé, Luzhin, accuses Sonya of theft at her father's wake. Pyotr Petrovich's initial interview with Sonya sets up a dynamic similar to the eavesdropping scenes examined above. The positioning of the three actors is highlighted through reference to Sonya's moving gaze (6:287), but now the third-person witness (Lebezyatnikov) moves into plain sight. The end of the scene repeats the emphasis on the position and senses of the witness, as Lebezyatnikov congratulates Luzhin on what he has just observed: "Throughout this scene Andrei Semionovich was either standing by the window or walking about the room [...] 'I heard everything, and *saw* everything,' he said with particular emphasis" (6:288; 332).

When Luzhin makes his accusation of theft public, Lebezyatnikov's refutation of the allegation against Sonya reprises the association of the senses and spatial arrangements with eavesdropping. His convoluted explanation, which begins, "although I was standing quite a way off, I saw it all, all of it [no ia vse, vse videl]," and ends "I saw it, I saw it [Ia videl, videl], and I'll swear on oath I did!" (6:306; 353). Moreover, his entire exposure of his mentor contains repeated reference to seeing, and the visual element is consistently combined with his commentary on his own position in the room in relation to Luzhin and the money: "I saw that because I was standing nearby just then." This gives his version of events an embodied dimension that survives its manifest deficiencies as a witness statement.[30] This suggests that although Lebezyatnikov is a figure of ridicule throughout the novel, his role here is serious. He espouses a form of witnessing that goes beyond mere looking by expressing itself in spatial, embodied terms. As Apollonio argues, his poor eyesight means he may well not have seen anything incriminating.[31] Undoubtedly, Luzhin is counting precisely on his witness *not* being able to witness – on him only hearing rather than seeing (thereby reinforcing the similarity of the scene to the earlier eavesdropping episodes). Yet Lebezyatnikov, because he is separated by his visual impairment and cannot "s[ee] with his own eyes," relies on the *various* forms of reality. In the essay "A Propos of the Exhibition" [Po povodu vystavki, 1873], Dostoevsky describes these various forms as leading to the "reality that really exists [deistvitel'no syshchestvuiushchee]" of Dickens, rather than the flat "evidence of their own eyes" of contemporary painters (21:75–6; 1:214–15). Allen's comment in relation to "A Gentle Creature" [Krotkaia, 1876] also appears to apply to Lebezyatnikov's unseeing act of witnessing: "Paradoxically, only the 'unrealistic' frame or vision can penetrate or bear witness to what is real, to what is seen not only *on* but also *from* the inside."[32] For all his other shortcomings as a character, Lebezyatnikov is able to perceive beneath the surface – of his own materialist beliefs and rejection of the notion of compassion as much as anything else – to understand what is essential in Sonya (and Luzhin). Paradoxically, he does so by focusing on the material elements of the scene he witnesses, emphasizing precisely the surface, physical arrangements. Thus, while the witness himself moves into view here – after two scenes of eavesdropping with a concealed third person – his own *in*ability to view the incident acts as a further form of distancing. The separation of the character from direct sense perception reinforces the embodied nature of the scene.

Lebezyatnikov's act of visually impaired witnessing to Sonya's innocence affirms the role of the third person in representing the characters' embodiment, even as the text pokes fun at his narratorial inadequacies. A much more assured act of narration/witnessing – ostensibly concerning Raskolnikov's guilt – occurs towards the end of the novel, in two adjacent scenes. At the end of their final conversation, in the dive on Obukhovsky Prospekt near the Haymarket, Raskolnikov follows Svidrigailov back to his lodgings. Upon arriving in the corridor he shares with Sonya, Svidrigailov changes tone to deliver an elaborate narrative of his own actions while he is performing them:

> Look [Vidite], here's Sofia Semionovna's door: see, there's no one there! [...] And look, it's Madame de Kapernaumov herself, isn't it? Well (she's a bit deaf [ona glukha nemnogo]), has she gone out? Where? So, did you hear that [slyshali teper']? [...] Well now, have a look [izvol'te videt']: I'm taking this five-per-cent bond out of my desk (see how many I've still got left!); this one's on its way to the money changer's today. So, did you see all that [videli]? [...] I lock the desk, I lock the flat, and here we are on the stairs again." (6:373–4; 430)

The pantomime of listening to the deaf Kapernaumova (as with the half-blind Lebezyatnikov), and the repeated exhortations to Raskolnikov to view what he is doing, reinforce the association of the senses with spatial arrangements that we have seen in other witnessing scenarios. Svidrigailov's narration casts not only Raskolnikov in the role of witness, but also Kapernaumova. Yet precisely *what* is being witnessed here, beyond Svidrigailov's superficial actions, is initially unclear.

A little over a page later, Svidrigailov recapitulates this scene and its triangular dynamic, this time with Dunya as his primary witness, and the porter as secondary: "I live right here, in this building we're coming up to. Here's the house porter; he knows me very well, look, he's bowing to me; he can see that I'm walking with a lady, and of course he's had time to notice your face" (6:375; 431–2). The repetition draws attention to his device, ultimately revealing its meaning as he proceeds to explain, in the same exaggeratedly theatrical manner, the spatial arrangement that enabled him to eavesdrop on Raskolnikov and Sonya. In doing so, Svidrigailov parodies the type of episodic doubling we have already seen in the appearance of the eavesdropping motif in consecutive scenes in both

Crime and Punishment and *The Adolescent*. In each case, it is the revelation in the second scene that endows the dynamic established in the earlier sequence with significance.

As we have seen, Svidrigailov's eavesdropping, which places him in the position of the third-person narrator, provides the extra dimension that embodies Raskolnikov. In turn, this forces him to see the other as an embodied being as well. In these recapitulations, Svidrigailov again takes over the function of the narrator by creating the doubled scene for his own purposes. Svidrigailov's refashioning of Raskolnikov's confession with his own intonation and evaluation[33] places the original conversation at two removes, first by his covert listening, and then by his re-enactment. The approach he adopts to performing these scenes, emphasizing the senses and the role of the space in enabling his eavesdropping, reinforces the idea that Raskolnikov's embodiment – once he has returned to relative health – occurs only at a distance and filtered through a third person. At the same time, Svidrigailov, by taking on the role of the witnessed, rather than the witness, also places himself in Raskolnikov's position. This happens, moreover, precisely at the point when Svidrigailov replaces Raskolnikov as focalizer in the only sustained passage of the novel that is removed from Raskolnikov's consciousness. The characters have effectively changed places: Svidrigailov's final movements (his walk towards the Petersburg side and his dreams that emphasize heightened senses and delineate the spaces of the tawdry hotel where he takes a room) parallel both Raskolnikov's earlier actions and his distorted sense experiences. Having lent his own embodiment to Raskolnikov, as the third person, to bring the hero closer to confession, Svidrigailov can now only access his own senses through dreams and delirium. This occurs precisely as he draws closer to the final disembodiment of non-being. In order to achieve their respective resolutions, each protagonist must take from the other what he lacks, and become what he is not.

Conclusion

The indirect embodiment of Dostoevsky's characters occurs through the distortion of their own senses, and in their filtered representation through the eyes and ears of witnesses, either concealed or in plain sight. Memory, dreams, and delirium form the basis of a mode of sense experience that distances characters from their own bodies and the reality around them. The distancing provided by witnesses is also subject to potential distortion, through the imperfect perception of the third person, or the recasting of the scene in another's words. As protagonists' relations to their material being and experience of the world become indirect, the more real becomes less real, and vice versa – including in perception of the self. The outer body of characters and the world they occupy lack the stability normally associated with realist novels. This transpires not only because of the association of the sense experience with abnormal states and the unconscious, but also because body and space become doubly relative constructions; the two come into being as a result of their interaction, and as perceived through the eyes of another. At the same time, that very instability enables the exchange of interior and exterior states, potentially giving the other (and the reader) access to the self.

Raskolnikov undergoes a radical transformation as a result of this model: from heightened sense perception associated with sickness, he is subsequently rendered through Svidrigailov's perspective, before their final exchange of places and characteristics. This suggests that embodiment through a third person – even if, as in this instance, it has a positive effect, leading to the acknowledgment of others and ultimately the hero's confession – can lead to a loss of unitary consciousness. This parallels Yuri Corrigan's identification of the "Vasia Shumkov paradigm" of the collective personality, in which the borders between individual characters become indistinct and permeable.[34] As the "I" becomes "not-I," for Raskolnikov and Svidrigailov (as well as Arkady in *The Adolescent*, when he moves into the position of the third person in order to gain the perspective and knowledge he needs to tell the story), the implications of indirect embodiment shift onto the ontological and narrative planes. It relates to the separation from the self not only of Dostoevsky's doubles, but also that which the author himself underwent in order to create his distinctive narrative voices. As he formulated in his earliest conception of *Poor Folk*: "They [readers] are used to seeing the author's mug in everything; I don't show mine. But it doesn't enter into their heads that it's Devushkin speaking, not I, and that Devushkin can't speak otherwise" (28.1:117).[35] Distorted sense perception, and embodiment that is distanced through a third person within the text, thus become Dostoevsky's mechanisms for depicting the limits of the material world, and its potential to be breached.

NOTES

I would like to thank the editors of the present volume for their extremely constructive advice, which helped me transform a rather messy first draft into the chapter I wanted to write, and for their friendship and support.

1 Recent treatments of symbolic space in Dostoevsky include: Ganna Bograd, "Metafizicheskoe prostranstvo i pravoslavnaia tsimvolika kak osnova mest

obitaniia geroev romana 'Prestuplenie i nakazanie,'" in *Dostoevskii: dopolne-niia k kommentariu*, ed. T.A. Kasatkina (Moscow: Nauka, 2005), 179–202; and Vladimir Ivantsov, "Digging into Dostoevskii's Underground: From the Met-aphorical to the Literal," *Slavic and East European Journal* 62, no. 2 (Summer 2018): 382–400. See also Katherine Bowers's and Vadim Shneyder's contri-butions to the present volume

2 For exceptions to this trend, see: Sharon Lubkemann Allen, "Reflection/ Refraction of the Dying Light: Narrative Vision in Nineteenth-Century Russian and French Fiction," *Comparative Literature* 54, no. 1 (2002): 2–22; Gabriella Safran, "The Troubled Frame Narrative: Bad Listening in Late Imperial Russia," *The Russian Review* 72, no. 4 (2013): 556–572; Anna Schur, "The Limits of Listening: Particularity, Compassion, and Dostoevsky's 'Bookish Humaneness,'" *The Russian Review* 72, no. 4 (2013): 573–589; and Daniel Schümann, "Raskolnikov's Aural Conversion: From Hearing to Lis-tening," *Ulbandus Review* 16 (2014): 6–23.

3 Mikhail Bakhtin, *Problems of Dostoevsky's Poetics*, trans. Caryl Emerson (Minneapolis: University of Minnesota Press, 1984), 59–60.

4 F.M. Dostoevskii, *Polnoe sobranie sochinenii v tridtsati tomakh*, ed. G. M. Fridlender et al. (Leningrad: "Nauka," 1972–90), vol. 8, 148. Subse-quent references to this edition will be indicated in the text with volume and page numbers. Translation: Fyodor Dostoevsky, *The Idiot*, trans. Alan Myers (Oxford: Oxford University Press, 1992), 185. Subsequent references to this translation will be indicated after the *PSS* volume and page number following a semicolon. On the rhetoric and thematics of vision in *The Idiot*, see A.B. Krinitsyn, "O spetsifike vizual'nogo mira u Dostoevskogo i seman-tike 'videnii' v romane Idiot'," in *Roman F M Dostoevskogo 'Idiot': sovremennoe sostoianie izucheniia*, ed. T.A. Kasatkina (Moscow: Nasledie, 2001), 170–205; and Robert Louis Jackson, *Dialogues with Dostoevsky: The Overwhelming Ques-tions* (Stanford, CA: Stanford University Press, 1993), 47–49.

5 William A. Cohen, *Embodied: Victorian Literature and the Senses* (Minneapolis: University of Minnesota Press, 2009), 1, 5.

6 N.G. Chernyshevskii, "Antropologicheskii printsip v filosofii," in *Izbrannye filosofskie sochineniia*, ed. M.M. Grigor'ian (Moscow: Gosudarstvennoe iz-datel'stvo politicheskoi literatury, 1951), 185–188. On Dostoevsky's polemic with Chernyshevsky, see Melissa Frazier's contribution to the present volume.

7 From a letter to Mikhail Dostoevsky, January–February 1847. My own translation.

8 Translation: Fyodor Dostoevsky, *The Double*, trans. Hugh Aplin (Richmond: Alma Classics, 2016), 8. Subsequent references to this translation will be in-dicated after the *PSS* volume and page number following a semicolon.

9 Translation: Fyodor Dostoyevsky, *A Writer's Diary*, trans. Kenneth Lantz, vol. 1, 1873–1876 (London: Quartet, 1994), 170. Subsequent references to this

translation will be indicated after the *PSS* volume and page number following a semicolon.

10   The Underground Man represents one of the most extreme cases of *disembodiment* in Dostoevsky's fiction. *Notes from Underground* [Zapiski iz podpol'ia, 1864] is notable for its absence of reference to the senses; the narrator seldom sees or hears, and is generally impervious to outside or sensual influence until he meets Liza. More than half of the novella's 21 uses of *slyshat'* (to hear) occur in the scenes with the prostitute.

11   See, for example, Adele Lindenmeyr, "Raskolnikov's City and the Napoleonic Plan," *Slavic Review* 35, no. 1 (1976): 39–40.

12   Translation: Fyodor Dostoevsky, *Crime and Punishment*, trans. Nicolas Pasternak Slater (Oxford: Oxford University Press, 2017), 68. Subsequent references to this translation will be indicated after the *PSS* volume and page number following a semicolon. Dmitry Merezhkovsky describes such moments of tension as leading to the "dukhovnost' ploti" (spiritualization of the flesh); D.S. Merezhkovskii, *L. Tolstoi i Dostoevskii*, ed. E.A. Andrushchenko (Moscow: Nauka, 2000), 146.

13   John Levin and Sarah J. Young, "Mapping Machines: Transformations of the Petersburg Text," *Primerjalna Književnost* 36, no. 2 (2013): 157.

14   Translation: Fyodor Dostoevsky, *The Adolescent*, trans. Dora O'Brien (Richmond: Alma Classics, 2016), 357.

15   The aural dimension of *Crime and Punishment* is discussed in ethical terms, highlighting the negative associations of eavesdropping and Raskolnikov's predatory listening instincts, in Schümann, "Raskolnikov's Aural Conversion," 12.

16   The emphasis on the senses, particularly hearing, in "The Peasant Marey" [Muzhik Marei, 1876] in *A Writer's Diary*, indicates the importance of memory to embodied experience in Dostoevsky's works.

17   Dostoevsky's use of eavesdropping goes back to his farcical 1848 story "Another Man's Wife and a Husband Under the Bed," and is central to various works, including "Uncle's Dream," [Dyadushkin son, 1859] and the chapter "Akul'ka's Husband" [Akul'kin muzh, 1861] in *Notes from the House of the Dead*. On the latter, see Schur, "The Limits of Listening," 581–588.

18   This particular sense of space associated with eavesdropping, in which the private realm is transgressed, is noted by Ann Gaylin, *Eavesdropping in the Novel from Austen to Proust* (Cambridge: Cambridge University Press, 2003), 2. Bakhtin associates the movement from private to public inherent in eavesdropping with the development of the novelistic form. Mikhail Bakhtin, "Forms of Time and of the Chronotope in the Novel," in *The Dialogic Imagination: Four Essays by M.M. Bakhtin*, ed. Michael Holquist, trans. Caryl Emerson and Michael Holquist (Austin: University of Texas Press, 1981), 123–124.

19 The repeated reference to doors in this scene, and those discussed below, indicates the connection between eavesdropping and the threshold chronotope and, therefore, the transformative potential of the eavesdropping dynamic. Bakhtin, *Problems*, 170.

20 Hansen-Löve notes the tension between Arkady's position as an outside observer in such scenes, and his desire to play a central role in the novel's drama. He indicates a psycho-sexual dimension to the frequency with which Arkady is trapped, eavesdropping, in a bedroom, which reprises the scenario of "Another Man's Wife and a Husband under the Bed." O. Khansen-Leve, "Diskursivnye protsessy v romane Dostoevskogo 'Podrostok'," in *Avtor i tekst: sbornik statei*, ed. V.M. Markovich and V. Shmid (St Petersburg: Izd-vo S-Peterburgskogo universiteta, 1996), 260–261.

21 As Gaylin argues, "Illicit listening in the novel stages the manner in which stories are generated and resolved." *Eavesdropping*, 2.

22 The connection of eavesdropping with interior space is explored in Peter Betjemann, "Eavesdropping with Charlotte Perkins Gilman: Fiction, Transcription, and the Ethics of Interior Design," *American Literary Realism* 46, no. 2 (2014): 95–115. Dostoevsky's preoccupation with interior design is apparent in the recurring motif of redecoration in *Crime and Punishment*, including of Alyona's apartment after the murder, the apartment downstairs where the decorators Mikolai and Mitrei are working, and the police bureau Raskolnikov visits at the beginning of part 2. These references draw the reader's attention to the delineation of the novel's interior spaces long before their significance to the eavesdropping scenes becomes clear.

23 The use of an initial interior description to set up future eavesdropping episodes also features in "Uncle's Dream"; a long description of the layout of Moskaleva's "salon" appears irrelevant until two chapters later, when her relative Nastasya Petrovna retreats to an adjoining cubby hole in order to eavesdrop on Moskaleva's conversation with her daughter Zina about the plan to ensnare the eponymous elderly Prince (2:319).

24 Eric Naiman, "Gospel Rape," *Dostoevsky Studies* New Series, no. 22 (2018): 11–40.

25 The connection between eavesdropping and the third-person voice in narrative is explored in John Vernon, "Reading, Writing, and Eavesdropping: Some Thoughts on the Nature of Realistic Fiction," *The Kenyon Review* 4, no. 4 (1982): 49.

26 This scene also associates sound and space with memory, thus recalling the forms of indirect sense perception discussed above, when Mikolka puts in his unexpected appearance: "Later on, when he thought back to that moment, Raskolnikov recalled it like this: The noise outside the door suddenly got much louder, and the door opened a fraction" (6:270; 310).

27 Raskolnikov considers only the crime he intended to commit, ignoring the murder of Lizaveta altogether until his first encounter with Sonya.

28 Bakhtin, *Problems*, 64.

29 As his sister, Liza, comments, "I've long since seen that you know nothing about anything" (13:133; 175).

30 Following Luzhin – the lawyer's – lead, both Lebezyatnikov and Raskolnikov frame their rebuttal of his allegation in terms of testimony (6:301–308), undermining the former's supposed authority and emphasizing the subjective status of witnessing, which becomes relevant not only to this novel, but to *Brothers Karamazov* in particular.

31 Carol Apollonio, *Dostoevsky's Secrets: Reading Against the Grain* (Evanston: Northwestern University Press, 2009), 91.

32 Allen, "Reflection/Refraction," 7. Italics in original.

33 Bakhtin, *Problems*, 89.

34 Yuri Corrigan, *Dostoevsky and the Riddle of the Self* (Evanston: Northwestern University Press, 2017), 18–21.

35 Letter to Mikhail Dostoevsky, 1 February 1846. My translation.

7 Under the Floorboards, Over the Door: The Gothic Corpse and Writing Fear in *The Idiot*

KATHERINE BOWERS

In August 1867 Fyodor Dostoevsky and his wife Anna Grigoryevna visited the Basel Museum and viewed Hans Holbein the Younger's painting *Body of the Dead Christ in the Tomb* (1521–2). Writing her memoirs in the 1910s, Anna Grigoryevna recalled Dostoevsky's reaction to it:

> The painting had a crushing [podavliaiushchee] impact on Fyodor Mikhailovich. He stood before it as if stunned [porazhennyi]. I did not have the strength to look at it – the first impression was too difficult for me, particularly in my sickly condition – and I went into the other galleries. When I returned ... I found Fyodor Mikhailovich riveted in the same place before the painting. On his agitated [vzvolnovannom] face was a frightened [ispugannoe] expression, one I had noticed more than once during the initial moments of an epileptic seizure.[1]

Anna's concern that Dostoevsky would have a seizure prompted her to lead the writer to rest in another room where he gradually calmed down, yet he "insisted on returning once more to view this astounding painting [porazivshuiu kartinu]."[2] Anna's 1867 diary records other details including her own reaction to the painting: "it is not at all aesthetic and only arouses disgust and some kind of horror in me" [eto vovse ne estetichno, i vo mne vozbudilo odno tol'ko otvrashchenie i kakoi-to uzhas].[3] Dostoevsky later incorporated *Dead Christ* into *The Idiot* [Idiot,1869], the novel he was working on in the fall of 1867.[4]

In his study of Dostoevsky's relationship to beauty, Robert Louis Jackson writes that the painting "deeply disturbs man's moral and religious tranquility; it is the embodiment of an aesthetics of despair."[5] Jackson likens the painting's aesthetics to atheism, a connection also made in *The Idiot* by the characters' reactions to it. In Part II Prince Myshkin famously exclaims that "that picture may cause some to lose their faith" (8:182),[6] a statement which articulates the central problem the painting represents within the novel, namely the challenge of believing in Christ's resurrection when faced with his apparent mortality in such an abject way. Ippolit extends this challenge outwards in Part III, asking the crucial question: "if death is so horrible and the laws of nature so powerful, how can they be overcome?" (8:339). How it is possible to believe in a higher power when confronted with brute nature as expressed in the finality of death?

Death is a point of fascination for Dostoevsky throughout *The Idiot*, more so than in any other of his works. Liza Knapp has described the novel as "a comprehensive study of death," observing: "*The Idiot* asks what we know about death and how we narrate about death."[7] In addition to the discussions of Holbein's painting, the novel includes myriad stories of death, from Myshkin's tale of the experience of a condemned man in the beginning of Part I to the revelation of Nastasya Filippovna's corpse in the conclusion of Part IV. One such narrated death anticipates the details of Nastasya Filippovna's: the "body under the floorboards," a murder victim buried in Rogozhin's house. Nastasya Filippovna describes it in a letter in Part III: "I kept thinking that, somewhere under the floorboards, perhaps hidden there by his father, there might be a dead man wrapped in oilcloth [kleenka], just like that Moscow case, and even surrounded in the same way with bottles of Zhdanov fluid [zhdanovskaia zhidkost']" (8:380). She has imagined this murder, but its details – the oilcloth and Zhdanov fluid – link it to a real case: the July 1866 murder of the jeweller Kalmykov in Moscow. The murderer, V.F. Mazurin, used a disinfectant called Zhdanov fluid to disguise the smell of the body. Later, when Myshkin witnesses Nastasya Filippovna's death tableau, the oilcloth and Zhdanov fluid again appear, and Myshkin remarks on its similarity to the Moscow case, "As it was there… in Moscow?" (8:504). As Jacques Catteau observes, the two murders (Kalmykov's and Nastasya Filippovna's) "endlessly echo and clarify each other."[8] Although Nastasya Filippovna's corpse is revealed only in the final scenes, Dostoevsky's hidden corpse is buried in the novel's narrative structure, remembered when objects, encounters, or dreams prompt characters to imagine Rogozhin as a murderer: for example, a silk-wrapped razor, an offhand comment that Rogozhin will slit Nastasya Filippovna's throat, or Nastasya Filippovna's fantasy of the body buried under the floorboards of Rogozhin's house.

This concealed corpse trope also links *The Idiot* to the gothic genre.[9] Another "body under the floorboards" famously appears in Edgar Allan Poe's gothic story "The Tell-Tale Heart" (1843). Poe's story tells of a murderer who is haunted by the beating of his victim's heart from underneath the floorboards. The audible heartbeat, which only the narrator can hear, denotes his guilty conscience.[10] Following Poe, the body under the floorboards takes on this association of transgression – a theme explored in depth by Dostoevsky in *Crime and Punishment* [Prestuplenie i nakazanie] and elsewhere. Additionally, in *The Idiot*, this imagined corpse joins a series of other dead bodies: victims of execution and violence, victims of poverty and deprivation, victims of illness, and *Dead Christ.*

A copy of *Dead Christ* hangs over a doorway in Rogozhin's house. Like the body under the floorboards, the body in the painting occupies gothic space: a liminal space – a threshold – in a house associated with darkness, suffering, and a violent past and, as Catteau notes, based on Mazurin the murderer's house. The novel's philosophical core centres on two key scenes in which *Dead Christ* figures prominently, foregrounding again the centrality of the dead body to the novel: Myshkin's discussion with Rogozhin about the nature of faith and Ippolit's "Essential Explanation."[11] Yet the impassioned discussion of Holbein's work in Part II, or even the detailed description Ippolit provides of it in Part III, fails to capture the affective experience the painting provokes, that which Dostoevsky had when he viewed it. This chapter will examine one tool Dostoevsky used in *The Idiot* to create an affective experience within his realist art – gothic narrative force – and focus on its utility in the discussion of the novel's gothic bodies: *Dead Christ* over the door and the imagined body under the floorboards.

Dostoevsky and Holbein's Gothic Corpse

Holbein's painting depicts Christ's bruised and cut corpse laid out in the tomb following the crucifixion, but in its unique depiction of a visibly mortal and vulnerable body rather than a body obviously destined for resurrection, its subject could be any body. Whereas in *The Idiot* the characters' ekphrastic discussions clearly indicate the theological implications of depicting Christ's body in this manner, Anna Grigoryevna describes her first encounter with the painting as a visceral reaction to the realistic depiction of the corpse itself.[12]

> He is depicted with an emaciated body, visible bones and ribs, arms and legs with pierced wounds, swollen and very blue, like a dead man who has already begun to rot. The face is also fearfully agonized, with half-open eyes, but already seeing nothing and expressing nothing. The nose, mouth and chin had turned blue; in general, it so closely resembles a real dead man, that, really, it seemed to me that I would not want to stay in the same room with him.[13]

She focuses on the body's features, but describes them liminally, that is, in a state of transition. The subject is like a corpse about to decompose, yet it is animated as, in her interpretation of the painting, the face is "agonized," as if expressing feeling, and the eyes half-open, as if they might see.

By emphasizing the fact that the eyes see and express nothing, Anna Grigoryevna underscores the liminality she senses in confronting the painting. She is disoriented as she faces the ambiguous space between life and death.[14] In Anna Grigoryevna's description this space between the familiar and the unknown is a locus of fear, and, indeed, she comments that she would not like to be left alone with the painting because it resembles a real dead man. For Julia Kristeva, "the utmost of abjection" is a corpse "seen without God and outside of science": "It is death infecting life. Abject. It is something rejected from which one does not part, from which one does not protect oneself as from an object. Imaginary uncanniness and real threat, it beckons to us and ends up engulfing us."[15] Anna Grigoryevna is compelled and engulfed by the portrait in the way Kristeva would later describe. Indeed, her reaction to *Dead Christ* underscores the painting's realism. In *The Idiot* Holbein's painting represents this fear, both in its role of *memento mori* and in its challenge to Christian faith.

Dead Christ provokes Anna Grigoryevna's fear, and when it appears in *The Idiot*, also charged with this affect, the painting functions as a gothic corpse. Yael Shapira defines a "gothic corpse" as "an image of the dead body rendered with deliberate graphic bluntness in order to excite and entertain."[16] Shapira argues that eighteenth-century English novelists included sensationalistic descriptions of dead bodies in their fiction as part of a new trend. Eschewing earlier didactic uses of these graphic passages, the new novelists rather used them to "seize the reader's attention and add a powerful charge to key moments in the plot."[17] While *Dead Christ* provokes strong reactions, it may seem counter-intuitive to equate the painting's appearance in Dostoevsky's novel with excitement and entertainment. Yet, in each scene where it specifically appears, the painting serves as a catalyst for storytelling; it sparks Myshkin's four parables about the nature of religious faith as well as Ippolit's "Essential Explanation." Intriguingly, while the graphic and sensationalistic nature of corpses is bound up with Kristevan abjection, Shapira's study instead argues that

> decisions about the graphic image of the corpse function as gestures of self-definition: the very fact that the corpse is there or not there, hinted at or abruptly revealed, riddled with worms or idealized into an object of ethereal beauty – these are not only representations of the dead body itself (replete as it is with cultural connotations, fears and longings) but statements

about the intentions of the writer and the way she or he perceives fiction's relation to the reader.[18]

The corpse in gothic literature is thus a narrative device that a writer deliberately and consciously deploys to create an affective connection with the reader. This connection is intrinsic to the gothic as, in M.H. Abrams's formulation, the best gothic novels "[open] up to fiction the realm of the irrational and [...] perverse impulses and nightmarish terrors that lie beneath the orderly surface of the civilized mind"– for both the characters and the reader.[19] *Dead Christ* assumes this function in *The Idiot*. As the gothic corpse, the painting's recurrence in the novel generates affective responses among the characters. Using *Dead Christ* as a catalyst for gothic narrative force in *The Idiot* enabled Dostoevsky the space within a realist framework to explore the nature of his characters' fear, but also his readers'.

Dostoevsky was an avid reader of gothic novels. In *Winter Notes on Summer Impressions* [Zimnie zametki o letnikh vpechatleniiakh, 1863], he recalls childhood encounters with Ann Radcliffe's works.[20]

> I used to spend the long winter hours before bed listening (for I could not yet read), agape with ecstasy and terror, as my parents read aloud to me from the novels of Ann Radcliffe. Then I would rave deliriously about them in my sleep. (5:46)[21]

This statement suggests gothic novels' effect on the reader (or, in this case, listener). First, they revolve around the solution of a mystery. This mystery's solution, constantly anticipated and deferred, spurs both reader and gothic heroine or hero onward. The reader keeps turning the pages, filled, like Dostoevsky, with ecstasy and terror, dreading and yet looking forward to the anticipated horrors. The heroine, similarly, often imprisoned in a gloomy castle, opens door after door to discover the castle's secrets, in spite of the constant expectation of stumbling upon something dreadful. Secondly, in addition to mystery, the novels' plots revolve around some broken taboo or transgression, which is sometimes the source of the mystery and other times simply lends atmosphere. Finally, the gothic is preoccupied with the exploration of psychologies such as fear, anxiety, and dread – both in depicting the way these psychologies manifest within the work and in evoking them from the reader.[22] These novels are intended to spark readers' imaginations and produce a temporary but strong affective reaction in them, as they do in the young Dostoevsky.

While Dostoevsky famously borrowed from multiple genres across his literary corpus, in *The Idiot*, a novel permeated by fear, he specifically deployed gothic narrative much more extensively than in his other works. Several scholars have observed gothic elements in Dostoevsky's work. Leonid Grossman was the first to recognize Dostoevsky's "borrowing" from gothic novels,[23] while George Steiner extended this argument and identified a particular connection between *The Idiot* and the gothic, noting that Dostoevsky's brand of realism applied techniques "translated" from the gothic genre.[24] Robin Feuer Miller was the first to examine in depth Dostoevsky's use of the gothic in *The Idiot*; she identifies a gothic narrator among the novel's multiple narrative voices and maps it to an organized system of narration.[25] In Miller's analysis, the gothic narrator's function in *The Idiot* is twofold: to rivet the reader's attention and also to enable a fantastic reality. Building on Miller's study, my work elsewhere examines the novel's narrative debt to the gothic, arguing that Dostoevsky's emplotment incorporates gothic master plots as a means to enable the philosophical experiment he puts forth in *The Idiot*.[26]

The present chapter is a counterpart to this work. Here I analyze the appearance of gothic narrative force in *The Idiot* to reveal a tightly interconnected and systematic exploration of the affective experience of viewing *Dead Christ*. When I refer to gothic narrative force, I mean the feeling of emotional momentum built using narrative devices common to the gothic genre in a text. The reader, encountering gothic narrative force, is plunged into a self-conscious state of anticipation characterized by affective responses such as dread, anxiety, and fear. By "the reader" here, I refer both to the actual reader and the documented effects of gothic narrative devices on readers and to the imagined reader, the reader that the author imagines as they write the literary text and that the actual reader imagines as they read it.[27] Peter K. Garrett describes gothic narrative force as "the force of the desire to disturb and to be disturbed that joins tellers and their audiences and the counterforces that seek to control disturbance, the force of destiny that overwhelms characters, the force of repetition that generates multiplying versions."[28] This gothic narrative force punctuates the novelistic fabric of *The Idiot* in three key episodes that evoke Holbein's painting: Myshkin's encounter with Rogozhin in Part II, Ippolit's "Essential Explanation" in Part III, and the discovery of Nastasya Filippovna's corpse in Part IV. The painting's religious and philosophical connotations are indelibly bound to its role as a gothic body in the text through these gothic narratives. More broadly, this network of gothic narrative episodes engages the reader on a visceral level, cultivating a feeling of terror and anxiety that comes to exist beyond the pages of the novel.

The First Narrative: The Gloomy House, the Knife, and the Corpse

The first gothic narrative arc begins with the uncanny feeling of Rogozhin's gaze in Chapter 2 of Part II. This episode prefaces the events of the next three chapters, all marked with gothic narrative force: Myshkin's visit to Rogozhin's house in Chapter 3, the discussion of *Dead Christ* and faith in Chapter 4, and, the conclusion, Myshkin's seizure in Chapter 5. Miller has called Chapter 5 "the most extended passage in the Gothic mode" in the novel: "the whole chapter, save the last two paragraphs, is like the tale of terror in its heightened mood and in the extreme use of the technique of arbitrary disclosure by the narrator. Fears merely intimated provoke a greater effect than ones that are fully described."[29] Miller identifies several gothic narrative tropes, including the narrator's "air of overbearing, all-encompassing mystery," the parallel between Myshkin's sense of foreboding and an oncoming storm, strong dramatic irony, and the chapter's culmination in the shocking scene of the Prince's seizure.[30] However, my analysis traces the cues of gothic narrative force and reveals both that the gothic arc in Part II begins earlier and that the gothic corpse appears at its centre.

The first gothic narrative marker appears when Myshkin, arriving in St Petersburg, "suddenly" has the uncomfortable sensation that "the strange, burning gaze of someone's two eyes" (8:158) is watching him.[31] The narrator almost immediately dismisses the feeling – "of course, he only imagined it" (8:158) – but the episode leaves the Prince with an "unpleasant impression" (8:158). While the moment seems inconsequential, the uncanny feeling of being watched by someone becomes a repeated theme in the novel, one felt by Myshkin, Ippolit, and, finally, Nastasya Filippovna. Each time a character feels this gaze, it signals the beginning of gothic narrative force in the text.

Myshkin goes to visit Rogozhin, whose house is described in strikingly gothic terms: "both inside and out the house appears somehow inhospitable and barren, everything somehow concealed and hidden" (8:170).[32] As the passage continues, Dostoevsky's reader enters into the mindset of the gothic novel reader. Recognizable narrative markers identify the build-up of gothic narrative force: Rogozhin's house is "gloomy" [mrachnyi] and labyrinthine, with Myshkin forced to traverse a zig-zagging maze of corridors and shut-up rooms to reach Rogozhin (8:170). Myshkin, taking in the house and Rogozhin's "extraordinarily strange and heavy gaze," remembers "something recent, painful, gloomy," but the specific memory is not articulated (8:171). These gothic markers indicate a mystery to be solved. When Myshkin connects the gloomy gothic house with Rogozhin himself, the mystery of the house transfers to its owner and the gothic objects it contains become clues for the reader to piece together: the soot-covered ancestral portraits, the knife, and *Dead Christ*, the gothic corpse.

When *Dead Christ* first appears, as Carol Apollonio has observed, the image is clearly divorced from any divine symbolism. It is a faded copy of unknown provenance hung above a threshold, surrounded by other faded prints, and, in Apollonio's words, "shows *an image of* dead nature, *not the living word.*"[33] This mundane description is quickly subsumed by the image's representation of a gothic corpse and that body's effect on its viewers. As Apollonio argues, "The key is beyond the frame, in the living people facing the challenge of the image."[34] I would argue, the key lies in the affective response of the image's viewers. The scene in Rogozhin's house details the characters' discussion of the painting and Myshkin's response to it. Yet, strikingly, the source of these reactions remains concealed; the painting itself is not described. *Dead Christ* becomes a deferred mystery, one to be taken up later in the novel. This narrative technique, which exposes characters' reactions but does not reveal their source, is common in gothic fiction as well as in *The Idiot*, and represents another narrative link between Dostoevsky's novel and the gothic. Taking my cue from Dostoevsky and gothic novelists, I will defer the discussion of *Dead Christ* for later in this chapter and, instead, focus now on the relationship between the painting's appearance in Chapter 4 and the conclusion to the gothic narrative arc, Myshkin's epileptic fit.[35]

Myshkin, before his fit, wanders the streets of St Petersburg while the gothic narrator describes his thoughts. Sarah J. Young links the painting and the fit as two parts of a whole: "In the Holbein and his confused mental state before his fit, Myshkin faces all the issues of how he has changed, what he has lost, and where he has failed."[36] During this process of self-reflection Myshkin wanders within the realm of the gothic.[37] Rogozhin's eyes appear again and once more Myshkin climbs a gloomy staircase. This repeated narrative structure in *The Idiot* is reminiscent of the gothic loci present in Ann Radcliffe's novels. Mark Pettus identifies a Radcliffean structure featuring circular movement between cell, scaffold, and turret as a chronotope in Dostoevsky's works.[38] In Pettus's analysis, climbing up to a turret – any elevated space – will lead to a shift in perspective, but does not enable escape from the cycle, as the turret itself is a space of entrapment. As Myshkin ascends this staircase, Rogozhin waits at the top with a knife, evoking the gothic objects encountered earlier – his secretive family line suggested in the sooty ancestral portraits and the garden knife concealed in a book – and represents a return of gothic narrative force. The reader anticipates the violence, waiting in suspense as Myshkin climbs the stairs. Here, Dostoevsky again uses the gothic narrative trick of deferring a key plot point to build suspense: the anticipated attack is deferred until after Myshkin's visit to Rogozhin.

And what of the third gothic object, the *Dead Christ? Dead Christ* manifests in the epileptic fit that strikes Myshkin, saving him from Rogozhin. Epilepsy, for Myshkin, is both a curse and salvation. Both times Myshkin suffers an epileptic fit in the novel, he feels confusion, anxiety, and dread as it approaches. This feeling is intrinsically linked to gothic narrative in Chapter 5 as the gothic narrator describes Myshkin's pre-epileptic thoughts in what Miller calls a "deliberately mysterious" way, connecting the oncoming fit with a premonition of Rogozhin's attack: "'something' pursues Myshkin, a 'demon' has attached itself to him."[39] When the fit strikes, however, Myshkin feels "an intense inner light" and is transfigured. The fits bring clarity of mind and new insights, but they are described, in both cases, in language that evokes horror. Myshkin's first fit saves him from Rogozhin's knife, but his experience is no less horrifying than the threat of swift murder: "he clearly and consciously remembered the beginning, the very first sound of his fearful scream, which tore out of his chest and which he could not have stopped with any force. In an instant his consciousness was extinguished and then complete darkness" (8:195). Written from Myshkin's perspective, this account of a fit resembles an out-of-body experience, as the prince hears himself scream. A more clinical description of a seizure follows:

> The face is suddenly, horribly distorted, especially the gaze. Convulsions and spasms overwhelm the whole body and all the facial features. A fearful, incomprehensible scream unlike anything else tears out of the chest; in that scream suddenly everything human seems to vanish and it is impossible, or at least very difficult, for the witness to comprehend and admit that the same person is screaming. One even imagines that someone else is screaming, someone inside this person … For many, the sight of a man having a seizure fills them with decided and impossible horror, in which there is even something mystical. (8:195)

This first fit instils in the reader the idea of seizures as violent, unnatural, and painful experiences. Myshkin's sublime transfiguration is quickly lost in the description of the fit that follows. The supernatural seems present, but the "mystical" horror of the onlookers watching the seizure and Myshkin's violent experience contrast sharply with the "extraordinary *inner light*" the prince feels (italics in original). Following his fit, Myshkin lies on the ground, unconscious, and bruised. In this he resembles the Holbein painting. Before the fit, the image of the gothic body was implied but deferred when *Dead Christ* was discussed but not described.

The description of Myshkin's seizure, then, fulfils the narrative arc; the anticipated gothic body appears in the end and the deferred mystery is revealed.

The Second Narrative: The Nightmare, the Monster, and the Death Sentence

The second gothic narrative arc occurs in Part III in the long section detailing Ippolit's "Essential Explanation." As in the first, Rogozhin's uncanny gaze signals the advent of gothic narrative force and the gothic corpse appears centrally in the discussion of *Dead Christ.* The "Explanation" is set apart from the rest of the novel by two events; it begins with Ippolit's account of Rogozhin's appearance in his room at night and concludes with his suicide attempt. The signal of Rogozhin's eyes indelibly links this gothic narrative arc with the first. The first gothic narrative arc introduced a gothic setting and objects, transferring the affective experience of fear onto Rogozhin. This second arc builds on the first, exploring the nuances of fear, dread, and anxiety through a first-person confession narrative similar to gothic novels such as James Hogg's *The Private Memoirs and Confessions of a Justified Sinner* (1824). The contrast between Rogozhin's gaze in the beginning of each passage illustrates this difference. In the first scene, Myshkin feels an unknown gaze upon him and it makes an unpleasant lingering impression, while in the second Ippolit describes a gothic cliché: a midnight intruder, possibly supernatural, who voyeuristically watches the sleeping subject. Ippolit's experience of this gothic trope results in visceral fear, described in terms of physiological response: shivering, trembling, and breathlessness. In this sense, fear becomes a more palpable actor in the second gothic arc. In the first, *Dead Christ* acted as a catalyst for storytelling; in the second, the gothic conventions of Rogozhin's voyeurism spark Ippolit's "Essential Explanation," but Holbein's gothic body is nonetheless embedded in Ippolit's text.

Prompted by a gothic nightmare cliché, the "Explanation"'s encoded terrors take the form of monsters. The narrative begins with a horrible creature that haunts Ippolit's dreams. Described very precisely and yet unlike any identifiable animal, this monster has a tortoise shell and long tail, paws wriggling like snakes, and an excess of whiskers. As it runs about the bedroom Ippolit remarks that he "was terribly afraid" it would sting him, but that he was most tormented by these questions: who had sent it into his room, what they had meant to do to him, and "what was its secret?" (8:324). Ippolit's dead dog, Norma, similarly fears the monster, but musters her courage to stand up to it and even grab it between her teeth. The disgusting image of the chewed-up creature spewing white fluid onto Norma's tongue concludes the dream. This nightmare sets the tone for the rest of Ippolit's "Explanation," which heavily incorporates elements of fear, mystery, and sensation into its narrative.

Dead Christ again appears centrally, but this time Ippolit supplies a detailed description of its subject:

> It's the face of a man, *only just* taken down from the cross, that is, still preserving much that is alive, warm; nothing has stiffened yet, such that suffering even appears on the face of the dead man, as if he were still sensate ... In the painting this face has been fearfully beaten with blows, is swelling, and is covered with fearful, swollen and bloodstained bruises, the eyes are open, the pupils have rolled to the side: the large broad whites of the eyes glint with a sort of dead, glassy reflection. (8:339)

Here Ippolit fixates on the pain and suffering that Christ must have endured as he died, dwelling on each wound. In this scene, the gothic corpse takes on a new layer of meaning because of this graphic description. Whereas earlier the corpse served to fulfil the role of mystery, here there is no mystery; suffering and death are laid bare along with the ravages of natural processes. Ippolit goes on to liken these processes to a monster, "nature appears in the guise of an enormous, relentless, and mute beast [zveria], or, more accurately... in the guise of some kind of huge machine of modern construction, which senselessly caught, crushed, and devoured, deaf and insensible, a great and priceless being" (8:339).

Ippolit's horrified description is similar to Anna Grigoryevna's diary account in that both view the gothic body in terms of projected suffering and pain.[40] Like the uncanny sensation of disembodied eyes gazing at a subject, the gothic body too carries an uncanny feeling for its viewer. Steven Bruhm connects this sensation, through Freud's essay on "The Uncanny," with the return of the repressed: "repressed violence returns, and the body – afflicted, severed, cut – proclaims its primacy, its irrepressibility, its material existence."[41] In Bruhm's study of the gothic body in Romantic fiction, the visibly vulnerable and mortal gothic body stands in opposition to "transcendent Romantic consciousness,"[42] a situation that parallels the role of *Dead Christ* in *The Idiot* vis-à-vis religious faith. In this sense, in addition to its religious implications, as a gothic body, *Dead Christ* represents a *memento mori*, a reminder of our mortality, a locus for repressed terror. The image of the dead Christ, like the creature that haunts Ippolit's dreams, becomes a manifestation of the pain and uncertainty of death, of Ippolit's own fears, but he cannot yet accept the unknown and, with it, his own mortality. Death becomes monstrous.

When Ippolit asks how to imagine an image that has no image, his answer comes in the form of other monsters: a giant tarantula first, and then Rogozhin.

Echoing his prefatory appearance in Ippolit's "Essential Explanation," Rogozhin appears again as a gothic harbinger. After the first narrative arc's conclusion, the reader anticipates the voyeuristic bedroom scene, already guessing its outcome. However, whereas in the first narrative arc Rogozhin is a source of gothic fear, the gothic villain wielding the knife in the shadows, in the second Ippolit identifies him as a manifestation of gothic fear, an apparition that, like the monsters in his nightmares, could be fantasy. In the confession, Ippolit's thoughts seem to have slowed down, as if the process of feeling fear were dragging them out.

> I'd no sooner thought I was afraid, then suddenly it was as if ice ran over my entire body; I felt a cold chill in my spine and my knees shook. At that very moment, as though he precisely guessed I was afraid, Rogozhin took back the hand on which he was leaning, straightened up, and began to move his mouth, as though he was about to laugh; he stared straight at me. Such rage seized me that I decidedly wanted to attack him. (8:341)

This fear feeds into the overarching feeling of anxiety that drives the novel. Ippolit, in breaking down the specific way he feels fear, its physical reaction, and what he is psychologically seeing and experiencing, manages to channel his fear into fury.

This transformation is a gothic convention: as Miller observes, "At the heart of the gothic tradition in literature lies a metaphysical, semi-mythic, frequently religious quest in which ... an individual, often a self-divided hero, seeks to discover his relationship to the universe."[43] As Ippolit relives his fears by retelling them, he has a sublime moment, and comes to new understanding through this experience of sublime anxiety. Whereas earlier he felt terror at the thought of Rogozhin in his room, after the transformation of his fear he is able to dispel Rogozhin's spectre. Although shaking with fear following the reading of his "Explanation," he no longer fears death.[44] Ippolit justifies his suicide as a solution to the torment and pain inflicted upon him by the "higher powers" who have given him the "death sentence" of consumption. Whereas earlier in the text, Myshkin provides descriptions of executions, and wonders openly what a condemned man must feel in his last moments, Ippolit's gothic narrative arc examines the myriad manifestations of fear upon a condemned man. Ippolit's terror drives him to the brink of madness, but also to the justification of great transgressions such as suicide. Here Dostoevsky analyzes the power that fear wields as well as the great existential terror felt in the face of death. Ippolit's "Explanation," with its monsters and tragedies, anxieties and mysteries, provides a much clearer psychological portrait of a condemned man than Myshkin's empathetic but distanced descriptions of beheadings. This gothic narrative gives context to the more nebulous existential anxiety that drives the novel's philosophical questioning.

The Final Narrative: Behind the Black Veil

The final gothic narrative arc in the novel is linked to the other two thematically, through gothic narrative force and through oblique references to *Dead Christ*. This narrative, like the others, is first grounded in the gothic trope of Rogozhin's uncanny gaze, the feeling of his disembodied eyes watching that so unnerved Myshkin in Part II and Ippolit in Part III. In the end of Part III Nastasya Filippovna reports feeling Rogozhin's gaze upon her, and in Part IV she seems to be haunted by his spectre, which she claims is hiding in the garden and will kill her in the night. While the narrator explains this as a mirage, Rogozhin's apparition again signals a gothic arc, accompanied by the gothic trappings associated with him: his secretive past, his knife, and *Dead Christ*.

As the marriage plan goes forward, gothic narrative force begins to shape the plot once more.[45] All seems well leading up to Nastasya Filippovna's appearance for her wedding, but when her escort to church arrives, she steps out of the house, "white as a sheet; but her large dark eyes flashed at the crowd like burning coals" (8:493). Later the escort reports that she is "pale as a corpse" (8:493). This description of the bride echoes an earlier passage, when Nastasya Filippovna, having cursed Rogozhin, chooses Myshkin: "The prince ran too, but on the threshold, he was seized by two arms. The crushed, contorted face of Nastasya Filippovna was gazing fixedly at him, and her blue lips moved" (8:475). This description, particularly the narrative severing of her parts – her limbs acting alone, her lips moving alone – recall the gothic body and, possibly, the epileptic body. Her threshold position, furthermore, suggests liminality, that she is in transition from one state of being to the next. At the church, she sees Rogozhin's eyes in the crowd, and runs to his gothic gaze, plunging the reader again into the gothic narrative mode. Here Myshkin becomes the central figure in the gothic narrative. In the first narrative Myshkin revealed the gothic body's power and in the second Ippolit learned how to depict the affective reactions associated with the gothic body. In this final gothic narrative, Nastasya Filippovna becomes the gothic body, the abject corpse that sits at the novel's centre.

Gothic narrative force colours Myshkin's search through St Petersburg's streets for Nastasya Filippovna. Searching in semi-darkness, he walks down street after street, always consumed with the most fearful dread. When Rogozhin reveals himself to the prince, confessing that he has been following him all day, Myshkin is again confronted with the gothic voyeurism of Rogozhin's uncanny gaze. Myshkin's repeated journey into Rogozhin's house and the uncanny gaze indelibly connect this gothic narrative arc with the first, but with the added anticipation of a gothic body behind one of the doors. When the pair enter Rogozhin's rooms, Myshkin is confronted by a new object to add to the inventory of gothic objects associated with the house: "a heavy green silk curtain" (8:502), which divides the room and conceals the bed.

One of the most famous passages in gothic literature also features a mystery hidden behind a curtain: the black veil scene in Radcliffe's *The Mysteries of Udolpho* (1794). Travelling to Udolpho, Emily St Aubert begins to hear rumours of the mysterious portrait of a former countess. Exploring the castle, she comes upon a chamber with a mysterious black curtain that she resolves to look behind. Thwarted in her first attempt, she returns later to lift the veil:

> Here again she looked round for a seat to sustain her, and perceived only a dark curtain, which, descending from the ceiling to the floor, was drawn along the whole side of the chamber. Ill as she was, the appearance of this curtain struck her, and she paused to gaze upon it, in wonder and apprehension. It seemed to conceal a recess of the chamber; she wished, yet dreaded, to lift it, and to discover what it veiled ... till, suddenly conjecturing, that it concealed the body of her murdered aunt, she seized it, in a fit of desperation, and drew it aside.[46]

In another instance of gothic narrative deferral, the reader does not discover for some time after this event what the veil concealed. The narrator, however, refers to the veil constantly, but always putting off the horror of what lies behind it, and, in that sense, building up the novel's tension.

Arriving at this final tableau in Rogozhin's room, the reader of *The Idiot* has already entered the mindset of the gothic novel reader through the careful construction of the gothic narrative arcs and the novel's gothic master plot; a mystery concealed behind a curtain in a gloomy room hardly seems out of place. When the curtain finally reveals its dark secret, the reader is not surprised to discover a gothic body. Indeed, Nastasya Filippovna's death has been predicted with gothic narrative markers since the beginning of this arc. Furthermore, the gothic corpse represented by *Dead Christ* has already been located within Rogozhin's house:

[The prince's] eyes had already grown acclimated, so that he could make out the whole bed; on it someone lay in a perfectly motionless sleep; not the faintest rustle, not the slightest breath could be heard. The figure was hidden by a white sheet from the head down, but the limbs were not clearly defined somehow; all that could be seen, from the protuberances of the sheet, was that a person was lying there, stretched out. All around, messily … discarded clothes had been thrown about; a luxurious white silk dress, flowers, ribbons … some lace had been crumpled into a heap, and … peeping out from under the sheet, the tip of a naked foot was revealed; it appeared as if carved out of marble and was fearfully still. The prince looked and felt, the more he looked, the more deathly still and quiet it became in the room. Suddenly, a fly that woke up began to buzz, flew over the bed, and settled by the headboard. The prince shuddered. (8:503).

Here, as in Radcliffe's novel, a curtain reveals a corpse, and the description of the corpse is less important than the build-up to its discovery. However, whereas Nastasya Filippovna's corpse is not described in graphic detail, in *Udolpho* the corpse revealed resembles *Dead Christ.*

Beyond, appeared a corpse, stretched on a kind of low couch, which was crimsoned with human blood, as was the floor beneath. The features, deformed by death, were ghastly and horrible, and more than one livid wound appeared in the face. Emily, bending over the body, gazed, for a moment, with an eager, frenzied eye; but, in the next, the lamp dropped from her hand, and she fell senseless at the foot of the couch.[47]

The corpse in *Udolpho* is horrifying because of the evidence of its violent death. The wounds on its face, the bright crimson of its spilled blood – the narrator recounts these shocking details, and Emily, aghast at her discovery, cannot look away. Radcliffe's use of the deferred mystery and gothic body are deliberately gruesome, fittingly shocking for the object of so much narrative tension. The description of Nastasya Filippovna's final repose deliberately avoids the graphic description that gothic horror demands, however. Dostoevsky's narrator focuses on the accessories of life that surround her. She seems to have undressed a moment ago; her dress, lace, flowers, and diamonds lay unthinkingly scattered about the room. The unnatural stillness of her foot and the silence of the room suggest death, as does the decomposition process suggested by the fly's buzzing, but the narrator avoids a lurid description of the corpse. Bruhm's Freudian discussion of gothic bodies as loci where repressed fears are confronted may shed light on this narrative choice. Nastasya Filippovna's death is ostensibly caused by Rogozhin wielding a knife, a foretold death and one nearly experienced by Myshkin in the first gothic narrative arc.[48] In this sense, the final scene of Myshkin and Rogozhin standing over a corpse in Rogozhin's house evokes the first gothic narrative arc and the experience of looking at Holbein's *Dead Christ*.[49] In both passages, the sensationalistic, graphic aspects of the corpse are left to the reader's imagination, although the reader has since encountered Ippolit's description of the painting in the second gothic narrative.

In the Radcliffean tradition, "all gothic novels [do] eventually reveal the dreadful secrets which ... are presented to the reader as potential sources of terror. Instead of producing this promised effect of terror, however, the revelation of such secrets actually dispels the reader's emotions of anticipatory dread."[50] The feverish pace built up by the constant mentions of fear and the string of destructive acts deflates as soon as Rogozhin draws back the curtain and allows Myshkin to see the corpse. As in a gothic novel, the final mystery's solution signals the end of the narrative arc, and all that remains is the footsteps' arrival and justice to be served. When the authorities discover the pair, the narrator describes them as though from a distance. One reason this ending is particularly harrowing is because the reader becomes complicit in the scene when Myshkin begins acting as Rogozhin's accomplice. Then, the sudden break of the third-person narration from Myshkin's perspective to an outside one throws the final tableau into sharp relief, exposing not only Nastasya Filippovna's corpse, but also Rogozhin and Myshkin's disordered mental states. This distancing technique lends a heightened degree of horror to the novel's overall ending that is lacking in Nastasya Filippovna's death scene.

The three perspectives explored in this final gothic narrative arc contribute to the novel's preoccupation with the experience of death. Rogozhin's passionate but strangely casual murder of Nastasya Filippovna shows the brevity of life as well as the potential for violent crime in day-to-day life. Of all the characters in the novel, Rogozhin is the most unsympathetic. We never gain access to his thoughts and feelings unless another character narrates it. This distance serves to make Rogozhin's ability to kill more horrifying. In other novels, Dostoevsky examines the murderer's conscience, but in *The Idiot*, he never elucidates Rogozhin's psychology. Rogozhin kills without explanation, violently and senselessly. On the other hand, Myshkin's encounter with such a violent and transgressive act as well as his abject reaction to Nastasya Filippovna's corpse drives him to idiocy, although we do not observe his internal psychological process. Death, so feared and analysed throughout the novel, remains as a final mystery for the reader.

Conclusion: The Gothic Corpse as Dostoevskian Image

In Dostoevsky's notebooks for *The Idiot*, *Dead Christ* appears only once, in the fifth plan, written 1–4 November 1867. The painting is merely mentioned; the entire reference is "The story about Holbein's *Christ* in Basel" (9:184). However, *Dead Christ* appears immediately after a reference to the thoughts of a man about to be decapitated, a clear link both to Myshkin's story about the execution he witnessed in Switzerland and Dostoevsky's own experience at his mock execution in December 1849. In this sense, *Dead Christ* becomes a visual representation of existential terror, a symbol that evokes the fear grounded in the conversation Dostoevsky had with another condemned man, Speshnev, while they waited for execution in 1849. In this episode, reported in Fyodor Lvov's memoirs, Dostoevsky said to a fellow prisoner called Speshnev, "We will be together with Christ," to which Speshnev replied, "A handful of dust."[51] The terror at the core of this exchange appears in *The Idiot* when Myshkin describes the thoughts of a condemned man: "Now he exists and lives, but in three minutes he will be *something else*, someone or something – but who? Where?" (8:52).

In his discussion of *Dead Christ* Ippolit asks one of the most important questions in Dostoevsky's aesthetic world: "Can one imagine as an image that which has no image?" [Mozhet li mereshchit'sia v obraze to, chto ne imeet obraza?] (8:340). Here, when Ippolit asks about the fear of the unknown – what happens after death – and the terror of the void, his question stems from the same place as the condemned man's. However, the question also stands more broadly at the forefront of Dostoevsky's artistic mission, namely in his conviction that the act of representing lived experience must include spiritual truths that challenge the boundaries of conventional realist form. This is what the writer meant when he called himself "a realist in a higher sense" (27:65). As Molly Brunson explains, "when Dostoevsky wonders whether an image will come forth from his pen, whether he will be able to fully incarnate an idea, he speaks not only of a desire to represent a Christ-like figure in a novel, but also of a desire to transfigure the materials of pen and page into a rounder, more complete realist image."[52] Brunson views the fusion of word and image as a crucial aspect of Dostoevsky's realism, which "desires to move beyond the mimetic divide, to transfigure reality into a perfect artistic form, and thus to transcend the very border between death and life."[53] Knapp specifically connects the representation of death with Dostoevsky's "fantastic realism," observing that, "because death itself lies at the limit of our reality and the laws that govern it, this process requires literary forms that approach the "fantastic."[54] *Dead Christ*, for Dostoevsky, presents a model for this kind of art; for this reason, when viewing the painting, Anna Grigoryevna remembers that he called Holbein "a great artist and poet" [zamechatel'nym khudozhnikom i poetom] who fused literary and visual aesthetics into one realist practice.[55] I would argue that the function of the gothic body in *The Idiot* further demonstrates that, for Dostoevsky, the realist depiction of spiritual truth is indelibly bound to the emotions that such experience generates, both positive and negative. Dostoevsky exploits the connection between gothic narrative and reader emotion in *The Idiot* to enable the creation of realist art that transcends the medium to exist beyond the text as palpable emotions evoked in the reader's lived experience.

The two gothic bodies in *The Idiot* and their accompanying affect function in the narrative as responses to Ippolit's question. In Ippolit's gothic narrative this image comes to be embodied by Rogozhin, who appears as if in answer to this question; as Young observes, "The aesthetic shock of the painting and Rogozhin, as its owner, therefore seem to be directly responsible for the scenes of violence that follow both appearances of the Holbein."[56] Rogozhin represents the fear *Dead Christ* symbolizes in the novel: he laughs in the face of Myshkin's fears, he manifests as the senseless machine of Ippolit's nightmare, and he carries out Nastasya Filippovna's death sentence. Whereas *Dead Christ*, hanging over the door, is a gothic body that carries with it the possibility of hope, Rogozhin represents its obverse: the gothic corpse under the floorboards surrounded by bottles of Zhdanov fluid and a razor wrapped in silk. The gothic body under the floorboards is an imagined victim, a stand-in for the fear of death and an affective image that generates an uncanny unease in both characters and readers.

After the first seven chapters of *The Idiot* were published in January 1868, Dostoevsky wrote to his friend Apollon Maikov to ask his impression of the novel. Maikov responded positively, particularly highlighting both the interest piqued by "personally experienced horrifying moments" [interes mnogikh lichno perezhitykh uzhasnykh momentov] and "the originality of the hero's challenge" [original'naia zadacha v geroe].[57] The relationship between these two aspects – the challenge of the "beautiful man" [prekrasnyi chelovek] and the vividness of the experience of existential terror – was a challenging one to articulate. In a March 1868 letter to Maikov he writes, "Regarding *The Idiot*, I'm so afraid, so afraid, you can't imagine. Even a kind of unnatural fear. It's never been like this" (28.2:274). But what specifically is the source of Dostoevsky's fear? Reading the gothic bodies in *The Idiot* reveals a clear connection between gothic narrative force, fear, and the existential terror that is so difficult to articulate in prose. The terror that emerges from *The Idiot* infects writer, reader, and characters and represents Dostoevsky's own lived experience as an image without an image, as affect generated by the two gothic bodies under the floorboards and above the door.

NOTES

I would like to thank my co-editor Kate Holland as well as Yuri Corrigan, Connor Doak, Tatiana Filimonova, Melissa Frazier, Ervin Malakaj, and Vadim Shneyder for their constructive comments on earlier versions of this chapter. I presented a version of this work in talks at Hokkaido University and the University of Tokyo in March 2019 and I am grateful to Daisuke Adachi for hosting me and to the scholars I met in Sapporo and Tokyo for the productive discussions that followed each seminar. This chapter was completed while I was a Wall Scholar in residence at the Peter Wall Institute for Advanced Studies at the University of British Columbia, 2019–20.

1 A.G. Dostoevskaia, *Vospominaniia* (Moscow: Pravda, 1987), 186. All translations in this chapter are my own unless noted otherwise.
2 Dostoevskaia, *Vospominaniia*, 186.
3 A.G. Dostoevskaia, *Dnevnik 1867 goda* (Moscow: "Nauka," 1993), 234. Robert Louis Jackson analyzes the exchange I include here in more depth, linking the conflicting reactions of Dostoevsky and his wife with aesthetics in "Once Again about Dostoevsky's Response to Hans Holbein the Younger's *Dead Body of Christ in the Tomb*," in *Dostoevsky beyond Dostoevsky: Science, Religion, Philosophy*, ed. Svetlana Evdokimova and Vladimir Golstein (Boston: Academic Studies Press, 2016), 179–92.
4 On the incorporation of the painting into the novel's structure, see Sarah J. Young, "Holbein's *Christ in the Tomb* in the Structure of *The Idiot*," *Russian Studies in Literature* 44, no. 1 (2007): 90–102.
5 Robert Louis Jackson, *Dostoevsky's Quest for Form: A Study of His Philosophy of Art* (New Haven, CT: Yale University Press, 1966), 67.
6 F.M. Dostoevskii, *Polnoe sobranie sochinenii v tridtsati tomakh*, ed. G.M. Fridlender et al. (Leningrad: "Nauka," 1972–90). Subsequent references to this edition will be indicated in the text with volume and page number(s).
7 Liza Knapp, *The Annihilation of Inertia: Dostoevsky and Metaphysics* (Evanston, IL: Northwestern University Press, 1996), 68.
8 Jacques Catteau, *Dostoyevsky and the Process of Literary Creation*, trans. Audrey Littlewood (Cambridge: Cambridge University Press, 1989), 185. Catteau discusses Dostoevsky's incorporation of the Mazurin case in detail, 185–6.
9 On the links between gothic literature and death, see the collection *The Gothic and Death*, ed. Carol Margaret Davison (Manchester: Manchester University Press, 2017); my chapter in the collection, while not on Dostoevsky,

examines the links between gothic narrative and the representation of
death in Russian realism: Katherine Bowers, "'Through the Opaque Veil':
The Gothic and Death in Russian Realism," 157–73.

10 Ian Conrich and Laura Sedgwick, *Gothic Dissections in Film and Literature: The
Body in Parts* (London: Palgrave Macmillan, 2017), 198–200.

11 Malcolm Jones identifies these discussions as the novel's "centre of gravity,"
and the painting as their "medium," the vehicle that enables the philosophical point of view to shift from Myshkin in Part II to Ippolit in Part III. See
Malcolm Jones, *Dostoevsky and the Dynamics of Religious Experience* (London:
Anthem Press, 2005), 88.

12 Tatiana Kasatkina has argued that whether or not the painting depicts
Christ is a matter of interpretation on the viewer's part and related to the
viewer's spatial position relative to the painting (whether viewing from
straight on, from above, or from below). See "After Seeing the Original,"
Russian Studies in Literature 47, no. 3 (2011): 73–97.

13 Dostoevskaia, *Dnevnik 1867 goda*, 234.

14 Kasatkina has analyzed the painting's liminality and argues the opposite:
that the painting depicts Christ at the moment he is just coming back to
life. See T.A. Kasatkina, "Posle znakomstva s podlinnikom: Kartina Gansa
Gol'beina Mladshego 'Khristos v mogile' v strukture romana F.M. Dostoevskogo 'Idiot,'" *Novyi mir* 2 (2006): 154.

15 Julia Kristeva, *Powers of Horror: An Essay on Abjection*, trans. Leon S. Roudiez
(New York: Columbia University Press, 1982), 4.

16 Yael Shapira, *Inventing the Gothic Corpse: The Thrill of Human Remains in the
Eighteenth-Century Novel* (London: Palgrave Macmillan, 2018), 1.

17 Ibid., 3.

18 Ibid., 5–6.

19 M.H. Abrams, "Gothic Novel," in *A Glossary of Literary Terms* (Boston: Thomson-Wadsworth, 2005), 118.

20 Boris Tikhomirov has analyzed Dostoevsky's childhood reading and determined that he extensively read pseudo-Radcliffiana, works in the vein of
Radcliffe and attributed to her, but not actually by her. See B.N. Tikhomirov, "K probleme genezisa 'ital'ianskoi mechty' Dostoevskogo: Radklif ili
psevdo-Radklif?" *Dostoevskii i mirovaia kul'tura* 10, no. 2 (2020): 128–52.

21 The translation is found in Fyodor Dostoevsky, *Winter Notes on Summer Impressions*, trans. David Patterson (Evanston, IL: Northwestern University
Press, 1997), 1–2.

22 This three-part definition is my own; see Katherine Bowers, "The City
through a Glass, Darkly: Use of the Gothic in Early Russian Realism,"
Modern Language Review 108, no. 4 (2013): 1238. It builds upon the work
of David Punter, Fred Botting, and Muireann Maguire, as well as from the
experience of reading a wide range of gothic novels. For its underpinnings,

see David Punter, *The Literature of Terror*, vol. 2: *The Modern Gothic* (London: Longman, 1996), 146; Fred Botting, *Gothic* (London: Routledge, 1996), 2–3; and Muireann Maguire, *Stalin's Ghosts: Gothic Themes in Early Soviet Literature* (Oxford: Peter Lang, 2012), 10–14.

23 Leonid Grossman, "Kompozitsiia v romane Dostoevskogo," in *Poetika Dostoevskogo* (Moscow: 39-aia tip. Internatsional'naia "Mospoligraf," 1925), 24–35.

24 George Steiner, *Tolstoy or Dostoevsky: An Essay in the Old Criticism*, 2nd ed. (New Haven, CT: Yale University Press, 1996), 210.

25 Robin Feuer Miller, *Dostoevsky and* The Idiot*: Author, Narrator, and Reader* (Cambridge, MA: Harvard University Press, 1981), 108–25.

26 Katherine Bowers, *Writing Fear: Russian Realism and the Gothic* (Toronto: University of Toronto Press, forthcoming), chapter 4.

27 On the imagined gothic novel reader in Russia, see Katherine Bowers, "The Gothic Novel Reader Comes to Russia," in *Reading Russia: A History of Reading in Modern Russia*, vol. 2, ed. Damiano Rebecchini and Raffaella Vassena (Milan: Ledizioni, 2020), 377–408.

28 Peter K. Garrett, *Gothic Reflections: Narrative Force in Nineteenth-Century Fiction* (Ithaca, NY: Cornell University Press, 2003), 10.

29 Miller, *Dostoevsky and* The Idiot, 116.

30 Ibid., 117–19.

31 This episode also demonstrates the narrative mechanics related to voyeurism, sensory perception, and embodiment analyzed by Sarah J. Young in the present volume.

32 Kasatkina has argued that Rogozhin's house is a collapsed sanctuary, a symbol of blasphemy, destruction, and failure. See T.A. Kasatkina, *O tvoriashchei prirode slova: Ontologichnost' slova v tvorchestve F. M. Dostoevskogo kak osnova "realizma v vysshem smysle"* (Moscow: IMLI RAN, 2004), 380–93. The relevant chapter has also been published in English translation: Tatiana Kasatkina, "History in a Name: Myshkin and the 'Horizontal Sanctuary,'" in *The New Russian Dostoevsky: Readings for the Twenty-First Century*, ed. and trans. Carol Apollonio et al. (Bloomington: Slavica, 2010), 145–64. In his chapter in the present volume, Vadim Shneyder discusses the way descriptions of Rogozhin and his house correspond to a broader spatial poetics within Dostoevsky's works.

33 Carol Apollonio, "*The Idiot*'s 'Vertical Sanctuary': The Holbein Christ and Ippolit's Confession," in *Dostoevsky's Secrets: Reading against the Grain* (Evanston, IL: Northwestern University Press, 2009), 95. Italics in original.

34 Ibid., 97.

35 On epilepsy's connection to the gothic, see Laurence Talairach-Vielmas, *Wilkie Collins, Medicine, and the Gothic* (Cardiff: University of Wales Press, 2009), 99–105.

36 Sarah J. Young, *Dostoevsky's* The Idiot *and the Ethical Foundations of Narrative: Reading, Narrating, Scripting* (London: Anthem Press, 2004), 118.

37 Brandy Lain Schillace has studied Emily St Aubert's internal reveries in Ann Radcliffe's *The Mysteries of Udolpho* as symptoms of an epileptic condition. Her analysis of Emily aligns well with Myshkin's reveries in this part of *The Idiot*. See Schillace, "'Temporary Failure of Mind': Déjà Vu and Epilepsy in Radcliffe's 'The Mysteries of Udolpho,'" *Eighteenth-Century Studies* 42, no. 2 (2009): 273–87.

38 Mark Pettus, "Dostoevsky's Closed Threshold in the Construction of the Existential Novel" (PhD diss., Princeton University, 2009), 239–40.

39 Miller, *Dostoevsky and* The Idiot, 116.

40 I recommend Young's analysis of Ippolit's relationship with *Dead Christ*; see Young, *Dostoevsky's* The Idiot, 140–2.

41 Steven Bruhm, *Gothic Bodies: The Politics of Pain in Romantic Fiction* (Philadelphia: University of Pennsylvania Press, 1994), xv.

42 Bruhm, *Gothic Bodies*, xvi.

43 Robin Feuer Miller, *Dostoevsky's Unfinished Journey* (New Haven, CT: Yale University Press, 2007), 134.

44 My gothic reading of the "Explanation" aligns with Apollonio's vertical reading of the "Explanation." See Apollonio, *Dostoevsky's Secrets*, 93–103.

45 On the expectations of the marriage plot in Dostoevsky's works, see Anna Berman's chapter in the present volume.

46 Ann Radcliffe, *The Mysteries of Udolpho* (Oxford: Oxford University Press, 2008), 348.

47 Radcliffe, *The Mysteries of Udolpho*, 348.

48 This reading aligns with Knapp's analysis of Nastasya Filippovna as a condemned woman. See Knapp, *The Annihilation of Inertia*, 77–80.

49 Young has observed that the two appearances of Holbein's *Dead Christ* and the scene of Myshkin and Rogozhin standing over Nastasya Filippovna's corpse are linked by virtue of the fact that these three scenes are the only one-on-one conversations between the pair. See Young, "Holbein's *Christ in the Tomb*," 94.

50 Chloe Chard, "Introduction," in Ann Radcliffe, *The Romance of the Forest* (Oxford University Press, 1999), viii.

51 See V.R. Leikina-Svirskaia, "Zapiska o dele Petrashevtsev: rukopis' F.N. L'vova s pometkami M.V. Butashevicha-Petrashevskogo," *Literaturnoe nasledstvo* 63 (1956): 188.

52 Molly Brunson, *Russian Realisms: Literature and Painting, 1840–1890* (DeKalb: Northern Illinois University Press, 2016), 163.

53 Brunson, *Russian Realisms*, 24–5.

54 Knapp, *The Annihilation of Inertia*, 68.

55 Dostoevskaia, *Dnevnik 1867 goda*, 234.

56 Young, "Holbein's *Christ in the Tomb*," 95.

57 A.N. Maikov, *Pis'ma k F.M. Dostoevskomu*, ed. N.T. Ashimbaeva (Moscow: Pamiatniki kul'tury, 1984), 67.

8 The Improbable Poetics of *Crime and Punishment*

GRETA MATZNER-GORE

In the 1860s, Russia was overrun by a craze for statistics. A Russian translation of Adolphe Quetelet's influential statistical work, *A Treatise on Man and the Development of His Faculties* [Sur l'homme et le développement de ses facultés, ou Essai de physique sociale, 1835], appeared in 1865.[1] Henry Buckle's *History of Civilization in England* (1857) (which took Quetelet's work as its starting point) was translated in 1861 and published again in 1863.[2] Excitement about statistical analysis – its potential for revealing the underlying causes of social ills and pointing the way to their solution – was reaching a fever pitch. As one enthusiastic reviewer declared in 1865: "Statistics – this is the philosopher's stone that antiquity searched for with such effort."[3] Even the imperial government got on board. In 1864, it established the Central Statistical Committee to collect and study sociological, geographical, and agricultural data from across the empire.[4]

Dostoevsky tackled his era's fascination with statistics head on. As scholars have long shown, Dostoevsky directly engaged with the language and logic of what was then called "moral statistics" in his works, especially *Crime and Punishment* [Prestuplenie i nakazanie, 1866].[5] The novel contains several overt, critical references to the fad. In an early scene, the murderous but conflicted protagonist, Raskolnikov, meditates on the danger of using words like "percentage" to describe living, suffering human beings. Imagining the probable future of prostitution and destitution awaiting an intoxicated young girl he meets on the street, Raskolnikov muses:

> That's how it should be, they say. A certain percentage, they say, must go that way every year ... Which way? ... To the devil, I suppose, so as to freshen up the rest and not get in their way. Percentage! What lovely words they use: so soothing, so scholarly. You hear a word like that and wonder what on

earth you were worrying about. Now if it were a different word, you might feel a little less comfortable.[6]

A later reference to statistics – this one played for comic effect – is equally overt. In that scene, the kindly but confused young socialist Lebezyatnikov recommends some educational reading material to his stuffy and prudish provincial lady neighbours: Adolph Wagner's recently translated "Regularity in Apparently Volitional Human Action from the Point of View of Statistics" (no doubt to their horror) (6:307).[7]

Yet *Crime and Punishment* also confronts the vogue for statistics in less obvious ways, which scholars have not yet fully recognized. In this novel, Dostoevsky not only takes a stand against statistical determinism (the belief that large-scale statistical regularities prove free will to be an illusion). He also takes a stand against an entire network of statistically inflected ideas about the essence of goodness, the path to human perfectibility, and the nature of verisimilitude in art. Crucially, Dostoevsky does this not by *rejecting* statistical thinking and the probabilistic reasoning that underlies it, but rather by *using* statistical reasoning in a different way, a way that inverts Quetelet's system of values. Quetelet and his followers valorized the probable, the average and the ordinary. *Crime and Punishment* suggests, to the contrary, that it is not ordinary people and events, but the statistical outliers – the odd, unusual, and unlikely – that reveal the true nature of reality. It cultivates what I (building on Yuri Lotman) will call "a poetics of improbability," which operates on every level of the text, from the methods of characterization, to the structure of the plot, to the protagonist's improbable moral resurrection at the end.[8]

As I will argue, in *Crime and Punishment* Dostoevsky does not adopt the anti-scientific, anti-rationalist position that so many critics have attributed to him. Instead, he tries to convince his readers that the realm of scientific possibility is vaster than they think, and that it allows for the most unexpected, miraculous-seeming events.[9]

From Probability Theory to "Social Physics"

First, some background on Quetelet and the movement he inspired. A Belgian astronomer with an enthusiasm for probability theory, Quetelet became convinced that it could be used not only in the study of celestial bodies, but in the study of social bodies as well. His logic went something like this. In order to track the movement of a planet, astronomers collect multiple observations of its coordinates. Each individual observation is subject to error (instruments are imprecise and astronomers make mistakes), but the aggregate is less so. By calculating the average of a large number of such observations, astronomers can predict the planet's future movements with great precision. What if you applied those same mathematical principles to different sets of data, say, to records of marriage, mortality, illness, and crime? By comparing the average heights of children from the ages of one to twenty, for example, you can see how growth rates tend to change as children get older. By comparing the ages of violent criminals, you can determine when "propensity to crime" reaches its peak. Quetelet dubbed his method "social physics," because he believed it would reveal the social and physiological "laws" that govern all human growth and behaviour, from the width of a Scottish soldier's chest, to the frequency with which women in their sixties marry men in their twenties.[10]

Quetelet's work sparked debates about the existence of free will, crime, and judicial punishment throughout Europe. Quetelet was careful to remind his readers that the "laws" he had discovered held true only for large social groups and could "be applied to individuals only within certain limits."[11] But his favourite metaphors tended to confuse matters (if we are subject to social "laws," how can we avoid conforming to them?), as did his most famous declarations, such as the oft-quoted: "*society prepares crime, and the guilty are only the instruments by which it is executed.*"[12] Moreover, Quetelet's devotees did not always draw the same distinctions between aggregates and individuals that he did. They often conflated the probable with the necessary, what *might* happen with what *must* happen in every single case.[13] Buckle, for example, used Quetelet's tables of crime statistics as grist for the mill of his own strict determinism. For Buckle, they provided virtual proof that human behaviour is fundamentally predictable. He makes his case in absolute terms:

> If, for example, I am intimately acquainted with the character of any person, I can frequently tell how he will act under some given circumstances. Should I fail in this prediction, I must ascribe my error not to the arbitrary and capricious freedom of his will, nor to any supernatural pre-arrangement, for of neither of these things have we the slightest proof, but I must be content to suppose either that I had been misinformed as to some of the circumstances in which he was placed, or else that I had not sufficiently studied the ordinary operations of his mind.[14] If, however, I were capable of correct reasoning, and if, at the same time, I had a complete knowledge both of his disposition and of all the events by which he was surrounded, I should be able to foresee the line of conduct which, in consequence of those events, he would adopt.[15]

Buckle's Russian populizer, V.A. Zaitsev, made the case for determinism with even more rhetorical flare. As he wrote in his 1863 article, "Natural

Science and Justice" [Estestvoznanie i iustitsiia]: "man in all his actions, from the most important to the most insignificant, obeys statistical laws."[16]

Dostoevsky knew the work of Quetelet's extreme and uncompromising acolytes better than he knew Quetelet himself. He repeatedly sparred with Zaitsev in the press, and he owned his own copy of Buckle's *History of Civilization in England* (which he mocked in *Notes from Underground* [Zapiski iz podpol'ia, 1864] [5:111–12]). It would be a mistake to assume that Dostoevsky rejected every single one of their ideas wholesale, however. In 1864, the same year that he published *Notes from Underground*, Dostoevsky drafted an open letter to his critics, in which he grants many of Buckle's main points:

> We are adherents of the native-soil philosophy [*pochvenniki*], first of all, because we believe that nothing on earth happens abstractly, outside of (real, historical) life, or discontinuously. If one can agree with Buckle about the influence of the climate and other things on peoples' development and sphere of understanding, then it is also clear that when these conditions cease, the understanding of the peoples who developed under these conditions will cease as well. Soil that has been cultivated changes the climate (the population), railroads shrink distances, and so on. If it really is true that the Mohammedan peoples could not be anything but Mohammedans, then it is also true that they could not convert to Christianity *as a whole people* before their time, but only as individual personalities. (Now they are all converting). (20:202; italics in original)

Dostoevsky agrees with Buckle that external forces like climate, soil quality, and technological change shape the development of peoples as a whole. But he disagrees about something just as important. Dostoevsky insists that such external forces do *not* determine the behaviour of "individual personalities," who can and do buck statistical trends. And he hints that, while these individual actions may be *statistically* insignificant, they are nevertheless highly revealing, at least for those with eyes to see. He strongly implies that these unexpected, singular conversions are the first signs of a mass turn towards Christianity that is yet to come.

The Moral and Aesthetic Value of Averages

The statistical enthusiasts provided more than just a sounding board against which Dostoevsky could develop his own ideas about historical change, however. They provided a sounding board for his evolving moral and aesthetic principles as well.

For Quetelet, for example, the statistically "Average Man" (*srednii chelovek* in Russian translation) was much more than a hypothetical being whose movements could be tracked in lieu of a planet. He was *the* human ideal. Again and again, Quetelet argues that the closer a person approaches the average – whether in height, weight, or degree of bravery – the closer he comes to "what is good and beautiful."[17] All significant deviations from the mean, by contrast, "constitute deformity and disease."[18] In a passage that reads very much like Raskolnikov's "extraordinary man" theory (with the values inverted), Quetelet emphasizes

> how much importance I attach to the consideration of *limits*, which seem to me of two kinds, *ordinary* or natural, and *extraordinary* or beyond the natural. The first limits comprise within them the qualities which deviate more or less from the mean, without attracting attention by excess on one side or the other. When the deviations become greater, they constitute the extraordinary class, having itself its limits, on the outer verge of which are things preternatural or monstrosities.[19]

According to Quetelet, any "extraordinary" human quality that deviates too far from the average becomes increasingly ugly, unnatural, even monstrous. This holds not only for physical characteristics like arm length or head size, but for moral characteristics as well. As Quetelet suggests in *On the Social System and the Laws That Regulate It* [Du système social et des lois qui le régissent, 1848] (which was translated into Russian in 1866, and included a chapter titled "Crime and Punishment" [Prestuplenie i nakazanie]), "in medio virtus" is a universal truth. Moral instincts like generosity are only as good as they are moderate: too much leads to profligacy; too little leads to avarice.[20]

Quetelet allocated the "Average Man" a central role in the arts as well. Although he acknowledges that artists are necessarily drawn to variety and particularity, he insists that the varieties and particularities they depict should always fall well within "the natural limits" of the "ordinary."[21] Staying within these probabilistic limits (within one standard deviation of the mean, perhaps) is both the key to beauty and the key to verisimilitude in art. As Quetelet puts it: "The necessity of veracity in faithfully representing the physiognomy, the habits, and the manners of people at different epochs, has at all times led artists and literary men to seize, among the individuals whom they observed, the characteristic traits of the period in which they lived; or, in other words, to come as near the average as possible."[22] For Quetelet, "veracity" in art requires statistically average subject matter.

The Poetics of Improbability

Dostoevsky may or may not have known Quetelet's theory of art first-hand. But he was intimately familiar with theories of verisimilitude *like* it, which was highly typical of its time.[23] As Maurice Lee has shown, by the mid-nineteenth century literary critics all over Europe were declaring fictions "subject to statistical laws" and demanding that literary plot-lines adhere to "the calculus of probabilities."[24] Russian literary critics were no exception. When, in 1860, Nikolai Dobrolyubov declared that works of literature should demonstrate "logical truth," he defined this as "reasonable probability [razumnoi veroiatnost'iu] and congruence with the existing course of affairs."[25]

From the very beginning of his post-Siberian career, however, Dostoevsky wanted to do something different. In 1858, he told his brother that he had written a "sharp" polemical article titled "On the Statistical School in Literature" (28.1:316). Although the article has not survived, Dostoevsky's later writings on realism hint at what it might have contained. In an 1869 letter that has since become famous, he explained:

> I have my own particular view of reality (in art), and that which the majority calls almost fantastic and exceptional sometimes contains the very essence of reality for me. The everydayness of phenomena and a requisite view of them is not yet realism, in my opinion, but even its opposite. In every issue of the newspapers you come upon an account of the most real facts and of the strangest ones. For our writers they are fantastic, and they don't engage with them. But they are reality, because they are facts. (29.1:19)[26]

For Dostoevsky, the average, ordinary, or probable does not always reflect the underlying reality. To the contrary, it is the statistically infrequent and seemingly exceptional events that often reveal the most about the times in which they occur, and point the way towards the future.[27] Donald Fanger puts it especially well: Dostoevsky is searching "not for the statistical average, or the recognizably universal, but rather for the statistical exception and the new guise of the universal that is just coming to birth."[28]

In *Crime and Punishment*, Dostoevsky realizes his improbable brand of realism more fully than ever before. First, he fills his novel with exceptional characters who nevertheless become representative of Russian life as he understood it. The saintly prostitute, Sonya, is extremely petite and unusually young-looking, with a face described as "terribly thin, terribly pale [...] quite irregular and somehow sharp" (6:183; 221). She is a statistical outlier not just physically, but morally as well: her extreme generosity, limitless capacity for self-sacrifice, and "*insatiable* compassion" rebuke Quetelet's beloved principle – "in medio virtus" (6:243; 297; italics in original).[29] Raskolnikov is also far from average in several important ways. His behaviour after the murder – especially the careless way he treats the goods he has stolen – strikes those who learn of it as highly unusual, almost impossible. It "seemed improbable" [pokazalos' neveroiatnym] to investigators that he never even checked to see how much money was in the pawnbroker's purse. This is part of what ultimately convinces them that Raskolnikov "did not really resemble an ordinary [obyknovennogo] murderer, felon and robber: this was something else" (6:410–11; 503–4).

Of course, Raskolnikov *wants* to seem out of the ordinary. He kills in order to prove himself an "extraordinary" [neobyknovennyi] man, who dares to break the law and fears no punishment. Ironically, however, Raskolnikov's theory – that a small percentage of the world's population has the moral right to commit crime – is one of the most ordinary things about him.[30] A mashup of popular ideas taken from the statistical enthusiasts, Utilitarianism, Social Darwinism, and the writings of Napoleon III, it is far from unusual.[31] As Razumikhin puts it, the theory "isn't new and resembles everything we've read and heard a thousand times before" (6:202; 245).[32] The murders that Raskolnikov's theory drives him to commit are also surprisingly *average*. According to Quetelet's calculations, the greatest number of violent crimes take place during the summer months (Raskolnikov kills in July) and the "propensity to crime" reaches its height near the age of twenty-five (Raskolnikov is twenty-three).[33] In other words, Raskolnikov's *really* extraordinary qualities are not the ones that he thinks they are. His lust for power and delusions of grandeur are commonplace. It is his heightened generosity and capacity for compassion that truly set him apart.[34]

The extraordinary heroes of *Crime and Punishment* live through a series of events that are just as exceptional as they are. Dostoevsky builds the novel's plot around a sequence of strange, almost miraculous coincidences, which are so abundant some have seen them as an artistic flaw. Ernest Simmons called it "the principal artistic blemish in the work. Coincidence, of course, may be justifiable in a novel, for it is a legitimate part of the pattern of reality. In real life, however, coincidental happenings do not violate the laws of probability, and in fiction our credibility is forfeited if coincidence is overworked."[35] The novel contains dozens of such "violations." Luzhin just happens to live in the same apartment as the Marmeladovs; Svidrigailov just happens to overhear Sonya talking to Raskolnikov on the street, and then just happens to move into the apartment next door to her. Raskolnikov just happens to overhear the pawnbroker's sister, Lizaveta, saying what time she will be out of the house (giving him the opportunity to commit murder); and when he cannot access his chosen axe, another one just happens to be waiting for him in the courtyard. Robert Belknap has argued that none of these events is strictly impossible.[36] But they *are* highly improbable. In fact, I would argue that Dostoevsky includes them largely *because* they "violate the laws of probability," the statistical norms that Quetelet and his followers believed governed human life (a thesis Dostoevsky rejects). Doing so allows Dostoevsky to depict a world that is both scientifically possible *and* bubbling with potentiality, a world in which the strangest and most unexpected things can happen.

Indeed, in Dostoevsky's fiction, the unexpected rules. For the past one hundred years, critics have been discussing how often the word "suddenly" [vdrug] punctures Dostoevsky's works. (According to Vladimir Toporov, the word "suddenly" appears around 560 times in *Crime and Punishment* alone, often several times over the course of a single paragraph.)[37] Mikhail Bakhtin famously traced the generic origins of Dostoevsky's novels back to Menippean Satire with its "*extraordinary freedom of plot and philosophical invention*," which regularly upends reader expectations.[38] Yuri Lotman has even argued that Dostoevsky's storylines operate according to a "law of *least* probability": "In a text by Dostoevskij the thing least expected by the reader (that is to say the least expected both according to the laws of life experience and literary constructs) turns out to be the one thing possible for the author [...] in a whole series of cases predictability is, in fact, present, only in reverse: episodes follow each other in not the most probable but the most improbable order."[39]

Lotman demonstrates his point with a sequence from *Demons*, but several from *Crime and Punishment* make his case just as well. One, which combines references to criminology and statistics with an intrusion of the unexpected, merits special attention. In this scene, the lead investigator, Porfiry Petrovich, works on Raskolnikov's nerves. He hints that he already knows who killed the pawnbroker, but is in no hurry to make an arrest, because he suspects the murderer (i.e., Raskolnikov) would actually *prefer* to get caught. After giving a few examples of this psychological phenomenon, Porfiry Petrovich makes the following aside:

> These are all particular cases [chastnye sluchai], I'll agree. The case I've just described really is a particular one, sir! But here's what we need to bear in mind, dear sweet Rodion Romanovich: the typical case [obshchego-to sluchaia-s], the very same one according to which all the legal forms and principles are tailored and calculated and written up in books, simply does not exist, sir, by virtue of the fact that each and every deed, each and every – for

want of a better example – crime, just as soon as it occurs in reality, immediately becomes a particular case, sir; in fact, sometimes it's like nothing that's ever gone before (6:261; 317; translation altered).

According to Porfiry Petrovich, the average, "typical" case has little to teach investigators, because each and every criminal and each and every crime is "particular" and unique unto itself.[40] Instead of assuming that a murderer will act according to some generalizable set of principles, the investigator must strive to understand the unique psychological "laws" governing his singular personality. And, Porfiry Petrovich hints, he has cracked Raskolnikov's code. A criminal like Raskolnikov "won't run away *psychologically*, heh-heh! What a lovely little phrase! The laws of nature won't let him run away, even if he did have somewhere to go" (6:262; 318; italics in original).

Perhaps Porfiry Petrovich truly believes that Raskolnikov's behaviour is controlled by psychological "law." (Or perhaps he is just trying to intimidate his suspect. Later he warns Raskolnikov to take everything he says with a grain of salt.) As for Dostoevsky, however, he strongly suggests that sometimes people act according to no law whatsoever. The chapter ends when "a strange incident occurred, something so very unexpected, in the ordinary course of events [pri obyknovennom khode veshchei], that there was simply no way either Raskolnikov or Porfiry Petrovich could ever have anticipated it" (6:270; 327, translation altered).[41] Another suspect, the painter Mikolka, suddenly confesses to the murder, ruining Porfiry Petrovich's plans and giving Raskolnikov an unexpected reprieve from interrogation. Here, Dostoevsky uses his improbable poetics to demonstrate a philosophical point: human actions are not as easy to predict as thinkers like Quetelet and Buckle imagine, or Porfiry Petrovich claims. Porfiry may have studied Mikolka's personality in great depth, but even he cannot anticipate what the painter will do next.

Dostoevsky revels in events like Mikolka's unexpected but perfectly timed confession that are so improbable, so out of the ordinary, they border on the miraculous. The narrator of *The Gambler* [Igrok,1866] describes his story in those terms: "Certain events occurred with me that were almost miraculous; in any case that's how I continue to see them, although, from another point of view – especially judging by the whirlwind in which I was turning at the time – they were perhaps merely not entirely ordinary" [ne sovsem obyknovennye] (5:281). The plot of *Crime and Punishment*, which Dostoevsky wrote at the same time, also plays out in this improbable zone, where the "not quite ordinary" approaches the miraculous. It is no wonder that Raskolnikov sees the coincidences that befall him as signs of divine or demonic intervention. When he unexpectedly stumbles upon an unattended axe in the courtyard, he blames the devil (6:60). When he happens upon Svidrigailov in a tavern, he calls their meeting a strange "chance" [sluchai], but does not deny that, in his heart of hearts, he believes it to be a "miracle" [chudo] (6:356; 438).

Like all of the "miracles" in Dostoevsky's fiction, however, this one has a (potentially) rational explanation. According to Svidrigailov, the meeting was no miracle at all: Raskolnikov has forgotten that Svidrigailov said he would be in precisely this tavern at precisely this time. The address must have "imprinted itself mechanically in [Raskolnikov's] memory," and, without realizing what he was doing, Raskolnikov "mechanically" walked straight there (6:357; 439; translation altered). In general, highly improbable events like this one can always be explained in more than one way. They can be read as the workings of natural law, the result of random chance, or even as signs of covert divine or demonic intervention – which is precisely what makes them so appealing to Dostoevsky. They suggest that something very much like a miracle can happen in real life, that the miraculous need not emanate from some extraterrestrial sphere, but instead (to quote Lotman once more) can be "discovered in the thick of life itself."[42]

The Improbable Ending of *Crime and Punishment*

I want to conclude this chapter by considering the part of *Crime and Punishment* that has struck generations of readers as the most improbable of all – the epilogue, when, after nine unrepentant months in prison, Raskolnikov undergoes a sudden change of heart. He is sitting on a log, overlooking the river, when Sonya "suddenly" [vdrug] appears by his side. Then, just as "suddenly" [vdrug] he falls down at her feet (6:421; 516). "There and then, in that same instant" Sonya understands what has happened, "that he loved her, loved her endlessly, and that the moment had finally come" (6:421; 516).

Raskolnikov's "resurrection" (6:421; 517) takes place so quickly and unexpectedly, however, that many critics have deemed it unconvincing. Bakhtin calls the ending "*conventionally monologic*," a rare moment when Dostoevsky's own Christian ideology threatens to overwhelm the polyphonic artistic structure of the novel as a whole.[43] Simmons declares it "neither artistically palatable nor psychologically sound."[44] Konstantin Mochulsky claims that even Dostoevsky did not believe in Raskolnikov's conversion, which he reads as the author's half-hearted attempt to appease a conservative readership. "We know Raskolnikov too well to believe this 'pious lie,'" Mochulsky opines.[45]

I want to suggest, to the contrary, that Raskolnikov's transformation does accord with the novel's larger aesthetic structure, not in spite of its improbability, but precisely *because* of it. For the entire novel, we have watched Raskolnikov swing back and forth like the pendulum of a tightly wound clock between his impulses towards pride, violence, and solitude, on the one hand, and towards faith, generosity, and human community, on the other, "as if two contrasting characters were taking turns inside of him" (6:165; 200). If the past predicts the future, he should keep moving back and forth between these two poles indefinitely, until he finally runs out of energy and stops moving altogether. Even his last name – which is famously built on the root of the Russian word for "schism" [raskol] – suggests that this divided state is fundamental to his identity, and thus unlikely to change. But what if Raskolnikov's transformation is *meant* to seem unlikely, truly *extra*ordinary? What if it is not supposed to be "artistically palatable," at least not to readers who equate probability with verisimilitude? When Mochulsky says that we know Raskolnikov too well to believe in his transformation, his logic approaches Buckle's: if we have "complete knowledge" of a man's character and the "ordinary operations of his mind," we should be able to foresee everything he will or will not do. But Dostoevsky has spent the entire novel trying to convince us that Buckle's theory does not hold. In that sense, Raskolnikov's improbable conversion is perfectly in harmony with the rest of the novel, not to mention with Dostoevsky's larger aesthetic project, which habitually grants signifying power to statistical outliers.

Yet it is equally important for Dostoevsky's project that Raskolnikov's transformation seem *plausible*, if improbable, *possible*, if atypical of his usual divided behaviour, and that readers believe that something like it could happen in real life (even if it *probably* wouldn't). Dostoevsky takes pains to establish the possibility of Raskolnikov's change of heart from page one, by emphasizing the hero's inner conflict about his crime, and his feelings of shame and horror at what he has done. But Dostoevsky also takes pains to establish the possibility that Raskolnikov could go another way as well. Porfiry Petrovich, for example, considers the possibility that "God has prepared a life" for Raskolnikov, which he will find when he repents; but Porfiry Petrovich also weighs the chances that Raskolnikov's potential will simply pass "like smoke," and even that he will commit suicide without confessing first (6:352; 433).[46] Svidrigailov identifies yet another road that Raskolnikov might go down, declaring that he "could be a proper rascal with time, once all this silliness is knocked out of him" (6:390; 475). Raskolnikov's future conversion, thus, is represented as a possibility, rather than an inevitability, a plausibility rather than a necessity. If it seemed too inevitable, if it became too easy to predict, then it would just end up reaffirming Buckle's deterministic logic.[47]

Another way that Dostoevsky tries to make Raskolnikov's sudden conversion seem plausible is by emphasizing its incompleteness. If Raskolnikov's entire personality were to transform instantaneously, completely and irrevocably, this might indeed strike readers as an impossibility, a "pious lie." But it doesn't. Instead, Dostoevsky balances out references to the instantaneousness of Raskolnikov's transformation with references to his enduring personal weaknesses. Even after his riverside conversion, Raskolnikov experiences no special renewal of religious faith. He "mechanically" [mashinal'no] picks up the copy of the New Testament that Sonya has given him, but puts it down again without opening or reading it. Worse, he continues to show little remorse for his crime. To the contrary, he mentally disowns his past. As we learn: "Everything, even his crime, even his sentence and exile, now seemed, in the first surge, somehow alien and strange, as if it were not even him they had happened to" (6:422; 517). But we also learn that Raskolnikov is wrong, that he has *not* become an entirely new person, and that he will not be able to escape his past as easily as he imagines: "He didn't even know that his new life was not being given to him for free, that it would still cost him dear, that it would have to be paid for with a great, future deed" (6:422; 518).

Characteristically, however, the narrator does not tell us what that "great, future deed" might be. Like almost all of the details of Raskolnikov's future life, this one remains hazy and undetermined.[48] Take the novel's famous final lines: "But here a new story begins: the story of a man's gradual renewal and gradual rebirth, of his gradual crossing from one world to another, of his acquaintance with a new, as yet unknown reality" (6:422; 518). The final lines assure us that, one way or another, Raskolnikov will eventually be reborn, that he will reach a "new" and "unknown reality" (whatever that might be). But these lines do not mark out the path he will take to get there, and they do not guarantee that his path will be a straight one.[49] They allow for a degree of continued unpredictability, for the possibility that Raskolnikov's life will be punctured by still more improbable and extraordinary events.

So if the ending of *Crime and Punishment* subverts reader expectations in some ways, in others it does not.[50] In one way, at least, it is paradoxically predictable. After all, this is not the first, not the second, but the 560th "sudden" turn of events in the novel – by this point, we should be expecting the unexpected. Robert Belknap has noted another way in which the ending hardly surprises. It concludes with the uniting in love of a beautiful young man and an attractive young woman, and what could be more expected of a novelistic ending than that?[51] Like so much of Dostoevsky's fiction, the epilogue to *Crime and Punishment* combines the expected with the unexpected, the gradual with the sudden, the literarily conventional with the anomalous. It exists in the liminal realm Dostoevsky likes best: the realm of the improbable, the statistically unlikely, the *almost* miraculous (but nevertheless scientifically *possible*).

NOTES

1 A. Ketle, *Chelovek i razvitie ego sposobnostei, ili Opyt obshchestvennoi fiziki*, vol. 1 (St Petersburg, 1865).

2 G.T. Bokl' [Buckle], *Istoriia tsivilizatsii v Anglii*, trans. K. Bestuzhev-Riumin, vol. 1 (St Petersburg, 1863), https://dlib.rsl.ru/viewer /01007496547#?page=2.

3 Kiriak Danilov, review of *Ugolovno-statisticheskie etiudy*, by N. Nekliudov, *Sankt-Peterburgskie vedomosti*, 28 March 1865.

4 Alexander Vucinich, *Science in Russian Culture, 1861–1917* (Stanford, CA: Stanford University Press, 1970), 89.

5 Georgii Fridlender, *Realizm Dostoevskogo* (Leningrad: Nauka, 1964), 150–7; Harriet Murav, *Holy Foolishness: Dostoevsky's Novels and the Poetics of Cultural Critique* (Stanford, CA: Stanford University Press, 1992), 55–9; Liza Knapp, *The Annihilation of Inertia: Dostoevsky and Metaphysics* (Evanston, IL: Northwestern University Press, 1996), 44–54; Irina Paperno, *Suicide as a Cultural Institution in Dostoevsky's Russia* (Ithaca, NY: Cornell University Press, 1997), especially 66–73 and 125–6.

6 F.M. Dostoevskii, *Polnoe sobranie sochinenii v tridtsati tomakh*, ed. V.G. Bazanov et al. (Leningrad: "Nauka," 1972–90), vol. 6, 43. Fyodor Dostoyevsky, *Crime and Punishment*, trans. Oliver Ready (New York: Penguin Books, 2014), 48. From here on I will cite Ready's translation parenthetically in the body of the text, following the volume and page number for the *PSS* and set off by a semicolon.

7 Wagner's work appeared in Russian translation in 1866. Adolph Wagner, "Zakonosoobraznost' v po-vidimomu proizvol'nykh chelovecheskikh deistviiakh s tochki zreniia statistiki," in *Obshchii vyvod polozhitel'nogo metoda*, ed. N. Nekliudov (St Petersburg, 1866), 297–383.

8 Dostoevsky knew something about the mathematics of probability himself. In his recent dissertation, Michael Marsh-Soloway explores Dostoevsky's likely familiarity with probability theory (along with other branches of mathematics). See Michael Marsh-Soloway, "The Mathematical Genius of F.M. Dostoevsky: Imaginary Numbers, Statistics, Non-Euclidean Geometry, and Infinity" (PhD diss., University of Virginia, 2016), especially his excellent chapter on *The Gambler* and the odds at the roulette wheel, 185–225.

9 My argument (that Dostoevsky works within the realm of scientific possibility, rather than outside of or against it) builds on a recent trend in Dostoevsky scholarship to which the essays in this volume make a substantial
   contribution. (See especially Alexey Vdovin's analysis of Dostoevsky's debt
   to Ivan Sechenov and Sarah J. Young's argument that the author "saw a
   spiritual existence grounded in the real world, rather than divorced from
   it, as the solution to the crisis of faith he associated with the age and depicted in his works" (119). Other important studies on the topic include
   Anna Schur [Kaladiouk], "On 'Sticking to the Fact' and 'Understanding
   Nothing': Dostoevsky and the Scientific Method," *Russian Review* 65, no. 3
   (2006): 417–38, and Melissa Frazier, "The Science of Sensation: Dostoevsky, Wilkie Collins and the Detective Novel," *Dostoevsky Studies* New Series,
   no. 19 (2015): 7–28. Also see Melissa Frazier, "Nauka realizma," in *Russkii
   realizm XIX veka: mimesis, politika, ekonomika*, ed. M. Vaisman, A. Vdovin, I.
   Kliger, K. Ospovat (Moscow: Novoe literaturnoe obozrenie, 2020), 408–30.
   In it, Frazier argues that, for all Dostoevsky's tendency toward the other-
   worldly, his realism is nevertheless inflected with "a certain scientific world-
   view" – not one in line with Quetelet's world of "averages," which was based
   on amateurish mathematics, but rather one in line with the more complex
   visions of scientific thinkers like James Maxwell, George Lewes, and Nikolai
   Strakhov.
10 Quetelet borrowed the term "Social Physics" from Auguste Comte, prompt-
   ing Comte (who was no fan of probability theory) to rename his own field
   of study "sociology" in protest. As Ian Hacking argues, Comte foresaw that,
   far from finally revealing the laws that determine social behaviour, the
   mathematics of probability would eventually lead to "hypotheses of the entire absence of Law." Ian Hacking, *The Taming of Chance* (Cambridge: Cambridge University Press, 1990), 143–4.
11 M.A. Quetelet, *A Treatise on Man and the Development of His Faculties* (Edinburgh: William and Robert Chambers, 1842), 7.
12 Ibid., 108.
13 As Theodore Porter puts it, "[m]ost statistical enthusiasts simply ignored
   the dependence of statistical reasoning on probability," and, therefore, a
   degree of uncertainty. See Theodore M. Porter, *The Rise of Statistical Thinking, 1820-1900* (Princeton: Princeton University Press, 1986), 10. They
   ignored the fact that the "new certainty" provided by applications of probability theory "was, finally, a particular valence of doubt." See Thomas M.
   Kavanagh, *Enlightenment and the Shadows of Chance: The Novel and the
   Culture of Gambling in Eighteenth-Century France* (Baltimore: Johns Hopkins
   University Press, 1993), 12.
14 In the 1863 Russian edition of Buckle's work, the phrase "the ordinary operations of his mind" reads "obyknovennyi khod ego mysli": Buckle, *Istoriia*

tsivilisatsii v Anglii, 14. As I discuss later in this chapter, Dostoevsky uses a very similar expression at a key moment of *Crime and Punishment.*

15 Henry Thomas Buckle, *History of Civilization in England*, vol. 1 (New York: D. Appleton, 1884), 14. Dostoevsky knew Buckle's work very well, and even owned a copy of *History of Civilization in England.* See N.F. Budanova, ed., *Biblioteka F.M. Dostoevskogo: opyt rekonstruktsii, nauchnoe opisanie* (St Petersburg: "Nauka," 2005), 135–6.

16 V.A. Zaitsev, "Estestvoznanie i iustitsiia," *Russkoe slovo* (July 1863), otd. i: 112.

17 Quetelet, *A Treatise on Man*, x.

18 Ibid., 99.

19 Ibid., x. Italics in original.

20 Adol'f Ketle, *Sotsial'naia sistema i zakony eiu upravliaiushchie*, trans. L.N. Shakhovskoi (St Petersburg: N. Poliakov, 1866), 278, http://xn–90ax2c.xn–p1ai/catalog/000199_000009_003577415/viewer/.

21 Quetelet, *A Treatise on Man*, vi.

22 Ibid., 96.

23 Quetelet's writings on art occupy a prominent place in the second half of *On Man and the Development of His Faculties*, but only the first half of the book had appeared in Russian translation by 1866 (and only the first half was widely discussed in the Russian press).

24 Maurice S. Lee, *Uncertain Chances: Science, Skepticism, and Belief in Nineteenth-Century American Literature* (Oxford: Oxford University Press, 2012), 29. Other critics, with different aesthetic tastes, used the language of probability as a form of disparagement. Louis-Edmond Duranty, for example, critiqued *Madame Bovary* for being overly dry and unemotional, "a literary application of the mathematics of probability." Cited in *Documents of Modern Literary Realism*, ed. George J. Becker (Princeton, NJ: Princeton University Press, 1963), 98.

25 Quoted in Charles A. Moser, *Esthetics as Nightmare: Russian Literary Theory, 1855–1870* (Princeton, NJ: Princeton University Press, 1989), 180. See N.A. Dobroliubov, *Sobranie sochinenii v deviati tomakh* (Moscow: "Khudozhestvennaia literatura," 1961–4), vol. 6, 311.

26 Maurice Lee argues that writers like Edgar Allen Poe strove to "liberate imaginative literature from probabilistic constraints, not by rejecting probabilistic verisimilitude as such but by insisting on its extravagant potential." See Lee, *Uncertain Chances*, 35. Dostoevsky, who always admired Poe, takes part in this larger literary trend.

27 When Dostoevsky insisted that highly improbable events could reveal as much (or more) about the nature of reality as "ordinary" ones, he was in good company. Just one year after he finished *Crime and Punishment*, the physicist James Maxwell also began toying with the possibility that something close to a miracle could take place in real life. Convinced that

"macroscopic regularities such as the second law of thermodynamics are only probable" rather than absolute, he argued that entropy in a closed system could decrease rather than increase, at least theoretically. In a thought experiment now referred to as "Maxwell's Demon," he posited that, given the right set of circumstances, even incontrovertible-seeming laws of physics could be bent, if not broken entirely. Porter, *The Rise of Statistical Thinking*, 194.

28 Donald Fanger, *Dostoevsky and Romantic Realism: A Study of Dostoevsky in Relation to Balzac, Dickens, and Gogol* (Evanston, IL: Northwestern University Press, 1998), 217.

29 Harriet Murav argues that the frequent comparisons of Sonya to a holy fool place her outside of the norm according to mid-nineteenth-century medical discourse as well. Murav, *Holy Foolishness*, 66–9.

30 For another take on Raskolnikov's mixed ordinary and extraordinary qualities, see Ilya Kliger's contribution to this volume.

31 Fridlender, *Realizm Dostoevskogo*, 150–67.

32 As Konstantine Klioutchkine has argued, Raskolnikov is a "modern media man," who regurgitates clichés that were circulating and re-circulating in the Russian press of the 1860s. Konstantine Klioutchkine, "The Rise of *Crime and Punishment* from the Air of the Media," *Slavic Review* 61, no. 1 (Spring 2002): 88–108.

33 Quetelet, *A Treatise on Man*, 95. The Russian statistician N. Nekliudov contests some of Quetelet's conclusions. Drawing from a larger sample set, he tries to show that the propensity to crime in fact peaks a bit later, between the ages of twenty-five and thirty. Even according to Nekliudov's revised calculations, however, someone of Raskolnikov's age makes for a fairly likely murderer. Nekliudov rates the age range of twenty-one to twenty-five as the third most "criminal period" in the human lifespan. N. Nekliudov, *Ugolovno-statisticheskie etiudy* (St Petersburg: Tip. Nikolaia Tiblena i Kompaniia, 1865), 59.

34 According to one familiar reading of *Crime and Punishment* – which has been proposed by Gary Saul Morson, for example – Raskolnikov's big mistake is that he desires extraordinariness, that he does not recognize the virtue of "small acts of prosaic goodness" or "ordinary decency" and "practical reason." As I have been trying to show, however, Dostoevsky values the extraordinary just as much as his protagonist does (although he sees the extraordinary in different places, people, and things). Gary Saul Morson, "The God of Onions: *The Brothers Karamazov* and the Mythic Prosaic," in *A New Word on "The Brothers Karamazov,"* ed. Robert Louis Jackson (Evanston, IL: Northwestern University Press, 2004), 108.

35 Ernest J. Simmons, *Dostoevsky: The Making of a Novelist* (New York: Vintage Books, 1962), 169.

36 Robert L. Belknap, *Plots* (New York: Columbia University Press, 2016), 115–21.

37 V.N. Toporov, "O structure romana Dostoevskogo v sviazi s arkhaichnymi skhemami mifologicheskogo myshleniia. (Prestuplenie i nakazanie), in *Structure of Texts and Semiotics of Culture*, ed. Jan van der Eng (The Hague: Mouton, 1973), 234–6.

38 Mikhail Bakhtin, *Problems of Dostoevsky's Poetics*, ed. and trans. Caryl Emerson (Minneapolis: University of Minnesota Press, 1984), 114. Italics in original.

39 Jurij M. Lotman, "The Origin of Plot in the Light of Typology," trans. Julian Graffy, *Poetics Today* 1, no. ½ (Autumn 1979): 175, 177.

40 As Kate Holland argues, confusing the typical and the particular, the probable and the actual, is precisely the mistake that the prosecutor makes in *Brothers Karamazov*. Kate Holland, "The Legend of the *Ladonka* and the Trial of the Novel," in *A New Word on "The Brothers Karamazov,"* ed. Robert Louis Jackson (Evanston, IL: Northwestern University Press, 2004), 194.

41 Note the echoing of Buckle's words in this line.

42 Lotman, "The Origin of Plot," 178. There was a long tradition in Western European philosophy of discussing miracles (sometimes classed in the larger category of "extraordinary facts" [faits extraordinaires]) in terms of probability. David Hume, for example, argued that miracles fly so completely in the face of our everyday experience that the probability of one actually taking place is effectively zero, amounting to a positive proof against it. The English theologian Richard Price offered a rebuttal that Dostoevsky might have found convincing. Just because miracles are unlikely, Price retorted, that does not make them impossible: "between *impossibilities* and *improbabilities*, however apt we are to confound them, there is an infinite difference." Qtd. in Lorraine Daston, *Classical Probability in the Enlightenment* (Princeton, NJ: Princeton University Press, 1988), 327. See Daston's subchapter on "Testimony and the Probability of Miracles," 306–42. Italics in original.

43 Bakhtin, *Problems of Dostoevsky's Poetics*, 39. Italics in original.

44 Simmons, *Dostoevsky: The Making of a Novelist*, 153.

45 Konstantin Mochulsky, *Dostoevsky: His Life and Work*, trans. Michael A. Minihan (Princeton, NJ: Princeton University Press, 1967), 312.

46 Taken as a whole, Porfiry Petrovich's words look less like novelistic foreshadowing (which hints at what will happen so many pages down the line), and more like what Gary Saul Morson calls "sideshadowing," a gesture toward the many different paths the protagonist *might* take. Gary Saul Morson, *Narrative and Freedom: The Shadows of Time* (New Haven, CT: Yale University Press, 1994), 117–72.

47 David Matual provides a convincing, in-depth analysis of the many ways in which the language, imagery, and events of the epilogue are connected

with the rest of the novel. I disagree with him on one point, however. He calls the novel's conclusion "the inevitable result of all that precedes it." I have tried to argue, by contrast, that Dostoevsky tries to make Raskolnikov's transformation seem possible, but not inevitable. David Matual, "In Defense of the Epilogue of *Crime and Punishment*," *Studies in the Novel* 24, no. 1 (Spring 1992): 33.

48　Kate Holland notes that the very reference to a "great, future deed" is ambiguous, because it resonates with Raskolnikov's "extraordinary man" theory (suggesting that he may not have moved beyond it after all). Kate Holland, "The Clash of Deferral and Anticipation: *Crime and Punishment*'s Epilogue and the Difficulties of Narrative Closure," *Canadian Slavonic Papers* 62, no. 2 (2020): 110. Indeed, as Eric Naiman has shown, the ending contains so many ambiguities that highly sceptical readings of Raskolnikov's transformation will always be possible. Eric Naiman, "'There was something almost crude about it all…' – Reading *Crime and Punishment*'s Epilogue Hard against the Grain," *Canadian Slavonic Papers* 62, no. 2 (2020): 123–43.

49　I make some of these observations in the third chapter of my book, in which I read the epilogue of *Crime and Punishment* both in the context of Dostoevsky's other "happy endings" and his eschatological thought as a whole. See Greta Matzner-Gore, *Dostoevsky and the Ethics of Narrative Form: Suspense, Closure, Minor Characters* (Evanston, IL: Northwestern University Press, 2020), especially 68–70.

50　Katherine Bowers analyzes this play of thwarted and fulfilled expectations in light of the novel's experiments with genre, specifically its "generic hybridity." Katherine Bowers, "Plotting the Ending: Generic Expectation and the Uncanny Epilogue of *Crime and Punishment*," *Canadian Slavonic Papers* 62, no. 2 (2020): 95–108.

51　Belknap, *Plots*, 124.

9 Illegitimacies of the Novel: Characterization in Dostoevsky's *The Adolescent*

CHLOË KITZINGER

In 1918, Georg Lukács published an essay on his friend Béla Balázs that includes the following credo: "Dostoevsky's people live, without distance, the essence of their souls. Meanwhile the problem of other writers, including even Tolstoy, consists in how a soul can overcome those obstacles by which it is prevented from an attainment, even a glimpse, of itself. Dostoevsky begins where the others end: he describes how the soul lives its own life."[1]

This comment draws on the extensive notes Lukács had made for his abandoned book on Dostoevsky, to which *The Theory of the Novel* (1916) was originally designated as a preface.[2] Together with the notes, it sheds light on Lukács's enigmatic pronouncement at the end of that essay that "Dostoevsky did not write novels."[3] For Dostoevsky's characters, as Lukács writes in his notes, thought is action; they have no professions and no central marriage plots. They "do not develop" over the course of the narrative; and their actions cannot be genealogically traced back to their family circumstances or environment. Instead, their "adventures" take place "in the soul," on the level of idea and dialogue rather than biographical plot.[4]

Lukács's ideas about Dostoevsky have ethical and political significance for his early thought, but their significance is also aesthetic. Characterized by a direct continuity between action and idea, Dostoevsky's characters place the fictional sphere of action beside the point. They are free from the "instrumental" centrality of the hero of a conventional novel that (as Lukács writes in *The Theory of the Novel*) "comprises the essence of its totality between the beginning and the end, and thereby raises an individual to the infinite heights of one who must create an entire world through his experience" (83). What Dostoevsky escapes is the novelistic simulacrum of the epic "rounded world": the illusion of a world divinely fitted for human selves that the novel imperfectly, because artificially, projects. He avoids the split between epic and novel by relinquishing the dream of divinely adequate creation itself.

A vital strand of twentieth-century criticism and theory extends both backwards and forwards from Lukács's reading of Dostoevsky's characters. An early predecessor is Dmitry Merezhkovsky's globally influential treatise *L. Tolstoi and Dostoevskii* (1900–2), with its argument that Dostoevsky departs from Tolstoy in building his characters primarily from speech – through characterizing remarks "as a result of which the portrait becomes too live ... as if it were just about to stir and step out of the frame like a ghost."[5] The line continues through Merezhkovsky's fellow symbolist Vyacheslav Ivanov, who began his 1911 lecture "Dostoevskii and the Novel-Tragedy" (published 1916) with his own arresting image of Dostoevsky's characters as "living ghosts": "they knock at our doors in dark and in white nights, they can be recognized on the streets in murky patches of Petersburg fog and they settle in to talk with us in insomniac hours in our own underground."[6] The eerie vividness of characters created by their "own" speech exempts Dostoevsky (as both Merezhkovsky and Ivanov suggest) from the novel's generic limitations. Using his characters' words to expose the transcendentally free essence of their personalities, Dostoevsky transposed them into the communal cultural realms of tragedy and myth. It is only a step from here to Mikhail Bakhtin's *Problems of Dostoevsky's Poetics* [Problemy tvorchestva Dostoevskogo, 1929; Problemy poetiki Dostoevskogo, 1963]. An attentive reader both of Lukács's *Theory of the Novel* and of symbolist Dostoevsky criticism, Bakhtin formalized and canonized the idea that Dostoevsky's characters are created by their "own" words rather than the words of a narrator, and unlike the young Lukács, he associated this apparent autonomy with the revolutionary and indispensable power of the novel form.[7]

And yet, for all his faith in the novel genre as epitomized in Dostoevsky, Bakhtin strikes a rare nostalgic note when he writes about the mimetic completeness, or what he calls the "embodiedness [voploshchennost']," of Dostoevsky's characters:

> The plot of the biographical novel is not adequate to [Dostoevsky's hero], for such a plot relies wholly on the social and characterological definitiveness of the hero, on his full embodiedness in life. Between the character of the hero and the plot of his life there must be a deep and organic unity ... The hero and the objective world surrounding him must be made of one piece. But Dostoevsky's hero in this sense is not embodied and cannot be embodied. He cannot have a normal biographical plot. The heroes themselves, it turns out, fervently dream of being embodied, they long to attach themselves to one of life's normal plots. The longing for embodiment

[zhazhda voploshcheniia] by the "dreamer," [by the "underground man"] born of an idea and by the "hero of an accidental family," is one of Dostoevsky's most important themes.[8]

The very quality that Merezhkovsky, Ivanov, Lukács, and Bakhtin all (differently) celebrate – the Dostoevskian character's "freedom" from narrated social, physical, and biographical traits – here emerges as a moment of loss. Adopting the character's viewpoint, Bakhtin nods towards the vividly "embodying" aspect of realist illusion that Dostoevsky's novels leave behind.

At the origins of the foundational branch of criticism and theory of the novel now associated most strongly with Bakhtin, there is thus a puzzle about Dostoevsky's characters that demands exploration. In one sense, their "reality" is unprecedented; it depends on the sustained illusion that these characters are painted by their *own* thoughts and words, and so (in Bakhtin's well-known argument) always exceed their characterization, retaining a "surplus" unconstrained by any particular plot, narrative circumstance, or trait.[9] In another sense, as readers throughout their reception history have commented, Dostoevsky's characters often seem less "real" than the more extensively narrated protagonists of Turgenev, Goncharov, or (especially) Tolstoy.[10] In the divide between Dostoevsky's indirect and Tolstoy's direct techniques of characterization, Merezhkovsky saw national and religious implications; Ivanov, Lukács, and Bakhtin, equally weighty generic ones.[11] But questions remain. Does a character with the quality of a "living ghost" take more or less vivid shape than a character fully "embodied" in the text that creates him? Did Dostoevsky himself embrace or lament the narrative techniques that set his characters apart from those of his contemporaries?

In this chapter, I will argue that the "longing for embodiedness" of Dostoevsky's characters, most often treated as peripheral to the true work of his novels, was in another sense at the very heart of his thought about characterization and about the novel's capacity to transform the world in which it is read. For Lukács, Dostoevsky bypasses what might be called the *foundling* plot of the novel – the novel as an "expression of … transcendental homelessness" (41), as the epic of a world "abandoned by God" (88). But could there in fact be a better summary of Dostoevsky's writings than (in Lukács's own iconic phrase) "the epic of an age in which the extensive totality of life is no longer given … yet which still thinks in terms of totality" (56)? In a struggle whose focus was realist characterization, Dostoevsky aimed not just to capture, but also to solidify, the contemporary "types" he saw – to fit them for the very conventional techniques of novelistic mimesis from which he was later seen to have liberated the genre.[12] I believe that this mimetic ambition has bearing on how we interpret his novels and their intended effects on the reader. In a line of works stretching from *Poor Folk* [Bednye liudi, 1846] to *Brothers Karamazov* [Brat'ia Karamazovy, 1880], Dostoevsky chronicled and strove to overcome what Lukács recognized as the realist novel's most tormenting illegitimacy: its separation from the terms of reality itself.

It is not coincidental that Dostoevsky reflected on this project most directly in a text that is itself about illegitimacy, his second-to-last novel *The Adolescent* [Podrostok, 1875]. Following a discussion of some problems that the reception of his earlier novels and mimetic characters posed, I will show how *The Adolescent* offers a response. Frequently though ever less sidelined in studies of Dostoevsky's works, *The Adolescent* holds out an unfamiliar vision of Dostoevsky as tormented by the limitations of his own novels, and also of the novel genre as such. It suggests a Dostoevsky both more and less conventional than the central line of twentieth-century criticism presents him – aspiring towards a mimetic standard that later readers thought he had far surpassed, but revealing a faith nothing short of radical in the spiritual power that such mimetic representation might hold.

During Dostoevsky's lifetime, his characters were often dismissed as diseased aberrations, drawn from the seediest corners of life and the human soul.[13] This criticism grew more heated throughout his career. While critics from across ideological camps praised the psychological nuance of Raskolnikov, many reviewers of *The Idiot* [Idiot, 1869] criticized the "fantasy [fantastichnost']," "phantasmagoria," and "soul-sickness" of its characters.[14] Thus, D.I. Minaev described *The Idiot* as "a fairy tale in which the less verisimilitude there is, the better. People meet, become acquainted, fall in love, slap one another, and all on the first caprice of the author, without any kind of artistic truth."[15] V.P. Burenin called it "a belletristic composition made up of a multitude of absurd characters and events, without a care for any artistic task at all."[16] By the time of *The Adolescent*'s publication in 1875, the hostile (Westernizer) critic V.G. Avseenko could treat the implausibility of Dostoevsky's novels as a known fact, seamlessly linking the charge of "abnormality" with the language of the insubstantial: "It has often been said that Mr. Dostoevsky succeeds best with the representation of phenomena of life that stand on the boundary separating reality from the world of ghosts ... It is *not people acting*, but some degenerates of the human race, some *underground shadows*."[17]

As in the cases of Minaev, Burenin, and Avseenko, such denunciations of Dostoevsky's realism were often politically and ideologically motivated. However, critics consistently couched these attacks – and Dostoevsky consistently received them – in terms of artistic technique. In an unpublished draft preface to *The Adolescent*, Dostoevsky responded to Avseenko's charges (among others) with a defence of his own "fantastic realism":

> Facts. They pass by. They don't notice. *There are no citizens*, and no one wants to make an effort and force himself to think and notice. I could not tear myself away, and all the cries of critics that I am representing an unreal life [nenastoiashchuiu zhizn'] have not deterred me … Our talented writers, who have been representing, with high art, the life of our mid-upper-class (family) circle – Tolstoy, Goncharov – thought that they were representing the life of the majority – I think it was they who were representing the life of exceptions. On the contrary, their life is the life of exceptions, and mine is the life of the general rule. Future generations who are less partial will recognize this; the truth will be on my side. . . I am proud that I was the first to depict the real man of the *Russian majority* [nastoiashchego cheloveka *russkogo bol'shinstva*] and the first to lay bare his monstrous and tragic side. The tragic element lies in his consciousness of monstrosity. (22 March 1875; 16:329; italics in original)

Dostoevsky answers the accusation of "unreality" by claiming that he is the one representing the "real man of the Russian majority," and the accusation of "ghostliness," by claiming that his unconventional subjects dictate these unconventional techniques. Raskolnikov, Stepan Trofimovich, and the Underground Man (paradigmatic examples that he lists elsewhere in the passage) become "tragic" not because of their monstrosity, but because of their *consciousness* of monstrosity; the representation of this consciousness fits them for literature when no pre-existing patterns can. In effect, Dostoevsky here inaugurates what would become the symbolist critics', and later Bakhtin's, explanation and argument for the vividness of his own characters. They are "real" precisely because they transcend the conventions of realist narrative and description. Because there is no template for these subjects' representation, the author has no choice but to characterize them (tautologically) through their "own" thoughts and self-perceptions.

However, in both his aesthetic writings and criticism and his art, Dostoevsky had long grappled with the question of whether these same contemporary subjects could be brought together with a different, less tenuous mode of representation. As Robert Louis Jackson suggests, Dostoevsky's "quest for form" – his reach towards a classical ideal of beauty from the depths of contemporary chaos and moral ugliness – was, by the same token, a quest for literary mimesis. In Dostoevsky's understanding, the writer introduces order and beauty into the human reality he sees by crystallizing it into literary "ideals" or types. The autonomous "life" of these typical characters reflects the aesthetic unity of the work itself, and types (in turn) are the work's main avenue for shaping readers' understanding and consciousness of their society.[18] But if a type is still historically unfinished, can it take compelling aesthetic shape? In their well-known exchange of letters on this question (February 1874), Ivan Goncharov had argued no and Dostoevsky yes – but Dostoevsky's own identification of "artistic truth" with finished aesthetic form suggests that he must (on some level) have shared Goncharov's misgivings.[19] The critics' failure to recognize the typicality of his "real men of the Russian majority" may demonstrate their incompetence as readers, but it also opens the possibility that something is missing from these protagonists' unconventional characterization.

Though Dostoevsky's draft preface to *The Adolescent* is most often read as an appeal (soon resoundingly answered) to "future generations" of readers, it thus also draws attention to a mimetic inadequacy by the standards of nineteenth-century realism – an illegitimacy resulting from the very "self-"characterization with which we now associate the vividness of Dostoevsky's characters. I think Dostoevsky not only acknowledged, but also used this inadequacy to further his vision of the realist novel's aesthetic, social, and spiritual task. The novel that inspired his defensive preface, *The Adolescent*, both thematizes his experimental (illegitimate) techniques of characterization, and deliberately stages their disintegration. In the process, *The Adolescent* places him closer to the conventional hopes and anxieties of the European novel than its wild eccentricity suggests.

The narrator-hero of *The Adolescent*, Arkady Dolgoruky, announces his illegitimate birth in the novel's first pages, together with his name:

> My last name is Dolgoruky, and my legal father is Makar Ivanovich Dolgoruky, a former household serf of the Versilov family. Thus I'm a legitimate, though in the highest degree illegitimate, son, and my origin is not subject to the slightest doubt. (13:6)[20]

This laborious opening statement, in divorcing Arkady from the line of his legal peasant father, also places him in a line of protagonists as old as the novel itself. Like Julien Sorel, Arkady faces "a choice among possible fathers from whom to inherit"; like Tom Jones or the Dickensian foundling, "he is characterized by desire, rather than possession."[21] By tracing the process of embodying the hero within his proper biography, illegitimacy plots underscore the fit between fictional character and fictional world that Lukács saw as the novel's foundational illusion.[22] As previous analyses have noted, in *The Adolescent* and through his choice of an illegitimate child as protagonist, Dostoevsky grappled unusually directly both with the legacy of his own work as a novelist, and with the legacy of the Russian novel itself.[23] We can extend this argument to suggest that he was engaged, further, with the legacy and purpose of the entire genre. A *Tom Jones* (1749) or *Oliver Twist* (1838) begins with a hero who must be restored to his rightful place; *The Adolescent* begins by asking what this narrative restoration would achieve.

This questioning stance springs, in part, from the additional historical and cultural weight that Dostoevsky lent to the narrative metaphor of illegitimacy. Arkady Dolgoruky realizes a set of fragmentary characters from Dostoevsky's notebooks – chief among them a draft version of Prince Myshkin, and the projected hero of the never-written epic "The Life of a Great Sinner [Zhitie velikogo greshnika, 1869–70] – whose "accidental families" underscore their kinship with post-Reform Russia. The image of Russia as the illegitimate child of East and West traces back at least as far as Pyotr Chaadaev's "First Philosophical Letter" [Lettres philosophiques adressées à une dame, Lettre première, 1829]: "We others [Russians], like illegitimate children, come to this world without patrimony... Each one of us must himself once again seek to tie the broken thread of the family line [le fil rompu de la famille]."[24] For Dostoevsky, the idea of Russia's inherent illegitimacy – its "isolation in the European family of peoples" (21:70) – was compounded after the 1861–4 Great Reforms' break with accumulated tradition. The illegitimately born hero as sketched in his 1860s–'70s notebooks and novels sees himself as both better and worse than everyone else; as a passage from the *Idiot* notebook put it, "To master everyone, to triumph over everyone and to get revenge on everyone (and for what – who knows). (He is an illegitimate son.) [Ovladet' vsemi, vostorzhestvovat' <nad> vsemi i otomstit' vsem (a za chto – neizvestno). (On pobochnyi syn.)] (9:178). This personal sense of rancour and exclusion also signals the bitter *national* bind of post-Reform Russia as Dostoevsky saw it, faced with the task of reconstructing foundations that it had never fully owned.

The illegitimate protagonist thus makes tangible a set of problems – individual, national, generic, and narrative – that run the length of Dostoevsky's career. Arkady caught between his legal peasant and his natural noble father allegorically mirrors Russia caught between its homegrown ("Eastern") traditions and its adopted Western ones. His illegitimacy, in turn, makes literal the plight of many Dostoevskian characters whose birth does not give them an identity – from the cripplingly "ordinary"

Ganya Ivolgin to the dramatically unmoored Raskolnikov – and these characters pose a challenge to the novelist akin to the challenge of Russian history itself.

It is no surprise, then, that Dostoevsky was determined to make the nonentity Arkady the protagonist of *The Adolescent* rather than his father Versilov, who was conceived as "already a genuine heroic type" (16:7). However, in a process recorded in unusual detail in his notebooks for *The Adolescent*, he found that he could place Arkady at the centre of the novel only by also making him its narrator (16:47 ff.) Arkady thus epitomizes (lastly) the formal plight of the "illegitimate" Dostoevskian character as such – of "real men of the Russian majority" who take shape only when they tell their own stories, and are thus cut off from any conclusively defining or omniscient narrative origin. As Dostoevsky's writings about type suggest, if the novelist could "embody" such characters in coherent and memorable figures, it would be a sign that he had found in them (and in the rootless aspects of contemporary Russia) something that answers to the vivifying form of the beautiful work of art. *The Adolescent* with its illegitimate protagonist shows especially clearly how, for Dostoevsky, conventional realist characterization took on a messianic national and spiritual significance. It is an extreme case, but just for that reason, an emblematic one – a vortex of all the complexities that Dostoevsky associated with mimetic representation in and of 1870s Russia. But with the stakes raised so high and made so visible, it is striking how spectacularly Dostoevsky lets the act of representation fall apart.

The Adolescent recounts the first year that Arkady Makarovich Dolgoruky spends in St Petersburg with his natural father, the dissolute landowner Andrei Petrovich Versilov, and his mother, born a peasant on Versilov's estate. While Arkady arrives intending to discover the truth about Versilov's moral character, he soon becomes infatuated with Katerina Nikolaevna Akhmakova, who is also an object of Versilov's affection. Arkady's "notes" tell the increasingly sordid story of the rivalry between himself and Versilov, and of his idyllic encounter with his legal peasant father, Makar Ivanovich Dolgoruky, just before the latter's death. An elaborate blackmail plot, revolving around a "document" in Arkady's possession that could give him power over Katerina Nikolaevna, runs through the novel and culminates in a crisis, averted by chance, in which Katerina Nikolaevna is almost raped by Arkady's former schoolmate Lambert and almost murdered by Versilov. The story ends, inconclusively, with the implication of a future relationship between Arkady and Katerina Nikolaevna and of Versilov's reunion with (though not marriage to) Arkady's mother; the novel's last section is the comments of Arkady's former tutor, Nikolai Semyonovich, on the manuscript of his "notes" (the main text of the novel).

This summary gives only the barest impression of the multitude of figures and events that crowd Arkady's narrative. Digressions and repetitious subplots hang from the basic plotline – suicides, other blackmails, gambling episodes, several other rumoured rapes, a host of abandoned or illegitimate children. Nevertheless, as many have argued, Arkady's "notes" follow a coherent pattern: they are structured as a Bildungsroman, a series of tests that attempt to illuminate Versilov's true character, and so to establish the chief model available for Arkady to define his future path on or against.[25] From the beginning, it is clear that Arkady's portrait of Versilov – "even now... in a great many ways a complete riddle to me" (13:6; 6) – will be inconclusive. However, the task of describing Versilov is the impetus from which the narrative unfolds.

It is notable, then, that Arkady's weaknesses as a narrator cluster around the introduction of new characters into his story. The incidental character Olimpiada is symptomatic:

> I looked at her quite closely and found nothing special: not a very tall girl, plump, and with extremely ruddy cheeks. Her face, however, was rather pleasant, the kind that the materialists like. Her expression was kind, perhaps, but with a wrinkle [so skladkoi]. She could not have been especially brilliant intellectually, at least not in a higher sense, but one could see cunning in her eyes. No more than nineteen years old. In short, nothing remarkable. We'd have called her a "pillow" in high school. (If I describe her in such detail, it's solely because I'll need it in the future.) By the way, everything I've been describing so far, with such apparently unnecessary detail, all leads to the future and will be needed there. (13:33; 39)

This passage is a parody of a realist character-portrait. Arkady qualifies each feature he mentions, blurring it even as it meets the page. Moreover, although he is putatively writing a year after the events he recounts, he misleads the reader about Olimpiada's significance – the *size* of the "character-space" she will occupy in his narrative.[26] Olimpiada demands close attention, but she turns out to be "nothing special"; the details of her appearance will be necessary "in the future," but as it happens, she returns only once. Arkady begins by signalling the conventions of omniscient characterization, but in the same breath, he disrupts them.

The same trend continues throughout the narrative. Arkady introduces almost every new character with a portrait like Olimpiada's, offering concrete physical details (as Dostoevsky dubbed them in notebook plans) "à la L[eo] T[olstoi]" (16:87; 16:73). But a reader attempting to associate these details with a stably recurring figure in a stably sized space (à la Leo Tolstoy) will be disappointed: Arkady's technical difficulties with characterization reflect and exacerbate the convolution of the story he is trying to tell. His frequent confusion at the changeability of faces culminates in the suspicion (as he writes of the blackmailer Stebelkov) that individual physical traits "not only did not personalize his character, but seemed precisely to endow it with something general, like everyone else ... He passes quickly from a laughing to a grave look, from a grave to a playful or winking one, but it is all somehow scattered and pointless [... ne tol'ko ne sposobstvovali ego kharakternosti, no imenno kak by pridavali emu chto-to obshchee, na vsekh pokhozhee ... So smeshlivogo on bystro perekhodit na vazhnyi vid, s vazhnogo na igrivyi ili podmigivaiush-chii, no vse eto kak-to raskidchivo i besprichinno]" (13:118; 142). The mobile face is a standard feature of physiognomic character-portraits in Dostoevsky's novels.[27] But in *The Adolescent* this mobility infects the entire project of characterization; the narrative, like a kaleidoscope, shifts among constellations of minor figures without specifying the connections between them.[28] There are two Princes Sokolsky, no relation to each other. Stebelkov, whose schemes dominate the middle third of the novel, is eclipsed without notice by a second blackmailer, Lambert. Incidental characters unfurl from their functional roles to give speeches that touch on the novel's most central preoccupations, then vanish for good. Even Makar Dolgoruky, the legal father who, late in the novel, offers Arkady a "seemly" alternative to the disorder around Versilov, dies before his influence can crystallize. Names too are unstable: the suicide Olya's mother, called Darya Onisimovna in Part One, becomes Nastasya Egorovna in Part Three.

The novel's secondary characters thus fail to satisfy one of the most basic definitions of realist character ever formulated, as that which results "when identical semes traverse the same proper name several times and appear to settle upon it."[29] Much of this chaos results from the circumstances of serial publication, but its effect on a reader's ability to construct a coherent fictional world is none the weaker for being unintentional. In a Bildungsroman built around two central projects of characterization – Versilov, and Arkady himself – it emerges that Arkady is telling a story in which almost *all* the figures struggle to take shape. Indeed, Versilov's hiddenness is the clearest preoccupation of Arkady's narrative – emblematized by the "wrinkle" that conceals whether he is sincere or mocking, sane or mad (13:171, 13:223, 13:372; 209, 244, 463). He ends as the most elusive of the novel's shifting points: still unmarried to Arkady's mother, still an uncertain Christian, and still shadowed by Arkady's attempts at explanation.[30]

The thrust of this analysis may be simply that Dostoevsky's approach to the novel's structure, as laid out in his notebooks, was successful. The narrator Arkady emerges as protagonist, characterized primarily by his own first-person "notes [zapiski]" In turn, the other characters (and notably Versilov) are screened or fragmented by the very text that pursues them, revealing the teller at the expense of the tale. In Dostoevsky's first published work of fiction, *Poor Folk*, he had brought new life to the Gogolian titular councillor by making him responsible for his "own" epistolary narration. In *The Adolescent* he takes this technique a step further, by making Arkady responsible for the cast of an entire novel. The result is hyperbolically "dialogic," a concatenation of voices cut off from the narrative selves that Arkady can only fleetingly make cohere. But perhaps it does lead to the single coherent character of Arkady himself, who spends the narrative mastering the technique of his "own" characterization and, in the process, his identity and future path.[31]

However, there is an aspect of the novel that this relatively optimistic reading does not capture: *The Adolescent's* orientation (beginning with its title) on its own present inadequacy – on the condition of not yet being fully instated or grown. Age is the hopeful metaphor for this condition. It is shadowed throughout by the more insidious trope of illegitimacy: a suggestion that the lack may never be fully remedied, the gap between "desire and possession" never entirely bridged. First attached to Arkady's birth, the image of illegitimacy shades into his "idea" of compensating for his lack of nobility by becoming "as rich as Rothschild," accumulating the capital that will turn him into an extraordinary man. He quickly becomes distracted from his "idea," but its logic does not end with him; it is mirrored in the theories of the intellectual Kraft, who kills himself because he has concluded that "the Russian people are a second-rate people ... whose fate is to serve *merely as material for a more noble race*" (13:44; 51; my italics). More surprisingly, Versilov's paean to his own nobility reflects a similar pattern of thought:

> I repeat to you that I can't help respecting my nobility. Over the centuries we have developed a high cultural type never seen before ... the type of universal suffering for all [tip vsemirnogo boleniia za vsekh] ... It preserves in itself the future of Russia. There are perhaps only a thousand of us ... but *the whole of Russia has lived up to now only to produce this thousand* ... Only the Russian ... is capable of becoming most Russian precisely only when he is most European. (13:376–7; 468–9; my italics)

A distortion of Dostoevsky's treasured notion of Russian "pan-humanism [vsechelovechestvo]," Versilov's vision of an élite "thousand" who are "most Russian" precisely when they are "most European" distinctly recalls the image of his own illegitimate son Arkady, kissing the hands of the French tutor who used to beat him to remind him of his lowly origins. What unites Arkady, Kraft, and Versilov is the dream of accumulation – the suppliant wish to live into [nazhit'] something that will compensate for the deficiencies of the present. In his representation of an "accidental family," Dostoevsky thus shows the sense of illegitimacy spreading outward, from the narrator-hero's birth to the entire world and historical moment that he portrays.

In the novel's enigmatic epilogue, Arkady's former teacher Nikolai Semyonovich invites us, at last, to extend the logic of illegitimacy and accumulation to its central narrative, the text of Arkady's first-person "notes [zapiski]":

> Yes, Arkady Makarovich, you are *a member of an accidental family* [chlen sluch-ainogo semeistva], as opposed to our still-recent hereditary types, who had a childhood and youth so different from yours. I confess, I would not wish to be a novelist whose hero comes from an accidental family! Thankless work and lacking in beautiful forms. And these types in any case are still a current matter, and therefore cannot be artistically finished ... What, though, is the writer to do who has no wish to write only in the historical genre and is possessed by a yearning for what is current? To guess ... and be mistaken. But "Notes" such as yours could, it seems to me, serve as material for a future artistic work [materialom dlia budushchego khudozhestvennogo proizve-deniia], for a future picture – of a disorderly but already bygone epoch ... the future artist will find beautiful forms even for portraying the past dis-order and chaos. It is then that "Notes" like yours will be needed and will provide material – as long as they are sincere, even despite all that is chaotic and accidental about them. (13:455; 563–4; italics in original)

With this implicit comparison to the "beautiful forms" of the Tolstoyan family novel, Nikolai Semyonovich frames Arkady's *zapiski* as "material for a future artistic work." Subtitled "A Novel [roman]," *The Adolescent* dares us to read this "future artistic work" as a reference to its own text. With equal daring, however, it challenges us to justify this reading. If Arkady's *zapiski* on their own are not a novel, then perhaps it is the self-reflexive epilogue that creates the "work of art." "Notes" become novel with the very move that delegitimizes them by the standard of "beautiful form" – insisting on what they are not yet, and what they could still become.

Read as a consistent aesthetic credo rather than an aberration, a failure, or even an innovative departure from Dostoevsky's previous work, *The Adolescent* lends a new slant to Lukács's idea that "Dostoevsky did not write novels," or, in Bakhtin's revision, that his works provide a basis for redefining what novels are. It suggests that far from portraying a world "remote from any struggle against what actually exists," or describing people who "live, without distance, the essence of their souls," Dostoevsky strove to rediscover the narrative "distance" and legitimating authority that could lend those souls fictional bodies. He imagined less that the novel could change to become more like the modern world than that the world could change to become more like the historical novel.

Dostoevsky's boldest generic move in *The Adolescent* thus depends, counter-intuitively, on compounding the sense of inadequacy figured in his protagonist's illegitimate birth and reflected in the "accidental" form of his *zapiski*. With the zealous self-abasement of a Fyodor Karamazov, *The Adolescent* trumpets its own distance from the vivid, ordered solidity of a Tolstoyan fictional world. But I believe that in the process, Dostoevsky grasps beyond both the finished beauty of Tolstoyan mimetic form, and the techniques by which he himself captures contemporary disorder, for a still bigger prize – the reclamation of the divinely "given" world of what Lukács calls the epic. As he has Versilov lament in a revealing notebook draft:

I have, my dear, one favourite Russian writer. He is a novelist, but for me he's almost a historiographer of our nobility ... He takes a nobleman from his childhood and youth, he draws him in his family ... and all so poetically, so unshakably and inarguably. He is a psychologist of the nobleman's soul. But the main thing is that this is given as inarguable, and of course, you agree. You agree and you envy. Oh, how they envy! There are children who from childhood already begin to become pensive about their families ... and, the main thing, already in childhood begin to understand the disorder and accidental quality [sluchainost'] of the foundations of their life, the absence of established forms and inherited wisdom [ustanovivshikhsia form i rodovogo predaniia]. These should envy my writer, envy (my) his characters and, perhaps, dislike them. Oh, these are not characters [eto ne geroi], they are sweet children, who have wonderful, sweet fathers, eating at the club, entertaining around Moscow ... (17:143)

Conceived in the generic setting of Arkady's *zapiski*, Versilov looks covetously over to the characters narrated "so unshakably and inarguably" by Tolstoy, and he sees "not characters, but sweet children, who have wonderful sweet fathers." Versilov's envy implies a mimetic standard that even Tolstoy could not meet: in the idyll he imagines, to be narrated authoritatively is to be not just vivid, but real. I suggest that the desire that he voices coincides with Dostoevsky's own: that a "future novel," filled with mimetically embodied characters, could restore a vision of contemporary reality as equally susceptible to benevolent divine creation. Much as (in Derrida's famous variation on Plato's *Phaedrus*) all claims to the transparency and legitimacy of speech hinge on the space that is opened by the illegitimacy of writing, so here, this extravagant hope for transcendence is grounded in the aesthetics of accident.[32]

On this interpretation, mimetic characterization in Dostoevsky traces the same dialectic between earthly, "living" struggle and heavenly, immortal perfection that (as many have argued) lies at the centre of his religious philosophy, articulated most directly in the 1864 notebook passage written while Dostoevsky was keeping vigil with the body of his first wife Mariya Isaeva ("Masha is lying on the table" [20:171–4]). Earthly life presupposes a state of "development" and struggle towards the ideal of Christlike "love for another as oneself"; immortality in paradise must be imagined as the state where this ideal has been achieved (20:172–3). A similarly absolute split between present imperfection and future transformation seems to structure Dostoevsky's thought about characterization and the novel. While the novelist can realize contemporary types only partially – as voices or ghosts rather than "embodied" characters – he is then free to envision their full "embodiment" as leading to the redemption of the very fallen world he represents.[33] Crucial to this vision, however, is an insistence on what is missing from the Dostoevskian character. In the space opened by these deficiencies, Dostoevsky imagines overleaping the bounds of the novel genre itself.

The Adolescent is unique among Dostoevsky's novels in laying bare this ambition, placing the metaphorical illegitimacy of all his characters at the visible centre of its narrative. His far more celebrated final novel, *Brothers Karamazov,* pursues a different strategy. Here the trope of illegitimacy is buried – albeit at the heart of the plot – in the person of Smerdyakov, Fyodor Karamazov's murderer and probable unrecognized son. A shadow fourth brother, Smerdyakov is excluded from the novel's title and its key family name; the suspense of the detective plot depends upon a calculation that the reader will ignore him. But his crime and eventual suicide serve to set Dmitry, Ivan, and Alyosha Karamazov on paths towards the living "struggle" for spiritual salvation. At once essential to the narrative and obscured by it, Smerdyakov raises the the possibility that by the end of his career, Dostoevsky was caught between the "illegitimacy" of his own characters, and the "illegitimacy" of the European novel. With its near-Tolstoyan composition around the Karamazov family and (so to speak) the "breed-force" of *karamazovshchina, Brothers Karamazov* comes close to endowing the autonomous Dostoevskian character with the fleshy vividness and stability of a conventional realist hero.[34] Might Smerdyakov's concealment help compensate for this change? Now using rather than deconstructing the established resources for mimetic "embodiment," does Dostoevsky hope to finesse the separation they make inevitable – the separation between the realist novel's wilfully "rounded" world, and chaotically unauthored contemporary reality?

A more detailed discussion of *Brothers Karamazov* lies beyond the scope of this essay. However, holding *Brothers Karamazov* or *Crime and Punishment* [Prestuplenie i nakazanie, 1866] in mind together with *The Adolescent* clarifies how completely Dostoevsky was committed to his indirect methods of characterization in his second-to-last novel – and how firmly his legacy is identified with other novels that actually put them *less* fully into practice. At its most experimental, his approach to the novel genre meant replacing the imitation of "embodiedness" with the longing for it. The revolutionary form of Dostoevsky's works undoubtedly outstrips the author's conservative nostalgia. But the structuring presence of nostalgia within those works should not be ignored.[35] Much as Dostoevsky deplored the absence of established forms in his chronicles of "real men of the Russian majority," many of his novels seem, when compared with *The Adolescent*, to take a more conventional approach to characterization than has often been acknowledged. When the barrier of the "rounded" novelistic world truly is eroded, as it is in *The Adolescent*, the prevailing mood is not triumph at an illusion overcome, but hope for its eventual restoration as reality.

Of course, it would be fruitless to hold that only one of these sides of Dostoevsky's approach to characterization and the novel is relevant – either the adventure of seemingly authorless fictional being, or the fantasy of the author's redemptive rediscovery. Nevertheless, the persistent dream of mimetic embodiment in Dostoevsky reveals something about the enduring source of the realist novel's power over its reader. In particular, it calls into question the vision (dominant since the symbolists, and especially since Bakhtin) of Dostoevsky's characters as the point where the novel genre comes closest to crossing into the reader's life. Dostoevsky himself holds out a vision of realist characters not as the most detachable elements of the novel, but rather as that which will always reach towards a "body," the stable textual presence that comes from the interchange between fictional hero and fictional world. On this view, characters at their most seductively embodied are woven into the act of reading – an act that separates them from the rest of what Bakhtin calls "the ongoing event of current life [prodolzhaiushcheesia i seichas sobytiie zhizni]."[36] The Dostoevsky who hopes to overcome the boundary between authored novel and created world challenges the Dostoevsky who makes characters look autonomous from their texts. Neither impulse may triumph, but equally, neither vanishes. Instead, they ensure one another's perpetual homelessness: the foundling plot of the novel, whose dimensions Dostoevsky ingeniously and anxiously explored.

NOTES

1 "Béla Balázs and His Detractors," 1918. Quoted and translated from Hungarian into German in G. Lukács, *Dostojewski: Notizen und Entwürfe*, ed. J.C. Nyiri (Budapest: Akademiai Kiado, 1985), 27–8. All English translations in the chapter are mine unless stated otherwise.

2 See the introductory note to the first journal publication of *The Theory of the Novel* in 1916, as discussed in Galin Tihanov, "Ethics and Revolution: Lukács's Responses to Dostoevskii," *Modern Language Review* 94, no. 3 (July 1999): 610 ff., and Galin Tihanov, *The Master and the Slave: Lukács, Bakhtin, and the Ideas of Their Time* (Oxford: Clarendon, 2000), 165–87.

3 Georg Lukács, *The Theory of the Novel*, trans. Anna Bostock (Cambridge, MA: MIT Press, 1971), 152. Further citations to this edition appear parenthetically in the text.

4 Lukács, *Dostojewski*, 42–62. In her chapter in this volume, Anna Berman takes up the theme of Dostoevsky's "missing marriage plots," and particularly his characters' failure to continue their family lines by producing legitimate children.

5 The immediate context for Merezhkovsky's reflection is the phrase "and to my little chicken [*i tsyplenochku*]" at the end of Fyodor Pavlovich's note for Grushenka in *Brothers Karamazov*. D.S. Merezhkovskii, *L. Tolstoi i Dostoevskii*, ed. E.A. Andrushchenko (Moscow: Nauka, 2000), 144. On the fundamental influence of his treatise on Dostoevsky criticism in Russia and Europe, see for example G.M. Fridlender, "D.S. Merezhkovskii i Dostoevskii," in *Dostoevskii: Materialy i isledovaniia* 10 (1992): 9–14; V.A. Keldysh, "Nasledie Dostoevskogo i russkaia mysl' porubezhnoi epokhi," in *Sviaz' vremen: Problemy preemstvennosti v russkoi literature kontsa XIX-nachala XX v.*, ed. V.A. Keldysh (Moscow: Nasledie, 1992), esp. 91–3; and Z.A. Feher, "Georg Lukács's Role in Dostoevskii's European Reception at the Turn of the Century" (PhD diss.,University of California, Los Angeles, 1978), 87n10.

6 V.I. Ivanov, *Sobranie sochinenii*, 4 vols., ed. D.V. Ivanov and O. Deshart (Brussels: Foyer Oriental Chrétien, 1971–87), vol. 4, 400.

7 On Bakhtin's knowledge and "appropriation" of Lukács's *Theory of the Novel*, see Tihanov, *The Master and the Slave*, 11–13.

8 Mikhail Bakhtin, *Problems of Dostoevsky's Poetics*, trans. Caryl Emerson (Minneapolis: University of Minnesota Press, 1984), 101–2 (translation modified); 1963 additions to the 1929 version in brackets. Cf. M.M. Bakhtin, *Sobranie sochinenii*, ed. S.G. Bocharov and N.I. Nikolaev, 7 vols. (Moscow: Russkie slovari, 1996–), vol. 2, 72–3. For the parallel passage in Bakhtin, *Problemy poetiki Dostoevskogo*, see vol. 6, 115. Further citations to this edition appear parenthetically (by volume and page) in the text.

9 See especially chapter 2 of Bakhtin's Dostoevsky book, where he writes of the Dostoevskian hero's "non-coincidence with himself" (6:70). In the 1941 essay "Epic and Novel," Bakhtin extended this "surplus of humanness" (3:640) to all novelistic characters.

10 Vladimir Nabokov makes an eager twentieth-century spokesman for this position: "Dostoevski characterizes his people through situation, through ethical matters, their psychological reactions, their inside ripples ... One feels that he does not see his characters physically, that they are merely puppets, remarkable, fascinating puppets plunged into the moving stream of the author's ideas." See Vladimir Nabokov, *Lectures on Russian Literature*, ed. Fredson Bowers (London: Picador, 1981), 104, 129.

11 I borrow these terms from Shlomith Rimmon-Kenan, who opposes characterization by "direct definition" (through overt "naming of qualities" by an authoritative narrator) to characterization by "indirect presentation" (through the narration of action, speech, appearance, etc.). She builds on work of Joseph Ewan, unfortunately available only in Hebrew. See Shlomith Rimmon-Kenan, *Narrative Fiction*, 2nd ed. (London and New York: Methuen, 2002), chapter 5.

12 For a different approach to the question of how Dostoevsky creates an impression of his characters as "embodied beings," see Sarah J. Young's essay in this volume. Young shows how Dostoevsky uses references to characters' sense perceptions to construct their embodied selves as well as the physical world around them. However, she argues that Dostoevsky "uses embodied characters to make the fantastic and imaginary more real" and that corporeal "instability" is key to the work of his novels. Here, I focus instead on the author's (and characters') vexed reach toward the solidity, vividness, and narrative authority that are more conventionally associated with realist illusion.

13 For a summary of this frequent criticism, see Keldysh, "Nasledie Dostoevskogo," 77–88.

14 I cite Dostoevsky's critics from the commentary notes to *The Idiot* in F.M. Dostoevskii, *Polnoe sobranie sochinenii v tridtsati tomakh*, 30 vols., ed. G.M. Fridlender et al. (Leningrad: Nauka, 1972–90), vol. 9, 410–20. Further citations to this edition appear parenthetically (by volume and page) in the text.

15 *Iskra*, May 1868; Dostoevskii, *PSS*, vol. 9, 414.

16 *Sankt-Peterburgskie Vedomosti*, September 1868; Dostoevskii, *PSS*, vol. 9, 415.

17 V.G. Avseenko, "Ocherki tekushchei literatury," *Russkii mir*, 1875, no. 55. Quoted in A. S. Dolinin, *Poslednie romany Dostoevskogo* (Moscow: Sovetskii pisatel', 1963), 197–8.

18 I am drawing on Robert Louis Jackson, *Dostoevsky's Quest for Form: A Study of His Philosophy of Art*, 2nd ed. (Bloomington, IN: Physsardt, 1978), 40–123. A

particularly important text for Jackson is Dostoevsky's 1861 essay "Mr. —bov and the Question of Art [Gospodin —bov i vopros ob iskusstve]," which notably focuses the question of artistic integrity through the question of mimetic characterization; see Dostoevskii, *PSS*, vol. 18, 89–98.

19 Jackson, *Quest*, 108–18; see I.A. Goncharov, *Sobranie sochinenii*, 8 vols. (Moscow: Gosizdat. khudozhestvennoi literatury, 1952–5), vol. 8, 456–8 and 459–61.

20 Fyodor Dostoevsky, *The Adolescent*, trans. Richard Pevear and Larissa Volokhonsky (New York: Knopf, 2003), 6. Subsequent citations to this translation of *The Adolescent* are parenthetical in the text following the *PSS*.

21 On Julien Sorel, see Peter Brooks, *Reading for the Plot* (New York: Knopf, 1984), 64; on Dickens's foundlings, see J. Hillis Miller, *Charles Dickens: The World of his Novels* (Cambridge, MA: Harvard University Press, 1958), 251.

22 On realist narrative's dependence on the family line (and modernist narrative's subversions), see Patricia D. Tobin, *Time and the Novel: The Genealogical Imperative* (Princeton, NJ: Princeton University Press, 1978).

23 Kate Holland offers a pivotal discussion of illegitimacy, narrative, and genre in *The Adolescent*, with which my account frequently intersects: Kate Holland, *The Novel in the Age of Disintegration: Dostoevsky and the Problem of Genre in the 1870s* (Evanston, IL: Northwestern University Press, 2013), 101–30. *The Adolescent* has long been read as Dostoevsky's most direct engagement with the legacy of the Russian novel, and especially with Tolstoy; see A.L. Bem, "Khudozhestvennaia polemika s Tolstym (K ponimaniiu 'Podrostka')," *O Dostoevskom*, vol. 3, 192–214 (Petropolis, 1936); K. Mochul'skii, *Dostoevskii: Zhizn' i tvorchestvo* (Paris: YMCA Press, 1947), 409 ff.; and others. Suzanne Fusso further illuminates *The Adolescent* as Dostoevsky's dialogue with his own early work in *Discovering Sexuality in Dostoevsky* (Evanston, IL: Northwestern University Press, 2006), 62–8.

24 P.Ia. Chaadaev, *Polnoe sobranie sochinenii i izbrannyie pis'ma*, ed. Z.A. Kamenskii et al., 2 vols. (Moscow: Nauka, 1991), vol. 1, 92.

25 On *The Adolescent* as Bildungsroman, see E.I. Semenov, *Roman Dostoevskogo Podrostok: Problematika i zhanr* (Leningrad: Nauka, 1979). The argument has recently been renewed by Lina Steiner, *For Humanity's Sake: The Bildungsroman in Russian Culture* (Toronto: University of Toronto Press, 2011), 135–73; Holland, *The Novel in the Age of Disintegration*; and others.

26 See Alex Woloch, *The One vs. the Many: Minor Characters and the Space of the Protagonist in the Novel* (Princeton, NJ: Princeton University Press, 2003), 13–14 ff.

27 For an exhaustive discussion, see Edmund Heier, *Literary Portraiture in Nineteenth-Century Russian Prose* (Cologne: Böhlau-Verlag, 1993), chapter 7.

28 The kaleidoscope image is developed in T.V. Tsiv'ian, "O strukture vremeni i prostranstva v romane Dostoevskogo 'Podrostok,'" *Russian Literature* 3 (1976): 243.

29 Roland Barthes, *S/Z*, trans. R. Howard (New York: Hill and Wang, 1974), 67.

30 As Peter Jensen has pointed out, Arkady's relationship to Versilov parodies that of an omniscient narrator to his protagonist; we see Arkady "in pursuit of the scattered potential fragments" of Versilov's biography. See P.A. Jensen, "Paradoksal'nost' avtorstva (u) Dostoevskogo," in *Paradoksy russkoi literatury*, ed. V. Markovich and V. Shmid (St Petersburg: Inapress, 2001), 231.

31 For two very different versions of this argument, see Holland, *Age of Disintegration*, 129–30; and T.A. Kasatkina, "Roman F.M. Dostoevskogo 'Podrostok': 'Ideia' geroia i ideia avtora," *Voprosy literatury*, no. 1 (2004): 181–212.

32 Jacques Derrida, "Plato's Pharmacy," in *Dissemination*, trans. Barbara Johnson (Chicago: University of Chicago Press, 1981), 63–171.

33 On this vision, see Robert Bird, "Refiguring the Russian Type: Dostoevsky and the Limits of Realism," in *A New Word on* The Brothers Karamazov, ed. Robert Louis Jackson (Evanston, IL: Northwestern University Press, 2004), 17–30.

34 On Tolstoy and "breed-force," see S. Bocharov, *Roman L. Tolstogo 'Voina i mir'* (Moscow: Khudozhestvennaia literatura, 1963), 89–100.

35 For a different take on the tension between Dostoevsky's conservative and radical impulses, see Kate Holland's discussion in this volume of failed duel plots in his late novels.

36 "Roman, kak literaturnyi zhanr," 3:634; see Mikhail Bakhtin, "Epic and Novel," in *The Dialogic Imagination*, ed. Michael Holquist and trans. Caryl Emerson and Michael Holquist (Austin: University of Texas Press, 1981), 31.

10 Sovereignty and the Novel: Dostoevsky's Political Theology

ILYA KLIGER

"The Only Entirely Social Art Form"

In theoretical work on the modern novel, there exists something like a consensus characterizing it as a symbolic form rooted in the imaginaries of civil society. Assumed from the start is the existence of autonomous private persons, endowed with certain characteristics (the givens of physical appearance and constitution, social standing, mental abilities, psychological traits, etc.), engaged in specific pursuits (of wealth, status, artistic or romantic fulfilment, etc.), and interacting with each other according to a set of norms. Where the very notion of the autonomous individual comes from, what supplies the range of worthwhile pursuits, how the norms are agreed upon and established – such questions ostensibly lie outside the scope of the novel's imagination. The novel presupposes the social life-world as a given and leaves the act of its making, the constitution of the polity itself, in oblivion. This is, more or less, what Hannah Arendt intends by characterizing the modern novel as "the only entirely social art form."[1] The political, which she understands as the site where fundamental decisions about human togetherness are made, remains for the novel a thoroughly alien problematic.

Literary scholars, scholars of the Western European novel in particular, seem to agree with this diagnosis. Margaret Cohen, for example, has described the dominant novelistic tradition in nineteenth-century France as coming into existence through the foreclosure of the political-constitutional dilemmas explored by the earlier generation of female writers of sentimental fiction.[2] Nancy Armstrong has extrapolated from the history of the British novel the principle that novelistic narratives draw on scenarios of conflict between individual desire and social morality and thus contribute to the sort of education – of the hero and the reader alike – that "does not impose the [political] general will on individuals but rather shapes individuals' wills to regulate their own desires."[3]

Still more forcefully, Fredric Jameson has argued that European realism is committed to an implicit conservatism precisely insofar as it leaves out political considerations. Realism's object is the world as it is, at least at the level of its basic social structure. "The very choice of the form itself," Jameson concludes, "is a professional endorsement of the status quo, a loyalty oath in the very apprenticeship to this aesthetic." Political concerns, questions about foundation and the common good as such, are either dismissed or treated with "satiric hostility," which is "the time-honored mode of dealing novelistically with political troublemakers."[4]

Underlying these and similar views on the modern novel is the work of social and political thinkers grappling with the process of what Arendt has designated as "the rise of the social."[5] Antonio Gramsci's notion of "hegemony," Louis Althusser's account of ideological "interpellation," and Michel Foucault's work on disciplinary techniques of power – all strive to register the emerging modes of subtle production and accommodation of individuals by means less of direct and visible force than of spontaneous and ostensibly non-coercive social interactions. Foucault's distinction between the regimes of sovereignty and discipline has been particularly productive for theorists and historians of the modern European novel since at least D.A. Miller's intervention in *The Novel and the Police* (1988). According to Miller, the nineteenth-century European novel in particular represents (and perpetuates) the world where subtle disciplinary power has triumphed over its spectacular, sovereign counterpart. "The sheer pettiness of discipline's coercions," he writes, "tends to keep them from scrutiny, and the diffusion of discipline's operations precludes locating them in an attackable centre. Disciplinary power constitutively mobilizes a tactic of tact: it is the policing power that never passes for such but is either invisible or visible only under cover of other, nobler or simply bland intentionalities (to educate, to cure, to produce, to defend)." Correspondingly, the novel tends to eschew depictions of centralized, clearly localizable and temporally concentrated acts of spectacular violence or coercion in favour of "a hidden and devious discipline [...] defined in terms of the spatial extension of its networks and the temporal deployment of its intrigues."[6]

Franco Moretti articulates a like-minded view, alluding to Gramsci's distinction between the subtly hegemonic civil society and the openly coercive state. For Moretti, the European Bildungsroman occludes the themes and logics of the state, because the latter "embodies a 'mechanical' and 'abstract' form of social cohesion, intrinsically remote and foreign to the countless articulations of everyday life: this is why its exercise of power appears of necessity to be an outside coercion, a force inclined by its very nature to be arbitrary, violent." By contrast, civil society provides proper material for novelistic exploration because it is "the sphere of 'spontaneous' and concrete bonds. Its authority merges with everyday activities and relationships, exercising itself in ways that are natural and unnoticeable."[7]

Moretti dedicates a separate essay to exploring the consequences of the elective affinity between civil society and the novel by contrast to a similar correlation between tragedy and the state. In his account, the opposing orientations of the novel to everyday social functioning and of tragedy to the imaginary of state crisis produce the following set of corresponding dichotomies: a genuine interest in the details and nuances of everyday life and a high valuation of its enjoyments vs. the sense that simply by being alive, we become entangled in myriad moral compromises and accumulate crushing guilt; focus on the routine, normal course of affairs vs. fascination with the striking exceptional event; a commitment to negotiation and compromise vs. their indignant refusal; an enthusiasm for the vicissitudes of (financial) exchange vs. the fascination with the way money (both its acquisition and its loss) can function as a test of who one really is; the proliferation of polite, potentially endless conversation vs. emphatic, performative speech as the medium for dramatic conflict.[8]

Political Theology in the Siberian Odes

Even a cursory acquaintance with Dostoevsky's novels is sufficient to convince one that the paradigm sketched out above is honoured only in the breach. To go down the list and show how the Russian novelist inverts each of these ostensibly novelistic features would amount to restating some of the best-rehearsed commonplaces of Dostoevsky scholarship: the temporality of his texts is one precisely of crisis; his conversation is far from polite; compromise is, at crucial times, impossible or ignoble; money is interesting primarily as a test of the truth about the self; and exception is more interesting than the norm. Thus, Moretti's rudimentary literary-historical model would seem to suggest that something like the starker problematics of state power (its legitimacy or illegitimacy, stability or instability, etc.) are encoded in the social imaginary of Dostoevsky's fiction, turning it into a zone of resistance or a blind spot vis-à-vis the dominant tradition of thinking about the novel as a socially symbolic form.[9]

It is not difficult to see why this might be the case. In the broadly Western European context, throughout the eighteenth and nineteenth centuries, the state tends to retreat from the position of privileged addressee and supreme overseer of literary production to become its distant legislator (e.g., through the establishment of intellectual property and authors' ownership rights, through more or less stringent censorship laws, etc.).

In Russia, this process remains evidently incomplete well into the nineteenth century.[10] Here, the direct and at times spectacular exercise of coercion was a perpetual feature of the relationship between Russian authors and the state. And I would suggest that this articulation of the lifeworld of cultural producers to the figure of the sovereign is worth taking seriously as a factor that can influence literary work at the level of form and genre, and can thus account for the inversion of categories which Dostoevsky's texts among others perform upon a model like Moretti's.

Put another way, the relationship between Russia's cultural elite and the state was structured by the perpetual possibility of the kind of dramatic encounter with sovereign power experienced by the young Dostoevsky as he stood in a group of political prisoners condemned to execution by the firing squad. Examining the official documents linked to the execution, Leonid Grossman concludes: "The ritual of the execution presupposed a most elaborate preparation of the ceremony, truly reminiscent of a large-scale staged production [...] No wonder that the correspondence between the highest ranked members of the government about the impending execution at times resembles the theatre director's copy of an unwieldy theatre play."[11] The exercise of power in the form of a public spectacle – the spectacle, furthermore, of the taking and subsequent giving of life – belongs to the regime of sovereignty as it has been delineated with particular starkness by Foucault: "a power which, in the absence of continual supervision, sought a renewal of its effect in the spectacle of its individual manifestations [and] was recharged in the ritual display of its reality as 'super-power.'"[12] Richard Wortman has referred to this type of spectacle as a "scenario of power," a symbolically laden ceremonial display of monarchical might, casting the ruler as a figure transcending everyday norms and normative judgments. Within Russian autocracy, writes Wortman, "the exercise of power and the representation of the monarch were reciprocal processes: absolute rule sustained the image of a transcendent monarch, which in turn warranted the untrammeled exercise of power."[13]

The script of the 1849 execution famously and fatefully contained an additional twist: the autocrat's last-moment granting of life through a commutation of the sentence. Sovereign power is the power "to take life or let live,"[14] and one might argue that only pardon transfers the relationship between the sovereign and the offender beyond the rule of law altogether into the sphere of an excruciatingly personal contact, revealing for the first time the true character of their relationship, its immediacy and directness. There exists a long tradition of political thought on the sovereign pardon,[15] but perhaps the most immediately relevant instance of such an act – relevant both because we can be sure it was known to Dostoevsky and because it appears directly in the dramatic shape of a "scenario of power" – can be found in Pierre Corneille's tragedy *Cinna or the Clemency of Caesar Augustus* [Cinna ou la Clémence d'Auguste, 1643]. In an 1840 letter to his brother, Dostoevsky raves about the play, and specifically about the moment when the Emperor Augustus forgives the political co-conspirators Cinna and Emilie for plotting to assassinate him:

> "Je suis maître de moi comme de l'univers;
> Je suis, je veux l'être. O siècles, o mémoire,
> Conservez à jamais ma dernière victoire!
> Je triomphe aujourd'hui du plus juste courroux
> De qui les souvenir puisse aller jusqua'à vous.
> Soyons amis, Cinna, c'est moi qui t'en convie ..."[16]

> I'm master of myself as of the world;
> I am. I wish to be. O days to come,
> Preserve for ever my last victory!
> I triumph over the most righteous wrath
> That ever can be handed down to you.
> Cinna, let us be friends. This I entreat ..."[17]

"Only offended angels speak this way," comments Dostoevsky.[18] The logic underlying this scene of Octavian's *générosité* [magnanimity, *velikodushie*] begins with the proclamation of self-mastery, the mastery over one's rage, even if it is most righteous. The staging of self-mastery signifies the existence of a principle that supersedes the offended individual himself. The rebels are pardoned for the sake of the stability of the state, which is thus placed beyond the persons of Octavian and Cinna. Or, put another way, pardon marks the site other than the person of the ruler himself at which sovereignty is ultimately located. In showing himself able – unlike the rebels – to act on behalf of the state, the sovereign proves himself worthy of his sovereignty and eminently superior to those he pardons. Hence the Empress Livia's concluding monologue asserting Octavian's place among the gods; hence also Dostoevsky's comparison of the pardoning Augustus to an angel. We will have an opportunity to return to this scenario later in the discussion. For now, it is sufficient to conclude that the staging of both execution and commutation (as a kind of qualified pardon, at least when it comes to the life itself of the accused) is readable as a paradigmatic scenario of sovereign power, asserting the sovereign's divine-like superiority to the subject, their ontological incommensurability – even (especially!) at the moment of their most intimate encounter.

To be sure, Dostoevsky's confrontation with sovereign power at its most distilled does not end with the encounter on Semyonovsky Square. It continues rather, changing media from a carefully scripted and staged ritual to the patriotic ode, embodied in two extant poems Dostoevsky composed in Siberia. Written at the end of the period of penal servitude, the poems – one composed on the occasions of the birthday of the recently widowed Empress Alexandra Fyodorovna, the other for the coronation of Alexander II – are addressed to members of the ruling family in the hopes that they might open the way for him to advance in the ranks and ultimately return to publishing.[19] We have two texts, then, whose proper "literary environment"[20] might be thought of as obsolete, invoking court literature and state patronage – a regime in which serious works are called upon to acclaim the majesty of the ruler.

The odes contain multiple images of royal charisma, consistently conflating the stately with the divine. The first poem, addressing the widowed empress, draws on the high classicist lexical register, framing the image of the recently deceased tsar with the help of the traditional topoi of divinization. Nicholas I is here presented as the solar deity, the fearsome archangel with a fiery sword; his grave is depicted as holy or saintly; his deeds are immortal; he is a god who is known through his works ["Kuda ni vzglianem my – vezde, povsiudu on!"]; he is an object of conversionary faith on the part of the formerly "schismatic" and "blind" lyrical persona ("V kogo uveroval raskol'nik i slepets"). Finally, towards the end of the poem, the heir to the throne makes an appearance as Christ ("Khrani togo, kto nam nisposlan na spasen'e!").[21] The second poem continues in the same vein. Here, Christ appears as "our tsar in a crown of thorns" ("nash tsar' v ventse ternovom"), while both newly crowned ruler and Christian saviour are united in their capacity – sorely needed by the lyrical persona – for "all-forgiveness" ("vseproshchen'e").[22]

Dostoevsky draws from the vast depository of politico-theological scenarios and topoi, at times refracted through the tradition of courtly poetry going back at least to the beginning of the eighteenth century. As Boris Uspensky and Viktor Zhivov have shown in their classical study of the sacralization of monarchical power in Russia, up until the fifteenth century, the tsar could be compared to God only figuratively, by way of rhetorical parallelism, underscoring "the infinite difference between the early tsar and the Heavenly Tsar."[23] The eschatological framework of the doctrine of "Moscow as Third Rome," emerging in the wake of the fall of Byzantium and the Florentine Union, resulted in the ascription to the ruler of the only remaining Orthodox kingdom of a messianic role. This accrual of charismatic power to the monarch allows later rulers to project even (especially!) their excesses as confirmation of their superhuman status. Anticipating one of the prominent images of royal charisma to which Dostoevsky resorts in his Siberian odes, the epithet "righteous sun" ("pravednoe solntse"), formerly used in liturgy with exclusive reference to Christ, is now applied to both legitimate rulers and pretenders to the throne. In fact, according to Uspensky and Zhivov, the process of sacralization of monarchical power triggers the emergence of the very problematic of pretendership: "The conception of the tsar's special charismatic power fundamentally altered the traditional notion, as the juxtaposition of just and unjust tsar now became that of genuine and false tsar."[24] Unlike the question of the tsar's justice, the question of authenticity cannot be resolved with reference to a pre-existing independent standard (e.g., adherence to divine commandments) but becomes a matter of sheer faith. Paradoxically, the secularizing reign of Peter I emerges as the apogee of this process, with the emperor now frequently referred to as Saviour ("Spas") or Christ. This could not but be perceived as blasphemy by the more traditional segments of the population.[25]

The Siberian odes then testify to the fact that Dostoevsky has thoroughly assimilated the imaginaries of sovereignty as they developed within the local tradition of political theology. As such, they continue what, at least on the scale of Dostoevsky's biography, began on the day of the execution: the unfolding of the scenario elevating the ruler to great charismatic heights through the display of mastery over life and death as well as through odic acclamation and sacralization. Of course, given the accumulated "genre memory" of odic address to the monarch, it is not altogether surprising to find a robust substratum of political-theological motifs structuring Dostoevsky's Siberian poems. But how would such a substratum enter into and interact with the generically hostile environment of the novel? Before addressing this question, and with an eye to adumbrating its stakes and terms, let us revisit briefly the main junctures of the argument so far:

1 The consensus critical view is that the genre of the modern novel tends to draw upon and reinforce the social imaginaries linked to the workings of civil society rather than the state. This entails focus on the spontaneous aggregation of individual wills and on impersonal/disciplinary rather than on personal/coercive modes of constraint.

2 It is not necessary to belabour the fact that Dostoevsky's fiction tends not only to flout but in fact to invert the narrative logics attributed to the novel by currently ascendant theories (as witness the particularly stark contrast with Moretti's description of the genre in "The Moment of Truth").

3 This raises the possibility that Dostoevsky's novels experience the warping effects of social imaginaries associated with the state. Such an affinity – at first glance certainly rather odd – would seem to be more justified within the Russian novelistic tradition, given the state's unusually active role in the literary field through much of the nineteenth century as well as Dostoevsky's own dramatic inclusion into the monarchy's scenarios of power.

4 Dostoevsky's Siberian odes both participate in these scenarios and thematize them, deploying an array of topoi from the tradition of Russian political theology. Could the elements of a political theology derived from the poems help us specify the logic whereby the imaginaries arising within the regime of sovereignty may produce a kind of mutation within the novel form? This is, most broadly understood, the wager of the discussion that follows.

The Sovereign in the Novel

In the remainder of the chapter I will attempt a brief reading of *Crime and Punishment* [Prestuplenie i nakazanie, 1866] and *Demons* [Besy, 1872] – the two late novels by Dostoevsky where the political-theological problematic is most clearly elaborated. In broad terms, both novels fall into what might be called "the Life of the Great Sinner" paradigm. *The Life of the Great Sinner* [Zhitie velikogo greshnika] is a provisional title for a novel Dostoevsky planned out in 1869–70. The novel remained unwritten, but the notes proved to contain something like a meta-plot, a mythos, for the last three novels he would complete as well as, anachronistically, for the earlier *Crime and Punishment*. The central plot arc of this quasi-hagiographic tale consists in the account of a turbulent sinner's path to moral regeneration.[26] At the core of the narrative is the notion that one's capacity to fall low in sin indicates a comparable ability to rise high in righteousness.[27] Thus, a certain elemental strength ("a raw, animal strength" [9:128]) emerges as a more fundamental category than sin or virtue themselves. The Great Sinner has been "elected" for greatness; greatness is his natural endowment. The slightly paradoxical ring of the phrase itself – "*great* sinner" – indicates that ethical considerations don't altogether overrule ontological ones: the positive connotations of the adjective are not entirely drowned out by the negative denotation of the noun. Conversion from sin to virtue, from blindness to faith, may or may not take place (it seems to at the end of *Crime and Punishment*, doesn't at the end of *Demons*), but for the time being, we are presented with a series of dramatizations and images of charisma, the aura of superior power, which allows the Great Sinner to say, in Dostoevsky's notes to the novel: "I myself am God" (9:130).

The representational priority of ontological categories (greatness/ mediocrity, power/weakness, intensity/tepidness, etc.) over ethical ones (virtue/sin, probity/corruption, kindness/cruelty, etc.) is central to a certain strain within political theology.[28] According to this logic, Uspensky and Zhivov write, the sovereign's "excesses may serve as the mark of charismatic exceptionalism."[29] The question of the ruler's justice is supplanted by the problem of his or her identity; identity is established through the process of (self-)representation on the part of the sovereign as well as faith and acclamation on the part of the subject. The question of the sovereign's identity cannot be resolved once and for all according to a pre-existing standard (i.e., of ethical or just rule). Thus, Peter may appear as Christ and Antichrist, god and idol at once.[30] This way of grasping the stakes of representation in Dostoevsky's late fiction would seem to reinforce – from a different direction – Mikhail Bakhtin's controversial claim for the priority of spatial over temporal categories in his poetics.[31] What Bakhtin calls finalization, which relies on plot to establish once and for all the identity of the hero – is he the real thing or a pretender? – would, in this account, too, withdraw to the background, giving way to an emphasis on moments of arrested time, which function not only as a stage for dialogic exchange but also, perhaps still more prominently, as dramatizations of charisma.

Both Raskolnikov and Stavrogin are endowed with such charisma, which accrues to them through scripts of exceptional, non-normative behaviour, stagings of enigmatic identity, scenarios of power over the lives of others, and striking outward appearance. The theme of sovereign rule is central to the novelistic trajectories of both. Raskolnikov tests himself against the paradigm of foundational politics, represented by the figure of the great lawgiver. The lawgiver is at the same time a criminal, who, in introducing new laws, spurns the laws of "the fathers." The lawgiver – Raskolnikov mentions Lycurgus, Solon, Muhammad, and Napoleon – acts from the place of normative exception, and so his actions invariably carry ambiguous ethical valences, depending on whether one views them from the point of view of their predecessors or successors. As sovereign, the lawgiver transcends ethics altogether and manifests himself – in a mode that mixes ontology with aesthetics – as a kind of higher, more intense being. This zone of indistinction between crime and the foundational act is illuminated during Raskolnikov's walk to the apartment of the old pawnbroker he intends to murder. Here, he entertains plans for expanding the Summer Garden to include the Field of Mars and the garden of the Mikhailovsky Palace. This plan happens to coincide precisely with Peter I's original design of the city. Peter, the one "lawgiver" whose name does not make it to Raskolnikov's list, repeatedly appears in the notes to the novel in the guise of "the Dutchman" as the model for the kind of world-transformative power Raskolnikov strives to possess ("I need power [...] I want everything that I see to be different [...] (the Dutchman Peter)" [7:153]).[32] Within the imaginary regime of sovereignty, the conflation between violent crime and the layout of the imperial capital ceases to sound like a mere detail from criminal psychopathology, emerging instead as yet another element in the coding of the crime as a foundational political act.[33]

In a similar vein, the entire central intrigue of *Demons*, as conceived by Petrusha Verkhovensky, hinges on whether or not Stavrogin will agree to be installed as Russia's new tsar once the "show-house" (balagan) of contemporary Russian society finally collapses. "It's nothing for you to sacrifice life, your own or someone else's," Petrusha acclaims, extolling Stavrogin's natural charisma. "You are a leader, you are a sun, and I am your worm" (10:324; 419).[34] At another point in the text, the ardent nationalist Shatov cries in disappointment: "And this is Nikolai Stavrogin's great exploit!" (10:193; 243). To this Stavrogin replies, anticipating Petrusha's later acclamations: "Forgive me [...] but you seem to look upon me as some sort of sun" [Izvinite [...] no vy, kazhetsia, smotrite na menia kak na kakoe-to solntse, a na sebia kak na kakuiu-to bukashku sravnitel'no so mnoi] (10:193; 243).

The royal emblem of the sun, the sovereign as a solar deity, already familiar to us from the Siberian odes, also appears in *Crime and Punishment* during the third conversation between Raskolnikov and the investigator Porfiry Petrovich. Urging Raskolnikov to embrace punishment, the investigator exclaims: "What matter if no one will see you for a long time? [...] Become a sun, and everyone will see you. The sun must be the sun first of all" (6:352; 460).[35] Thus, Raskolnikov is not alone in drawing on the register of sovereign charisma for means of self-definition. His ostensible nemesis, too, despite layers of novelistic equivocation and irony, sees him as an extraordinary man.[36]

Both protagonists are further associated with the figure of the tsar as it is delineated in contemporary folklore. Petrusha wishes to install Stavrogin as the newly revealed "Hidden One," the legendary figure of the legitimate monarch who has miraculously escaped his courtiers' attempt to assassinate him and will soon reveal himself as the people's legitimate ruler and redeemer.[37] In the context of the same speech, Petrusha identifies Stavrogin with yet another such figure, the folkloric Ivan Tsarevich. The same association appears in *Crime and Punishment*, when Raskolnikov is greeted at the police station at the end of the novel with the formula with which unclean powers greet Ivan Tsarevich (and other folk heroes) in fairytales: "Fee, fi, fo, fum, I smell the smell of a Russian man" (6:406; 527).

The charismatic aura with which the protagonists of the two novels are endowed is reinforced by Christological associations. Stavrogin's very name is derived from the Greek for "cross." Raskolnikov is linked to Christ explicitly in the notebooks to the novel as well as, more subtly, in the novel itself.[38] Less directly but perhaps more interestingly, the association comes through in the crucial passages depicting the reading of the Gospel story of the resurrection of Lazarus. Here, Raskolnikov is matched to several potential doubles: the "blind Jews" who come to believe in Christ at last; Lazarus, who is brought back from the dead; and finally Jesus, who allows Lazarus to die in order to be able to perform the greatest miracle of all by resurrecting him. As he says to his disciples: "For your sake I am glad I was not there [to prevent him from dying], so that you may [see the great deed of resurrection and] believe [in me]."[39] Raskolnikov operates within a parallel compulsion: to make it so that a death will have been worth it.

We have unmistakably before us, then, protagonists endowed with political-theological majesty. Thoroughly unsurprising in a patriotic ode or in a tragedy,[40] such an imaginary might be expected to trouble the more traditional representational strategies of the novel. One simple instance of such a troubled relationship between sovereignty and novelistic thematics can be detected at the level of Raskolnikov's motivations for the murder. Here, on the one hand, we have the assertion of godlike, sovereign power over life and death – a miraculous power whose deep-seated political-theological referent can be located at the point of convergence between the figures of Peter I and Christ. At stake here is the sovereign's assertion of the right to act beyond all constraints. On the other hand, the murder is also endowed with more mundane, more properly private or social motivations: his family's poverty, his sister's potentially disastrous betrothal, his need to make a career, certain contemporary ideas circulating in his cultural milieu, and so on. Thus, the central act of the novel is committed at the point of intersection between two symbolic regimes: the regime of sovereignty, asserting ultimate power over life and death in the name of the "new word," and focused on scenes of (self-)acclamation and (self-)doubt; and the regime of socialization, casting the crime and its aftermath as a sequence of social transgression, subsequent alienation, and eventual reintegration.

The second site at which the representational regime of sovereignty traverses the novelistic logics of social everydayness marks the distinction between the private and public domains. This is vividly rendered during the scene depicting an exchange between Raskolnikov and the police clerk Zamyotov. The two of them meet accidentally at a tavern, where Raskolnikov has stopped by to look for accounts of his own crime in newspapers. Zamyotov sits down next to him and starts a conversation. Raskolnikov taunts the clerk while gradually implicating himself until he comes close to admitting his guilt:

> A terrible word was trembling on his lips [...] another moment and it would jump out; another moment and it would let go; another moment and it would be spoken!
> "And what if it was I who killed the old woman and Lizaveta?" he said suddenly – and came to his senses.
> Zamyotov looked wildly at him and went as white as a sheet. (6:128; 165)

It is possible to read this scene, among similar others in which Raskolnikov brings himself to the edge of exposure, as an index of his conflicted desire to be apprehended. According to this interpretation – which arises by default within the horizon of novelistic psycho-social normativity – having committed the crime, Raskolnikov cannot bear the weight of the guilt and the isolation it imposes on him and begins to seek out exposure and punishment. The trouble with this interpretation is not only that Raskolnikov's feelings of guilt are explicitly ruled out (6:417; 543); the deeper issue is that it covers up the construction of the episode as a kind of scenario of power, in which a witness is called upon to gaze spellbound at the hero, who flickeringly manifests himself as a godlike figure with mastery over life and death; no wonder this profane theophany makes the witness look "wildly" and go "white as a sheet." In other words, Raskolnikov's act of self-revelation is doubly emplotted. On the one hand, we have a violation of the law committed by a private person – and this must remain hidden if the protagonist is to avoid getting caught. On the other hand, we have the crime as the pivotal point in a certain scenario of power – the sovereign's power "to take life and let live" – which must by definition be performed in the open, publicly establishing the identity of the actor through the act. Within the psychological code, we might say that the crime thus conceived produces in the protagonist the contradictory desire at once to remain hidden and, not so much to get caught, as to always be seen.[41]

The interaction of these two regimes (sovereignty and socialization) forms the dramatic kernel of the three extended conversations between Raskolnikov and Porfiry Petrovich. The encounters trace the investigator's struggle first to understand and then to realign the very structure of the protagonist's subjectivity, including, and perhaps most prominently, his sense of time. In Foucault's terms, Porfiry appears here as a paradigmatic "disciplinarian," less concerned with apprehending the criminal than with observing and trying to understand him, less driven to establish his formal identity than to get to the core of his way of thinking, less preoccupied with punishment than with correction and reform. Put another way, the investigator anchors the techniques and voices the values traditionally understood as novelistic: psychic transparency (to the omniscient gaze of the author/reader), malleability under the pressure of social interactions, openness in biographical time, and so on. Meanwhile, the protagonist adheres to a set of incommensurable imaginaries, associated with the regime of sovereignty: a vision of the subject as a mysterious source of exceptional, norm-destroying deeds, deeds that are on display for public viewing and acclamation (hence, the profound humiliation of having to hide) and thus establish, test, and fortify the identity of the doer.[42] Equally telling in this respect are the agonists' competing notions of identity in time. Here Porfiry is once again on the side of the novelistic impulse to see individuals as relatively mobile and fluid, insisting that confession and imprisonment would not empty Raskolnikov's life of meaning. For the investigator, the double murder, in other words, is only one among the many acts Raskolnikov will perform. For Raskolnikov himself, by contrast, the crime is *the* act, the moment of truth, the ordeal of his calling to law-giving greatness. Here, identity is given once and for all; it may be tested, but not changed.[43]

Somewhat schematically, then, we might say that the titular crime of the novel, and the enigma of identity to which it gives narrative foundation, can be specified as a locus of generic interference, internalizing the mutually contradictory imaginaries of disciplinary sociality on the one hand and sovereignty on the other. The protagonist is both ordinary, socially uprooted, novelistic; and extraordinary, endowed with a political-theological aura. Here, the traditional nineteenth-century novelistic motif that might be designated as "the young man in the city" is traversed by what might be regarded as the "alien" motif of "the sun of righteousness." The latter carries with it a set of distinct narrative logics, such as moment of truth, scene of acclamation, scenario of power, dualistic and ambiguous (rather than fluid) identity, etc.

Narratives of sovereignty, especially inflected by political-theological motifs, tend to rely for their dramatic arc on the opposition between legitimacy and pretendership. Uspensky invokes instances when pretenders to the throne demonstrated their sovereign status to the followers by displaying certain distinctive marks on their bodies.[44] In a similar vein Porfiry expresses concern about the possibility of a mistake about someone's extraordinary status and ironically suggests that it would be easier to tell the special people from the ordinary ones if the former wore distinctive clothes or were marked by brandings [kleimy]. The motif of impostership emerges still more prominently in *Demons*. One of the most striking passages in this respect depicts Stavrogin's conversation with the lame madwoman Marya Lebyadkina, who is secretly his wife. In the course of the scene, it becomes clear that Marya is expecting to meet a certain "Prince," her redeemer, but by the end of the exchange believes she is speaking to the Prince's murderer instead. Once again, we are confronted by the rigid opposition: Redeemer or Antichrist, Prince or Prince-killer, tsar or anti-tsar. The scene ends with what might be called "disclamation," the exposure and renunciation of the Prince as pretender, encapsulated in the shriek with which Marya chases Stavrogin out of the room: "Grishka Otrepev, anathema!" (10:219; 278).[45]

Central to both texts are the thematics of social disintegration. The stakes of redemption are high, and the yearning for the ruler-redeemer intense when everyone perceives with more or less clarity that the "show-house" of contemporary social life is about to collapse. Alternatively, the order's relative stability might be associated, as in *Crime and Punishment*, with the kind of revulsion Raskolnikov feels at the sight of Sonya prostituting herself for her family. Learning that the Marmeladovs live off of their daughter's misery, Raskolnikov thinks: "What a well they've dug for themselves, however! [...] And they got accustomed to it [...] Man gets accustomed to everything, the scoundrel [podlets]!" (6:25; 27). Social life does not produce "spontaneous bonds" (Moretti) but spontaneous turpitude [podlost'], unconscious accommodation to horror. What is needed, then, is the non-scoundrel, the one who will refuse to compromise and be compromised, who will have the strength to overstep and begin it all anew (6:25; 27). Thus, Raskolnikov proclaims the "state of exception" and goes on to stage the enigma of his own election.[46]

Stavrogin's election, in turn, is acclaimed or disclaimed by everyone around him. Even members of the older generation indulge in such – similarly ambiguous – speculations. His former tutor Stepan Trofimovich suggests that Stavrogin's scandalous behaviour should be explained as "merely the first stormy impulses of an overabundant constitution [...] and that it all resembled Shakespeare's description of the youth of Prince Harry, carousing with Falstaff, Poins, and Mistress Quickly" (10:36; 42). The invocation of the Henriade is significant here precisely as a precedent for exploring the problem of legitimacy. The two parts of *Henry IV* in particular trace out the consequences of Bolingbroke's usurpation and (indirect) murder of the divinely ordained king Richard II. Prince Hal's carousing with vagabonds is explicitly cast as his father's punishment for the (perhaps necessary) transgression; the political-theological essence of the punishment consists in the production of uncertainty about whether or not Bolingbroke's newly established royal line is divinely acceptable after all.

The question that is raised by the drama of legitimacy/pretendership pertains to the enigmatic emptiness of absolute power as such. In a farewell letter to Darya Shatova, Stavrogin writes: "I've tested my strength everywhere [...] This testing for myself and for show proved it to be boundless [...] In front of your very eyes, I endured a slap from your brother; I acknowledged my marriage publicly" (10:514; 675). The motif of "the test of strength," already familiar to us from *Crime and Punishment*, returns here with the added emphasis on the dimension of publicity, the "for show." Raskolnikov tests his strength with the murder, feels humiliated by the need to hide what he has done, and seeks out ways to put himself on display. Stavrogin tests his strength repeatedly and directly in public, "posing riddles" that attract the almost mystical fascination of the members of society. What happens to be "for show" here is the very capacity to spurn the opinions of those to whom this capacity is being shown. What the public witnesses is the power that rises above the public, utterly transcends it, constitutes a state of exception in its midst.

The first of the two episodes Stavrogin mentions in his letter is especially intriguing in our context. At issue is the scene during which he receives a blow in the face from his former disciple Shatov and does not respond. The episode is set up as the culmination of a long, nearly fifty-page sequence, gathering together most of the significant characters of the novel, whose complex relationships with each other (and to themselves) converge on the figure of the protagonist. Approximately halfway into the scene, Stavrogin himself arrives after a prolonged absence from the provincial town, and all attention focuses on him. Finally, we reach the event of the blow itself. Shatov walks up to Stavrogin, a hush settles over the room; Shatov strikes with all his might, someone cries out, everyone freezes again; silence (10:164; 203).[47] What follows in the dilation of the dramatic moment is a quasi-odic *exemplum*, an extended digression describing a precedent for the hero being acclaimed. Here we have an extended character portrait of the Decembrist Mikhail Lunin, valiant officer known for his recklessness in war and peace alike, whose regicidal plans of 1816 served as a pretext in 1825 for the verdict of life in penal servitude. Thus, indirectly invoked once again, thanks to the extended comparison of Stavrogin to Lunin, is the image of the protagonist as a participant in the drama of sovereignty, this time in the capacity of regicide.[48]

The digression concludes with the narrator's assertion that he has always considered Stavrogin to be the sort of man who would kill an offender on the spot, without even challenging him to a duel (10:165; 205). Yet – and herein lies the ultimate enigmatic exception – Stavrogin does not respond. We are thus confronted by a layered scenario in which the hero is cast not only as someone in possession of superior power – especially the power for violence – but also as someone capable of mastery over it. The narrator dwells on the scene of self-mastery in particular, comparing Stavrogin's ostensible feelings in the immediate aftermath of the blow to those of a man who tests his strength by clutching a red-hot bar of iron in his hand (10:166; 205). We are thus reminded of Dostoevsky's favourite scene in *Cinna*, the staging of Octavian's capacity to master his righteous rage, transcend even the logic of what is just through the act of pardon, the act whereby one shows oneself capable not only of punishment but of refusing to punish. Traditionally, the ruler's self-mastery, especially mastery over rage, functions as an index of legitimacy, and, in Corneille, this is indeed the act that founds stable rule in Rome. Stavrogin's scenario of power, on the other hand, serves to deepen the charismatic mystery, which projects the self-limitation of power as a mark of its boundlessness. The trouble is that power is limited here by nothing outside the self, no idea or ideal for the sake of which the ruler choses to limit his capacity for violence. What Stavrogin lacks, according to his own confession in the letter quoted above, is precisely Corneille's "générosité" [velikodushie], a dedication to a principle that stands outside and as it were above his own self. Like Raskolnikov, who (at least for the time being) has no "new word" with which to legislate but is preoccupied with capacity alone, so Stavrogin embodies the drama of pure power, beyond all determinations, beyond the distinction between legitimacy and pretendership, the drama, in short, of sovereignty itself.[49]

Entirely Social?

Comically blind to the real stakes of Stavrogin's journey through the novel, members of the older generation in *Demons* – in particular his mother and his former tutor – expect much from the handsome, promising young protagonist. They hope that he will one day stop behaving so strangely, come to his senses, marry a beautiful heiress, and become a brilliant member of society.[50] These properly "social" hopes do not simply go unfulfilled; they seem to be invoked only to highlight their ultimate pettiness by comparison with the novel's more authentic preoccupations. As we have seen, these preoccupations are, in *Demons* as well as in *Crime and Punishment*, better understood as political, or, more properly still, political-theological, foregrounding scenarios of power, acts of violence, scenes of acclamation, scripts of exception, and mysteries of charisma. These novels thus appear to draw upon the imaginaries of sovereign rule just as much as, and in certain ways more than, those of civil society, belying the consensus view of the novel as the genre of sociality par excellence. The notion that the novel, in order to be a novel, must be preoccupied with the negotiation of the boundaries between individual ambition or desire and social cohesion (Nancy Armstrong) or that the novel predominantly concerns itself with "the sphere of 'spontaneous' and concrete bonds" (Moretti), or that its version of power is subtle rather than brute (Foucault, Miller) – all these notions encounter a stumbling block in Dostoevsky.

When it comes to understanding why that may be the case, three concentric explanatory horizons seem relevant. The first and narrowest is the horizon of Dostoevsky's own ideological commitment, shared with many of his contemporaries of course, to an idealized vision of the monarchy as the political form most proper to the aspirations of the Russian people: "For the people, the tsar is not an external force, not the power of some conqueror (as was the case with the dynasties of former kings in France), but a nation-wide, all-unifying force that the people themselves desired, cultivated in their hearts, loved, suffered for, because from it alone was it expecting its deliverance from Egypt. For the people, the tsar is the embodiment of itself, of its whole idea, of its hopes and beliefs" (27:21; my translation).[51] The symbiosis of the people and the tsar leaves no room for the intermediation of society, understood as a more or less disciplined aggregation of self-seeking individuals. Within this model, the tsar is the One in whom, as in the famous frontispiece to Hobbes's *Leviathan*, the Many are contained. And insofar as the Many are a chosen people, the One is – according to the tradition of political theology that predates Dostoevsky's work by several centuries – their messiah and "earthly god."

This is the vision Dostoevsky offers already in his Siberian poems by drawing on the traditional odic themes, and it opens out onto the broader horizon of his experience as a writer in nineteenth-century Russia. Extensive problems with censorship aside, this experience spans the extremes of staged execution and exile at one end of the spectrum (coercion) and association with the royal family and the affairs of the state towards the end of his life at the other (collaboration). The point to emphasize here is not so much the fact, nor even the constant possibility of persecution, but rather *intimacy* with sovereign power, intimacy that could with comparable probability break a life or endow it with high meaning (sometimes both in the same gesture). In this respect, Dostoevsky's experience may have been among the most breathtaking to contemplate, but it was certainly closer to paradigmatic than to unprecedented.

Paradigmatic, too, because – and here we reach the third and outermost horizon – Dostoevsky's life and work unfolded in a world in which, to quote Antonio Gramsci, "the State was everything, civil society was primordial and gelatinous."[52] The hypothesis that animates the preceding discussion, then, is that in the midst of this distinctive historical formation, the novel begins to eschew the standard realist scripts of the pacification and accommodation of individuals within civil society and to focus instead on dramatizations of absolute power. The question of how these dramas play out in the work of other nineteenth-century Russian writers evidently reaches far beyond the scope of this chapter. Here, I would only like to suggest that when it comes to the prevalence of the imaginaries of sovereignty, Dostoevsky's work, much like his biography, presents what may be an especially vivid case but certainly not an exception.[53]

NOTES

I would like to thank Boris Maslov and Kirill Ospovat for their thought-provoking responses to an earlier version of this paper. For detailed feedback and editorial help, I am grateful to Katia Bowers, Melissa Frazier, Kate Holland, and Vadim Shneyder.

1 Hannah Arendt, *The Human Condition* (Chicago: Chicago University Press, 1998), 39.

2 Margaret Cohen, *The Sentimental Education of the Novel* (Princeton, NJ: Princeton University Press, 1999), 77–118.

3 Nancy Armstrong, "The Fiction of Bourgeois Morality and the Paradox of Individualism," in *The Novel*, vol. 2: *Forms and Themes*, ed. Franco Moretti (Princeton, NJ: Princeton University Press, 2006), 371.

4 Fredric Jameson, "The Experiments of Time: Providence and Realism," in *The Novel*, vol. 2, 113.

5 Hannah Arendt. *The Human Condition*, 38–49.

6 D.A. Miller. *The Novel and the Police* (Berkeley: University of California Press, 1988), 23. Foucault himself seemed to view the genre of the novel in this way, suggesting in a lecture course from 1975–76, that there exists an "essential kinship between the novel and the problem of the norm." Michel Foucault. *Society Must Be Defended: Lectures at the Collège de France 1975–1976*. (New York: Picador, 1997), 175.

7 Franco Moretti. *The Way of the World: The Bildungsroman in European Culture*, trans. Albert Sbragia (London and New York: Verso, 2000), 53.

8 Franco Moretti, "The Moment of Truth," *New Left Review* 1, 159 (September–October 1986): 42–5.

9 The correlate question of whether or not Dostoevsky's novel can be meaningfully described as tragic remains outside the purview of this study. I

have attempted to address this issue in Ilya Kliger, "Dostoevsky and the Novel-Tragedy: Genre and Modernity in Ivanov, Pumpiansky and Bakhtin," *PMLA* 126, no. 1 (January 2011): 73–87, and in Ilya Kliger, "Tragic Nationalism in Nietzsche and Dostoevsky," in *Nietzsche and Dostoevsky: Philosophy, Morality, Tragedy*, ed. Jeff Love and Jeffrey Metzger (Evanston, IL: Northwestern University Press, 2016), 143–72.

10 No doubt the trend away from sovereign display and towards discipline and market regulation is visible also in nineteenth-century Russia. See William Mills Todd, III, *Fiction and Society in the Age of Pushkin: Ideology, Institutions, and Narrative* (Cambridge, MA: Harvard University Press: 1986), 45–105, as well as William Mills Todd, III, "The Ruse of the Russian Novel" in *The Novel*, vol. 1: *History, Geography and Culture*, ed. Franco Moretti (Princeton, NJ: Princeton University Press, 2006), 401–13. But even here important qualifications must be made. We might invoke, for example, the distinctiveness of the Russian case with regard to the regulation of authorial ownership: "The 'police' character of the copyright system was unique to Russia: unlike other European legislation, Russian laws on copyright formed a part of the censorship regulation, and only in 1887 finally entered the Civil Code." See Ekaterina Pravilova, *A Public Empire: Property and the Quest for the Common Good in Imperial Russia* (Princeton, NJ: Princeton University Press, 2014), 220. Thus, the establishment of literary ownership in nineteenth-century Russia – an important factor in a properly functioning literary market –remained closely linked to the scenarios of direct prohibition and control.

11 Leonid Grossman, "Grazhdanskaia smert' F.M. Dostoevskogo," *Literaturnoe nasledstvo*, vols. 22–4 (Moscow: Nauka, 1935), 683.

12 Michel Foucault, *Discipline and Punish: The Birth of the Prison*, trans. Alan Sheridan (New York: Vintage Books, 1979), 17.

13 Richard Wortman, *Scenarios of Power: Myth and Ceremony in Russian Monarchy from Peter the Great to the Abdication of Nicholas II.* (Princeton, NJ: Princeton University Press, 2006), 1. See also the discussion of the symbolic implications of the ritual performance on the occasion of the execution of the five Decembrists, in *Scenarios of Power*, 132

14 Foucault. *Society Must Be Defended*, 241.

15 For a recent overview, see Bernadette Meyler, "Liberal Constitutionalism and the Sovereign Power," in *The Scaffolding of Sovereignty: Global and Aesthetic Perspectives on the History of a Concept*, ed. Zvi Benite, Stephanos Geroulanos, and Nichol Jerr (New York: Columbia University Press, 2017), 208–29. For a congenial discussion of the scenarios of power associated with execution and pardon in connection with the genre of tragedy, see Kirill Ospovat. *Terror and Pity: Aleksandr Sumarokov and the Theater of Power in Elizabethan Russia* (Boston: Academic Studies Press, 2016), 216–34.

16 Pierre Corneille, *Corneille's Cinna ou la Clémence D'Auguste*, ed. John E. Matzke (Boston: D.C. Heath, 1905), 91.

17 Pierre Corneille, *The Cid/Cinna/The Theatrical Illusion*, trans. John Cairncross (London, New York: Penguin, 1975), 189

18 F.M. Dostoevskii, *Polnoe sobranie sochinenii v tridtsati tomakh*, 30 vols., ed G.M. Fridlender et al. (Leningrad: "Nauka," 1972–90), vol 28, bk. 1, 71. Subsequent references to this edition will appear in parentheses in the text with volume and page numbers.

19 Leonid Grossman, "Grazhdanskaia smert' F.M. Dostoevskogo," 686.

20 This is one of the standard translations for the term "literaturnyi byt" coined by the Russian Formalists Boris Eikhenbaum and Yuri Tynianov to mean specific forms of human behaviour and social relations that constitute the immediate context in which literary works are produced and received.

21 Leonid Grossman, "Grazhdanskaia smert' F.M. Dostoevskogo," 710.

22 Ibid., 720.

23 Boris Uspensky and Viktor Zhivov, *"Tsar and God" and Other Essays in Russian Cultural Semiotics*, trans. Marcus C. Levitt, David Budgen, and Liv Bliss, ed. Marcus Levitt (Boston: Academic Studies Press, 2012), 6. See also Iurii Kagarlitskii, "Sakralizatsiia kak priem: resursy ubeditel'nosti i vliiatel'nosti imperskogo diskursa v Rossii XVIII veka," *Novoe literaturnoe obozrenie* 4 (1999), n.p. https://magazines.gorky.media/nlo/1999/4/sakralizacziya-kak-priem.html.

24 Uspensky and Zhivov, *"Tsar and God,"* 10.

25 Ibid., 26.

26 For a brief account of the project that gives justice to its complexity, see Kate Holland, *The Novel in the Age of Disintegration: Dostoevsky and the Problem of Genre in the 1870s* (Evanston, IL: Northwestern University Press, 2013), 50–3.

27 In Russian fiction, this motif probably originates with Gogol's *Dead Souls*, whose crooked protagonist is meant for future moral regeneration. See Juriy Lotman, "Gogol's 'Tale of Captain Kopejkin': Reconstruction of the Plan and Ideo-Compositional Function," trans. Julian Graffy, in Ju.M. Lotman and B.A. Uspenskij, *The Semiotics of Russian Culture*, ed. Ann Shukman (Ann Arbor: Michigan Slavic Contributions, 1984), 227.

28 The Western counterpart of this distinction can be found in Thomas Hobbes's influential formula "Auctoritas, non veritas facit legem." Reinhart Koselleck comments: "Laws are made by authority, not by truth. The prince is above the law and at the same time its source; he decides what is right and what is wrong; he is both law-maker and judge [...] To the traditional moral doctrines, [Hobbes] opposes one whose theme is political reason." Reinhart Koselleck, *Critique and Crisis: Enlightenment and the Pathogenesis of Modern Society* (Cambridge, MA: MIT Press, 1988), 31.

29 Uspensky and Zhivov, *"Tsar and God,"* 8.

30 This is indeed the underlying political-theological paradox of Alexander Pushkin's *Bronze Horseman.*

31 Mikhail Bakhtin, *Problems of Dostoevsky's Poetics,* ed. and trans. Caryl Emerson (Minneapolis: Minnesota University Press, 1984), 28.

32 For further invocations of Peter-the-Dutchman, see Dostoevskii, *Polnoe sobranie sochinenii,* vol. 7, 189, 190.

33 Much has been made of Raskolnikov's preoccupation with the figure of Napoleon, but it is important to distinguish among the various valences of the "Napoleonic myth" mobilized by different novelists and in different novelistic traditions. For the protagonists of Balzac, Napoleon symbolizes the unscrupulous energy of a parvenu; for Stendhal's heroes, he stands for spontaneity, impetuousness, and valour; for Raskolnikov, Napoleon is first and foremost a criminal law-giver, a usurper-sovereign, a(n) (imposter) redeemer. See Yuri Lotman's relevant discussion in Iu. Lotman, "Siuzhetnoe prostranstvo russkogo romana XIX stoletiia." *Izbrannye stat'i (v 3-kh tomakh)* (Tallinn: Aleksandra, 1993), vol. 3, 91–106. For Petrine motifs in *Crime and Punishment,* see Clint Walker, "On Serfdom, Sickness, and Redemption: The Peter the Great Subtext in *Crime and Punishment,*" *Dostoevsky Studies* New Series, no. 13 (2009), 93–108; Gary Rosenshield, *Challenging the Bard: Dostoevsky and Pushkin, a Study of Literary Relationship* (Madison: University of Wisconsin Press, 2013); and, most recently, Kathleen Scollins, "From the New Word to the True Word: *The Bronze Horseman* Subtext of *Crime and Punishment,*" *Russian Review* 78, no. 3 (July 2019): 414–36.

34 This translation can be found in Fyodor Dostoevsky, *Demons,* trans. Richard Pevear and Larissa Volokhonsky (New York: Vintage Books, 1995), 419. From now on references to this translation will be supplied in parentheses in the body of the text following the *PSS* reference and set off by a semicolon.

35 This translation can be found in Fyodor Dostoevsky, *Crime and Punishment,* trans. Richard Pevear and Larissa Volokhonsky (New York: Vintage Books, 1993), 460. From now on references to this translation will be supplied in parentheses in the body of the text following the *PSS* reference and set off by a semicolon.

36 On the concept of the extraordinary in Dostoevsky, and especially in *Crime and Punishment,* see Greta Matzner-Gore's contribution to this volume.

37 For a detailed discussion of the use of folk traditions in the characterization of Stavrogin, see Linda Ivanits, *Dostoevsky and the Russian People* (Cambridge: Cambridge University Press, 2008), 106–32. For a similar discussion of *Crime and Punishment,* see pp. 45–76 in the same work.

38 See Dostoevskii, *PSS,* vol. 7, 166, 192, 198. Also see Susan McReynolds, *Redemption and the Merchant God: Dostoevsky's Economy of Salvation and*

Antisemitism (Evanston, IL: Northwestern University Press, 2008), 117–32.
McReynolds notes the centrality of political theology for Raskolnikov's way
of imagining his act: "In Raskolnikov's imagination, Christ and political figures like Napoleon merge as 'great men' bringing a 'new word,' benefiting
humanity in general but exacting a high price from many individuals" (121).

39 *The New Oxford Annotated Bible: New Revised Standard Version with the Apocrypha*, ed. Michael Coogan (Oxford: Oxford University Press, 2007), 167.

40 When it comes to tragedy, the link of the genre to the problematic of sovereignty is well attested. See, for example, Glenn Most, "Sad Stories of the
Death of Kings: Sovereignty and Its Constraints in Greek Tragedy and Elsewhere" in Benite, Geroulanos, and Jerr, eds, *The Scaffolding of Sovereignty*,
57–79. In a classical text on medieval and early modern political theology
Ernst Kantorowicz develops his analysis of kingship with persistent reference to William Shakespeare's *Richard II*. See Kantorowicz. *The King's Two
Bodies: A Study in Medieval Political Theology* (Princeton, NJ: Princeton University Press, 2016). Also see Foucault, *Society Must Be Defended*, 174–7.

41 Hence, too, the ambiguity of searching for one's crime in the newspapers to
begin with: is it to make sure he is not a suspect, or is it to find the mark he
left upon the universe of public deeds?

42 I can do no more here than suggest a relationship between the notion of
sovereignty as the source of exception and Mikhail Bakhtin's well-known
thesis on the unfinalizable nature of Dostoevsky's heroes. The unfinalizable
self, the self who inevitably breaks out of societal norms and expectations,
evidently bears at least a structural resemblance to the self of the unlimited
ruler, the one who gives laws rather than obey them.

43 To be sure, the protagonist and the investigator should not be regarded
as pure embodiments of the imaginaries of sovereignty and disciplinarity
respectively. Raskolnikov, for one, turns out to lose control of the crime
and must in the aftermath reckon with the need to keep it secret. On the
other hand, as we have seen, Porfiry Petrovich invokes the solar metaphor
in relation to his suspect and acclaims him in other ways (6:351; 460). The
investigator's penchant for seeing the crime less as a moral outrage or an
infringement of the law than as an episode in Raskolnikov's – after all "exceptional" – biography should also indicate his partiality for at least an attenuated interpretation of the protagonist within the regime of sovereignty.

44 Boris Uspensky, "Tsar and Pretender: Samozvanchestvo or Royal Imposture
in Russia as a Cultural-Historical Phenomenon," in Lotman and Uspensky,
The Semiotics of Russian Culture, 264, 278. Among other pieces of evidence,
Uspensky cites documents from the Pugachev investigation:

> When we had sat down, Karavaev said to Emel'ka: "You call your-
> self a sovereign, yet sovereigns have the royal signs on their bodies,"

whereupon Emel'ka stood up and, ripping open the collar of his shirt, said: "There! If you do not believe that I am the sovereign, just look – here is the royal sign." First of all he showed the scars under his nipples left by an illness, and then the same kind of mark on his left temple. The Cossacks – Shigaev, Karavaev, Zarubin, Miasnikov – looked at the signs and said: "Well, now we believe you and recognize you as sovereign." (264–5)

45 In a different context, Bakhtin notes the motif of pretendership in one of Raskolnikov's dreams, linking it to the dream of the False Dmitry in Push- kin's *Boris Godunov.* "Before us is the image of communal ridicule on the public sphere decrowning a carnival king-pretender." (Bakhtin, *Problems of Dostoevsky's Poetics,* 168). For more comments on the motif of pretendership (again, in the context of carnival decrowning) in Dostoevsky, see Mikhail Bakhtin, *Sobranie sochinenii v semi tomakh,* vol. 5 (Moscow: Russkie slovari, 1996), 43–4. Harriet Murav dedicates a detailed discussion to the topic of pretendership in *Demons,* once again linking the protagonist-pretender to *Boris Godunov* and, more broadly, to the historical period of the Time of Troubles. See Harriet Murav, *Holy Foolishness: Dostoevsky's Novels and the Poetics of Cultural Critique* (Stanford, CA: Stanford University Press, 1992), 99–123. In an attempt to make sense of the "Ivan Tsarevich" motif in *Demons,* Olga Maiorova provides an especially pertinent account of the broader post-emancipation mytheme of royal pretendership in Maiorova, "Tsarevich-samozvanets v sotsial'noi mifologii poreformennoi epokhi," in *Rossia-Russia 3 (11): Kul'turnye praktiki v ideologicheskoi perspektive. Rossia XVII-nachalo XX veka.* (Moscow: OGI, 1999), 204–32. In Maiorova's account, the motif invokes contemporary folk legends conflating various members of the royal family with leaders of past peasant uprisings and sectarian leaders in the figure of the sovereign-redeemer. One important distinction that emerges in the process is between bureaucratic and popular notions of mo-narchical rule. The pretender-redeemer-tsar's legitimacy is evidently based on his messianic charisma rather than of legality or reason. For the role of schismatic-revolutionary imaginaries of sovereignty, see Irina Paperno, "The Liberation of Serfs as a Cultural Symbol" in *Russian Review* 63, no. 4 (October 2004): 417–436, especially 421–36.

46 The term "state of exception," indicating the situation that warrants the sus-pension of all constitutional norms in the face of an immediate danger to the state, has a long history. For overview and analysis, Giorgio Agamben, *State of Exception,* trans. Kevin Attell (Chicago: University of Chicago Press, 2005).

47 For a discussion of a Dostoevskian poetics of the slap, especially in relation to realized and unrealized scenarios of the duel, see Kate Holland's contri-bution to this volume.

48 The regicide partakes of the charisma of the sovereign by entering what
    Clifford Geertz has called "concentrated loci of serious acts": "an arena in
    which the events that most vitally affect its members' lives take place. It is
    involvement, *even oppositional involvement*, with such arenas and with the mo-
    mentous events that occur in them that confers charisma. It is a sign [...] of
    being near the heart of things." See Clifford Geertz, *Local Knowledge: Further
    Essays in Interpretative Anthropology* (New York: Basic Books, 2000), 122–3.
49 We find the same motif in Arkady Dolgoruky's fantasy of enrichment for the
    sake of power (mogushchestvo) in *The Adolescent*. Arkady imagines his own
    much richer version as Jupiter who is confident enough in his powers to no
    longer need to display it. Congenial, too, is the script according to which
    he reaches the heights of power and wealth only in order to renounce it
    all. Arkady's absolute wilfulness is thus expressed in the rejection of his will
    (13:74–6).
50 For a discussion of Dostoevsky's suspended marriage plots, see Anna Ber-
    man's contribution to this volume.
51 For detailed discussions of Dostoevsky's views on the monarchy, and espe-
    cially on the relationship between the monarchy and the Russian people,
    see Igor Volgin, *Poslednii god Dostoevskogo: Istoricheskie zapiski* (Moscow:
    AST, 2010), 265–7; V.G. Odinokov, *Khudozhestvenno-istoricheskii opyt v poetike
    russkikh pisatelei* (Novosibirsk: Nauka, 1990), 40–8; V.P. Popov, "Problema
    naroda u Dostoevskogo," *Dostoevskii: Materialy i issledovaniia* 4 (1980): 41–54;
    Richard Wortman, "Russian Monarchy and the People," in *Dostoevsky in Con-
    text*, ed. Deborah A. Martinsen and O.E. Maiorova (Cambridge: Cambridge
    University Press, 2015), 77–85.
52 Antonio Gramsci. *Selections from the Prison Notebooks*, trans. Quintin Hoare
    and Geoffrey Nowell-Smith (New York: International Publishers, 1971), 238.
53 I have attempted to explore the ways in which the imaginaries of sover-
    eignty and of state coercion more broadly affect the formal-thematic texture
    of Russian realist fictions in Ilya Kliger, "Hegel's Political Philosophy and
    the Social Imaginary of Early Russian Realism," *Studies in Eastern European
    Thought* 65, nos. 3–4 (September 2013): 189–99, as well as in Ilya Kliger,
    "Scenarios of Power in Turgenev's 'First Love': Russian Realism and the Al-
    legory of the State," *Comparative Literature* 70, no. 1 (March 2018): 25–45.

Works Cited

Dostoevsky Editions and Translations

F.M. Dostoevskii. *Polnoe sobranie sochinenii v 30 tomakh.* Edited by G.M.
  Fridlender et al. Leningrad: "Nauka," 1972–90.
– *Polnoe sobranie sochinenii i pisem v 35 tomakh.* Edited by V.E. Bagno et al.
  St Petersburg: "Nauka," 2013–.
Fyodor Dostoevsky. *The Adolescent.* Translated by Dora O'Brien. Richmond, UK:
  Alma Classics, 2016.
– *The Adolescent.* Translated by Richard Pevear and Larissa Volokhonsky. New
  York: Knopf, 2003.
– *The Brothers Karamazov.* Translated by Richard Pevear and Larissa
  Volokhonsky. London: Vintage Books, 2004.
– *Crime and Punishment.* Translated by Richard Pevear and Larissa Volokhonsky.
  New York: Vintage, 1993.
– *Crime and Punishment.* Translated by Oliver Ready. New York: Penguin Books,
  2014.
– *Crime and Punishment.* Translated by Nicolas Pasternak Slater. Oxford: Oxford
  University Press, 2017.
– *Demons.* Translated by Richard Pevear and Larissa Volokhonsky. New York:
  Vintage Books, 1995.
– *Demons.* Translated by Robert Maguire. London and New York: Penguin
  Classics, new edition, 2008.
– *The Double.* Translated by Hugh Aplin. Richmond, UK: Alma Classics, 2016.
– *The Double; The Gambler.* Translated by Richard Pevear and Larissa
  Volokhonsky. London: Everyman's Library, 2005.
– *The Idiot.* Translated by Alan Myers. Oxford: Oxford University Press, 1992.
– *Notes from Underground.* Translated by Boris Jakim. Grand Rapids, MI, and
  Cambridge, UK: William B. Eerdmans, 2009.
– *Poor Folk and Other Stories.* Translated by David McDuff. London: Penguin
  Books, 1988.

– *Winter Notes on Summer Impressions*. Translated by David Patterson. Evanston, IL: Northwestern University Press, 1997.
– *A Writer's Diary*. Translated by Kenneth Lantz. 2 vols. London: Quartet, 1994.

Other Works

Abrams, M.H. "Gothic Novel." In *A Glossary of Literary Terms*. Boston: Thomson-Wadsworth, 2005.

Agamben, Giorgio. *State of Exception*. Translated by Kevin Attell. Chicago: University of Chicago Press, 2005.

Allen, Elizabeth Cheresh. "Unmasking Lermontov's *Masquerade:* Romanticism as Ideology." *Slavic and East European Journal* 46, no. 1 (Spring 2002): 75–97.

Allen, Sharon Lubkemann. "Reflection/Refraction of the Dying Light: Narrative Vision in Nineteenth-Century Russian and French Fiction." *Comparative Literature* 54, no. 1 (2002): 2–22.

Apollonio, Carol. *Dostoevsky's Secrets: Reading against the Grain*. Evanston, IL: Northwestern University Press, 2009.

Arendt, Hannah. *The Human Condition*. Chicago: Chicago University Press, 1998.

Armstrong, Nancy. "The Fiction of Bourgeois Morality and the Paradox of Individualism." In *The Novel*, vol. 2: *Forms and Themes*, edited by Franco Moretti, 349–88. Princeton, NJ: Princeton University Press, 2006.

Auerbach, Erich. *Mimesis: The Representation of Reality in Western Literature*. Translated by Willard R. Trask. Princeton, NJ: Princeton University Press, 2003.

Avseenko, V.G. "Ocherki tekushchei literatury." *Russkii mir* 55 (1875).

Bakhtin, M.M. *Sobranie sochinenii*. Edited by S.G. Bocharov and N.I. Nikolaev. 7 vols. Moscow: Russkie slovari, 1996–.

Bakhtin, Mikhail. *The Dialogic Imagination*. Translated by Caryl Emerson and Michael Holquist. Edited by Michael Holquist. Austin: University of Texas Press, 1981.

– *Problems of Dostoevsky's Poetics*. Translated by Caryl Emerson. Minneapolis: University of Minnesota Press, 1984.

Balzac, Honoré de. *Eugénie Grandet*. In *Études de moeurs au XIXe siècle. Scènes de la vie de province*. 12 vols. Madame Charles-Béchet, 1834.

– *Eugénie Grandet*. Translated by Sylvia Raphael. Oxford: Oxford University Press, 1990.

Barthes, Roland. "The Reality Effect." In *The Rustle of Language*, translated by Richard Howard, 141–8. Berkeley: University of California Press, 1989.

– *S/Z*. Translated by R. Howard. New York: Hill and Wang, 1974.

Becker, George. J. *Documents of Modern Literary Realism*. Princeton, NJ: Princeton University Press, 1963.

Beer, Gillian. *Darwin's Plots: Evolutionary Narrative in Darwin, George Eliot and Nineteenth-Century Fiction.* Cambridge and New York: Cambridge University Press, 2009.

Beizer, Janet L. *Family Plots: Balzac's Narrative Generations.* New Haven, CT: Yale University Press, 1986.

Belknap, Robert L. *Plots.* New York: Columbia University Press, 2016.

– *The Structure of* The Brothers Karamazov. The Hague: Mouton, 1967.

Belopol'skii, V.N. *Dostoevskii i drugie: Stat'i o russkoi literature.* Rostov-on-Don: Foundation, 2011.

– "S kem polemiziroval Dostoevskii v povesti 'Zapiski iz podpol'ia'?" In *Dostoevskii i filosofiia. Sviazi i paralleli,* 20–30. Rostov-on-Don: Izdatel'stvo Instituta massovykh kommunikatsii, 1998.

Bem, A.L. "Khudozhestvennaia polemika s Tolstym (K ponimaniiu 'Podrostka')." In *O Dostoevskom,* vol. 3, 192–214. Berlin: Petropolis, 1936.

Berman, Anna A. "Incest and the Limits of Family in the Nineteenth-Century Novel." *Russian Review* 78, no. 1 (2019): 82–102.

– "Lateral Plots: Brothers and the Nineteenth-Century Russian Novel." *Slavic and East European Journal* 16, no.1 (2017): 1–28.

– *Siblings in Tolstoy and Dostoevsky: The Path to Universal Brotherhood.* Evanston, IL: Northwestern University Press, 2015.

Berman, Marshall. *All That Is Solid Melts into Air.* New York: Verso, 1983.

Bernard, Claude. *An Introduction to the Study of Experimental Medicine.* New York: Dover, 1957.

– *Introduction à l'étude de la médecine expérimentale.* Paris: Garnier-Flammarion, 1966.

Bethea, David M. *The Shape of Apocalypse in Modern Russian Fiction.* Princeton, NJ: Princeton University Press, 1989.

Betjemann, Peter. "Eavesdropping with Charlotte Perkins Gilman: Fiction, Transcription, and the Ethics of Interior Design." *American Literary Realism* 46, no. 2 (2014): 95–115.

Bialyi, G.A. "O psikhologicheskoi manere Turgeneva (Turgenev i Dostoevskii)." *Russkaia Literatura* 4 (1968): 34–50.

The New Oxford Annotated Bible: New Revised Standard Version with the Apocrypha. Edited by Michael Coogan. Oxford: Oxford University Press, 2007.

Bird, Robert. "Refiguring the Russian Type: Dostoevsky and the Limits of Realism." In *A New Word on* The Brothers Karamazov, edited by Robert Louis Jackson, 17–30. Evanston, IL: Northwestern University Press, 2004.

Bocharov, S. *Roman L. Tolstogo 'Voina i mir'.* Moscow: Khudozhestvennaia literatura, 1963.

Bograd, Ganna. "Metafizicheskoe prostranstvo i pravoslavnaia simvolika kak osnova mest obitaniia geroev romana 'Prestuplenie i nakazanie.'" In *Dostoevskii: dopolneniia k kommentariiu,* edited by T.A. Kasatkina, 179–202. Moscow: Nauka, 2005.

Bokl' [Buckle], G.T. *Istoriia tsivilizatsii v Anglii*. Vol. 1. Translated by
K. Bestuzhev-Riumin. St Petersburg, 1863. https://dlib.rsl.ru/viewer
/01007496547#?page=2.
Boone, Joseph Allen. *Tradition Counter Tradition: Love and the Form of Fiction*.
Chicago: University of Chicago Press, 1987.
Botting, Fred. *Gothic*. London: Routledge, 1996.
Bowers, Katherine. "The City through a Glass, Darkly: Use of the Gothic
in Early Russian Realism." *Modern Language Review* 108, no. 4 (2013):
1237–53.
– "The Gothic Novel Reader Comes to Russia." In *Reading Russia: A History of
Reading in Modern Russia*, vol. 2, edited by Damiano Rebecchini and Raffaella
Vassena, 377–408. Milan: Ledizioni, 2020.
– "Plotting the Ending: Generic Expectation and the Uncanny Epilogue of
Crime and Punishment." *Canadian Slavonic Papers* 62, no. 2 (2020): 95–108.
– "'Through the Opaque Veil': The Gothic and Death in Russian Realism." In
The Gothic and Death, edited by Carol Margaret Davison, 157–73. Manchester:
Manchester University Press, 2017.
– *Writing Fear: Russian Realism and the Gothic*. Toronto: University of Toronto
Press, forthcoming 2021.
Braithwaite, Dawn, Betsy Bach, Leslie Baxter, Rebecca DiVerniero, Joshua
Hammonds, Angela Hosek, Erin Willer, and Bianca Wolf. "Constructing
Family: A Typology of Voluntary Kin." *Journal of Social and Personal
Relationships* 27, no. 3 (2010): 388–407.
Brooks, Jeffrey. *When Russia Learned to Read: Literacy and Popular Literature,
1861–1917*. Princeton, NJ: Princeton University Press, 1985.
Brooks, Peter. *Reading for the Plot: Design and Intention in Narrative*. Cambridge,
MA: Harvard University Press, 1984.
Bruhm, Steven. *Gothic Bodies: The Politics of Pain in Romantic Fiction*.
Philadelphia: University of Pennsylvania Press, 1994.
Brunson, Molly. *Russian Realisms: Literature and Painting, 1840–1890*. DeKalb:
Northern Illinois University Press, 2016.
Buckle, Henry Thomas. *History of Civilization in England*. New York, 1884.
Budanova, N.F. *Biblioteka F.M. Dostoevskogo: opyt rekonstruktsii, nauchnoe opisanie*.
St Petersburg: "Nauka," 2005.
– "Zapiski iz podpol'ia: zagadki tsenzurnoi istorii povesti." *Dostoevskii: Materialy i
issledovaniia* 21 (2016): 236–45.
Calder, Jenni. *Women and Marriage in Victorian Fiction*. New York: Oxford
University Press, 1976.
Catteau, Jacques. *Dostoyevsky and the Process of Literary Creation*. Translated by
Audrey Littlewood. Cambridge: Cambridge University Press, 2005.
Chaadaev, P.Ia. *Polnoe sobranie sochinenii i izbrannye pis'ma*. 2 vols. Edited by Z.A.
Kamenskii et al. Moscow: Nauka, 1991.

Chard, Chloe. "Introduction." In Ann Radcliffe, *The Romance of the Forest*, vii–xxiv. Oxford University Press, 1999.

Chernyshevskii, N.G. "Antropologicheskii printsip v filosofii." In *Izbrannye filosofskie sochineniia*, edited by M.M. Grigor'ian, 162–254. Moscow: Gosudarstvennoe izdatel'stvo politicheskoi literatury, 1951.

– *Chto delat'?* Leningrad: Nauka, 1975.

Chernyshevsky, Nikolai. "The Russian at the *Rendez-vous*." In *Belinsky, Chernyshevsky, and Dobrolyubov: Selected Criticism*, edited by Ralph E. Matlaw, 108–29. New York: E.P. Dutton, 1962.

– *What Is to Be Done?* Translated by Michael Katz. Ithaca, NY: Cornell University Press, 1989.

Cohen, Margaret. *The Sentimental Education of the Novel.* Princeton, NJ: Princeton University Press, 1999.

Cohen, William A. *Embodied: Victorian Literature and the Senses.* Minneapolis: University of Minnesota Press, 2009.

Cohn, Dorrit. *Transparent Minds: Narrative Modes for Presenting Consciousness in Fiction.* Princeton, NJ: Princeton University Press, 1978.

Collins, Margery L., and Christine Pierce. "Holes and Slime: Sexism in Sartre's Psychoanalysis," *Philosophical Forum* 5, nos. 1–2 (Fall-Winter 1973–4): 112–27.

Comer, William J. "Rogozhin and the 'Castrates': Russian Religious Traditions in Dostoevsky's *The Idiot.*" *Slavic and East European Journal* 40, no. 1 (Spring 1996): 85–99.

Conrich, Ian, and Laura Sedgwick. *Gothic Dissections in Film and Literature: The Body in Parts.* London: Palgrave Macmillan, 2017.

Corneille, Pierre. *The Cid/Cinna/The Theatrical Illusion.* Translated by John Cairncross. London, New York: Penguin Books, 1975.

– *Corneille's Cinna ou la Clémence D'Aususte.* Edited by John E. Matzke. Boston: D.C. Heath, 1905.

Corrigan, Yuri. "Dostoevskii on Evil as Safe Haven and Anesthetic," *Slavic and East European Journal* 63, no. 2 (2019): 226–43.

– *Dostoevsky and the Riddle of the Self.* Evanston, IL: Northwestern University Press, 2017.

Dal', V.I. *Tolkovyi slovar' zhivogo velikorusskogo iazyka.* Moscow: Tipografiia lazaretskogo instituta vostochnykh iazykov, 1865.

Dames, Nicholas. "1825–1880. The Network of Nerves." In *The Emergences of Mind: Representation of Consciousness in Narrative Discourse in English*, edited by David Herman, 215–39. Lincoln: University of Nebraska Press, 2011.

– *The Physiology of the Novel: Reading, Neural Science and the Form of Victorian Fiction.* Oxford: Oxford University Press, 2007.

Danilov, Kiriak. Review of *Ugolovno-statisticheskie etiudy*, by N. Nekliudov. *Sankt-Peterburgskie vedomosti*, 28 March 1865.

Daston, Lorraine. *Classical Probability in the Enlightenment*. Princeton, NJ: Princeton University Press, 1988.

Dau, Duc, and Shale Preston. *Queer Victorian Families: Curious Relations in Literature*. New York: Routledge, 2015.

Debrezceny, Paul. *The Other Pushkin: A Study of Alexander Pushkin's Prose Fiction*. Stanford, CA: Stanford University Press, 1983.

Derrida, Jacques. "Plato's Pharmacy." In *Dissemination*, translated by Barbara Johnson, 63–171. Chicago: University of Chicago Press, 1981.

Dilaktorskaia, O.G. *Peterburgskaia povest' Dostoevskogo*. St Petersburg: Dmitrii Bulanin, 1999.

Doak, Connor. "Masculine Degeneration in Dostoevsky's *Demons*." In *Russian Writers and the* Fin de Siècle: *The Twilight of Realism*, edited by Katherine Bowers and Ani Kokobobo, 107–25. Cambridge: Cambridge University Press, 2015.

– "Myshkin's Queer Failure: (Mis)reading Masculinity in Dostoevskii's *The Idiot*." *Slavic and East European Journal* 63, no. 1 (2019): 1–27.

Dobroliubov, N.A. *Sobranie sochinenii v deviati tomakh*. Moscow: "Khudozhestvennaia literatura," 1961–4.

Dolinin, A.S. "F.M. Dostoevskii i N.N. Strakhov." In *Shestidesiatye gody*, edited by N.K. Piksanov and O.V. Tseknovitser, 238–54. Moscow: Izdatel'stvo Akademii nauk SSSR, 1940.

– *Poslednie romany Dostoevskogo*. Moscow: Sovetskii pisatel', 1963.

Dostoevskaia, A.G. *Dnevnik 1867 goda*. Moscow: "Nauka," 1993.

– *Vospominaniia*. Moscow: Pravda, 1987.

Edelman, Lee. "The Future Is Kid Stuff: Queer Theory, Disidentification, and the Death Drive." *NARRATIVE* 6, no. 1 (1998): 18–30

– *No Future: Queer Theory and the Death Drive*. Durham, NC: Duke University Press, 2004.

Engel, Barbara Alpern. "The 'Woman Question,' Women's Work, Women's Options." In *Dostoevsky in Context*, edited by Deborah A. Martinsen and O.E. Maiorova, 58–65. Cambridge: Cambridge University Press, 2015.

Engels, Friedrich. "Old Preface to Dühring. On Dialectics." In Karl Marx and Friedrich Engels, *Collected Works*, vol. 25, 336–344. New York: International Publishers, 1975.

Evdokimova, Svetlana, and Vladimir Golstein. *Dostoevsky beyond Dostoevsky: Science, Religion, Philosophy*. Boston: Academic Studies Press, 2016.

Fanger, Donald. *Dostoevsky and Romantic Realism: A Study of Dostoevsky in Relation to Balzac, Dickens, and Gogol*. Cambridge, MA: Harvard University Press, 1967.

Feher, Z.A. "Georg Lukács's Role in Dostoevskii's European Reception at the Turn of the Century." PhD diss., University of California, Los Angeles, 1978.

Fletcher, Angus. *Allegory: Theory of a Symbolic Mode*. Ithaca, NY: Cornell University Press, 1962.

Fludernik, Monika. *The Fictions of Language and the Languages of Fiction. The Linguistic Representation of Speech and Consciousness.* London; New York: Routledge, 1993.

– *Towards a 'Natural' Narratology.* London; New York: Routledge, 1996.

Forster, E.M. *Aspects of the Novel.* London: Penguin, 1963.

Foucault, Michel. *Discipline and Punish: The Birth of the Prison.* Translated by Alan Sheridan. New York: Vintage Books, 1979.

– *Society Must Be Defended: Lectures at the Collège de France 1975–1976.* Translated by David Macey. New York: Picador, 1997.

Frank, Joseph. "The Masks of Stavrogin." *Sewanee Review* 77, no. 4 (Autumn 1969): 660–91.

– *Dostoevsky: The Stir of Liberation, 1860–1865.* Princeton, NJ: Princeton University Press, 1986.

Frazier, Melissa. "Minds and Bodies in the World: Dostoevskii, George Eliot, and George Henry Lewes." *Forum for Modern Language Studies* 55, no. 2 (2019): 152–70.

– "Nauka realizma." In *Russkii realizm XIX veka: mimesis, politika, ekonomika,* edited by M. Vaisman, A. Vdovin, I. Kliger, and K. Ospovat, 408–30. Moscow: Novoe literaturnoe obozrenie, 2020.

– "The Science of Sensation: Dostoevsky, Wilkie Collins, and the Detective Novel." *Dostoevsky Studies* New Series, no. 19 (2015): 7–28.

Fridlender, Georgii. "D.S. Merezhkovskii i Dostoevskii." *Dostoevskii: Materialy i isledovaniia* 10 (1992): 9–14.

– *Realizm Dostoevskogo.* Leningrad: Nauka, 1964.

Frost, Elisa S. "The Hut on Chicken Legs: Encounters with Landladies in Russian Literature." PhD diss., University of Wisconsin Madison, 2002.

Furneaux, Holly. *Queer Dickens: Erotics, Families, Masculinities.* Oxford: Oxford University Press, 2009.

Fusso, Susanne. *Discovering Sexuality in Dostoevsky.* Evanston, IL: Northwestern University Press, 2006.

– "Dostoevskii and the Family." In *The Cambridge Companion to Dostoevskii.* Edited by William J. Leatherbarrow. Cambridge: Cambridge University Press, 2002.

Garrett, Peter K. *Gothic Reflections: Narrative Force in Nineteenth-Century Fiction.* Ithaca, NY: Cornell University Press, 2003.

Gaylin, Ann. *Eavesdropping in the Novel from Austen to Proust.* Cambridge: Cambridge University Press, 2003.

Geertz. Clifford. *Local Knowledge: Further Essays in Interpretative Anthropology.* New York: Basic Books, 2000.

Gibian, George. "Traditional Symbolism in *Crime and Punishment.*" *PMLA* 70, no. 5 (December 1955): 982–5.

Girard, René. *Deceit, Desire and the Novel: Self and Other in Literary Structure.* Translated by Yvonne Freccero. Baltimore: Johns Hopkins University Press, 1966.

– *Mensonge romantique et vérité Romanesque.* Paris: Grasset, 1961.

Goncharov, I.A. *Sobranie sochinenii.* 8 vols. Moscow: Gosizdat. khudozhestvennoi literatury, 1952–5.

Gramsci, Antonio. *Selections from the Prison Notebooks.* Translated by Quintin Hoare and Geoffrey Nowell-Smith. New York: International Publishers, 1971.

Gregory, Frederick. *Scientific Materialism in Nineteenth-Century Germany.* Boston: D. Reidel, 1977.

Grossman, Leonid. *Bal'zak i Dostoevskii.* In *Poetika Dostoevskogo,* 92–107. Moscow: Gosudarstvennaia akademiia khudozhestvennykh nauk, 1925.

– "Grazhdanskaia smert' F.M. Dostoevskogo," *Literaturnoe nasledstvo,* vols. 22–4 (1935): 683–736. Moscow: Nauka, 1935.

– *Poetika Dostoevskogo.* Moscow: 39-aia tip. Internatsional'naia tip. "Mospoligraf," 1925.

Gus, M.S. *Idei i obrazy Dostoevskogo.* Moscow: Gosudarstvennoe izdatel'stvo khudozhestvennoi literatury, 1971.

Hacking, Ian. *The Taming of Chance.* Cambridge: Cambridge University Press, 1990.

Halberstam, Judith. *In a Queer Time and Place: Transgender Bodies, Subcultural Lives.* New York: New York University Press, 2005.

Halperin, David M. *Saint Foucault: Towards a Gay Hagiography.* New York: Oxford University Press, 1995.

Heier, Edmund. *Literary Portraiture in Nineteenth-Century Russian Prose.* Cologne: Böhlau-Verlag, 1993.

Heldt, Barbara. *Terrible Perfection: Women and Russian Literature.* Bloomington and Indianapolis: Indiana University Press, 1987.

Helfant, Ian. *The High Stakes of Identity: Gambling in the Life and Literature of Nineteenth Century Russia.* Evanston, IL: Northwestern University Press, 2002.

Hinz, Evelyn J. "Hierogamy versus Wedlock: Types of Marriage Plots and Their Relationship to Genres of Prose Fiction," *PMLA* 91, no. 5 (1976): 900–13.

Holland, Kate. "From the Pre-History of Russian Novel Theory: Alexander Veselovsky and Fyodor Dostoevsky on the Modern Novel's Roots in Folklore and Legend." In *Persistent Forms: Explorations in Historical Poetics,* edited by Ilya Kliger and Boris Maslov, 340–68. New York: Fordham University Press, 2015.

– "The Clash of Deferral and Anticipation: *Crime and Punishment*'s Epilogue and the Difficulties of Narrative Closure." *Canadian Slavonic Papers* 62, no. 2 (2020): 109–22.

– "Hurrying, Clanging, Banging and Speeding for the Happiness of Mankind: Railways, Metaphor and Modernity in *The Idiot.*" Presentation, Annual Convention of the American Association for Slavic, East European and Eurasian Studies, Chicago, IL, 9–12 November 2017.

– "The Legend of the *Ladonka* and the Trial of the Novel." In *A New Word on "The Brothers Karamazov."* Edited by Robert Louis Jackson. Evanston, IL: Northwestern University Press, 2004.

– *The Novel in the Age of Disintegration: Dostoevsky and the Problem of Genre in the 1870s.* Evanston, IL: Northwestern University Press, 2013.

Holquist. Michael. "Bazarov and Secenov: The Role of Scientific Metaphor in Fathers and Sons." *Russian Literature* 6, no. 4 (1984): 359–74.

– *Dostoevsky and the Novel.* Princeton, NJ: Princeton University Press, 1977.

– "Gaps in Christology: *The Idiot.*" In *Dostoevsky: New Perspectives,* edited by Robert Louis Jackson, 126–44. Englewood Cliffs, NJ: Prentice-Hall, 1984.

Hunt, Lynn. *Measuring Time, Making History.* Budapest: Central European University Press, 2008.

Ivanits, Linda. *Dostoevsky and the Russian People.* Cambridge: Cambridge University Press, 2008.

Ivanov, V.I. *Sobranie sochinenii.* 4 vols. Edited by D.V. Ivanov and O. Deshart. Brussels: Foyer Oriental Chrétien, 1971–87.

Ivantsov, Vladimir. "Digging into Dostoevskii's Underground: From the Metaphorical to the Literal." *Slavic & East European Journal* 62, no. 2 (Summer 2018): 382–400.

Jackson, Robert Louis. *The Art of Dostoevsky: Deliriums and Nocturnes.* Princeton, NJ: Princeton University Press, 1981.

– *Dialogues with Dostoevsky: The Overwhelming Questions.* Stanford, CA: Stanford University Press, 1993.

– *Dostoevsky's Quest for Form: A Study of His Philosophy of Art.* New Haven, CT: Yale University Press, 1966.

– "Once Again about Dostoevsky's Response to Hans Holbein the Younger's *Dead Body of Christ in the Tomb.*" In *Dostoevsky beyond Dostoevsky: Science, Religion, Philosophy,* edited by Svetlana Evdokimova and Vladimir Golstein, 179–92. Boston: Academic Studies Press, 2016.

– "Preface." In *A New Word on* The Brothers Karamazov, edited by Robert Louis Jackson, ix–x. Evanston, IL: Northwestern University Press, 2004.

Jameson, Fredric. "The Experiments of Time: Providence and Realism." In *The Novel., vol. 2: Forms and Themes.* Edited by Franco Moretti, 95–127.

Jensen, P.A. "Paradoksal'nost' avtorstva (u) Dostoevskogo." In *Paradoksy russkoi literatury,* edited by V. Markovich and V. Shmid, 219–233. St Petersburg: Inapress, 2001.

Jones, Malcolm. *Dostoevsky and the Dynamics of Religious Experience.* London: Anthem Press, 2005.

Kagarlitskii, Iurii. "Sakralizatsiia kak priem: resursy ubeditel'nosti i vliiatel'nosti imperskogo diskursa v Rossii XVIII veka." In *Novoe literaturnoe obozrenie* 4 (1999): n.p. https://magazines.gorky.media/nlo/1999/4/sakralizacziya-kak-priem.html.

Kaladiouk. A.S. "On 'Sticking to the Fact' and 'Understanding Nothing': Dostoevskii and the Scientific Method." *Russian Review* 65, no. 3 (July 2006): 417–38.

Kantorowicz, Ernst. *The King's Two Bodies: A Study in Medieval Political Theology.* Princeton, NJ: Princeton University Press, 2016.

Karaulov, Iu.N. et al., eds. *Slovar' iazyka Dostoevskogo: Leksicheskii stroi idiolekta,* issue 1, Moscow: "Azbukovnik," 2001.

– *Slovar' iazyka Dostoevskogo.* Moscow: "Azbukovnik," 2012.

Kasatkina, T.A. "After Seeing the Original." *Russian Studies in Literature* 47, no. 3 (2011): 73–97.

– "History in a Name: Myshkin and the 'Horizontal Sanctuary.'" In *The New Russian Dostoevsky: Readings for the Twenty-First Century,* edited and translated by Carol Apollonio et al., 145–164. Bloomington: Slavica, 2010.

– *O tvoriashchei prirode slova: Ontologichnost' slova v tvorchestve F.M. Dostoevskogo kak osnova "realizma v vysshem smysle."* Moscow: IMLI RAN, 2004.

– "Posle znakomstva s podlinnikom: Kartina Gansa Gol'beina Mladshego 'Khristos v mogile' v strukture romana F.M. Dostoevskogo 'Idiot.'" *Novyi mir* 2 (2006): 154–68.

– "Roman F.M. Dostoevskogo 'Podrostok': 'Ideia' geroia i ideia avtora," *Voprosy literatury,* no. 1 (2004): 181–212.

Katz, Michael. "Dostoevskii's Homophilia/Homophobia." In *Gender and Sexuality in Russian Civilization,* edited by Peter I. Barta, 239–53. London: Routledge, 2001.

Kavanagh, Thomas M. *Enlightenment and the Shadows of Chance: The Novel and the Culture of Gambling in Eighteenth-Century France.* Baltimore, MD: Johns Hopkins University Press, 1993.

Keldysh, V.A. "Nasledie Dostoevskogo i russkaia mysl' porubezhnoi epokhi." In *Sviaz' vremen: Problemy preemstvennosti v russkoi literature kontsa XIX-nachala XX v.,* 76–115. Moscow: Nasledie, 1992.

Kelly, Aileen. *The Discovery of Chance: The Life and Thought of Alexander Herzen.* Cambridge, MA: Harvard University Press, 2016.

Ketle [Quetelet], Adol'f. *Chelovek i razvitie ego sposobnostei, ili Opyt obshchestvennoi fiziki,* vol. 1. St Petersburg, 1865.

– *Sotsial'naia sistema i zakony eiu upravliaiushchie.* Translated by L.N. Shakhovskoi. St Petersburg, 1866. http://xn–90ax2c.xn–p1ai/catalog/000199_000009_003577415/viewer/.

Khansen-Leve O. "Diskursivnye protsessy v romane Dostoevskogo 'Podrostok.'" In *Avtor i tekst: sbornik statei,* edited by V. M Markovich and V. Shmid, 229–67. St Petersburg: Izd-vo S-Peterburgskogo universiteta, 1996.

Kichigina, G. *The Imperial Laboratory: Experimental Physiology and Clinical Medicine in Post-Crimean Russia.* New York: Rodopi, 2009.

Kitzinger, Chloë. *Mimetic Lives: Tolstoy, Dostoevsky, and Character in the Novel.* Evanston, IL: Northwestern University Press, forthcoming 2021.

Kliger, Ilya. "Dostoevsky and the Novel-Tragedy: Genre and Modernity in Ivanov, Pumpiansky and Bakhtin." *PMLA* 126, no. 1 (January 2011): 73–87.

– "Hegel's Political Philosophy and the Social Imaginary of Early Russian Realism." *Studies in Eastern European Thought* 65, nos. 3–4 (September 2013): 189–99.

– *The Narrative Shape of Truth: Veridiction in Modern European Literature.* University Park, PA: Pennsylvania State University Press, 2011.

– "Scenarios of Power in Turgenev's 'First Love': Russian Realism and the Allegory of the State." *Comparative Literature* 70, no. 1 (March 2018): 25–45.

– "Shapes of History and the Enigmatic Hero in Dostoevsky: The Case of *Crime and Punishment.*" *Comparative Literature* 62, no. 3 (2010): 228–45.

– "Tragic Nationalism in Nietzsche and Dostoevsky." In *Nietzsche and Dostoevsky: Philosophy, Morality, Tragedy,* edited by Jeff Love and Jeffrey Metzger, 143–72. Evanston, IL: Northwestern University Press, 2016.

Klioutchkine, Konstantine. "The Rise of *Crime and Punishment* from the Air of the Media." *Slavic Review* 61, no. 1 (Spring 2002): 88–108.

Knapp, Liza. *The Annihilation of Inertia: Dostoevsky and Metaphysics.* Evanston, IL: Northwestern University Press, 1996.

– "Dostoevsky and the Novel of Adultery: *The Adolescent.*" *Dostoevsky Studies* New Series, no. 17 (2013): 37–71.

– "Realism." In *Dostoevsky in Context,* edited by Deborah A. Martinsen and O.E. Maiorova, 229–35. Cambridge: Cambridge University Press, 2016.

Koselleck, Reinhart. *Critique and Crisis: Enlightenment and the Pathogenesis of Modern Society.* Cambridge, MA: MIT Press, 1988.

– *Futures Past: On the Semantics of Historical Time.* Translated by Keith Tribe. Cambridge, MA: MIT Press, 1985.

Koshtoyants, K.S. *Essays on the History of Physiology in Russia.* Translated by D.P. Boder et al. Washington, DC: American Institute of Biological Sciences, 1964.

– *Ocherki po istorii fiziologii v Rossii.* Moscow, 1946.

Krieger, Murray. "'A Waking Dream': The Symbolic Alternative to Allegory." In *Allegory, Myth, and Symbol,* edited by Morton W. Bloomfield, 271–88. Cambridge, MA: Harvard University Press, 1981.

Krinitsyn, A.B. "O spetsifike vizual'nogo mira u Dostoevskogo i semantike 'videnii' v romane 'Idiot.'" In *Roman F.M. Dostoevskogo 'Idiot': sovremennoe sostoianie izucheniia,* edited by T.A. Kasatkina, 170–205. Moscow: Nasledie, 2001.

Kristeva, Julia. *Powers of Horror: An Essay on Abjection.* Translated by Leon S. Roudiez. New York: Columbia University Press, 1982.

Latour, Bruno. *Pandora's Hope.* Cambridge, MA: Harvard University Press, 1999.

Lednicki, Waclaw. *Russia, Poland and the West: Essays in Literary and Cultural History.* Port Washington, NY: Kennicat Press, 1966.

Lee, Maurice S. *Uncertain Chances: Science, Skepticism, and Belief in Nineteenth-Century American Literature.* Oxford: Oxford University Press, 2012.

Leikina-Svirskaia, V.R. "Zapiska o dele Petrashevtsev: rukopis' F.N. L'vova s pometkami M.V. Butashevicha-Petrashevskogo." *Literaturnoe nasledstvo* 63 (1956): 165–90.

Lermontov, M. Iu. *Sobranie sochinenii v chetyrekh tomakh.* 2nd ed., 4 vols. Edited by V.A. Manuilov et al. Leningrad: Nauka, 1980.

Levin, John, and Sarah J. Young. "Mapping Machines: Transformations of the Petersburg Text." *Primerjalna Književnost* 36, no. 2 (2013): 151–62, 293–7, 305.

Lewes, George Henry. *Problems of Life and Mind: First Series, the Foundations of a Creed.* Vol. 1. Boston: Houghton, Osgood, 1875–80.

– *Ranthorpe.* Athens: Ohio University Press, 1974.

Lindenmeyr. Adele. "Raskolnikov's City and the Napoleonic Plan." *Slavic Review* 35, no. 1 (1976): 39–40.

Livingston, Sally A. *Marriage, Property, and Women's Narratives.* New York: Palgrave Macmillan, 2012.

Lotman, Iurii M. "Duel'." In *Besedy o russkoi kul'ture: Byt i traditsii russkogo dvorianstva* (XVIII–nachalo XIX veka), 164–79. St Petersburg, 1994.

– "Siuzhetnoe prostranstvo russkogo romana XIX stoletiia." *Izbrannye stat'i (v 3-kh tomakh),* vol. 3. (Tallinn: Aleksandra, 1993): 91–106.

Lotman, Juriy. "Gogol's 'Tale of Captain Kopejkin: Reconstruction of the Plan and Ideo-Compositional Function." Translated by Julian Graffy. In Ju.M. Lotman and B.A. Uspenskij, *The Semiotics of Russian Culture,* edited by Ann Shukman, 213–30. Ann Arbor: Michigan Slavic Contributions, 1984.

– "The Origin of Plot in the Light of Typology." Translated by Julian Graffy. *Poetics Today* 1, no. 1/2 (Autumn 1979): 161–84.

Lounsbery, Anne. "Dostoevskii's Geography: Centers, Peripheries and Networks in *Demons.*" *Slavic Review* 66, no. 2 (Summer 2007): 211–29.

Lukács, Georg. *Dostojewski: Notizen und Entwürfe.* Edited by J.C. Nyiri. Budapest: Akademiai Kiado, 1985.

– *The Theory of the Novel.* Translated by Anna Bostock. Cambridge, MA: MIT Press, 1971.

Maguire, Muireann. *Stalin's Ghosts: Gothic Themes in Early Soviet Literature.* Oxford: Peter Lang, 2012.

Maikov, A.N. *Pis'ma k F.M. Dostoevskomu.* Edited by N.T. Ashimbaeva. Moscow: Pamiatniki kul'tury, 1984.

Maiorova, Olga. "Tsarevich-samozvanets v sotsial'noi mifologii poreformennoi epokhi." *Rossia-Russia. Novaia Seriia: kul'turnye praktiki v ideologicheskoi perspektive* 3, no. 11 (1999): 204–32.

Marcus, Sharon. *Between Women: Friendship, Desire, and Marriage in Victorian England.* Princeton, NJ: Princeton University Press, 2007.

Marrese, Michelle Lamarche. *A Woman's Kingdom: Noblewomen and the Control of Property in Russia, 1700–1861.* Ithaca, NY: Cornell University Press, 2002.

Marsh-Soloway, Michael. "The Mathematical Genius of F.M. Dostoevsky: Imaginary Numbers, Statistics, Non-Euclidean Geometry, and Infinity." PhD diss., University of Virginia, 2016.

Martinsen, Deborah A. "Dostoevsky's 'Diary of a Writer': Journal of the 1870s." In *Literary Journals in Imperial Russia*, edited by Martinsen, 150–68. Cambridge: Cambridge University Press, 1998.

Matual, David "In Defense of the Epilogue of *Crime and Punishment.*" *Studies in the Novel* 24, no. 1 (Spring 1992): 26–34.

Matzner-Gore, Greta. *Dostoevsky and the Ethics of Narrative Form: Suspense, Closure, Minor Characters*. Evanston, IL: Northwestern University Press, 2020.

– "Kicking Maksimov Out of the Carriage: Minor Characters, Exclusion, and *The Brothers Karamazov.*" *Slavic and East European Journal* 58, no. 3 (Fall 2014): 419–36.

McCrea, Barry. *In the Company of Strangers: Family and Narrative in Dickens, Conan Doyle, Joyce, and Proust.* New York: Columbia University Press, 2011.

McReynolds, Louise. *The News under Russia's Old Regime: The Development of a Mass Circulation Press.* Princeton, NJ: Princeton University Press, 1991.

McReynolds, Susan. *Redemption and the Merchant God: Dostoevsky's Economy of Salvation and Antisemitism.* Evanston, IL: Northwestern University Press, 2008.

– "'You Can Buy the Whole World': The Problem of Redemption in *The Brothers Karamazov.*" *Slavic and East European Journal* 52, no. 1 (Spring 2008): 87–111.

Meerson, Olga. *Dostoevsky's Taboos.* Dresden: Dresden University Press, 1998.

Mel'nikov-Pecherskii, P.I. *Sobranie sochinenii v vos'mi tomakh.* Moscow: Izdatel'stvo "Pravda," 1976.

Menke, Richard. "Fiction as Vivisection: G.H. Lewes and George Eliot." *ELH* 67, no. 2 (Summer 2000): 617–53.

Merezhkovskii, D.S. *L. Tolstoi i Dostoevskii.* Edited by E.A. Andrushchenko. Moscow: Nauka, 2000.

Meyer, Priscilla. *How the Russians Read the French: Lermontov, Dostoevsky, Tolstoy.* Madison: Wisconsin University Press, 2008.

Meyler, Bernadette. "Liberal Constitutionalism and the Sovereign Power." In *The Scaffolding of Sovereignty: Global and Aesthetic Perspectives on the History of a Concept*, edited by Zvi Benite, Stephanos Geroulanos, Nichol Jerr, 208–29. New York: Columbia University Press, 2017.

Miller, D.A. *The Novel and the Police.* Berkeley: University of California Press, 1988.

Miller, J. Hillis. *Charles Dickens: The World of His Novels.* Cambridge, MA: Harvard University Press, 1958.

– "The Two Allegories." In *Allegory, Myth, and Symbol*, edited by Morton W. Bloomfield, 355–70. Cambridge, MA: Harvard University Press, 1981.

Miller, Robin Feuer. "Afterword. In the end is the beginning." *Canadian Slavonic Papers* 62, no. 2 (2020): 144–53.

– *Dostoevsky and* The Idiot*: Author, Narrator, and Reader.* Cambridge, MA: Harvard University Press, 1981.
– *Dostoevsky's Unfinished Journey.* New Haven, CT: Yale University Press, 2007.
Mochul'skii, K. *Dostoevskii: Zhizn' i tvorchestvo.* Paris: YMCA Press, 1947.
Mochulsky, Konstantin. *Dostoevsky: His Life and Work.* Translated by Michael A. Minihan. Princeton, NJ: Princeton University Press, 1967.
Moretti, Franco. "The Moment of Truth," *The New Left Review* 1, no. 159 (September–October 1986): 42–5.
– *The Novel,* vol. 1: *History, Geography and Culture.* Edited by Franco Moretti. Princeton, NJ: Princeton University Press, 2006.
– *The Novel,* vol. 2: *Forms and Themes.* Edited by Franco Moretti. Princeton, NJ: Princeton University Press, 2006.
– *The Way of the World: The Bildungsroman in European Culture.* Translated by Albert Sbragia, London and New York: Verso, 2000.
Morson, Gary Saul. *The Boundaries of Genre: Dostoevsky's* Diary of a Writer *and the Traditions of Literary Utopia.* Austin: University of Texas Press, 1981.
– "The God of Onions: *The Brothers Karamazov* and the Mythic Prosaic." In *A New Word on "The Brothers Karamazov,"* edited by Robert Louis Jackson, 107–24. Evanston, IL: Northwestern University Press, 2004.
– *Narrative and Freedom: The Shadows of Time.* New Haven, CT: Yale University Press, 1994.
Moser, Charles A. *Esthetics as Nightmare: Russian Literary Theory, 1855–1870.* Princeton, NJ: Princeton University Press, 1989.
Most, Glenn. "Sad Stories of the Death of Kings: Sovereignty and Its Constraints in Greek Tragedy and Elsewhere." In *The Scaffolding of Sovereignty: Global and Aesthetic Perspectives on the History of a Concept,* edited by Zvi Benite, Stephanos Geroulanos, and Nichol Jerr, 57–79. New York: Columbia University Press, 2017.
Muñoz, José Esteban. *Cruising Utopia: The Then and There of Queer Futurity.* New York: New York University Press, 2009.
Murav, Harriet. *Holy Foolishness: Dostoevsky's Novels and the Poetics of Cultural Critique.* Stanford, CA: Stanford University Press, 1992.
Nabokov, Vladimir. *Lectures on Russian Literature.* Edited by Fredson Bowers. London: Picador, 1981.
Naiman, Eric. "Gospel Rape." *Dostoevsky Studies* New Series, no. 22 (2018): 11–40.
– "Kalganov." *Slavic and East European Journal* 58, no. 3 (Fall 2014): 394–418.
– "'There was something almost cruel about it all …' – Reading *Crime and Punishment*'s Epilogue Hard against the Grain." *Canadian Slavonic Papers* 62, no. 2 (2020): 123–43.
Nazirov, R.G. "Ob eticheskoi problematike povesti "Zapiski iz podpol'ia." In *Dostoevskii i ego vremia,* 145–146. Leningrad, 1971.

– "Sotsial'naia i eticheskaia problematika proizvedenii F.M. Dostoevskogo 1859–1866 godov." Kand. diss., Moscow, 1966.

– *Tvorcheskie printsipy F.M. Dostoevskogo.* Saratov: Izdatel'stvo Saratovskogo universiteta, 1982.

Nechaeva, V.S. *Rannii Dostoevskii 1821–1849.* Moscow: Nauka, 1979.

Nekliudov, N. *Ugolovno-statisticheskie etiudy.* St Petersburg, 1865.

Nelson, Margaret K. "Fictive Kin, Families We Choose, and Voluntary Kin: What Does the Discourse Tell Us?" *Journal of Family Theory & Review* 5 (2013): 259–81.

Odinokov, V.G. *Khudozhestvenno-istoricheskii opyt v poetike russkikh pisatelei.* Novosibirsk: Nauka, 1990.

Oniks [V. Petersen]. "Vstuplenie k romanu angela." *Literaturnaia gazeta* 6 (1881).

Ospovat, Kirill. *Terror and Pity: Aleksandr Sumarokov and the Theater of Power in Elizabethan Russia.* Boston: Academic Studies Press, 2016.

Paine, Jonathan. *Selling the Story: Transaction and Narrative Value in Balzac, Dostoevsky and Zola.* Cambridge, MA: Harvard University Press, 2019.

Paperno, Irina. "The Liberation of the Serfs as a Cultural Symbol." *Russian Review* 50, no. 4 (October 1991): 417–36.

– *Suicide as a Cultural Institution in Dostoevsky's Russia.* Ithaca, NY: Cornell University Press, 1997.

Peace, Richard. *Dostoyevsky: An Examination of the Major Novels.* Cambridge: Cambridge University Press, 1971.

Pettus, Mark. "Dostoevsky's Closed Threshold in the Construction of the Existential Novel." PhD diss., Princeton University, 2009.

Pisarev, D.I. *Polnoe sobranie sochinenii i pisem v 12-i tomakh.* Moscow: Nauka, 2001.

Popov, V.P. "Problema naroda u Dostoevskogo." *Dostoevskii: Materialy i issledovaniia* 4 (1980): 41–54.

Porter, Jillian. "The Double, The Rouble, The Real: Counterfeit Money in Dostoevskii's *Dvoinik.*" *Slavic and East European Journal* 58, no. 3 (2014): 378–93.

– *Economies of Feeling: Russian Literature under Nicholas I.* Evanston, IL: Northwestern University Press, 2017.

Porter, Theodore M. *The Rise of Statistical Thinking, 1820–1900.* Princeton, NJ: Princeton University Press, 1986.

Pravilova, Ekaterina. *A Public Empire: Property and the Quest for the Common Good in Imperial Russia.* Princeton, NJ: Princeton University Press, 2014.

Punter, David. *The Literature of Terror,* vol. 2: *The Modern Gothic.* London: Longman, 1996.

Quetelet, M.A. *A Treatise on Man and the Development of His Faculties.* Edinburgh, 1842.

Radcliffe, Ann. *The Mysteries of Udolpho.* Oxford: Oxford University Press, 2008.

Ragussis, Michael. *Acts of Naming: The Family Plot in Fiction.* New York: Oxford University Press, 1986.

Rebecchini, Damiano, and Raffaella Vassena, eds. *Reading Russia: A History of Reading in Modern Russia.* Vol. 2. Milan: Ledizioni, 2020.

Reyfman, Irina. *Ritualized Violence, Russian Style: The Duel in Russian Culture and Literature.* Stanford, CA: Stanford University Press, 1999.

Rimmon-Kenan, Shlomith. *Narrative Fiction,* 2nd ed. London and New York: Methuen, 2002.

Rosen, Nathan. Review of *Dostoevsky and the Jews,* by David I. Goldstein. *Dostoevsky Studies* Old Series, no. 3 (1982): 200–2.

Rosenshield, Gary. *Challenging the Bard: Dostoevsky and Pushkin, a Study of Literary Relationship.* Madison: Wisconsin University Press, 2013.

Ruzhitskii, I.V. "Atopony Dostoevskogo: K proektu slovaria." *Voprosy leksikografii* 1, no. 5 (2014): 56–75.

Safran, Gabriella. "The Troubled Frame Narrative: Bad Listening in Late Imperial Russia." *Russian Review* 72, no. 4 (2013): 556–72.

Said, Edward W. *Beginnings: Intention and Method.* New York: Basic Books, 1975.

Sartre, Jean-Paul. *Being and Nothingness: An Essay on Phenomenological Ontology.* Translated by Hazel E. Barnes. New York: Washington Square Press, 1966.

Scanlan, James P. *Dostoevsky the Thinker.* Ithaca, NY: Cornell University Press, 2002.

Schillace, Brandy Lain. "'Temporary Failure of Mind': Déjà Vu and Epilepsy in Radcliffe's 'The Mysteries of Udolpho.'" *Eighteenth-Century Studies* 42, no. 2 (2009): 273–87.

Scholle, Christina. *Das Duell in den russischen Literatur: Wandlungen und Verfall eines Ritus.* Munich: Peter Lang, 1977.

Schor, Naomi. *Reading in Detail: Aesthetics and the Feminine.* New York: Methuen, 1987.

Schümann, Daniel. "Raskolnikov's Aural Conversion: From Hearing to Listening." *Ulbandus Review* 16 (2014): 6–23.

Schur, Anna. "The Limits of Listening: Particularity, Compassion, and Dostoevsky's 'Bookish Humaneness.'" *Russian Review* 72, no. 4 (2013): 573–89.

Scollins, Kathleen. "From the New Word to the True Word: *The Bronze Horseman* Subtext of *Crime and Punishment.*" *Russian Review* 78, no. 3 (July 2019): 414–36.

Sechenov, I.M. "Refleksy golovnogo mozga." *Meditsinskii vestnik* 47 (1863): 461–84.

– "Refleksy golovnogo mozga," *Meditsinskii vestnik* 48 (1863): 493–512.

– *Reflexes of the Brain.* Translated by S. Belskii. Cambridge, MA: MIT Press, 1965.

Semenov, E.I. *Roman Dostoevskogo 'Podrostok': problematika i zhanr.* Leningrad: Nauka, 1979.

Shaikevich A. Ia. et al. *Statisticheskii slovar' iazyka Dostoevskogo.* Moscow: Iazyki slovianskoi kul'tury, 2003.

Shapira, Yael. *Inventing the Gothic Corpse: The Thrill of Human Remains in the Eighteenth-Century Novel.* London: Palgrave Macmillan, 2018.

Shaternikóv, M.N. "The Life of I.M. Sechenov." In *I.M. Sechenov. Biographical Sketch and Essays,* edited by Howard Gardner and Judith Kreiger Gardner, ix–xxxvi. New York: Arno Press, 1973.

Shideler, Ross. *Questioning the Father: From Darwin to Zola, Ibsen, Strindberg, and Hardy.* Stanford, CA: Stanford University Press, 1999.

Shotskaia, L.I. "Leksiko-semanticheskie gruppy s narodno-razgovornymi slvoobrazovatel'nymi priznakami v proze 30–40-kh godov XIX veka." In *Voprosy stilistiki russkogo iazyka,* edited by L.I. Shotskaia et al., 10–17. Irkutsk: Irkutskii Gosudarstvennyi Pedagogicheskii Institut, 1973.

Shneyder, Vadim. "Myshkin's Million: Merchants, Capitalists, and the Economic Imaginary in *The Idiot.*" *Russian Review* 77, no. 2 (2018): 241–58.

– *Russia's Capitalist Realism: Dostoevsky, Tolstoy, and Chekhov.* Evanston, IL: Northwestern University Press, 2020.

Simmons, Ernest J. *Dostoevsky: The Making of a Novelist.* New York: Vintage Books, 1962.

Sobol, Valeria. *Febris Erotica: Lovesickness in the Russian Literary Imagination.* Seattle: University of Washington Press, 2011.

Stein, Faith Wilson. "Wallpapering the Novel: Economics, Aesthetics, and the Realist Home." PhD diss., University of Illinois at Urbana-Champaign, 2013.

Steiner, George. *Tolstoy or Dostoevsky: An Essay in the Old Criticism,* 2nd ed. New Haven, CT: Yale University Press, 1996.

Steiner, Lina. *For Humanity's Sake: The Bildungsroman in Russian Culture.* Toronto: University of Toronto Press, 2011.

Straus, Nina Pelikan. *Dostoevsky and the Woman Question.* New York: St Martin's Press, 1994.

– "'Why Did I Say 'Women'?" Raskolnikov Reimagined." *Diacritics* 23, no. 1 (1993): 53–65.

Stromberg, David. "The Enigmatic G-v: A Defense of the Narrator-Chronicler in Dostoevsky's *Demons.*" *Russian Review* 71, no. 3 (July 2012): 460–81.

Talairach-Vielmas, Laurence. *Wilkie Collins, Medicine, and the Gothic.* Cardiff: University of Wales Press, 2009.

Tanner, Tony. *Adultery in the Novel: Contract and Transgression.* Baltimore, MD: Johns Hopkins University Press, 1979.

Tapp, Alyson. "Embarrassment in *The Idiot.*" *Slavic and East European Journal* 60, no. 3 (2016): 422–46.

Thackeray, William Makepeace. *Vanity Fair.* London: Penguin Books, 2012.

Thompson, Diane Oenning. The Brothers Karamazov *and the Poetics of Memory.* Cambridge: Cambridge University Press, 1991.

– "Dostoevskii and Science." In *The Cambridge Companion to Dostoevskii,* edited by William J. Leatherbarrow, 193–202. Cambridge: Cambridge University Press, 2002.

Tihanov, Galin. "Ethics and Revolution: Lukács's Responses to Dostoevskii." *Modern Language Review* 94, no. 3 (July 1999): 609–25.

– *The Master and the Slave: Lukács, Bakhtin, and the Ideas of Their Time.* Oxford: Clarendon, 2000.

Tikhomirov, B.N. "K probleme genezisa 'ital'ianskoi mechty' Dostoevskogo: Radklif ili psevdo-Radklif?" *Dostoevskii i mirovaia kul'tura* 10, no. 2 (2020): 128–52.

Tkachev, P.N. "Bol'nye liudi: 'Besy,' roman Fedora Dostoevskogo, v trekh chastiakh." In *Kritika 70-kh godov XIX veka*, edited by S.F. Dmitrenko, 67–123. Moscow: Olimp, 2002.

Tobin. Patricia D. *Time and the Novel: The Genealogical Imperative.* Princeton, NJ: Princeton University Press, 1978.

Todd, William Mills, III. "*The Brothers Karamazov* and the Poetics of Serial Publication." *Dostoevsky Studies* Old Series, no. 7 (1986): 87–93.

– "Dostoevsky as a Professional Writer." In *The Cambridge Companion to Dostoevsky*, edited by W.G. Leatherbarrow, 66–92. Cambridge: Cambridge University Press, 2002.

– *Fiction and Society in the Age of Pushkin: Ideology, Institutions, and Narrative.* Cambridge, MA: Harvard University Press: 1986.

– "The Ruse of the Russian Novel." In *The Novel*, vol. 1: *History, Geography and Culture*, edited by Franco Moretti, 401–13. Princeton, NJ: Princeton University Press, 2006.

Todes, Daniel Philip. "From Radicalism to Scientific Convention. Biological Psychology from Sechenov to Pavlov." PhD diss., University of Pennsylvania, 1981.

Todorov, Tzvetan. *Genres in Discourse.* Cambridge: Cambridge University Press, 1990.

Tolstoi, Lev. *Polnoe sobranie sochinenii (Iubileinoe izdanie).* 90 vols. Moscow: Gosudarstvennoe izdatel'stvo "Khudozhestvennaia literatura," 1928–59.

Tolstoy, Ivan. *James Clerk Maxwell: A Biography.* Chicago: University of Chicago Press, 1981.

Tolstoy, Leo. *Anna Karenina.* Translated by Richard Pevear and Larissa Volokhonsky. New York: Penguin Books, 2000.

Toporov, V.N. "O strukture romana Dostoevskogo v sviazi s arkhaichnymi skhemami mifologicheskogo myshleniia. (Prestuplenie i nakazanie). In *Structure of Texts and Semiotics of Culture*, edited by Jan van der Eng, 234–6. The Hague: Mouton, 1973.

Tsiv'ian, T.V. "O strukture vremeni i prostranstva v romane Dostoevskogo 'Podrostok.'" *Russian Literature* 3 (1976): 203–55.

Ulianova, Galina. *Female Entrepreneurs in Nineteenth-Century Russia.* London: Routledge, 2009.

Uspensky, Boris. "Tsar and Pretender: Samozvanchestvo or Royal Imposture in Russia as a Cultural-Historical Phenomenon." In Lotman and Uspensky, *The Semiotics of Russian Culture*, 113–152.

Uspensky, Boris, and Viktor Zhivov. *"Tsar and God" and Other Essays in Russian Cultural Semiotics*. Trans. Marcus C. Levitt, David Budgen, and Liv Bliss. Edited by Marcus Levitt. Boston: Academic Studies Press, 2012.

Vaisman, M., A. Vdovin, I, Kliger, and K. Ospovat, eds. *Russkii realizm XIX veka: Mimesis, politika, ekonomika*. Moscow: Novoe literaturnoe obozrenie, 2020.

Valentino, Russell. *Vicissitudes of Genre in the Russian Novel*. New York: Peter Lang, 2001.

Vdovin, A. "Dostoevskii i refleksy golovnogo mozga: 'Zapiski iz podpol'ia' v svete otkrytii I.M. Sechenova." In Vaisman et al., *Russkii realizm XIX veka: obschestvo, znanie, povestvovanie*, 431–51.

Vetlovskaya, Valentina A. "Alyosha Karamazov and the Hagiographic Hero." Translated by Nancy Pollak and Suzanne Fusso. In *Dostoevsky: New Perspectives*, edited by Robert Louis Jackson, 206–26. New York: Prentice Hall, 1984.

Vernon, John. "Reading, Writing, and Eavesdropping: Some Thoughts on the Nature of Realistic Fiction." *Kenyon Review* 4, no. 4 (1982): 49.

Vladiv, Slobodanka B. *Narrative Principles in Dostoevskij's Besy: A Structural Analysis*. Bern: Peter Lang, 1979.

Vogt, Carl. *Physiologische Briefe für Gebildete aller Stände*. Stuttgart, 1846. http://www.mdz-nbn-resolving.de/urn/resolver. pl?urn=urn:nbn:de:bvb:12-bsb10477770-0.

Volgin, Igor. *Poslednii god Dostoevskogo: Istoricheskie zapiski*. Moscow: AST, 2010.

Vucinich, Alexander. *Science in Russian Culture, 1861–1917*. Stanford, CA: Stanford University Press, 1970.

Wagner, Adolph. "'Zakonosoobraznost' v po-vidimomu proizvol'nykh chelovecheskikh deistviiakh s tochki zreniia statistiki." In *Obshchii vyvod polozhitel'nogo metoda*, edited by N. Nekliudov, 297–383. St Petersburg, 1866.

Walker, Clint. "On Serfdom, Sickness, and Redemption: The Peter the Great Subtext in Crime and Punishment." *Dostoevsky Studies* New Series, no. 13 (2009), 93–108.

Watt, Ian P. *The Rise of the Novel: Studies in Defoe, Richardson, and Fielding*. Berkeley and Los Angeles: University of California Press, 1957.

Weiner, Adam. *By Authors Possessed: The Demonic Novel in Russia*. Evanston, IL: Northwestern University Press, 1998.

Wellek, René. *A History of Modern Criticism*. Cambridge: Cambridge University Press, 1955.

White, Hayden. *Figural Realism: Studies in the Mimesis Effect*, 87–100. Baltimore, MD: Johns Hopkins University Press, 1999.

Wilson, Jennifer. "Dostoevsky's Timely Castration." *Transgender Studies Quarterly* 4, no. 5 (2018): 565–73.

Woloch, Alex. *The One vs. The Many: Minor Characters and the Space of the Protagonist in the Novel.* Princeton, NJ: Princeton University Press, 2003.

Woolf, Virginia. "The Russian Point of View." In *The Essays of Virginia Woolf,* vol. 4: *1925–1928,* edited by Andrew McNeillie, 181–9. Orlando: Harcourt Books, 2008.

Wortman, Richard. "Russian Monarchy and the People." In *Dostoevsky in Context,* edited by Deborah A. Martinsen and Olga Maiorova, 77–85. Cambridge: Cambridge University Press, 2015.

– *Scenarios of Power: Myth and Ceremony in Russian Monarchy from Peter the Great to the Abdication of Nicholas II.* Princeton, NJ: Princeton University Press, 2006.

Young, Sarah J. *Dostoevsky's* The Idiot *and the Ethical Foundations of Narrative: Reading, Narrating, Scripting.* London: Anthem Press, 2004.

– "Hesitation, Projection and Desire: The Fictionalizing 'As If' in Dostoevskii's Early Works." *Modern Languages Open* 1 (2018): n.p. http://doi.org/10.3828/mlo.v0i0.183.

– "Holbein's *Christ in the Tomb* in the Structure of *The Idiot,*" *Russian Studies in Literature* 44, no. 1 (2007): 90–102.

Zagidullina, M.V. "Dostoevskii glazami sootechestvennikov." In *Roman F.M. Dostoevskogo "Idiot": Sovremennoe sostoianie izucheniia,* edited by T.A. Kasatkina, 508–39. Moscow: Nasledia, 2001.

Zaitsev, V.A. "Estestvoznanie i iustitsiia." *Russkoe slovo* (July 1863).

Zakharov, V.N. *Sistema zhanrov Dostoevskogo: tipologiia i poetika.* Leningrad: Izdatel'stvo Leningradskogo universiteta, 1985.

Zebrikoff, Marie. "Chapter XIV: Russia." In *The Woman Question in Europe: A Series of Original Essays.* Edited by Theodore Stanton, 390-423. London: Sampson Low, Marston, Searle, and Rivington, 1884.

Zelinskii, V. *Kriticheskii komentarii k sochineniiam F.M. Dostoevskogo. Sbornik kriticheskikh statei. Chast' chetvertaia: "Brat'ia Karamazovy,"* 3rd ed. Moscow: Tipo-lit V. Rikhter, 1906.

Contributors

Anna A. Berman is Associate Professor in the Department of Languages, Literatures, and Cultures at McGill University. She is the author of *Siblings in Tolstoy and Dostoevsky: The Path to Universal Brotherhood* (Northwestern University Press, 2015).

Katherine Bowers is Associate Professor in the Department of Central, Eastern, and Northern European Studies at the University of British Columbia. She is the author of *Writing Fear: Russian Realism and the Gothic* (University of Toronto Press, forthcoming 2021). She is Vice-President of the North American Dostoevsky Society.

Melissa Frazier is Professor of Russian Language and Literature and Associate Dean of the College at Sarah Lawrence College. She is the author of *Romantic Encounters: Writers, Reading, and the Library for Reading* (Stanford University Press, 2007), and *Frames of the Imagination: Gogol's Arabesques and the Romantic Question of Genre* (Peter Lang, 2000).

Kate Holland is Associate Professor in the Department of Slavic Languages and Literatures at the University of Toronto. She is the author of *The Novel in the Age of Disintegration: Dostoevsky and the Problem of Genre in the 1870s* (Northwestern University Press, 2013). She is President of the North American Dostoevsky Society.

Chloë Kitzinger is Assistant Professor in the Department of German, Russian, and East European Languages and Literatures at Rutgers, the State University of New Jersey. She is the author of *Mimetic Lives: Tolstoy, Dostoevsky, and Character in the Novel* (Northwestern University Press, forthcoming 2021).

Ilya Kliger is Associate Professor in the Department of Russian and Slavic Studies at New York University. He is the author of *The Narrative Shape of Truth: Veridiction in Modern European Literature* (Penn State University Press, 2011).

Greta Matzner-Gore is Assistant Professor in the Department of Slavic Languages and Literatures at the University of Southern California. She is the author of *Dostoevsky and the Ethics of Narrative Form: Suspense, Closure, Minor Characters* (Northwestern University Press, 2020).

Vadim Shneyder is Assistant Professor in the Department of Slavic, East European and Eurasian Languages and Cultures at the University of California, Los Angeles. He is the author of *Russia's Capitalist Realism: Tolstoy, Dostoevsky, and Chekhov* (Northwestern University Press, 2020). He is Secretary-Treasurer of the North American Dostoevsky Society.

Alexey Vdovin is Associate Professor in the School of Philological Studies at the National Research University-Higher School of Economics in Moscow, Russia. He is the author of *Dobroliubov: A Raznochinets between the Spirit and the Flesh* (Moscow: Molodaia Gvardia, 2017).

Sarah J. Young is Associate Professor at the School of Slavonic and East European Studies, University College London. She is the author of *Dostoevsky's 'The Idiot' and the Ethical Foundations of Narrative: Reading, Narrating, Scripting* (London: Anthem, 2004).

Index